The Rule of Law and Governance in Indigenous Yoruba Society

African Philosophy: Critical Perspectives and Global Dialogue

The African Philosophy: Critical Perspectives and Global Dialogue book series aims to promote emerging critical perspectives in different branches of African philosophy. It serves as an avenue for philosophers within and between many African cultures to present new arguments, ask new questions, and begin new dialogues within both specialized communities and with the general public. By merging the critical and global dimensions of thoughts pertaining to important topics in African philosophy, this series beams the lights and rigour of philosophical analysis on topical as well as classical questions reflective of the African and African diaspora search for meaning in existence. Focused on the best of African philosophy, the series will introduce new concepts and new approaches in philosophy both to intellectual communities across Africa, as well as the rest of the world.

Titles in the Series

The Rule of Law and Governance in Indigenous Yoruba Society: A Study in African Philosophy of Law, by John Ayotunde Isola Bewaji

The Rule of Law and Governance in Indigenous Yoruba Society

A Study in African Philosophy of Law

John Ayotunde Isola Bewaji

LEXINGTON BOOKS
Lanham • Boulder • New York • London

Published by Lexington Books
An imprint of The Rowman & Littlefield Publishing Group, Inc.
4501 Forbes Boulevard, Suite 200, Lanham, Maryland 20706
www.rowman.com

Unit A, Whitacre Mews, 26-34 Stannary Street, London SE11 4AB

British Library Cataloguing in Publication Information Available

Library of Congress Cataloging-in-Publication Data

Names: Bewaji, John Ayotunde Isola, author.
Title: The rule of law and governance in indigenous Yoruba society : a study in African philosophy of law / John Ayotunde Isola Bewaji.
Lanham : Lexington Books, 2016. | Series: African philosophy: critical perspectives and global dialogue | Includes bibliographical references and index.
Identifiers: LCCN 2016023690 (print) | LCCN 2016024502 (ebook) | ISBN 9781498518376 (cloth : alk. paper) | ISBN 9781498518383 (Electronic)
Subjects: LCSH: Law, Yoruba. | Yoruba (African people)—Social life and customs. | Customary law—Nigeria. | Rule of law—Nigeria.
Classification: LCC KQ8401 .B49 2016 (print) | LCC KQ8401 (ebook) | DDC 340.5/208996333--dc23 LC record available at https://lccn.loc.gov/2016023690

∞™ The paper used in this publication meets the minimum requirements of American National Standard for Information Sciences Permanence of Paper for Printed Library Materials, ANSI/NISO Z39.48-1992.

Printed in the United States of America

Contents

Introduction 1

1 The Social Contract, Democracy, Law and Order in Africa 13
2 The Concept of Law in an Indigenous African (Yoruba) Society 31
3 The Rule of Law, Leadership and Development 57
4 Aspects of Legal Education and Sociopolitical Order in Indigenous Yoruba Society 81
5 Parallel Epistemologies, Parallel Justice Systems 103
6 Human Rights and Law in Indigenous and Contemporary Africa 119
7 Traditional Religion, Constituted Authority, Law and Order 147
8 Social Ethics, Law and Development 167
9 Law, Order, Èṣù and Liminality in the Yoruba Legal System 191
10 Culture, Property Rights and Risk Management in African Development 219

Conclusion 245
Bibliography 255
Index 277

Introduction

This book has two main goals. The first is to provide an exploration of aspects of indigenous Yoruba philosophy of law. The second is to relate this philosophy of law to the Yoruba indigenous traditions of governance, with a view to appreciating the relevance of the Yoruba traditions of law and governance to contemporary African experiments with imported Western democracy in the twenty-first century. There is no doubt that Africa's survival and flourishing largely depends on solving the perennial governance problems, whereby the disregard for rule of law by leaders of many African societies places these African societies in perpetual developmental paralysis and deprive the populations of most countries of the benefits of the good life which the rich human and material/natural resources of the continent promise.

In *Narratives of Struggle* (Bewaji 2012), it was argued that part of the problems plaguing Africa derive from how, from the middle of the last millennium, Africa has been the target of predatory invasions and denudation of her human, intellectual, cultural and material resources on a scale never visited on any other continent in human history. The centrality of Africa, the ease of access, the fecundity of its varied climate, the wealth of resources which exist above and below the earth of the continent and the hospitality of the populations of the continent, have made Africa attractive to greedy individuals and group fortune-seekers, at the expense of Africans.

In the process of the expropriation of Africa's human and natural resources through colonization and enslavement, one of the critical elements of human civilization which Africa lost was confidence in its ability to run its affairs efficiently and productively for the benefit of its people, using well-tested and time-honored indigenous legal, ethical, social, religious, cultural practices. Other effects of the invasion and subjugation of Africa and Africans have been annotated as epistemicide (Bewaji 2008b, 2012). Epistemicide is the deliberate act, behavior, exercise or crime, violent or nonviolent, overt or benign, of omission or commission, committed against a group or groups with the sole or ultimate intent to destroy the existence of the group or groups through the destruction of the indigenous knowledge systems, traditions and propagating mechanisms. It is a coordinated plan of different actions and inactions aimed at the destruction of essential foundations of the life of national or racial group or groups, with the aim of annihilating the group itself or groups themselves, or with the intention of making a nullity the identity, self-esteem, self-awareness or corporate existence, as autonomous or separate being, of a group or groups. It is the deliberate, calculated, concerted and systematic destruction, in whole or in part, of an ethnic, racial, religious, or national group identity or belief in such separate identity and existence, through the negations of their indigenous knowledge systems, denial and expropriation of their intellectual traditions and property and the foisting on the intellect of the target group, groups or society a mendicant and supplicant genuflecting approach to existence.

This epistemicide has led to what may become a terminal epistemic deficit on the part of African leaders. As it was used or intended in that discourse, "deficit" is not total lack, rather it is more of an inadequacy, it is a falling below or short of expectation, and it is a quality of being less than required; thereby leading to poor, weak, incomplete or below par performance or understanding. What is critical is that in the case of Africa's leadership, when there is epistemic deficit on the emasculating scale that we have witnessed since nominal independence were attained in many of these ex-colonies, there is always a need to look to outside sources to make up for the shortage, and there are often conditionalities attached to the granting of the balance. In itself it is arguable that all things and beings suffer some form of deficit or the other. But this will miss the point and is tantamount to deflecting the critical issue at stake and pandering to the advocates of mediocrity, who would have Africa continue on the pan-handling mendicancy train it has been on for so long and, therefore, succeed in preventing the kind of introspective reflection and engagement necessary to utilize the resources of Africa for the upliftment of the lives of African peoples.

The new struggle which Africa faces in the twenty-first century is how to liberate itself from literal and virtual domestic occupation forces, in the form of various externally determined, imposed and controlled local/national governments for the continued exploitation, subjection and destruction of the human and material resources of the continent; these are the parodies of modern "nation" states which Davidson (1992) has called Africa's burden. Indeed, the only thing modern about these states is the degree of moral bankruptcy which inhabit the chambers of these governance structures, where all ideas of moderation, legal responsibility or self- and group-respecting decorum are the most derided elements of public and private lives of leadership, in the pursuit of the worst form of primitive individual material accumulation, corruption and pandering to basest instincts in the quest for naked power, which exhibit crude incapacity to understand either the virtues of enlightened self-interest or social altruism. Because the externally determined governance systems were not designed to benefit the societies being ruled, but only that of the groups wielding the power at the material times, at the expense of every other segment of society, it has led to deadly zero-sum struggles for state power and do-or-die contestations for political offices. It is the position of the present work that most of the leadership cadres in Africa, being products of educational systems fundamentally flawed by the epistemicide perpetrated by Europe and Arabia, display a degree of epistemic deficit which leads to destructive policies which impoverish African peoples in the extreme.

In the last two millennia, Africa was first victim of trans-Sahara slave trade and colonization from Arabia. This was followed by western Europeans invading Africa for trading initially but leading to the trans-Atlantic slave trade and the forced enslavement of tens of millions of Africans in the so-called new world. This was capped with the partitioning of the entire African continent for economic exploitation and political colonial occupation. But more significantly, in the last few decades, America has joined with Europe and Asia—Japan, China and India—with the active connivance of domestic leadership in various African societies, to continue the process of complete emasculation of Africa, to the point where the entire continent of Africa is now virtually prostrate.

Walter Rodney (1982) presented these matters in *How Europe Underdeveloped Africa,* Frantz Fanon (2001) described the process poignantly in *The Wretched of the Earth,* and Claude Ake (2009) saw the same syndrome as critically as possible in *Social Science as Imperialism,* while Olufemi Taiwo (2010) characterized it well in *How Colonialism Preempted Modernity in Africa.* These point to a desperate challenge that faces Africa, through what I categorize as leadership deficit, a leadership successfully fed on a diet of deliberate epistemicide—a mind-wipe that destroys every intellectual and institutional value system of indigenous societies—and is graduated (certificated) by an inept educational system meant to keep Africa dependent.

While it may be contended that we should stop blaming others for the failings of Africa's leadership, there can be no disputing the fact that African leadership agency has been compromised by the fact that the intellectual traditions to which their consciousness was attuned was not tethered in the indigenous traditions which would encourage them to chart paths favoring their own societies. Agency in this regard is hollow and weak, to the point that the issue of epistemicide becomes extremely critical, because of its importance to the overall diagnosis of the African leadership condition. In our view, epistemicide is not merely an evolution occasioned by competing interests in the modern system of self-rule in Africa. There are serious problems caused by this epistemicide and the lack of confidence occasioned amongst Africans in their indigenous knowledge systems (epistemicide), as this is not simply a matter of choosing the kind of attitude one likes or admires, as African agency has been compromised since real choice does not exist in a fundamental sense. Our point is to show how a good number of Africans, aping other systems, may make recourse to choice to explain their faulty disposition.

Overall, there is the question of agency at two levels, namely, at the level of causation and at the level of displacement of the contemporary status quo in Africa. On the one hand, the question of agency with regard to causation concerns the tools, methods or instruments that brought about the neglect of African traditional systems. This has bred an "as-if-agency" which, to the outsider, would make a mockery of choice alternatives, because when one's indigenous traditions have been condemned as primitive, barbaric, ungodly and irrational, to say discarding such odious tradition is a choice is disingenuous at best, and hypocritical at the worst. On the other hand, the question of causation, with regard to the displacement of the status quo, concerns the means of liberating African cultural space from its current state and has within it the need to redeem African leadership agency through wholesome educational elaboration, analysis and establishment of genuine alternative governance systems, especially ones tethered on indigenous traditions of excellence within African ancestry. We believe that it is surely important for contemporary African leadership to learn how to think about these matters, especially as it relates to the inadequacy of merely postulating external agency as the culprit of causation and internal agency as the sole burden bearer of liberation struggle.

This book is, therefore, devoted to what can be described as a juridical forensic investigation of Nigeria's predicament of developmental deficit, leading to gross and unconscionable impoverishment of large segments of the population, in the midst of so much natural resources and abundant human capital, using Yoruba indigenous legal traditions as a reflective template. It is argued that, at the base, these fundamental factors, which have combined to underwrite African social, economic, political, cultural and other developmental weaknesses, have been successful in undermining and destroying indigenous legal systems, practices and philosophies.

It is suggested that the biggest incapacitating challenge that members of any society could face with respect to developing empowering tropes for wholesome identity construction and mental and spiritual liberation is to allow themselves to be convinced that their historical antecedents are naught. The Yoruba of West Africa were always conscious that *ise ni oogun ise*, that is, work is the medicine (antidote/cure) for (to) poverty, which instils in them the commitment to honest labor, in the believe that you cannot hunger if you are hardworking; while they understand that *ile ti a fi ito mo, iri ni i wo*; that is, a house built with spittle is easily blown away by drizzle; which in their view probably accounts for the vicious cycle of poverty of the politicians in Nigeria, and that *ina o mo oju eni t'o da* when it comes to the way law works, it like the bush fire which does not respect those who set it, as the law is no respecter of persons.

Marable (1995) ably described the black predicament regarding leadership as the infusion of messianism into autocracy and patriarchy to confound the developmental capacity of black Americans—a paradox which stems from how people who have been laid low by Christianity now uses the tropes of their emasculation to further their developmental incapacitation, which is not all too different from how the Rastafarians loath Babylon, yet could not extricate themselves from the shackles of Christianity in their own search for agency and authenticity, predicated on Zion. And while he suggests that democratization and infusion of confidence in the individual and groups would make a difference, it seems that this was more or less a product of hindsight, which is always better, given the challenges of the times. It would seem that the institutional structures, provided through the church, was partly responsible for this, given the diabolical role of the church in the enslavement of Africans in the West and their colonization in the continent in the name of God. But in the case of Africa, the destruction of the checks and balances of the various cultural institutions of Africa, replaced as it was by such alien warring and mutually antagonistic cultures emanating from the Middle East, through the agency of the two desert religions of Christianity and Islam, have developed a leadership that has no understanding of what indigenous concept of the rule of law was, not to mention the idea of conventions and traditions which underwrite sociopolitical and economic order in indigenous African societies.

These have provided me with the motivation to investigate the role of law, the rule of law, respect for law and order and legal traditions among Yoruba people in the development of their sophisticated society, with a view to understanding how the future generations of Africans can begin, introspectively, to map the strategies for development on the basis of justice, respect for law and protection of the common humanity of all, regardless of clime, gender, economic status, physical disabilities or orientations inherent in highly civilized indigenous African traditions. In doing this I have been very concerned to understand how the dilution of the indigenous legal traditions (with the clear prohibitions of evil, deception, greed, avarice, cruelty, dishonesty, corruption, crimes against the person and against society, etc.) with the imposition of the poorly understood European legal traditions (the worst being the English common law heritage), on the one hand, and the bombardment of the African culture space by an adulterated version of the Islamic political Sharia law, on the other hand, have created a vacuum that has not been properly filled, except in the ways in which Nigerians and Africans have found accommodationist (syncretisms, bastardization and dilution) approaches to escape the metaphysical implications of these two imported destructive legal traditions. I have been very fascinated by the factors of exceptionalism that have become the practice—you do what fits your imagination during the "unholy" days of the week, you go and make atonement on the "holy" days (compared with the Yoruba tradition in which each day of the week has its deity), and life goes on, regardless of what harm you have inflicted on the society or other people; you believe that by asking for forgiveness through weekly confessions to the holy father, paying tithes, giving alms, of building grandiose churches and mosques, you are absolved of, and protected from, consequences of your crimes against yourself, society and humanity at large. Hence, regardless of the challenges, I believe that there is need to engage the indigenous Yoruba (African) legal traditions, notions of rule of law, ideas about order, crime and punishment, with a view to appreciating the fundamental factors which have combined to facilitate the developmental impasse with which Africa is saddled, so that the insights gained can be meaningfully harnessed to provide pathways for the channeling of African energies to truly emancipate the African people from poverty, squalor and sociopolitical degradation to which the continent seem to have been condemned at the present time.

In chapter 1, we consider the concept of society and ideas of social communities in indigenous Yorubaland, through the prism of what has become known in Western scholarship as the classical social contract tradition of Hobbes, Locke, and Rousseau, which, in Western political theory and philosophy, has enjoyed such fame and acceptance as being basic to the development of liberal democratic theory and practice. It is often considered heretical for any scholar, especially one from the fringes, to meaningfully critique or deliberately ignore this so-called Western invention of how human communities and society came to emerge (Mills 1997). It is argued that the Western narrative of contract tradition, predicated on individualism, poses challenges that must be carefully interrogated, given the flux in the contemporary sociopolitical universe that at once impels paradoxically extreme nationalism and equally unavoidable self-serving globalism which disempowers the poorer countries of the world to further enrich the industrialized countries of Europe and North America.

The Western social contract tradition makes pronouncements on what is natural and what is non-natural. It offers what many have contended are rigorous arguments for these pronouncements that are supposedly "intuitive," "empirical," "logical," "psychological," "moral," "religio-metaphysical." What is offered to this bogus theory in this chapter is a challenge from the outside. I ask: 1) On what empirical data is the material presuppositions of contractarianism built? 2) What is the epistemological foundation of contractarianism? 3) Is contractarianism not derivable from any other form of sociological presupposition except that of the state of nature? 4) Does any human know a "state of nature"? 5) Given the answers to the above questions, to what extent are the legal and moral foundations of contractarianism sacrosanct? It is argued that it is very presumptuous of the Western social contract protagonists to suppose that they have captured *the only logically valid* basis of democratic practice universally—individualism.

In chapter 2, we examine the concept of law in Yoruba society. I begin the investigation against the backdrop of the presumption that the state of cultural development, and indeed the level of civilization, of any society can be discerned and measured by the evidence of many factors. Some of these factors are, a) the extent to which there is security of sustenance resources of food, water and energy for members of society, b) the protection of members of society from the devastation of the forces of nature through the development of habitat structures that conduce to good existence, c) the avenues for the expression of the talents and intuitions of members of the society through the arts and crafts, d) minimization of energy expended by members of society in the process of garnering basic means of existence through the use of creative technologies, e) the level of leisure and luxury that members of society are able to enjoy in order to be able to indulge in the arts, plan for their individual demise, make wars on other competing societies and secure dominance for the in-group by contrast to the out-group, f) the development of resources for the care of the sick, the weak and the old, and last but not the least, g) the development and procurement of means for ensuring that institutions, structures, resources and mechanisms are in place for the determination and protection of the rights of members of the society.

In this chapter, attention is focused only on the last factor, and this focus is in a limited way concerned with a philosophical analysis of the nature or, more accurately, the concept of law in indigenous Yoruba society before the interface with colonial experience. We provide an initial critical philosophical overview of the Yoruba legal system as developed, theorized and practiced within the purview of statecraft and polities of the empires, kingdoms, city-states and villages, which this writer believes is long overdue. The goal of the discussion is to elicit the fundamentals of the Yoruba legal system before the imposition of the English common law and the attendant manufacturing of various culturally alien constitutions for Nigeria.

This discussion helps us in the process of coming to terms with the heritage of colonialism in the jurisprudential domain on the one hand; while on the other hand, it provides an opportunity for a retrospective analysis of the factors that contribute to the dysfunctionality and debilitating retrogression of state-craft in Nigeria. The goal is to challenge our legal luminaries, ethicists, political philosophers, legal philosophers, politicians, political scientists, historians, sociologists, educationists and all interested students of African cultures to take the study of indigenous societies more closely to find solutions to challenges facing African societies.

In chapter 3, we examine the interface between the rule of law, morality and leadership in indigenous Yoruba society which conduced to the development of the highly sophisticated, urbane, economically and culturally diverse civil systems found in Yoruba land. The thesis which I defend in this chapter is that the cultures of impunity, nonaccountability and nonobservance of the rule of law, which pervades African leadership systems and practices, inherited from colonialism's intrinsic exogenous nature of the locus of power derivation and allegiance, cemented by miseducated, visionless and immoral post-colonial governance systems and further compounded by reckless, myopic, and unconscionable military dictatorships, are largely responsible for the recursive, permanent and vicious cycles of underdevelopment of African societies; it is not anything inherited from the Yoruba and Africa cultural traditions.

In this chapter, we examine first the concept of the rule of law, tracing the historical and cultural indigenous antecedents of the concept in the political systems of Yoruba society, indicating the strength and weaknesses of these systems, the checks and balances that reinforce moral, accountable, responsible and disciplined leadership in such indigenous societies. Second, I examine the theory and practice of colonialism and the kinds of leadership it generated in order to show the combined effects of colonialism, modernity and post-modernity on the governance systems foisted on post-colonial states in Africa. Third, I show that, given the defective preparation and appreciation of what constitute modern society by the leadership which inherited power at independence, married to instabilities of the political arrangements pervading the African landscape at independence, it is not strange to see how these combination of tragedies led to circumstances culminating in the debilitating governance structures and morally bankrupt socioeconomic, political, religious, educational and aesthetic systems found in most African societies today. Finally, it is argued that for as long as African societies continue not to take the rule of law seriously, for so long will our developmental efforts be fraught with in-built recipes for disaster and impoverishment.

In chapter 4, we examine some of the salient aspects of legal education in an indigenous African (i.e., Yoruba) society which conduced to the existence of civil society in which the rule of law pervaded the consciousness of the people and guaranteed liberties and pursuit of happiness of members of such a society, be they young or old, rich or poor, indigene or stranger. It is argued in this chapter that indigenous Yoruba society, prior to the European misadventure in West Africa, which culminated in the farce that is Nigeria as a polity, developed a highly sophisticated judicial system, backed up with advanced sociocultural structures of epistemological, metaphysical, axiological and practical ideas and principles for ensuring and maintaining order within its borders.

In chapter 5, I explore the fundamental reasons for the existence and continued virile survival and vibrancy of parallel indigenous justice systems along-side the British common law in Nigeria since colonization and after almost half a century of independence and deliberate acceptance of the English common law system as the official judicial system for Nigeria. I argue that this survival of these indigenous justice systems among the various nationalities of Nigeria is not intrinsically dependent on the convenience or cost-effectiveness of the indirect rule system which the British colonizer used in administering the country after amalgamation in 1914. I suggest that the survival of these justice systems is a reflection of the divergent foundations of the cultures of these societies from that of the alien imposed British system; these foundations include a) metaphysics, b) existential praxis, c) ecological spaces, d) cultural values, e) axiological beliefs, f) religious nexus of existence and, more importantly, and g) epistemologies of existence. In this discussion, I will be commenting on all the first six issues prefatorily, but my main interest lies in subjecting the last foundation to careful critical examination, to show that it is the epistemological incommensurability of indigenous and the imported common law legal systems that underwrite the survival of three parallel justice systems in Nigeria, whether under colonial existence or in the post-colony.

The conclusion that is reached is that the Nigerian legal theory and practice runs three parallel, almost acutely contradictory and schizophrenic life histories, because of the distorted and distorting nature of the colonial experiment on the one hand, and because of the poor capacity of post-colonial Nigerian leadership to appreciate the value of indigenous judicial and legal systems and practices in the face of the practical and theoretical incapacity, alienating disorientation and humiliating insensitivity of the English common legal system bequeathed to Nigeria with regard to the cultural values of the various ethnicities that make up the fabricated entity called Nigeria. This British legacy has failed to advance the course of Nigerian national development or national integration, but it has managed to continue to be an agent of division, perpetuation of inequities and enthronement of injustice, because of the adversarial nature of its epistemological, metaphysical, logical, methodological and theoretical underpinnings and the privileging of the capacity of the wealthy to impose his/her wish on society by being able to buy justice while leaving the weak, poor and vulnerable to languish in a limbo of judicial dispossession, desperation and nonexistence.

It is, therefore, not surprising that the recrudescence of the Islamic legal system and practice, in the form of Sharia law, has become rather contentious as an alternative to the British-English common law that the Nigerian Constitution enshrines in the form of notional secularism of the Nigerian nation-state. What is surprising is that a careful examination will show that many indigenous legal systems of Nigeria would not find the Islamic legal system alien to their indigenous cultural jurisprudence, both in its theoretical, epistemological, metaphysical, as well as humanistic determination to enthrone justice, and are consequently not in the least threatened by it. Thus, politics apart (though politics is what makes everything interesting and destructive in Nigeria and most African societies for that matter), the apparent tripartite (should we say multipartite?)

legal systems in Nigeria is a product of the distinctively tripartite (multipartite) legal epistemological and metaphysical traditions that inhabit the contemporary Nigerian soul. And it is only when clear attention is paid to these diverse foundations of law in Nigeria that cohesive development and growth would be possible.

In chapter 6, we to explore the Yoruba epistemological, metaphysical and axiological presuppositions of the concept of "person", "humanity" and "self", as the foundation and locus of legal and moral rights, either within the construct of the human person as a self in the process of being and existence, or as social construct deriving from the consciousness of the mediation of interaction of persons in a variety of spaces—communal, religious, political, economic, filial, professional and more.

In chapter 7, we examine the place of religion in indigenous Yoruba society, whether as the solution to the anxieties and uncertainties that confront human beings relating to the unpredictability of the forces of nature, or the acts of some human beings engaging in various machinations steeped in apparent or real negative actions aimed at making the lives of other human beings miserable. Under such circumstances, various religions have played very important roles in the validation of constitutional authority structures designed to oversee social stability and the legitimation of governance structures, thereby conducing to interpersonal peace and cooperative existence of members of society in the various communities. It is suggested that, within the context of African traditional religions, so much of what passes for religion in the contemporary societies, especially as pursued by the two invading Arabian Desert religions of Christianity and Islam, would be regarded as alien, nonreligious, against the will of the Supreme Being, and contrary to the wishes of the ancestors; this would have the consequence of consigning these so-called religions into the pantheon of the ungodly.

In chapter 8, we examine social ethics or moral reflection in indigenous Yoruba society by contrast with analytic ethics in Western society. We contrast this with the inability of Western philosophers to determine the purview of ethics and its nature which constitute an indictment of their prevarication while social order and interpersonal trust disintegrates.

In chapter 9, we examine law, order, Èsu and liminality in Yoruba society. This chapter explores the component of law enforcement, with a view to understanding the derivation of law, the sanctity of legal traditions, and the process of ensuring that society and individuals are protected with a legal system that is judiciously enforced without fear or favor to any segment of society. Given that Yoruba society is hierarchical, there is the ever present danger that the weak and vulnerable may be given short shrift; unless mechanisms are in place to ensure that the law is no respecter of persons or deities for that matter.

In chapter 10, it is argued that for indigenous Yoruba culture the whole universe is like one huge society, with contemporary human society within it being a society in which there is unavoidable mutual interdependence of all humans and other sentient beings that inhabit the universe. The rich need the poor to survive, and the poor need the rich to continue to exist. The technologically advanced need the technologically backward to continue to maximize the benefits of technology, and the technologically stunted need the technologically advanced to have a psychological feeling of being a part of humanity, through their attachment to the outward appearances of the age and being relevant to the new age of information consumption and manipulation. The "Christian" need the "other" (non-Christian) in order to have a point of contrast, and the non-Christian need a religio-metaphysical point of departure from the Christian in order to justify not being a Christian—whether fanatically or otherwise. The scientifically hi-tech "civilized" person and her society needs the scientifically under-privileged in order to be able to continue the supremacy of science, while at the same time pretending that scientific knowledge and technology is open and accessible to everyone who dare wish to attain the nirvana that it promises; yet science is, metaphysically and realistically, as closed a knowledge area as any in the esoteric mysteries of various reclusive orders in the world. There is even a sense in which the ecosphere is one in which animals, plants, and even the so-called inanimate objects need each other for the systemic continuance of the general equilibrium that sustains the multiverse. This is why it is important to pay attention to the extinction of plants, animals, and the depletion of sources of energies—be they fossil or otherwise. This shows why Yoruba does not place so much emphasis on individual contribution to knowledge, outside of the context of the society which makes such contribution possible, thereby placing reward with moderation on creativity, ingenuity and superior capacity.

The conclusion harnesses the major contributions of this chapter to Philosophy of Law and Governance in Africa, indicating the necessity to take seriously the obedience, observance, enforcement and operation of law as no respecter of persons, groups, affiliations and pedigrees. It is concluded that while Africa has much to offer humanity by way of its originary contribution to human civilization, the current situation where in most African countries, the burden of statehood, law enforcement and observance of the laws remain mainly that of poor, minorities or vulnerable segments of society cannot conduce to the renaissance which Africa seeks in the twenty-first century or beyond. And it does not assist in the process to argue that since Rome was not built in a day, there is time enough in the future to enable the African people to realize the human dreams of happiness, protection of life and property and, even more significantly, human dignity to live a tolerable existence in an environment of so much wealth and resources.

ONE

The Social Contract, Democracy, Law and Order in Africa

The worst thing that could ever happen to a people is for them to lose their history and allow themselves to be dememorialized. Societies have always been invaded, conquered and subjugated in human history, but in most cases the societies have not totally forgotten their identities, nor have they allowed others to determine the conditions on which they were to be human, conditions which give them a sense of identity or meaning of life and existence. The case of Africa is a different and very curious one, as European domination, conquest and subjugation carried with it the project of total nullification of the sense of humanity and historical antecedents of the various peoples of Africa, which allowed for various civilizations and empires, kingdoms and cultures to develop and flourish on the continent, while Europe and many other parts of the rest of the world were still wallowing in barbarity, thereby becoming the feeder centre and path of the human spread to the entire globe. There have been so many factors which have contributed to this complete destruction of African humanity, among which one could mention military superiority, economic superiority, "superior" savagery of primitive, untempered appetite for meaningless violence, religious sabotage, political ambiguation and artistic cum ethical derogation. In this chapter we will begin our investigation of the rule of law and the role of law in Africa against the background of the complete destruction of African legal and jurisprudential traditions as a factor in the complete destruction of African humanity and society by looking at the political project of centering reality and civilization against the background of an ahistorical projection of a fictive account of governance, government, statecraft and social existence, on a fake and fraudulent social contract theory.

The classical social contract tradition of Hobbes, Locke and Rousseau has enjoyed such fame and acceptance as being basic to the development of liberal democratic theory and practice that it would be almost sacrilegious heresy for any scholar, especially one from the fringes or margins of mainstream (sociopolitical) philosophical academia, to post serious attack and critique. But the social contract tradition poses challenges that must be accepted on various counts, with new insights and interpretations, given the fluxed reality in a contemporary sociopolitical universe that at once impels extreme (rabid) nationalism (as in the case of the United States of America) and unavoidable globalism (as in the case of the technological integrations of the whole world). This becomes all the more important, not simply in order to dislodge the primacy of the loyalty and the reverence of devotion from the historically ignorant and critically befuddled followers of this tradition as well as its most virulent critics, but from another perspective which hopes to, if possible, encourage that the anchorage of disclosure be completely implemented—derobbing the ideological king of Western political theory for critical anatomical examination, so as to show exactly what it is: a fraud perpetrated to entrench the domination of one segment of society by another with the acquiescence of the dominated. This is not an easy task, but it is one that is very compelling, in order to liberate humanity from the ideological prison into which one version of understanding human social existence has become a tool in the hands of those who have mastered the art of weapons of mass deception, ideological intimidation of opposing views and clinical orchestration of destruction of opposition.

The hallowed social contract tradition makes certain unusual pronouncements regarding what is natural, what is non-natural and what is merely contrived or constructed by humans. It supposes that these unsubstantiated pronouncements are valid and offers what many have contended are rigorous "intuitive," "empirical," "logical," "psychological," "moral," "religio-metaphysical" and other forms of arguments for its assertions regarding contractarianism. Seminal contemporary contributions to the further entrenchment of the intellectual place of this tradition in Western and non-Western political discourse, either by way of affirmation or through coherent critiques, have been Rawls, Wolff, Raphael, McBride and others. I do not intend to go over grounds which they have effectively and efficiently covered, as such a task cannot devolve on me, as I would be totally unsupportive of any form of valorization which such tacit approbation may suggest, given the fact that their perspectives bear a verisimilitude with that of the original authors of the contractarianism discussed here, a progeny that I disclaim. In fact, the whole project of the social contract, as it has been employed in contemporary scholarship, has been to de-historicize the traditions of governance of peoples of other climes, while vainly affirming the false originality of the vapid greed that inhabit the tenacity of the contraption that is the social contract, based on individualism and the vacuous modernism which underpin it.

What I offer in this chapter is a challenge from the outside. As an outsider who shares no patrimony to the mystique of social contractarianism and the Western fraud of historical manipulation of knowledge on which it stands, I am of the considered opinion that the time is ripe to ask a number of pertinent endogenous and exogenous questions, namely: a) On what empirical data are the material presuppositions of social contractarianism built? b) What are the epistemological and methodological foundations of social contractarianism? c) Is social contractarianism not derivable from any other form of sociological presupposition except that of state of nature? d) Does any living human adult even know a state of nature? Or, framed variantly, can any human adult really conjecture a true state of nature? And, finally, e) Given the answers to the above questions, to what extent are the legal and moral foundations of social contractarianism sacrosanct, or was it merely an intellectual experiment (explanatory device) brought about by the economic differentiation and impoverishment which was being visited on the hordes of poor Europeans in the modern period?

So, what I have attempted to do in this chapter is to provide an answer to these questions in what can only be a sketch, as time and space constraints preclude a longer presentation, because my interest in this book is not to interrogate Western political philosophy and its foundationalist exceptionalist contractarian essentialism built around a decadent individualism derived from the Cartesian "sum" of modernism. My goal in the chapter is to use my answers to suggest that it is very presumptuous of the social contractarians (Hobbes, Locke and Rousseau, and by extension, those who have embraced the tradition lock, stock and barrel—apologists of capitalism and its many masquerades in the form of democracy, globalization, etc.) to suppose that they have captured the basis of social contract and, hence, provide the only logically valid account of "democratic practice" universally, as the form of sociopolitical arrangement best suited for human existence. The challenge has the effect of calling for care in understanding the internal turmoil that "democratic practice" has persistently generated over the centuries and especially in this century as humanity progresses into the new millennium with a decade and a couple of years already gone, without any sign that Western democracy is anything but the contraption devised by the haves to continue to dominate and dispossess the poor legitimately. Evidence is the collective failed state status the European Union is turning into, while the United States of America is locked into the stranglehold of conservative plutocrats who will not even consider the poor Americans human enough to deserve decent health care taken for granted by inhabitants of other "civilized" countries of the world, while embracing individual greed in the name of democracy.

One final note is apposite in this introduction. I have deliberately elected to speak here of "democratic practice" and of Western democracy. I have not indicated whether liberal or otherwise. This is because, as a bystander to the American political system—a system acclaimed to be the best case of democratic practice in contemporary human polity—I am miffed by the cantankerousness of its principal players (especially the legislators in their ability to vainly pillory the American presidency for political gain), the freedom without responsibility of the populace and the "holier than thou, I see you today, I am blind tomorrow" foreign policy of official Washington. If I were to qualify "democratic practice" as I have observed the American system negate the ideals of liberalism as I understand it, I will not use "liberal," because of the odium it has generated in its real-life American situation; I will prefer "disciplined" democracy.

In *The Leviathan*, Thomas Hobbes (1651) executes one of the most poignant statements of the Western cultural psyche, an understanding of the moving force behind the evolution and development of what is known as "culture" in the West, without which there would have been unimaginable suffering and destruction, that is, *the right to private property*. This has resulted in the postulation by Hobbes of what he called the *social contract, the state of nature, or the sovereign* as the arbiter, the superior power that holds in check the mutual antagonism and the destructive self-annihilative war that Western human nature involuntarily, instinctively and compulsively engenders. As Hobbes states,

> Again, men have no pleasure, but on the contrary a great deal of grief, in keeping companies, where there is no power able to over-awe them all. For every man looketh that *his companion should value him at the same rate he sets upon himself; and upon all signs of contempt, or undervaluing, naturally endeavours, as far as he dare (which amongst them have no common power to keep them in quiet, is far enough to make them destroy each other), to extort a greater value from his contemners, by damage, and from others by example* (p. 264, emphasis added).

When Hobbes indicates that each human looks to have by force if necessary that "his companion should value him at the same rate he sets upon himself," we note that it dramatically inverts the Kantian Categorical Imperative and the Golden Rule of Jesus Christ. While the Kantian principle will have it that we act such that the rule of our action can become a universal law, that is, we should act such that the maxim of our action or the example of the intent and content of our behavior may be legislated for humanity because of the justness and moral probity and other regarding nature of such act, and while similarly the position of Jesus Christ would be that we love others as we love ourselves, on the contrary the Western Hobbesian position inverts this perspective and only speaks to our valuing ourselves alone and demanding (ensuring by force, where we can) that others respect this value. It enshrines an egoistic individualism, without a parallel in previous human history, that pervades the Western psyche, an individualism that craves respect without wishing to give the same to others as their full due, except under duress or threat of calamity by an overarching third party ganged up to impose by those who have the resources in the society in the form of the state; in fact, as is obvious from the Western Hobbesian understanding of human nature, the "other" person is conceived in purely oppositional adversarial terms—an enemy that must be contained, subjugated or destroyed.

Hobbes identifies three causes of strife in the state of nature as: a) competition, which causes the invasion of others for gain; b) diffidence, which causes invasion for safety; and c) glory, which causes invasion for the maintenance of reputation and defense of the same among *their kindred, their friends, their nation, their profession, or their name* (p. 264). He argues that when humans lived in a state of nature, life was full of misery:

> Hereby it is manifest, that during the time when men lived without a common power to keep them all in awe, they are in that condition which is called war; and such a war, as is of every man, against every man . . . on society; and which is worst of all, continual fear, and danger of violent death; and *the life of man, solitary, poor, nasty, brutish, and short* (pp. 264–65, emphasis added).

In Hobbes's reasoning, it is clear that the sovereign occupies the position that Deity occupies in monotheistic religious schemes. The sovereign is the law giver (as is drilled into unsuspecting Christian youth in patriarch Moses' Decalogue and the Christ's Sermon on the Mount), the upholder of such laws that he deems fit to give and the watchdog over the obedience of such laws as he gives. Without the sovereign, Hobbes is of the opinion that there would be no right or wrong, no justice or injustice, no common values and every act would be permitted, for there would be no liberty or commodious living. He says,

> The passions that incline men to peace are fear of death; desire of such things as are necessary to commodious living; and a hope by their industry to obtain them. And reason suggesteth convenient articles of peace, upon which men may be drawn to agreement. These articles, are they, which otherwise are called the Laws of Nature (p. 266).

It is curious that Hobbes did not tell us what happened before this ganging up to impose a sovereign, nor did he tell us whether all societies lived on the basis of strife and mutual distrust.

He went on to elaborate, with care, the distinction between "right of nature," and "law of nature" and the nature of the "contracts" deriving therefrom. But the contracts emanating from the law of nature, which is only a euphemism for the protection of self-interest or self-preservation, becomes void unless there be a sovereign, a "common power" to monitor obedience of the (egocentred and otherless) contracts so formed by striking fear of punitive expedition greater than the benefits derivable from breaking a covenant into the hearts of those who would have tried to break their sides of the contract; thereby creating *injustice,* which is no more than the *nonperformance of covenant* (see pp. 268–269). In this regard, Hobbes says,

> The only way to erect such a common power, as may be able to defend them from the invasion of foreigners, and the injuries of one another, and thereby to secure to them in such sort, as that by their own industry, and the fruits of the earth, they may nourish themselves and live contentedly; is, to confer all their power of strength upon one man, or upon one assembly of men, that they reduce all their wills, by plurality of voices, unto one will: which is as much as to say, to appoint one man, or assembly of men, to bear their person . . . as if every man should say to every man. *I authorize and give up my right of governing myself, to this man, or to this assembly of men, on this condition, that thou give up thy right to him, to authorize all his actions in like manner.* This done, the multitude so united, is called a COMMONWEALTH, in Latin CIVITAS. This is the generation of that great LEVIATHAN, or father, to speak more reverently, of the *mortal god,* to which we owe under the *immortal God*, our peace and defense (p. 271).

For Hobbes, then, many consequences, contractual rights, duties and obligations flow from this pact. Some of these are a) that all prior covenants contrary to this new one are voided by the new one; b) that the sovereign cannot do wrong to his subjects or be so accused (as the mortal god) because *volenti non fit injuria*; c) that the Leviathan cannot be committed to die, and d) he alone can institute what opinions and doctrines are conducive to peace, as he has acquired the collective wisdom of the people who agreed to appoint him, by some strange quirk of delegation of collective imagination and understanding of what would constitute and contribute to the overall welfare of the individual person and collective happiness of the people.

We see in the above the fact that this effort is based on rights conceived in a sense that privileges the persons who are already in control of the resources which enable them to be propertied, by contrast to the general populace who are contracted out of the equation, because they are not able to assert their rights against the Leviathan, nor do they have the wisdom to take part in the process of the contract formulation and enforcement—for example, the general peasantry of Europe who were being made virtual slaves in their own countries. It was this which led Marx to formulate his dialectical materialism thesis, as an antidote to the Hegelian Aristocratic and racist dialectical idealism. It is remarkable that at the same time Hobbes was pontificating about social contract hordes of Amerindians were being decimated as the "enlightened" Europeans were marching west in what became the United States of America and claiming from indigenous civilizations the wealth of the Americas. It was also while these hifalutin theories were being formulated by the Janus-faced intellectuals in Europe that the Haitians were being destroyed and the Africans were being shipped in millions to plantations in the "new" world (the Americas), away from their advanced sociocultural, scientific, agricultural and political climes into bondage as mere property, and in the process totally destroying their civilizations.

We may observe here that the Hobbesian social contract ultimately ends in a dictatorship of the Leviathan, as it had no other logical destiny, given its deliberate obfuscation of the critical importance which other-regarding respect and ego-sacrifice plays in the development of human society. Consequently, Hobbes's contractarianism ends in a *cul de sac*—a dead end, as a philosophical theory of political organization, an intellectual experiment, as a historical account and a disaster as a forward-looking predictor of international sociopolitical arrangement for the adjudication of clashes during human interaction on a local or on a global level. We shall examine this further presently; for now, let us turn our attention to the second of our trio contractarians, John Locke.

John Locke was, in my own judgement, to a very limited extent and in some sense, one of the most civilized of the intellectuals of his time. His *Two Treatises of Civil Government*, it could be argued, is a great testimonial to his intellectual genius and integrity; this is very much so when we examine what the European age of his day was doing in the Atlantic and in Asia. He started Book 1 with a consideration of the rationality of slavery and Sir Robert Filmer's apologia for totalitarianism. He concluded, contrary to the general trend of the period, that both slavery and totalitarianism were inconceivable debasements of human nature and rationality; this was a great achievement on his part, given the fact that this was an indictment of his own economic investment in slavery, or even as suggested, that he himself owned slaves.

Locke carefully examined the views of Sir Robert, and raised fundamental questions regarding the religious, moral, political, economic, cultural and natural grounds for the supposition that humans were destined to either divine rulership from Patriarch Adam or, for that matter, from parentage, conquest or necessity. In Book II, titled "An Essay Concerning The True Original, Extent and End of Civil Government," Locke advanced his ideas concerning the true origin of the state and that of political authority in society. While Hobbes postulated a state of nature in which there was perpetual war between contending individuals for the scarce resources available, and the state as the only possible check on the rancour that is innate to human nature, Locke understood human nature as one of "perfect freedom to order their actions, and dispose of their possessions and persons as they think fit, within the bounds of the law of Nature, without asking leave or depending upon the will of any other man" (p. 118).

It is interesting that Locke had this view of "freedom." It is an irresponsible view of freedom, because it assumes that human beings are autonomous, with no responsibilities to themselves so as not to do things which would harm themselves and that if they so carelessly exercise their perceived freedom as to compromise themselves, no one should care or hold them accountable. Apart from that, it assumes that there is any meaningful way in which humans are sole owners of "possessions," which no other person would have vested interest in, either because they had contributed to the process of one's upbringing or facilitation of the process of development of one, which has made the acquisition of the property possible in the first instance. Apart from that, this notion of personal freedom to dispose of one's possession assumes that filial obligations are obliterated by the factor of individual autonomy, which would ensure that under no circumstances is one compelled to make provisions for one's off-spring, especially to provide them opportunity for development of capacity for self-support.

Thus, the state of nature that Locke describes is one of "equality, wherein all power and jurisdiction is reciprocal, no one having more than another" (p. 118), it is clearly not a state of "license," it is a state in which "reason, which is that law, teaches all mankind who will but consult it" (p. 119). But this state of nature is only applicable to adults, who are also property owners; in fact, it is property that is most important here for Locke. Locke went further to discuss what constitutes a serious theory of punishment, based on reason and derivable from law of nature that unconditionally binds humans everywhere.

Compared with Hobbes, it is obvious that Locke was almost an incurable optimist, regarding human nature and the goodness and rationality innate to that nature. Locke then argues that humans get out of the state of nature through the voluntary choice of entering a compact, contract or consent of association with other humans for the procurement of the facilities of life which would have been beyond their reach had they gone solo (p. 124). But one cannot contribute what one does not have, and one of the powers that humans lack is that of taking the life of oneself or that of the other. Thus, when thieves or enemies attack one, the only justification for the use of force that may ensue in death to an aggressor, according to Locke, is only for the purpose of self-preservation, so that irreparable damage or mischief may not be done to oneself in the unlikely event that civil society fails to ensure the protection of one's life (p. 126). For this reason, one cannot, even in the extreme social aberration called slavery, enter into any compact that does not ensure personal safety or promote one's happiness (pp. 127–128).

While one may grant Locke the above with the proviso that it applies to matured humans who have the full understanding of the responsibilities to the self and to others that attend the freedom that they can claim under the Lockean system, it is important that we note that a crude interpretation that ahistorically attributes this freedom to all humans will be errant. It is not obvious the level of freedom that infants can appreciate or properly claim. If we are ready to treat some offenses as originating from minors and mete out corrective measures rather than punishment, then we would be indicating that minors need assistance to mature and be responsible adults. This notion is seriously abridged in the Western world, as painfully illustrated by the consequential events of misplaced education and a culture a-drift in the United States of America and other Western societies where child discipline is thrown overboard, creating a culture bred of state-of-nature theory inured in extreme liberalism and fattened on extreme individualism, weighing more on the side of superficial rights of children and less on responsible child-rearing, forgetting that before children become responsible adults there must be responsible parenting.

One other minor digression is indicated here. To be very charitable to Locke, one would have to suppose that he was most probably thinking of peonage, not Western slavery, when he asseverated that systems that promote personal safety and happiness override other matters. If one does not use this principle of charity, taking Locke in the most favorable reading, one will not be able to understand the failure on the part of Locke to see the evilness of the type of slavery that took place in the New World, by contrast to systems of "slavery" in various other traditional societies except the West. In various traditional systems of servitude, except in ancient Greece, the human rights of the serves were not denied and the barest essentials of safety and happiness were instituted. In ancient Greece, as in transatlantic slavery, the humans involved (that is, the slave owners, the slave masters and the slaves) were not humans: the slave owners were property-owning sub-human animals of the state-of-nature construct, the slave masters were sub-human despots with terrible complexes only assuaged by tyranny over the defenseless slaves; while the slaves were sub-human as they were property, to be treated any way their owners saw fit or unfit. Hence, Locke was either too ignorant or too civil to understand the Western psyche regarding the enslaved "other," and his theory of state was also too civil for his associates—especially those who have found his theories handier in explaining government and state.

Locke provides a very detailed examination of the origin of civil government; for he examined the fact that children and infants are not forced to remain in the commonwealth, except for as long as they are minors. In providing the contractarian account of the origin of the state and government, Locke says,

> Men being, as has been seen, by nature all free, equal, and independent, no one can be put out of his (her) estate and subject to the political power of another without his (her) own consent, which is done by

> agreeing with other men (women), to join and unite into a community for their comfortable, safe, and peaceable living, one amongst another, in a secure enjoyment of their properties, and a greater security against any that are not of it (p. 164, parentheses added).

While this statement by Locke may not have been recorded in history for direct verification by posterity for accuracy, it is important that we note that this is Locke's understanding of the origin of civil government. The notion of estate indicates property, which is common to other contract theorists, but his notion of estate does not cover property rights in other human beings, such as slavery mentioned above. To doubt this or think otherwise would be tantamount to embracing false theories or doctrines.

Jean Jacques Rousseau started the *Social Contract* with the assertion of the natural freedom of human beings at birth. This freedom is innate, inalienable and basic. It is common to all of humanity. But somehow humans find themselves in chains, in a state of alienated freedom or in a state of contrived unfreedom. Humans lose the natural freedom with which they were born and they are left with only a semblance of the real thing. He says, "Man is born free; and everywhere he is in chains. One thinks himself the master of others, and still remains a greater slave than they" (p. 181).

He was concerned about how this change came about. In trying to unravel the causes of the change, Rousseau took account of diverse factors. The first that he noticed is *force* (p. 181). Force, for Rousseau, means compulsion. And compulsion means making a person or people do things against his/her or their will. This, he argues, is unnatural; and if a person or people voluntarily obey such force, one cannot complain; while if they resist such force, it is better still; and, to regain their freedom is infinitely better still. All the processes of establishing the system under which members of the society shall live constitute the process of determining the *social order* (p. 182), and the social order is not a natural order; it is devised by humans in society. In my view, Rousseau is correct in regard to the fact that social order is not natural to the extent that it involves the creation of a complex social milieu with complicated educational and sustenance mechanisms that civil society entails. However, it seems to me that Rousseau is flagrantly mistaken in supposing that humans are born free. For the human fetus is a peculiar anomaly which is indefinitely attached to its progeny and parentage through physical, genetic, economic and social forces, first through the umbilical cord, second through provision of first life-sustaining facilities without which the infant is doomed to certain death, and lastly through skill forming and culture providing education, which makes independence possible for the individual that emerges from years of parental and community nurture and environmental care. It is this singular fact which makes the transmission of cultures and survival of societies a serious possibility; and further, it is this factor of gradual inheritance of independence and learning through apprenticeship to take care of the young which make Rousseau's position valid in his fear of how social order could arise out of force and be maintained by force.

If the process of establishing the social order is determined through the use of superior force, Rousseau would be amazed as to the type of sustenance the arrangement would have and whether it would endure. For, according to Rousseau, force cannot establish right, and the wish of the strongest can only subsist for as long as the strongest remains the strongest. Immediately the position is reversed, or whenever there is the possibility of disobedience without penalty, the *obligation,* out of need to avoid untoward consequences, to obey the dictates of the force, vanishes, for *force does not create right* (p. 185):

> The most ancient of societies, and the only one that is natural, is the *family*; and even so the children remain *attached* to the father *only so long as they need him for their preservation*. As soon as this need ceases, the natural bond is dissolved. The children (are) released from the obedience they owe to the father, and the father, released from the care he owed his children, return equally to independence. If they remain united, they continue so no longer naturally, but voluntarily, and the family itself is then maintained only by convention (p. 182, italics and parentheses added).

We may immediately note two things in passing here. First, Rousseau spoke of father and son or children because he wrote during a period when there was no gender consciousness that would have informed discourse in the patriarchal, male-dominated society in which he lived. This, I believe, accounts for why he speaks as if when the child is born *to* a father the child is born *by* the father. The second thing craving our notation is this: Rousseau conjectures that humans were born *naturally* free, which we mentioned earlier. But the fact is that infants were not born naturally free, as they remain attached to their mothers through the umbilical cord and remain dependent, as he observed, for a long time after birth for what he called *preservation,* sustenance and protection. Since we have commented above on the natural unfreedom of the infant, it remains only to insist here that it may be that the same reason that accounted for the gender bias of his discourse indirectly informs the inability of Rousseau to see that infants (the human young generally) were never born free. The recognition of this factor would be momentous toward a proper understanding of what educational attitude would be beneficial to society. More will be said on this later, time and space permitting.

For Rousseau, the second factor that leads people into unions, apart from force, as noted earlier, is *self-preservation*. It is this need for self-preservation which makes the child voluntarily relinquish his freedom to his father, in return for care, provision, and protection. The members of the family *alienate their liberty* (equality and freedom which they possess in their natural states as human beings) *only for their own advantage* to the head of the family who is their father (p. 182). This deliberate alienation of liberty, freedom and equality by members of the family is repaid by the *love* that the father has for members of the family. This love, going by Rousseau's understanding of the relationship, is also not an altruistic one; it derives from self-interest, as the father derives pleasure and satisfaction from leading and commanding the family. In the cases of the state, for Rousseau, since there is no immediate filial relationship to engender love for the followers or members of the community and society, the *chief* derives pleasure from commanding the people.

The third factor that leads people to association, according to Rousseau, is *conventions*. By convention, Rousseau understands the *first original gathering and agreement process* by which a people become, so to say, a *people*. This he calls an original *unanimity, on one occasion at least,* which, by inference, gives the majority the right to lead the minority electorally (p. 190). But this convention is also a product of expedience, and it is a contrivance that comes about from the necessity to maximize the innate individual self-interest intrinsic to the Western psyche, using the greater pool of force available to more people. This is in contrast with each person trying to accomplish similar objectives separately and at cross purposes. It is also a fiat that may lose its force because of any individual violation of its clauses due to any unilateral minimal modification, without the consent of the persons who have entered into the compact, thereby returning to each the original *conventional* liberty they had voluntarily renounced in the hope of a greater liberty derivable from the common pool of greater protection that derives from the commonwealth.

Thus, Rousseau says, in chapter 6 on "The Social Compact" (I wish to quote at length from the passage to allow Rousseau to speak for himself here), that,

> I suppose men to have reached the point at which the obstacles in the way of their preservation in the state of nature show their power of resistance to be greater than the resources at the disposal of each individual for his maintenance in that state. That primitive condition can then subsist no longer, and human race would perish unless it changed its manner of existence.
>
> But, as men cannot engender new forces, but only unite and direct existing ones, they have no other means of preserving themselves than the formation, by aggregation, of a sum of forces great enough to overcome the resistance. These they have to bring into play by means of a single motive power, and cause to act in concert.
>
> The sum of forces can arise only where several persons come together: but, as the forces and liberty of each man are the chief instrument of his self-preservation, how can he pledge them without harm-

> ing his own interests, and neglecting the care he owes to himself? This difficulty, in its bearing on my present subject, may be stated in the following terms:
>
> "The problem is to find a form of association which will defend and protect with the whole common force the person and goods of each associate, and in which each, while uniting himself with all, may still obey himself alone, and remain as free as before." This is the fundamental problem of which the social contract provides the solution (pp. 190–91).

The important consequence of the contract so ordained by each man with the other man is the creation of the *sovereign*. The sovereign, in Rousseau's reasoning, is not a person, but an authority. It is not even an aristocratic group, but an aggregation of the individual voices and wills of the contracting members of the society. Because of this, the sovereign cannot become law unto itself in a way inimical to the interest of the contracting parties. Thus,

> Each of us puts his person and all his power in common under the supreme direction of the general will, and in our corporate capacity, we receive each member as an individual part of the whole.
>
> At once, in place of the individual personality of each contracting party, this act of association creates a corporate and a collective body, composed of as many as the assembly contains voters, and receiving from this act of unity, its common identity, its life, and its will (p. 192).

The social contract, once formed, engenders minor inconvenience for those who may not realize that it is in their interest to be obedient to its authority. It involves the possibility of coercion, where "renegades" are "forced to be free" or forced to obey the laws that they have freely made for their self-protection (p. 195). This is not an evil as such, for it prevents the greater evil of individuals fending for themselves and failing in the process, ending up with the greater inconvenience of having to live in the state of nature. Through the aggregation of the individual wills there emerges the collective will which is stronger and more able to effectively and efficiently guarantee the individual rights that would otherwise have been threatened because of individuals' incapacity to protect their rights on their own.

The appeal of this theory, like the creation story found in the book of Genesis, consists first and foremost in its intuitiveness, conceptual simplicity and theoretical elegance. In fact, the social contract theories have captured the imagination of many, becoming almost as divine as the system of Euclid in Western scholarship. And one cannot but be impressed by the acuity and perspicacity of the trio of contractarians that we have examined here. But the genius that provided the impetus to the development of this type of democratic construct has not gone without serious challenges from various directions. Before we conclude this discussion, we will examine some of the criticisms of the social contract theory—both the exogenous types that have suggested complete rejection of the theory and those endogenous ones that have suggested emendations to remove the weak points of the theory.

The usual criticisms of contractarianism have been endogenous to Western cultural orientation and, because of that, they have not been audacious enough to challenge the fundamental bogus assumptions of contractarianism. Some of the criticisms have, in fact, been anticipated by the contractarians. For example, the criticism that the state of nature was never a historical reality experienced by humans was carefully discussed by John Locke, who, perhaps, was the most intellectually robust of the three classical contractarians we have discussed in this essay. His response was that the history of human society makes clear determination difficult for the historicity or nonhistoricity of the postulated compact. In a sense, the admission that this contract was never supposed to have been a real-life one deflates the seriousness of the critique, but nevertheless, it is clear that after admitting that the compact was not a historical one, one still finds that contract theorists use their postulate to warrant the sovereign and the allegiance people are supposed to owe to state authority as "constituted authority."

Another, similar but not the same, criticism has been the argument that the "social contract" indicated in the contractarian theory is simply a hypothetical one, designed as an analogical apologia to justify the legitimacy of democratic principles and practice on which Western societies have sought to found governmental systems and nothing more. But then, it is suggested by the critic, this hypothetical methodology is prospectively stretched too far as if it were a factual reality, thus creating the logical gap between the intention and the actual outcome of discourse. Hobbes and Rousseau are partly guilty of this error, but it is clear that what the contractarians were doing was more important than mere hypothesizing. They were concerned with the justification, more than the mere historical origin, of government.

It has also been argued that the government that is derivable from the contractarian contraption is not uniformly the same; that Hobbes derives a Leviathan dictator, Locke a state that is shot through with democratic principles that surpasses the mere legalisms of contractarianism; while Rousseau came up with a state that indicates minor incongruities of *forcing dissenting members to be free*, even against the wishes of these "recalcitrant" members. One way of assuaging the implications of this particular criticism is to look at the historical factors that led to the development of these contrasting contract approaches by each of the contractarians. These are complex social, historical and intellectual issues beyond the scope of this present discussion, and as such, could be addressed in another study.

The contractarians all suppose that the state of nature is one in which *human nature* tends only toward *negative expressions*. This is very much similar to the understanding of human nature found the Christian religion where the negation of the good in human personality, *albeit* through the sinister artifice of the Serpent, typified as the Great Fall of Patriarch Adam and Mother Eve from Divine Grace, leads to the projection of the good *ad infinitum* to the supernatural, such that a dependency of humans on the supernatural becomes inevitable, to counterbalance the inherent weakness and predatory nature of humans, and also to bring about redemption and ultimately lead to the realization of the positive that has been in abeyance, latent and negativized by the negatives in human nature.

In the case of the contractarians, the balance of the negatives in the human sociopolitical and economic nature inexorably leads to the creation of the state, a big brother who is permanently breathing down the necks of the recalcitrant humans who would never have done the right thing unless coerced. Or, minimally, the state enforces the wiles and ideas of the individual person who needs the enforcer.

By painting the picture of gloom and doom, the stage is perfectly set for the state authority as inevitability. But even if we grant this gloomy picture of human nature in its "natural" state, the inevitability of the contractarian state as the only possible arbiter is not logically established, as there are societies that have not, given this picture, gone to the point of setting up state powers as they have remained stateless societies. Hence, it has been contended, that if the fear of the gloom has not compelled some societies to statecraft, it can only evidence the logical gap in the contractarian argument, namely, that the gloomy picture painted in which humans in the state of nature are in perpetual grief because of mutual suspicion, the avarice and covetousness that arise as a result of the natural scarcity of resources and mutual exclusivity of conflicting needs are not inevitable paths to statecraft.

Upon a careful analysis of the contractarianism of Hobbes, Locke and Rousseau, it will be seen that there is no doubt that the position which *private property* has occupied in Western consciousness has indicated the contractarian apologia for statecraft as the only means of averting the extinction of humanity through inordinate greed, dispossessive quest for personal enrichment—to the detriment of other equally deserving humans in the same environment and the mutual self-destruction that would have followed the war of all against all—which is intrinsic to human nature in Western culture.

It is clear that Western culture is built on the position that only the fear of violence and mutual annihilation impels humans, through passions, to peace. In other words, peace arises out of the recognition of the futility of the antagonistic war of all against all (*omnium bellum contra omnes*). On the contrary, the critic will argue that it is not passion but *reason* that leads to the human need to contemplate the arrangement for peace and statecraft; that is, the state as a craft, a contrivance of the highest human genius. This is evident from the simple fact that passion has no time to contemplate, but only to gratify in whichever way possible, but only reason can be used in the service of passion to *work* out the best means of gratifying the needs of passion.

Also, when Hobbes conjectures that humans place a value upon themselves and desire that others recognize this value, exerting through force this recognition, if need be, it is clear that Hobbes has inverted the Kantian Categorical Imperative and the Golden Rule of Jesus Christ. Clearly, it is obvious that forming a compact with others to pursue the recognition of the store of value one places on oneself only goes to show that one should place equal value first on the other human, in order to be able to get into a contractual relation with the other, based on trust. Obviously, the development of concepts of self-valuation, contract formation and trust are not concepts that passion is capable of forming, nor ones which persons in states of passion can adumbrate. Hence, the conviction, on our part, that the contractarians did humanity a disservice by enunciating a one-sided notion of human nature. This failure on the part of the contractarians deliberately creates a fiat; it supposes that there was a point in the human past that steps were left unadopted to protect the weak and the young insofar as it did not pander to the glory and psychological gratification of some person(s), the strong. Herein lay the weakness of the suggestion that fatherly love is selfish gratification of base ingratiation and that leadership could not have developed from a genuine need to create a better society.

Finally, the idea of the dependence of infants on parents as arising from the need for self-preservation is jejune. If the human infant ever has any serious ability to procure self-preservation at all, it is as a dependent, as the severance of the umbilical cord that unites the infant to the mother is a painful one, as this cord had always been the means of nurture for the infant *in situ*. At birth the dependence is natural, and no amount of contractarian contraption could will away the dependence of the human infant, unlike most other animals, on their parents. Saying that the father (one would imagine here that the contractarian here properly means the mother) derives pleasure (and fulfillment from maternal caring for the infant) for the service provided, through directing and presiding over the affairs of the family, is not good reason to warrant the labors that go into the nurture of the human infant. In fact, this is good enough reason to say that humans were never born free, but only come to acquire freedom in maturity; that is, for human beings, there never was anything like natural freedom.

The state of nature theories (and, by extension, theorists) and Western political philosophy (*mutantis mutandis*, Western political philosophers) have assumed that the only way for deriving representative, just, humane, democratic culture and practice is through the formal consent, compact, or contract that the electoral systems have formalized. In making the assumption, they have undertaken to impose on other societies a mode of civil government that is not intrinsically indigenous, though not totally alien to their historical experience and the aspirations that their civilizations have developed over numerous millennia. In other words, Western intellectuals only conceive of civil society as a means of preserving individuality while other older societies have seen that such individuality has no meaning outside of community.

Thus, while the expedience of electoral practice might be the only "objective" barometer for clear measurement of contemporary governmental popularity and legitimacy in the complex arena of international politics, it is important that the point be made that democratic cultures had developed and thrived in ancient civilizations outside the West without the acute contentiousness, intrinsic mutual antagonisms and warring fratricidal destructiveness that is typical of the possessive Western individualist, whose sense of community is forged only as a matter of self-preservation and not because of the natural and inescapable innate social inclinations of humans. Not to recognize this fact will tantamount to telling only one side of the story about human political organization. It will be telling one true story as if it were the only true story instead of telling that one story as one of the many true stories about the development of similar phenomena.

In cultures where ownership of property is not the first principle of association, where the recognition of the existence of others as the crucible within which one's existence is made possible and meaningful is understood, where there is mutual trust between members of family that transcends that temporary link forged by incapacity on the part of infants to fend for themselves and the transient obligation of parents and adults to provide for minors, where, even when there are wants and needs that scarcity may make difficult not to contend with others to fulfil but such contentiousness are not without the primary understanding that life is more important and associations and associates more permanent than immediate material satisfaction and gratification, it will not be difficult to see why deriving good political cultures from neighborliness, and, consequently, hypothesizing political cultures that endorse first social and communal well-being as the harbinger of individual and personal well-being of members, may be a better alternative and why civil society would have developed and prospered without any prejudice to the nature and internal peculiarity of Western political history. It is no wonder that civil society developed in older civilizations of the world before Western civilization was midwifed by these older civilizations, especially that of the Nile Valley.

TWO

The Concept of Law in an Indigenous African (Yoruba) Society

The state of cultural development, and indeed the level of civilization, of any society can be discerned and measured by the evidence of many factors. Some of these factors relate to a) the extent to which there is security of sustenance resources of food, water and energy for members of society, b) the protection of members of society from the devastation of the forces of nature through the development of habitat structures that conduce to good existence, c) the avenues for the expression of the talents and intuitions of members of the society through the arts and crafts, d) minimization of energy expended by members of society in the process of garnering basic means of existence through the use of creative technologies, e) the level of leisure and luxury that members of society are able to enjoy in order to be able to indulge in the arts, plan for their individual demise, make wars on other competing societies and secure dominance for the in-group by contrast to the out-group, f) the development of resources for the care of the sick, the weak and the old, and last but not least, g) the development of and procurement of means for ensuring that institutions, structures, resources and mechanisms are in place for the determination and protection of the rights of members of the society.

In this chapter attention is focused only on the last factor, and this focus is in a limited way concerned with a philosophical analysis of the nature or, more accurately, the concept of law in indigenous Yoruba society before the interface with colonial experience and the attendant coercion of the various nationalities that existed within the geographical space of Nigeria into that federated political contraption (of various nationalities) known as Nigeria. It means that we are going to try to provide an initial critical philosophical overview of the Yoruba legal system as developed, theorized and practiced within the purview of statecraft and polities of the empires, kingdoms, city-states and villages, which this writer believes is long overdue. The goal of the discussion is to elicit the fundamentals of the Yoruba legal system before the imposition of the English common law and the attendant manufacturing of various culturally alien constitutions for Nigeria (constitutions which have never worked, because of their insensitivity to the cultural foundations of the numerous ethnicities that make up the artifice called Nigeria).

It is hoped that a philosophical discourse of this kind would, as we celebrate two hundred years of abolition of slavery in the new world and sixty years of the independence of the first black country (Haiti) to be nominally liberated from the clutches of colonialism, on the one hand, help us all in the process of coming to terms with the heritage of colonialism in the jurisprudential domain, while on the other hand, it would provide an opportunity for clear-sighted and retrospective analysis of the factors that contribute to the dysfunctionality and debilitating retrogression of state-craft in Nigeria, for example, to the point of anarchy, with the suggestion that there probably isn't something in the nature of the black person that impels him/her to self-destruction! If this effort is meaningful, it would challenge our legal luminaries, ethicists, political philosophers, legal philosophers, politicians, political scientists, historians, sociologists, educationists and all interested students of African cultures to undertake a holistic approach to the study of indigenous societies from multi-disciplinary perspectives and with more circumspection than has hitherto taken place. More importantly, such effort will lead to self-critical reflection of the goals of existence and the ends of humanity, especially in the search for an Africana agenda in the face of the monster of globalization, which is just a new name for the new form of colonization of the peoples of the South, whereby cattle and grains in Europe and America get more subsidy to cushion the effects of market forces than Africans and Caribbeans obtain from their governments for the contrived WTO-, IMF-, and World Bank-enforced declining prices of the primary products such as cocoa and sugar.

There is an openly recognized fact that humans are social animals, but this is an oft-repeated platitude that is normally taken for granted as true without adequate attention to the elements of sociocultural differences that create various distinct and irreconcilable identities for members of various societies. However, advocates of individual freedom, personal liberties, individual identity, self-determination and pursuit of personal happiness as absolute values often derogate from this truism by superimposing and super-ordinating the unit over the source of its being. To the extent that humans need a nonconstricting environment to fully realize their humanity, to that extent the humanity of humans need other humans—that is, persons are only persons within the context of the personhood of other humans/persons. This means that society as a whole must attend to issues of justice and fairness, with a view to ensuring the minimum occurrence of friction in order to assure individual members predictable warrants for fulfilling personal existence within the space provided in/by society.

With regard to the nature of human interaction in society, especially Yoruba society, Akinsola Akiwowo (1980) is very perceptive when he averred of what we call society that:

> The result is, among human beings, a complex network of *isesi* bond which unites every man, woman, or child to another. This network is what I have called *Aşuwada* or the purposeful knitting together of conscious beings for the attainment of a goal. In the case of conscious human beings, the purpose of such knitting together is social.
>
> Hence-from, according to this view, that which is called human society is what we call *asuwada eniyan*. Human society, *asuwada eniyan*, provides for each member who makes it up, five categories of inalienable social values, which constitute the purpose and goal of human collectivities. These are:
>
> a. *Ire aiku* (the value of good health until old age or meaningful long life)
> b. *Ire-owo* (financial security or economic prosperity)
> c. *Ire oko-aya* (the value of intimate relationship and love or enduring marriage)
> d. *Ire omo* (the value of parenthood or the blessing of having children); and
> e. *Ire abori ota* (the value of assured self-actualization or the blessing of/over enemies) (pp. 13–14)

What Akiwowo is celebrating here is that by nature conscious human beings are beings sensitive to the dimensions of existence and how these originate meaningfulness of selves on the one hand, and group histories and destinies on the other hand. Because of this, humanity in Yoruba context must transcend individuality into community if existence is to be meaningful.

From the foregoing, it is clear that no civilized society, in the true sense of society or community of humans and civilization, could exist without a system of laws devoted to the procurement and protection of values such as are set out above; that is, no society or community can survive without what can be regarded as a "legal system." But it is necessary to recognize that there are systems of laws in virtually all societies which are usually similar in major ways, even though there may be significant variations emanating from cultural, environmental, and historical differences—inclusive of the fact that a law that may look on the face of it as similar may be differently interpreted in different societies, as a result of cultural differences. Further, the humanity of humans indicate that we have some basic needs which are general to all humans, but these needs are met in different ways because of different existential circumstances and cultural experiences of members of different societies. To this end, the physical and social environments are crucial in the determination of the relations that facilitate the adequate meeting of the needs—some of which are basically survival in nature, while some others are of enrichment add-on in nature. Whatever the case may be, systems of laws are necessary to ensure the orderliness of the society to protect both society and members from destructive forces.

It is safe to suppose that wherever there are laws and systems of laws, there would be legal theories that underwrite them. Indigenous African communities were societies with norms, both moral and legal, before the advent of European destructive engagement interruption in the modern period. For this reason, it is contended here that, a) the task of careful examination and analysis of these structures and systems is long overdue and b) it is safe to assume that close scrutiny would unveil the legal systems of indigenous African societies as well as the legal theories that found them. The overall objective of this effort is to enrich our knowledge of the indigenous legal systems before European colonialism in the modern period, and in this regard the Yoruba legal system, as one of the legal systems often recognized by the foreign colonial office as essential to the proper running of the colonized societies, but which was derogatorily regarded as "native law and custom" or "customary laws" of the colonial societies, such as the Yoruba society, upon the introduction of English common law, thereby creating parallel and often conflicting or irreconcilable legal systems—with distinct and conflicting metaphysics, epistemologies, moral foundations and logic. To this end, based on the discussion by Hart, we could see a legal system primarily as a system of:

> (i) rules forbidding or enjoining certain types of behavior under penalty; (ii) rules requiring people to compensate those whom they injure in certain ways; (iii) rules specifying what must be done to make wills, contracts or other arrangements which confer rights and create obligations; (iv) courts to determine what the rules are and when they have been broken, and to fix the punishment of compensation to be paid; (v) a legislature (we would add, "authorities") to make new rules and abolish old ones (Hart 1961: 3).

Apart from the third element here, that is, (iii) above, and specifically the section referencing the making of wills within it, which in Yoruba society would mostly be regarded as an aberration (as no one shares his/her property in anticipation of the time he/she would be dead), there are other elements, such as a) processes for apprehending offenders or rewarding sterling performers incorporated in enforcement mechanisms that are clearly spelt out; b) properly defined institutional structures for holding those legally incarcerated; c) structured processes for confiscating or obtaining redress from offenders in compensation for the injury suffered by the aggrieved and by society; and d) structured processes for determining legitimacy and obedience to law. These additional elements are necessary in order to prevent chaos and resort to vigilantism by aggrieved persons and their sympathizers.

A complete examination of the concept of law in any society would have to address the issues raised above. But such discussion would not end at such a level, if it was to be meaningful and useful to interested students, scholars, the general public and policy makers. Such an examination will also have to devote attention to other matters, such as, first, how does legal obligation (i.e., the law) differ from orders backed by threats? Or, how do we separate the obligations of laws from obligations of duress, force, or intimidation? Second, how do we differentiate morality from law, given that both are concerned with ensuring just, fair, good, right relationships between humans in society? Are law and morality aspects of the same coin? And third, what constitute the origin or validating foundation of legal rules? What is the founding principle on which the force of law is built—the dictates of the rules, the choices of the judges, the maker or giver of the laws, proper law-making authority, the overall interest of society or the individual interest of members of society? We would also have to attend to the content of law, application of law and origin of law; these are important in showing how traditions, conventions, precedents, evidence, facts, witnesses, testimonies, proverbs, the ancestors and the determinations of good reason are used in the adjudication of disputes in the Yoruba indigenous legal system.

To this end, it clear that this essay is specifically devoted to an examination of the concept of law, and the various legal and moral issues to which it may give rise in the indigenous Yoruba legal system. We will examine the various theories of the origins of law within this legal system with a view to indicating the tenuous relation between indigenous Yoruba legal practice and contemporary Nigerian legal practice. Our discussion will be methodologically located within a philosophical approach within the sub-discipline of philosophy known as Philosophy of Law. We observe that this is a kind of engagement that is rare but which is necessary in the effort to see how Nigeria (Africa) can begin to embrace its history, traditions, customs and culture as a compulsory springboard to homegrown development, regardless of the fact that this is an effort which has now been compromised by the dearth of confidence and the outsourcing of knowledge to other geo-cultural regions of the world to the eternal peril of Africa.

Before closing this section I would like to say a word about my unapologetic reference to "indigenous Yoruba legal system" as "indigenous." Critics of references to such ideas as "indigenous," "traditional," and "pre-colonial" as descriptions of periods in African past are worried of the possibility of reinforcing the so-called idea of "folk philosophy," "ethno-philosophy," "cultural unanimity," "group philosophy" or other such universalizing and generalizing descriptive nomenclatures with regard to Africa. Such concerns are justified, but this does not remove from the validity of carefully annotated reference to parts of African past as belonging to the domestic, classical and indigenous or traditional intellectual heritage of Africa. Thus, my use of "indigenous" to describe the Yoruba legal system before the interface with the English legal system is to show that Yoruba civilization developed carefully orchestrated and sensitively tailored legal ideas, theories, beliefs and practices that conduced to well-ordered society centuries, if not millennia, before their interface with their kith and kin whose complexion have been affected (bleached) by inclement weather as a consequence of their wandering away from the homeland, hence their becoming *oyibo,* what in Jamaica is called "pale-face."

In this regard, we insist that this is not any different from the reference to the "English legal system" or "American legal system" or "French legal system" or "Japanese legal system" or any other indigenous legal system. While in the case of the American legal system, it was largely imported from Europe, in the case of the indigenous Yoruba legal system that I am seeking to understand here, it was a system totally native to Yoruba land, developing over hundreds, if not thousands, of years before colonial times. This does not mean that Yoruba society was insulated from influences from other societies around her, but what is affirmed here is that the legal system that is described as indigenous to Yoruba societies of the period under consideration was totally a result of sociocultural, environmental, filial, religious, intellectual, political and economic evolution of society of the Yoruba people. And, in my view, it is only fair that due respect be paid to the legal ideas and systems that sustained societies of Africa before the irruptions of colonization created the dislocation of the systems and ideas that conduced to meaningful existence for those who lived in these societies before our time.

LAWS AND MORAL NORMS IN INDIGENOUS YORUBA SOCIETY

In *The History of the Yorubas* (1969 [1921]), Rev. Samuel Johnson documented the highly urbanized nature of Yoruba society, whereby from time immemorial there were cities, towns, villages, and rural communities. For the Yoruba, the mythological cradle of humanity, not just Yoruba people, is Ile-Ife, "the place from which the day dawns" (Idowu 1962: 11). Oyo was the seat of central government, under a monarchical system of government, which built a large empire or kingdom spanning a large geographical area of West Africa at the peak of its power (p. 40). But the monarch, who is referred to as the King or *Ọba,* is elected by a body of noble men, or chiefs, comprising of "the seven principal councilors of state" after consultation with Ifa. At the peak of its power, the King of Oyo, known as Alaafin, had dominion over all Yoruba land—whereby "vassal or provincial kings and ruling princes were 1060," (p. 41) with these social and political units "completely organized" along the same pattern as that of the central government in Oyo. Hence, Johnson says,

> The Alaafin is the supreme head of all the kings and princes of the Yoruba nation, as he is the direct lineal descendant and successor of the reputed founder of the nation. The succession, as above said, is by election from amongst the members of the royal family, of the one considered as the most worthy, age and nearness to the throne being taken into consideration. It might be mentioned in passing that the feelings and acceptance of the denizens of the harem towards the king-elect are often privately ascertained and assured previously.
>
> In the earliest days, the eldest son naturally succeeded the father, and in order to be educated in all the duties of kingship which must one day devolve upon him, he was often associated more or less with the father in performing important duties and thereby he often performed royal functions, and thus gradually he practically reigned with his father under the title of AREMO (p. 41).

Johnson documented, in some detail, the system of government of the Yoruba society, with the highly specialized activities of various individual personages and groups in society which conduce to urbanization, a highly developed cultural foundation manifesting in the arts, religion, politics, commerce and other elements of civilization. For him, Yoruba people consider themselves leaders in all circumstances and assume leadership in whatever situations they find themselves, but they also have a proclivity for destructive independence of spirit, hence having a tendency toward dissension, leading in the end to strife, for which the internecine wars were a direct result and consequence which constituted an evil that brought the Yoruba nation to a lot of ruin (Johnson 1969: xxi, 69). What he did not set out for his readership was the precise system of laws that made for order and good governance, and how the disregard and or abuse of these laws led to discord, decadence and the implosion of the empire that emerged in Yoruba land—an empire which spanned most of present-day southern Nigeria, Togo, Benin, and Ghana. But indications are scattered throughout the book as to the nature of law, the concept of law, the origins of law, origins of legitimacy, procedures for law enforcement, dispute resolution and mediation, mechanisms for legal redress, dispensation of reward and punishment, and what constituted due process so that justice was not only done but is clearly seen to have been fairly carried out.

Yoruba society is generally one that is highly sensitive to the existence of laws, norms, rules, regulations and ideas regarding right, wrong, justice, proper behavior, deportment and clear attention to each person being moral and obedient to law. It is only when all persons, rich or poor, big or small, male or female, noble or peasant, king or chief, priest or laity, deformed or otherwise, young or old, native or foreigner, are observant of and obedient to the ethos and rules and laws that social order is maintained, and prosperity assured to society by the ancestors and Olodumare—the Supreme Being in Yoruba religion (Bewaji 1998). And because of the deliberate efforts made to educate Yoruba children to properly become responsible individuals, cognizant of their duties, it meant that there were few instances of existential angst, whereby individuals are in a quandary as to what their proper roles, duties or obligations were in society at any point in time (Crowder 1968: 372). Bolaji Idowu (1962) conflated the existence, types and nature of the laws, customs, rules and regulations with religio-metaphysical beliefs and activities in society when he says:

> It is to be noted that the same Yoruba word, with its cognate verb, is used for both "sin" and "offence." The word is *Ẹ̀ṣẹ̀*. This is a word which has been popularized by Christian evangelism and Islam. It is the word used for "sin" in the Yoruba translation of the Bible. The word *Ĕwò* is more comprehensive, however, and goes deeper to the heart of the matter. Obviously, it was connected originally with the breach of "ritual" laws. The phrase *j'ĕwò* . . . literally means "To eat the *tabu*"; it is a Yoruba expression for "break the *tabu*" or "commit sin" (p. 149).

The reason why he did that was clear. He was concerned with understanding the nature of moral values in Yoruba society from a clearly religious foundation. This led him to seek an understanding, not only of moral values but also of laws and regulations governing secular interaction of members of society within the domain of religion. This practice has been very popular among scholars not sensitive to the fact that even when practical secular rules have no religious foundations, yet to cement such laws, rules and regulations in unassailable validity and respect, they are often couched in religio-metaphysical terms—referring such laws, rules and regulations either to Olodumare and the divinities, the ancestors or other supernatural forces responsible for the sustenance of humanity and society.

Contrary to Idowu, it is clear that the Yoruba society has a distinct word for "law" outside of the religious domain, which is *Òfin*. This *òfin* is made principally by the Oba in Council or arises through the conventions and traditions of the people in the process of interaction and experience over a long period of time, and inscribed in the memory of the culture through various literary devices such as story-telling and proverbs, which are drawn upon in all walks of life and in all relevant situations to resolve conflicts and maintain order in society. And it must be emphasized that in Yoruba society, no person is above the law, because *"bí a se b' erú, bệ la b'ọmọ"*—that is, since there is no distinction in the process of giving birth to the noble infant and the peasant infant, there can be no differential treatment before the law for anyone.

Since Òfin is law, what then is "breaking the law" in Yoruba society? This is quite easy to answer. To "break the law" is to *ru ofin* or *ru'fin*, while the process of "breaking the law" is *i ru ofin*, and "someone who has broken the law" is regarded as *a ru'fin*. Thus, when there is an allegation (*ifisun, fifi sun, ifi ejo sun* or reporting of an offence or reporting the breaking of a law) that someone has broken the law of a society, of a family, a club or association, the person is considered to be under suspicion until the matter has been properly investigated, canvassing of evidence, calling upon all the creative measures to bring forward witnesses and other necessary and relevant ideas, where the person does not confess to the accusation or where there were no witnesses to confront the accused on being brought to answer to the system, and either the person is cleared of allegation of breaking the law or is found guilty of breaking the law.

As is clear from the above, this does not have much to do with religion as suggested by Idowu. However, within the context of religion, there is the notion of sin—*Èşè*—related to *tabu* outlined by him, where the infringement of *tabu* is as articulated by him. But this only makes ambiguous the relation between what the law and religion commands and the application of the same word to the infringement of legal and religious prescriptions. For legal purposes, it is clear that the use of religious terminology in a social setting that has nothing to do with religion does not pose any confusion to the Yoruba, for there is an appreciation that one can break the law of the society as well as one may break the commands of the religious powers—ancestors, deities, and the Supreme Being. When one breaks the law of the society, one would have *ru ofin* or *ru'fin* or *şè s' ofin*; where *şè* here means "break," "offend," "infract" or infringe," and what the person has broken or infringed could be a secular law or a religious *tabu*. While the first kind of infraction has no relation to "sin," except in an elliptical manner, because it is within social interaction as such, the second directly relate to religious issues. But both kinds of infringements could have repercussion for secular as well as religious order and the practical well-being of society at large, and probably this was responsible for the rather undifferentiated manner in which Idowu discussed the matter; that is, apart from the religious interests of his scholarship.

A third layer of interpersonal norms relate to morality in society, and this is where the concept of *Ọmọlúàbí*—a highly cultured person of high social, moral and religious integrity—is very important, as it describes how an upright, trustworthy, truthful, loyal, honest, hard-working, responsible, respectful person (indeed it refers to a highly moral individual) would be regarded in the context of Yoruba society—just like the idea of a "perfect gentleman" in English, with the proviso that it is not just gentlemen that can be accorded such respect and acclamation in Yoruba society but rather members of both genders (Bewaji 2003: 222). In Yoruba society, the context of morality is *asuwada eniyan*. *Ọmọlúàbí* (*omo ti Olu Iwa bi*—the human that was delivered and raised by god of character) is the total embodiment of the moral, social, cultural, religious and educated manifestation of the best that any human being can aspire to be. In this context, it is better to be an *Ọmọlúàbí* than to have the greatest material wealth, as *Iwa l'ewa omo eniyan*, that is, "good character is the beauty of a human being" (Bewaji 2003: 220). We should note that the line between legal and moral regulations are often very thin in indigenous Yoruba society, as rules relating to filial and conjugal relations border on both realms and are subject to moral approbation and legal sanctions. Also, ideas related to cleanliness and respect for elders are not purely moral in nature, but they may lead to physical and social ostracism to the party that fail to make the required standard (Bewaji 1994). Thus, while many moral norms are not actionable in the sense of being subject to legal enforcement in many societies, this is not totally the case in Yoruba society. Thus, according to Akiwowo,

> The primordial forms of *asuwada eniyan*, that is human society, are *Ajobi* and *Ajogbe* whose English equivalents as mentioned earlier are *consanguinity* and *co-residentship* (p. 18)
>
> As forms *asuwada eniyan*, therefore, *ajobi* and *ajogbe* are distinctive social relationships and social processes with established observable patterns . . . called *Sociation* (p. 20).

It is within the context of this *asuwada eniyan* that the social, political, economic, moral, legal and other relations of interaction take place; and often these are a complex nexus of interactions which demand perceptivity on the part of leadership to attenuate friction and discord, because on these planes it is to be observed that humans even with the best intentions may do things which have the capacity to be injurious to themselves, to others and to corporate social existence. And it is in the occurrence of these interactions that humans in Yoruba society device enforcement mechanisms backed by laws and apparatuses of social and moral sanctions.

Yoruba society, largely being a nonexclusively patriarchal society, without necessarily being gender exclusive, the symbol of the law then is the King in Council (Oba in Council), as he embodied the authority of his people, the traditions of the elders, the customs and deeds of the ancestors and the center of justice for society. We must note there are Obabirin also, who are not the wives of the king in many towns and cities. It is very important to understand this, because it may be supposed that because the Yoruba society embraced a monarchical system of government this automatically translated into a nondemocratic authoritarian dictatorship. On the contrary, the legal system functioned, was effective, and maintained the state authority only because the Oba in Council was supported by clearly all the other layers of society. Being a hierarchical society,

Yoruba society priced highly order and clear determinations of bounds of power and authority, hence the layers of authority spiral upward from the *baale*—male head of each family, the *ijoye*—the chiefs in each ward of the town, the *baale*—the head of each village, to the Oba in Council, in all Yoruba societies. This makes for the clear understanding of the moral and legal duties, obligations and requirements of each member of society—as defined within the context of social existence and appreciated as being beneficial to all members of society regardless of their stages of existence in life. And deriving from this, it is clear that, indeed, the legitimacy of authority of the Oba in Council was retained and maintained only to the extent that there was popular support from the populace, based on the extent to which the government reflected the wishes, interests, aspirations and overall objectives of the population.

This does not mean that there were no aberrations to this, where either the Oba (King) became despotic and lost the support of his Council, hence becoming isolated in his palace and consequently ineffectual within his domain, or the whole body politic as embodied by the Oba in Council could become so corrupted that they defined the societal interest in their own parochial way to reflect the interest of the Oba in Council. When this has ever happened in the past, the carpet is pulled from the feet of the Oba in Council, isolating the band of tyrants and making control and governance of society impossible, thereby generating chaos, decay, discord and anarchy in society. In fact, Johnson (1969) wrote that some of the internecine wars in Yoruba land are to be seen as a consequence of such moral and political decadence that often attend societies that have been able to assure leadership unhindered wealth and a luxurious, opulent lifestyle, which led to the demise of the Oyo Empire (p. 69). In extreme instances of monarchical tyranny, the king is either excommunicated from the domain or he is asked to commit suicide—a request that he cannot refuse, given the oath of office to which he has sworn!

The reason why we would say, along with Akiwowo, that the context of morality is human society is that it is not only human beings who have to obey laws—all things in nature have to obey natural laws that govern their existence. In this regard, animals, plants and all things in nature are subject to natural laws, infringement of which laws has consequences for their welfare. In this regard, Yoruba society takes care to understand the environmental conditions of all things around them, so that even when they have to utilize any of these existents, they do not do so in manners that contradict their being, otherwise the consequences for doing things that go contrary to the natural laws would imperil the existence of the beings and all things in their environ. In the case of humans, the laws that must be obeyed are not only those that are natural to our physiology and anatomy but those that arise as a consequence of experience of the need for good society and good relations with other humans in society. And the kinds of sanctions that attend infractions of these laws are weighed proportionately to the negative consequences that malfeasance would originate to society as a whole. Morality, on the other hand is, in some sense, unlike laws, peculiar to human society as only humans have the conscious capacity nurtured in deliberate moral education to choose to be moral or immoral.

There are various symbols of legal authority of the Oba in Council. These vary from the simple idea of recognizing the messenger of the king sent on an errand, and respecting the messenger the same way one would respect the king wherever one were to accost the messenger, to the messenger being accompanied by the staff of office—*Ọpa Aṣẹ*—of the King in Council, to the presence of any instrument of office of the King in Council—such as *Ìrùkẹrẹ*, *Abẹbẹ*, or *Ìlẹkẹ* of the Oba or King, and to the presence of one of the officers or chiefs of the state (Johnson 1969: 51). When the King in Council (that is, the king sitting with his council of chiefs) is performing his office in accordance with the expressed interest of members of the society, he and his chiefs receive the due respect and obedience of the people. What is also important here is to understand that each segment of the society and professional associations have representation directly or indirectly in the council on which the king presides. As it were, the society makes direct input into the legislations and laws that are passed through the democratic system of delegated representation, whereby the various families and their heads represent the views of their members, while these are carried forward to the ward- and street-level meetings which inform the positions of the chiefs in their deliberations with the King in Council.

Since the body (Oba in Council) entrusted with the proper administration law and order in society have a responsibility for the judicious dispensation of their obligation, it is not an accident that resources and support mechanisms are provided for them to perform their duties. While indigenous Yoruba society may not have developed specialized professionals like lawyers and prison warders, there was no doubt that measures were in place to address these needs. In the first place, when an accusation is levelled against anyone, clear effort is made for fair hearing and due process. Each party to the dispute are brought to face each other, usually at the house of the head of the "court," to state their positions as they deem fit, without any fear or threat from any source. This is usually presented before the council presided over by either the *baalé*—male head of each family, the *ìjòyè*—the chiefs in each ward of the town, the *baalè*—the head of each village, or the Oba in Council, depending on the importance of the issue to the individual, the community and the society at large. The reason for the parties being given equal opportunity is so that both parties can ventilate their claims in the most appropriate manner they may deem fit. While witnesses are usually encouraged to present evidence for either party, and the evidence is considered fairly—given the degree of veracity of the content of evidence—there is usually the clear aversion to third parties taking over the presentation of cases for aggrieved parties, for it is not expected that such parties would be more privy to the issue than the aggrieved, as *gbà ràn mi kò ye kó lè d'ẹlẹru*—that is, someone helping one to carry a luggage should not become the owner of the luggage! Anecdotally, I remember clearly when I was contemplating going to university for undergraduate studies and my father asked what I was going to study. I told him I was not sure, as I could do economics, political science or law. When he heard about law, he asked whether I was planning to become a lawyer (*a gb'ẹjọ rò*—one who accepts others' cases to state for them as if those others have no mouth to state their own cases), and I indicated that was possible. His counsel was that I should do something more fitting or human, as lawyers were known to be liars and heartless! While this may not be the case in reality, this was not far from the way in which lawyers were generally perceived in Yoruba land.

Since humans live in society, and there are various levels of interaction, it follows that there would be different kinds of friction in interpersonal and community relations. For this reason, though, the general rubric for dispute articulation is to identify the kind of law that has been infringed, and there are levels of seriousness. This is annotated by the kinds of accusations levelled, the process for adjudication and kinds of punishment or remedy sought or instituted. It is in the light of this that reporting the dispute (that is, *ifi ẹsun kan,* or *ifi ẹjọ sun*) requires that it be done in the presence of more than one single person, so that the matter may begin to be properly addressed. When someone has done something that is of very grave matters, it is said that the person *da oran*—where it is recognized that *oran* is more serious than merely infringing on interpersonal rules, as it involves a threat to the total cohesion of society. This is taken very seriously and the matter must be resolved with dispatch. And there may be requirements for stating the case (*ẹjọ*), such as that the litigant indicate specifics of the case (*okodoro ọrọ*), along with proper notice to the witnesses (*ẹlẹri*) to the issue in question.

At this stage, both parties are brought together, with the view to understanding the basis of the dispute and finding amicable settlement. If the details of the case indicate clear infringement of the accuser's rights, and the accused acknowledges the offence (confesses to the offence—*mọ ẹjọ ẹ l'ebi*), then matters would not drag for long, and the accused would not suffer too much. In such cases, if the offence is not of grave consequence to the overall welfare of the society, then judgment—*idajọ*—may involve *ibawi, ikilọ*—reprimand and warning. This may end the matter if no damages or retribution—*ẹsan* or *ẹtọ*—is required by the litigant. On the other hand, if the gravity of the matter requires that damages be paid, this leads to a fine which may cover the replacement of the cost to the litigant and for the troubles caused to society. In this case, there are many possibilities; these may include *public disgrace (ẹsin* or *ẹlẹya*), retribution (*ẹsan*), punishment as means of deterrence to other who may contemplate similar behavior or action (*ifi j'ofin*), remand or detention in prison form (*a ti mọ'le* or *ihamọ*), and in extreme situations, where the offence constitutes a threat to the corporate existence of the society, the offender may be asked to leave the community, either permanently or temporarily (excommunicated) or even the person may be sentenced to death (*idajo iku)*.

To prevent miscarriage of justice, various precautions are taken. These include ensuring that the reporting of the problem is done in the presence of others who can bear testimony to the veracity of the claims of the aggrieved. Hearing the matter must also be in the presence of both parties, because it is both unjust and immoral to judge a case on the hearing of only one side to the dispute—*a gb'ẹjọ ẹnikan da, agba osika* (one who hears one side and judges a case is a wicked elder or judge unworthy of being called elder or judge). Also, when the case comes up for mention or resolution, both parties must be present, as it is believed that it is wrong to conclude or determine a case in the absence of the parties to the case—*a ki i fa ori l'ẹhin olori* (it is impossible to shave someone's head in his absence).

Determining any issue may involve community service, payment to the ancestors and gods in the form of sacrifice, especially if what was involved was a big *ọràn*—like transgressing the memory of the ancestors, defiling the religious foundations of society, insubordinating to the authorities of the leadership of the community, grand theft, horrible sexual escapades as incest and more. The *èèwọ* or taboo must be expiated and the society cleansed of the abomination, so that restoration of social cohesion and trust be established promptly. Not doing this may become a danger to the leadership, which has sworn to maintain the integrity of the society above self-interest at all times. Having taken such oaths, they face extreme dangers if they were to renege for whatever reason—even at the pain of death—in the performance of their duties and obligations to the society. These duties are also framed in the form of duties to the Olodumare, the gods (divinities), the ancestors, the living and the yet unborn. And if one were to privately fail to perform these duties, or do whatever contradicts the oath to which he/she has sworn, even when this has not been observed, the person should never expect that the offence will not be punished, for *bí ènìyàn bá nyọ ilẹ dà, oun abẹnu a maa yọ ènìyàn se*—which means that "if one should be secretly doing evil, very evil things will be secretly affecting the person," and *adìẹ irànà ni, kì í se oun à je gbé,* that is, "the fowl used to announce death is never eaten without payment."

In the preceding sections of this discussion we have looked at the concept and nature of law in indigenous Yoruba society. We have sketched what could constitute an analogous Yoruba legal system in response to the issues raised by Hart, vis a vis Yoruba society before the advent of Nigeria as a country, and we have found that it must consist of:

> (i) rules forbidding or enjoining certain types of behavior under penalty; (ii) rules requiring people to compensate those whom they injure in certain ways; (iii) rules specifying what must be done to make wills, contracts or other arrangements which confer rights and create obligations; (iv) courts to determine what the rules are and when they have been broken, and to fix the punishment of compensation to be paid; (v) a legislature to make new rules and abolish old ones (Hart 1961: 3).

We also looked at elements dealing with our response to the emendation to Hart's view, that is, in terms of,

> a) processes for apprehending offenders or rewarding sterling performers incorporated in enforcement mechanisms that are clearly spelt out; b) properly defined institutional structures for holding those legally incarcerated; c) structured processes for confiscating or obtaining redress from offenders in compensation for the injury suffered by the aggrieved and by society; and d) structured processes for determining legitimacy and obedience to law. . . .

which we suggested. But the other aspect of our discussion deals with how law relates to other similar ideas or phenomena in society. We formulated these in the form of the following questions. First, how does legal obligation (i.e., the law) differ from orders backed by threats? Or, how do we separate the obligations of laws from obligations of duress, force, or intimidation? Second, how do we differentiate morality from law, given that both are concerned with ensuring just, fair, good, right relationships between humans in society? Are law and morality aspects of the same coin? And third, what constitute the origin or validating foundation of legal rules?

It is necessary to look at these matters because, a) contemporary experience has shown that, as preached by the West through colonialism and educational subjugation of Africana societies, human societies in Africa now crave individualism and freedom as absolute values which make European societies superior to African societies and which Africa must attain in order to be on par with the West; b) conflicts arise ever so often regarding how to understand and/or treat indigenous African legal traditions which are pejoratively described as native law and custom (as if the English common law is not the native law and custom of England); c) the contradictions in the application of English common law and indigenous Yoruba legal systems, especially where these relate to marital issues (land ownership, gender issues, will, property, types of marriage, sexual orientations in relationships, circumcision, etc.); and d) the chronic and intractable brigandage that have dominated Africana polities at the behest of Western imperialist efforts to ensure that Africa remains pauperized in order to continue to fulfil the prediction that Africans are incapable of governing themselves.

At the beginning of our discussion we noted that it was only within the context of *asuwada eniyan* that the various tangible and intangible goods that conduce to the proper existence of human beings can take place, for no individual human can guarantee the security of sustenance resources of food alone and outside of society, nor protection from the devastation of the forces, while guaranteeing avenues for the expression of her talents and intuitions and minimizing the energy in garnering basic means of existence through the use of creative technologies, leaving room for leisure and taking adequate care of herself in sickness and old-age. This is the reason why Yoruba metaphysic of existence does not recognize how a single individual can proclaim that "we have arrived"!

Based on this, it is clear that a Yoruba person does not see herself as succeeding as *a nikan j'ọpọn* or *aso, a nikan da rin* regardless of how wealthy or successful she may have become in any endeavor of life, because, for them, the reason why snakes are easy to kill is due to the fact that snakes are loners. This is indicated in the proverb that *a i tọwọ rin ejò, lo n se'ku pa wón*; that is, if snakes were to move in groups, who would be strong enough to face them? More importantly, within the culture of Yoruba society, young ones are not trained to make distinctions between siblings and relatives, as all related persons, either by blood or by humanity are seen as brothers and sisters. For the above reason, Yoruba society does not allow members see disputes as issues that must end with absolute finality, where separation becomes total, as there is no virtue in individualism.

Apart from the unnecessarily exorbitant cost of litigating disputes in the formal judicial system in Nigeria and the fact that lawyers are involved in replacing the parties in presenting their cases—thereby preventing the truth from coming out—there is also the fact that it is believed that even when we have problems, disagree or offend each other and fight, it is never to the death—*bi a ba n ja, bi ka ku ko*. Akiwowo (1980) cited Ifa Literary Corpus—*Otua—ariwafin,* which celebrates the virtue of *ajogbe,* while lamenting the dangers of individualism (p. 29).

What the above indicates is clearly that the origin of legitimacy and efficacy of law derives from the fact that humans in Yoruba society recognize that no one can be an island (*igi kan ko le da igbo se*), for there is no need to resort to the most violent of means to compel individuals to perform their duties in society and to respect other members of society. Thus, while individuals may have to use force to obtain respect for rights in certain respects, the society does not need to resort to such draconian measures, as individuals recognize the corporate body as superior in rights and in demands for her obedience over any other individual rights. In consequence, the individual accedes to the supremacy of the moral and legal dictates of society. And where individuals or segments of society attempt to use duress or force to coerce individuals unjustly—even in cases where debt repayment, for example, is at issue—society may intercede to allow for a more humane resolution to the problem, without demeaning the humanity of any one to the dispute.

As to the second question, differentiating between law and morality, we have said that this distinction is clear in many instances, but that they interweave in other areas, as what is more emphasized in Yoruba polities is being an *Omoluabi,* which involves being a good citizen as well as being a morally upright person. In any case, it is difficult to see how one could be a good citizen when one is not a morally decent, truthful, trustworthy, diligent and responsible individual. For this reason, the selection of kings and leadership in Yoruba societies involves taking into consideration every quality a human being needs to have to function properly in society. The suspicion that Yoruba people have of "book people" who have undergone years of tutelage in the English educational system is borne out by the split personality that it inflicts on products of such education—they are highly read but virtually useless as human beings capable of functioning as morally decent persons in society. In any case, they often wonder how it is possible that there is no requirement of moral stature of leaders in Western societies, while in indigenous Yoruba polities, rascals and delinquents will ever have aspired to leadership positions.

Now, this is not to indicate that there were no instances in Yoruba history where unscrupulous, vile individuals had occupied positions of power. When such occur, there were clear means of dealing with them. And in the extreme, where there are other complicit officers in the court of the ruler who collude with the tyrant or evil ruler, at the end such leaders come to very horrible ends. Stories are told of the terrible demise that such leaders have met in the past. Such stories are effective in detailing the potential tyrant to show restraint or face the music. Apart from this, individuals are most mindful of their family name, their community image, and their society's best interest over and above their own personal interest; as they are often reminded that *ọba to jẹ, t'ilu tu ka, oruko rẹ ko ni pa rẹ; eyı to jẹ t'ilu toro, oruko rẹ ko ni parẹ*; that is, "the name of the king who reigned and the city was deserted will never be forgotten, and likewise the name of the king who reigned and the city became prosperous will not be forgotten."

With regard to the final question regarding the validating force of law in Yoruba society, it could be indicated that suasion is largely responsible. But to simply indicate this may be glossing very important factors which come together to ensure that members of Yoruba society recognize that obeying the law is in their best interest. We may note the following important elements here: a) proper home training and social, political, cultural and professional education (all round education) meant that each individual Yoruba person knows what is right and does it. This does not mean that there are no criminals or ignorant persons who break the rules or infringe moral codes in society, but such are in the minority and are easy to deal with; b) the place of social cohesion in the consciousness of the people ensures that humans put clear stock in maintaining the order and success of social and community forces. For the Yoruba person, the Cartesian "Cogito, ergo sum" is meaningless, because without the *we* there can be no *I*, hence "I am, because we are" (Hord and Lee 1995), for it always takes a whole village to raise a child. Even when one should become very rich through one's personal effort and all one's siblings and relatives are dirt poor, there can be no joy in the success or wealth, as it is true that *Olowo kan l'arin otosi m'ẹwa, otosi di m'ọkanlaa*; that is, "a single rich person among a family of ten other very poor persons make eleven very poor persons."

The purpose of law is to equalize, as much as possible, the interactive process in society, and thereby to ensure that members of society are assured that the trust which each individual reposes in the collective arrangement of protection, security and individual pursuit of happiness are not undermined by those who may have the power or the intent to so do. If the law does not provide equal treatment for persons in society, then the process of cooperative facilitation of the interests of members of society would be undermined. It appears that it is assumed that freedom is an end in itself in contemporary scholarship, as it is an ultimate good in itself. This appearance is based on the fact that without freedom, the human capacity would be impaired and circumvented as the process of developing autonomy of personhood and consciousness would be affected negatively. According to Shyllon,

> personal freedom is the freedom of every law abiding citizen to think what he will, to say what he will, and to go where he will on his lawful occasions without let or hindrance from any other persons. The only duties which should restrict this freedom are those which are necessary to enable everyone else to do the same. Whenever the interest of individual liberty and public order are nicely balanced, the scale should go down on the side of freedom (Shyllon 1987: 4).

I can imagine the reason why Shyllon is of this view in the last portion of the quotation above. It is because of the epistemological and metaphysical anonymity of what constitute "public order." But I would argue that this kind of guarantee of individual freedom presupposes that the individual is a highly responsible person, who not only appreciates the fact that his/her responsibility is not only to the self, to take advantage of society as much as possible in furtherance of his/her personal happiness, but that there is within him/her a consciousness of the fact that not exercising self-control in the choices made would lead to not only the destruction of personal liberty in the long run, but also the destruction of the context within which the liberty makes sense—community.

I am aware of the possibility of taking the absolutist view of liberty or freedom which may be inferred from the above, as is often done by those who buy into the contract theory which we have discussed in chapter 1 in an essentialist manner, which looks at society as intrinsically a hindrance on personal autonomy which must be curtailed in order for the individual to maximize happiness. The other issues which they raise is that society would not have come into being had it not been that the individual voluntarily gave up some of his liberty in order to gain additional leverage on those who may wish to deprive him or her of the liberties which would make his/her happiness secure. The danger involved in this kind of emphasis on the individual unfettered liberty is the fact that it creates the possibility of having an impostor individuality, which assumes supremacy at the expense of society, and consequently takes for granted that he/she could not have been endowed with the so-called inalienable liberties except within the collectivity that society alone can make possible. The necessity for legal restraints on both the individual and collective is to ensure that there is moderation in all things that are done, either by the individual or by the collective. Often the importance of proper moral and legal education is of significance in ensuring that each side of the equation is notified well in advance of the consequences of taking for granted, at the expense of either party, the necessity of fulfilling the personal or corporate side of the equation.

In indigenous African societies, especially where there were highly developed urban communities, the instance of individual liberty and freedom is well articulated and guaranteed to ensure that each person is not encumbered in any way in developing himself or herself and hence in contributing to the maximum to the welfare and advancement of society. For this reason proper care is taken in individual and group education to ensure that the norms, rules, regulations and laws of the society (big and small) are brought to the attention of the individual, *nitori ilu ti ko si ofin, ese ko si*. Punishment and reward are based on laws which are unambiguously formulated and well known. What Shyllon calls the prospective nature of law is what ensures that all members of society are aware of the bounds that must be preserved in intra and inter personal relations, in order for the liberties and freedoms which are assured to be protected. According to Shyllon,

> That the spirit of liberty is so deeply rooted in our traditional constitutional structure; and that our forefathers believed that the essence of man is freedom is reflected in the following remarks of T. J. Bowen (1857) who after [spending] six years in Yorubaland, noted that "The highest excellence of the best governments among white people consists in constitutional checks or limits to prevent abuses. Strange as it may seem, the Central Africans had studied out the balance of power and reduced it to practice long before our fathers settled in America—before the barons of England had extorted the great charter from King John" (p. 6).
>
> William Henry Clarke, another keen observer who spent four years in Yorubaland from 1854 to 1858, while confirming the statement of

> Bowen, added: "However, such a statement may be spurned by those whose incredulity is equaled only by their prejudice of colour: it is nevertheless true.
>
> Finally . . . Commander F. E. Forbes quoted in the *Church Missionary Intelligencer* in 1853 wherein he marveled at the remarkable Egba federal structure: "Abeokuta has four presidents. Each town has a *warafa* or civil council of six and an average twenty *ogboni* or magistrates. It has also according to its size, one, two or three *baloguns* or military chiefs. Hence there are in office—taking the towns at 140–840 principal rulers or a "House of Lords," 2,800 secondary chiefs or 'House of Commons', 140 principal military chiefs and 280 secondary ones; and I hold this to be the most extraordinary republic in the world (Shyllon 1987: 7).

What follows from the above is that modernity had existed in Yorubaland before the contract theorists who were mainly motivated by greed, private property and oppression of the poor devised the theories of governance based on the worst elements in the depraved human. As Fela Anikulapo Kuti would formulate it, it is impossible for the animal to teach the human humanity, because the only thing that could happen when the animal leads the human is for humanity to become like the animal.

Let me use a stark example, earlier hinted at, that I find most apposite here. Part of what constitutes Western modernity and European civilization is the substitution of domesticated animals and pets for the friendship and sharing of space with other human beings for love, affection, intimacy and pleasure because, with modernity and the inordinate claiming of absolute rights against the other equally self-centered and hedonistically inclined persons, it imposes the impossible situation on Western humanity where each human becomes an unnecessary encumbrance on the other. This then supposes that animals are better companions than siblings, off-springs, parents, relatives—especially when they reach a certain age, because each person must covet their space, protect it, and ensure that it is not shared by anything that has the capacity to talk back at one, unless invited and with time limit for departure. Two consequences flow from this: while on the one hand there is now a reduction in the potential for incest, there is the pervasive, though unquantified upswing in bestiality; while on the other hand, we find the tolerance level of other humans to have reduced, because we find it very difficult to communicate effectively with each other, as the pets though they may suspect what we are saying to them, could not respond back to further aggravate our displeasure.

But that is the least of the problem. It is absolutely amazing when we look at what happens to those who walk their dogs and see that it is now a case of the tail wagging the dog. In most instances, instead of the owner walking the dog, in urban areas of the United States, for example, it is the dog that is now walking the owner, because whatever the dog likes it does and the owner must go along with them. In such instance, the dogs control the human, and the human has absolutely no control. It is like what happens with modern child rearing, because under the guise of civilization, the kids are brought up on heavy doses of bribery, whitemail and false sense of reality, to the point that they grow up to become addicted to mercenary behavior, thinking quid pro quo in every instance and expecting always to get something for every little thing they give. The result is that they find human relationships most difficult to tolerate, and as a consequence are condemned to the perfidy of the solipsistic lonesomeness; simply because what they do not know how to give, natural selfless kindness they vainly expect to receive, making conjugal relationships impossible and family commitments lacking in selfless devotion. And because they are not ever brought up to understand a world in which it is possible to give without expecting, the reciprocal nature of kindness is lost on them, meaning that old ideas of family, love, friendship are being redefined or expunged on the altar of reality shows and cyber counseling.

What we have shown here is that given the fact that culture is the foundation of law, based on the experiences of members of society, and as a forward-looking predisposition to understand humanity, it would follow that the law is a key element of societal relations, as a bonding mortar for the preservation of order against those instances where the process of interaction throws up possibilities of chaos—not in anticipation of perpetual chaos as the contract theories would have us believe. If, in the nineteenth century, Abeokuta had developed the highly specialized, differentiated, sophisticated governance structures that was described above, could one imagine what had happened in older kingdoms, empires and republics such as Ife, Ekiti, Ibadan, Oyo, Ghana, Mali, Kanem Bornu, Sokoto, Songhai, Zimbabwe, etc. In many instances, some of the states that existed were not just federations; they were confederations, extending over expanses of geographical space bigger than the whole of the United States of America and Europe. In any case, the point of the matter is, *ojo lo pa'werepe to d'eni a ko lu, ere lo b'edun n'le to da'la i mo o sa*. It is the situation of reality which reversed the process and historicity of civilization which has consigned the senior partner to nothingness which makes for the situation where peoples whose cultures midwifed the other cultures of the world to become mendicants, taking and living on the remnants of cultural wastes from other climes.

There is need for law because of the contingency of situations where there may exist conflict of interest in which the public or society has vested interest, as such situations, if not properly addressed, may lead to disassociation and disintegration of society. Laws are necessary to take care of situations where moral suasion is not enough, and where individuals and groups in society need a) clarity in the recognition of desert, b) for the assurance that all humans in society have recourse where there is unfairness and injustice, and c) to prevent the necessity of persons and groups taking matters into their own hands by resorting to vigilantism or violence in the pursuit of their perceived or real legitimate interest. As a consequence, law in Yoruba society does not address microscopically all aspects of human existence and interaction. A well-cultured individual, an *Omoluabi,* does not need the threat of laws or the compulsions of regulations to do that which is right or to perform his/her duty to her/himself, to other persons and to society as a whole.

With the above in mind, we will mention some specific areas of law that are critical to the existence of a well-ordered society, as perceived in Yoruba culture. These are laws relating to land ownership and use, marriage and family relationships—including widowhood, extended family ties and the human society as the larger extension of one's family, property ownership and transfer—including inheritance after the demise of one's parents and relatives, trades and professions—such as smithery, building, carpentry, hunting, traditional medicine doctors, cattle and other animal husbandry, fishery and seafaring, trading and contractual obligations related to such matters, cooperative ventures and partnership arrangements either for work or for savings, commerce, debt servicing and collection, war making, chieftaincy titles and rites of passage, death, burial and capital punishment and more.

The fact that society evolves new needs and forms of interaction implies that at various times, and given the contingency of various circumstances, the society would have to bring about new laws or do away with ones that become obsolete. This is part of the functions performed by the Oba in Council in various communities and at various levels. What remains to emphasize in Yoruba society is the fact that recognition of the fact that what works today may not work in the future—whatever one may wish—leads to the sayings that *igba kò tọ lọ bi òrere, aye kò gun lọ bi ọpá ibọn*—that is, time is not unidimensional and the world is not as straight as the barrel of a gun, and *b'òní ti rí, ọla le ma ri bẹẹ, ló mú kí babaláwo máa d'Ífá ojojúmọ*—that is, "as today is, tomorrow may not be like that, hence the divines must diviners Ifa everyday."

And it is recognized that there is need for the cooperation of all members of society for the social cohesion that is necessary for every member of society to have a good life to be realized. Various stories—*àlọ* and *ìtàn,* that is moonlight stories and history—are told to children and young people to drive this point home; the scripture of Yoruba theology, Ifa Literary Corpus, reinforces this at every turn both in the process of divination as well as in the process of illumination of issues, and references are made to precedents—positive and negative—in the determination of cases brought for adjudication before the Oba in Council. These all serve the purpose of cementing the laws of society and ensuring that all are aware of their obligations and duties to themselves and to society, to obey and ensure that others obey the laws of the land.

In concluding this discussion, there are three points that become obvious from our examination of the nature and concept of law in indigenous Yoruba society. In the first instance, it is clear that Rawls's understanding of the purpose of law and justice does not apply to Yoruba society. Hence, there could be nothing more alien to the Yoruba notion of law and justice than for Rawls (1971) to say that:

> Each person possess an inviolability founded on justice that even the welfare of society as a whole cannot override. For this reason justice denies that the loss of freedom for some is made right by a greater good shared by others. It does not allow that the sacrifices imposed on a few are outweighed by the larger sum of advantages enjoyed by many. Therefore in a just society the liberties of equal citizenship are taken as settled; the rights secured by justice are not subject to political bargaining or to the calculus of social interests (pp. 3–5).

The fact that leaders of contemporary Nigeria and Yoruba society have embraced this deception, which assumes that an individual has some rights which they could enjoy without or outside of human societies, is misguided. Being a social being does not mean that the human being must not obey any laws. The irrational acceptance of the ideas of liberty without responsibility has been particularly pernicious to African societies, making social cohesion impossible, and leading to various actions of persons in positions of authority and power to be outside of the norms and laws of the land. But when such persons are asked to swear before indigenous deities and ancestors, they balk and claim that they are now Christians or Muslims and they must not take oath before "pagan" gods, as they know that they cannot get away with defiling the indigenous deities and ancestors—while they blithely take oaths with the Bible and Koran without any negative consequences, as the Jewish and Arab gods and ancestors care not a hoot what happens to African humanity, integrity or identity.

The second point relates to the negative effects of the imposition of the laws of alien cultures on Nigeria and the Yoruba in particular. It has meant that Nigerians and Yoruba people, not being familiar with the culture that underwrite the English law, are happy to operate with deliberate intention not to obey the alien laws, and since they have been made to disregard their own culture, they equally become liberated from existing under the indigenous legal system of Yoruba society. For example, while land cannot be sold in indigenous Yoruba society, persons now sell the same land to more than one single person at the same time, creating not only an abomination but also terrible conflict between the unsuspecting persons who have been duped. Hence, by being able to operate under confused legal systems, the people are now living in state of near anarchy, whereby leadership blatantly abuse their positions and powers without any means of redress to society or offended individuals. The factor of military dictatorship in the history of Nigeria has compounded this situation of lawlessness and chaos, which may only have been replicated in Yoruba history during the period of internecine wars before colonialism.

The offshoot of legal alienation, bordering on judicial schizophrenia, is the farce being exploited by criminal leaders and their conscienceless legal fraternity collaborators to hold society to ransom for bogus fundamental human rights of "innocent until proven guilty" when crooks who have robbed society of resources are apprehended and arraigned before the courts. How else does one explain the situation where even when it is clear that a leader has abused his/her office and the trust of the people to enrich the self, with tons of inexplicable wealth, accumulated over a short period of doing nothing else but being in office, yet the leader enlists hundreds of criminal lawyers to do everything to prevent justice being done for the millions of people whose capacity for decent existence has been destroyed by the acts of primitive greed, abominable disregard for law and justice to the people and despicable abuse of power. For Yoruba legal tradition, just as in French legal tradition, the onus is on the accused to show/prove innocence, rather than that the society having to prove the opposite. *Loogun ii jale, loogun ii ji nnkan eni, be e, loogun ii wa'le eni k'obe silo o ma sonu*; how is it the responsibility of the robbed to show where in the turban or *gbariye loogun* has hidden the loot? The charade that goes on under EFCC trials of looters of the Nigerian commonwealth only help to confirm the needs of Africans for a return to indigenous legal tradition, judicial systems and sociocultural value systems in order to ensure that African posterity does not continue to drift rudderlessly under the yoke of English common law designed for only one thing—the continued impoverishment of the poor, the weak and the vulnerable members of society.

Finally, it must be acknowledged that while there is no perfect legal system in any part of the world, the advent of colonialism and the imposition of the fiat that is Nigeria has negatively impacted the legal system of the Yoruba people. It has truncated the development and evolution of the Yoruba legal system to meet new challenges and adapt to current situations in the world. As such, the kinds of education that would have conduced to social order and cohesion, steeped in the traditions of the people have been abrogated without any rational warrant, and hence the decadence in all strata of contemporary Nigerian and Yoruba society, which allows thieves to claim human rights when apprehended for theft, and there is no protection of the human rights of the people whose commonwealth has been stolen

While nostalgia is always psychologically comforting, it is difficult to see how the golden age of Yoruba civilization can be recaptured, but as a first step in the direction of ensuring the enthronement of order and justice and fairness in Nigerian body politic it is imperative that we make the effort to excavate some of the foundations of indigenous legal systems in Nigeria and use those aspects that would conduce to order and humane society. Hence, in conclusion, it is suggested that our educational system must ensure that we teach aspects of the indigenous legal system to our young ones, so that the legal "fish out of water" despondency that pervade Nigeria in terms of responsibilities, duties, obligations to self and the state, and respect for law and corporate existence of society can be ameliorated. Additionally, there is need to stop the aberration of impunity that pervade the social domain of Nigeria, to the extent that Nigerian leaders not behave as if they are not accountable to anyone, using and abusing their offices to rob the national treasury and take their loot to European and American countries, thereby perpetuating the colonial government system where government was an alien system imposed with no responsibility to the governed. For Yoruba people, this is particularly a sorry state of existence, where *omo onile olona wa di a s'agbe jeun*—that is, a nation of free-born people have become beggars in their own land!

THREE

The Rule of Law, Leadership and Development

In this chapter I examine the interface area between leadership, law and morality. The thesis which I defend in this chapter is that the cultures of impunity, nonaccountability and nonobservance of the rule of law, which pervades African leadership systems and practice, inherited from colonialism's intrinsic exogenous nature, cemented by mis-educated, visionless and immoral post-colonial governance systems and further compounded by reckless, myopic, and unconscionable military dictatorships, are responsible for the recursive, permanent, vicious cycle of underdevelopment of African societies.

To underwrite my argument, I examine first the concept of the rule of law, tracing the historical and cultural indigenous antecedents of the concept in the political systems in many parts of pre-colonial Africa, indicating the strengths and weaknesses of these systems, the checks and balances that reinforce moral, accountable, responsible and disciplined leadership in such indigenous societies. Second, I examine the theory and practice of colonialism and the kinds of leadership it generated in order to show the combined effects of colonialism, modernity and post-modernity on the governance systems foisted on post-colonial states in Africa, without the fundamental cultural foundations to underwrite the systems, which all served to undermine the developmental trajectories of Africana societies. Third, I show that, given the defective preparation and appreciation of what constitute modern society by the leadership which inherited power at independence, married to instabilities of the political arrangements pervading the African landscape at independence, leading to a slew of military dictatorships and their pretense to saving society from implosion, it is not strange to see how these combination of tragedies have led to circumstances culminating in the debilitating governance structures and morally bankrupt socioeconomic, political, religious, educational and aesthetic systems found in most Africana societies today. Finally, I argue that for as long as African societies continue not to take the rule of law seriously, for so long will our developmental efforts face in-built recipes for poverty.

THE RULE OF LAW—THE WESTERN PERSPECTIVE

One of the major achievements of human civilization, in its march to ensure the survival and prosperity of all members of society, in peaceful co-existence, for the protection of the individual, regardless of their peculiar states of being, and for the collective advancement, progress and good, has been the development of the idea, notion, concept and practice of "the rule of law." There is no doubt that human beings have proclivities toward excess, and can be tempted to take advantage of the vulnerable, the weak and the poor. More curious, however, is the fact that fortunes are difficult to predict, such that there is always the possibility of changes or accidents, which may make the rich become poor and the poor become rich. This possibility constitutes a cautionary for those who may find themselves in positions of power to temper their behavior and actions with humility, for no one knows what tomorrow may bring! But even more important is the fact that, as rational beings who have always found strength in numbers, therefore pandering to their gregarious nature, human beings discovered very early in the evolution of society that order is better than chaos, discipline better than indiscipline, moral existence better that immoral (amoral) existence, and obedience to rules, norms and law better than otherwise. In any case, there was never any time when human beings could have survived under a strict "state of nature" (Bewaji 1998), one in which it was survival of the fittest, based strictly on the basest of instincts, as no infant human being was fit for survival at birth, without the support and nurturing of the immediate family and the collaboration of society at large. Show me an adult human being, and I will show you a product of human commitment to self-sacrifice and self-denial in the process of ensuring the survival of another human being.

However, contrary to the fictive unidirectional social contract between human adults, there are various ways in which human society could be, and has been, organized in order to ensure the protection and welfare of members of society. Indeed, there have been various forms of political organizations or governance arrangements, from dictatorship to oligarchy, from feudalism to monarchy and from aristocracy to the most liberal and the now most popular democratic form of arrangement. There is no gainsaying the fact that rules (laws) have always governed human interaction from the dawn of human social interaction, even though who maintains it and how it is maintained may differ from society to society. In some instances some of the features of laws are similar to what obtains with morality, to the extent that some scholars may even want to say that laws are formalized moral codes; but there is no doubt that often there may be conflict between what is regarded as moral and what is regarded as lawful/legal, and individuals can choose to break the law, while doing what they consider right/moral, with some degree of justification, even if they are punished under the law. However, there are very few who would suggest that it would not be more acceptable, more justifiable, if what was legally stipulated were also morally acceptable to the members of society.

Before the advent of the destructive incursions of Europeans in the modern period, and of marauding Arabs before them, into Africa, most African societies had evolved various forms of arrangements for governance. Some of these arrangements have been noted as being very sophisticated, complicated and highly specialized. There was no doubt that to keep order and maintain prosperity in empires and kingdoms or even city states, there had to be political arrangements which were conducive to the expansion of the domains of the various empires, kingdoms and city states. Indeed, to build the hamlets, villages, towns and cities of various sizes, there had to be norms, ethics, laws, regulations and various enforcement mechanisms for infractions of these various regulations. In Yoruba land, for example, very sophisticated systems of governance were evolved, from the village level to the towns and the cities, to the extent that the empires in Yoruba land were monarchical, federalist and also con-federalist, depending on the distance between the center and the peripheries, the consanguinity of relationships, the levels of trust between the center and the outer bands of the empire and kingdom and also the probability of insurgency or threats to the central power in the polity (Akinyemi 1980). And while still reflecting on the Yoruba example, there is ample evidence from the history of the Yorubas that there was serious attention to morality and law, to the extent that conventions, precedents and new rules and regulations were passed and followed as the evolution of society took place over many millennia. This allowed for clarity about what is expected of the individual in various circumstances, while at the same time ensuring that each person was treated with ultimate respect for their humanity and integrity of personhood. Even while there were various forms of social and economic stratifications in society, it was clear that there was expected a level of uniform respect and equity in dealings between the various strata of society, because *bi a se bi eru, be e la bi omo*; that is, slaves and free born were born in the same process. This is even more forcefully emphasized when it is said that no one has two heads—*ko si eni t'o l'ori meji*, so that no one can claim undue privilege on account of either pedigree of birth or happenstance of wealth or poverty!

Extant literature reflects long-standing pondering about human nature. The popular narrative in Western scholarship indicates that human nature, understood dually as both positive and negative, is susceptible to creating challenges for mutual coexistence, hence modalities were developed or evolved over time to attenuate the strictures that would create discord, compromise human existence and disrupt the balance of societal well-being. Top on the list are the norms, ethos, taboos, conventions, rules, regulations and laws, all of which were jealously guarded by all members of society, young and old, male and female, bearing in mind that when things go wrong, all will be affected. For the kinds of security of life and property referenced, which never allowed for the kinds of theories of human nature celebrated in the West as leading to the social or political contract, and which allowed the Western man to treat another human being like a thing, a nonbeing, it must be that there was careful attention to proper conduct, good behavior, respect for others predicated primarily on respect for self. This means that there must be careful attention to the rule of law, proper process, attention to ethical behavior, and the assurance that justice is not just done, but is seen manifestly to be done.

But what is "the rule of law?" I will use the concept of the rule of law as enunciated in Western scholarship as stalking horse to gain an ingress into the understanding of the concept and its practice in Africa before colonialism, and show that in indigenous legal systems and practices, the residues of this indigenous system, still pervade what is known as the parallel justice system regarded as native law and custom—customary law. The reason for starting with the Western annotation is because as a people mis-educated into epistemic deficiency, we (the academics) are often ignorant of our indigenous intellectual heritage, having been convinced of being heirs to "the empty baggage syndrome"—a people with no intellectual heritage, only now being tutored by Europe to become human!

There is no precise definition of "the rule of law," just as "law" itself is subject to various equally plausible definitions. For this reason, I will present some of the features of "the rule of law," and use these to synthesize its purport and practice, as it obtains in the common law. The first thing to note about the rule of law is its prescription that the state/society/polity must be governed by rules which are made, or prescribed, or laid down in advance. This means that it is not possible to be punished for a crime/offense that did not exist in the statutes already, and it means that one's actions could not be retroactively criminalized. Let me use an example here. Sometime in the mid-90s, the government of Jamaica retroactively imposed taxation on financial institutions. Apart from the fact that this contravened the rule of law, it was unfair, unjust and irresponsible. It was effectively a case of arrogance of power. But even more critically for the society, it contributed in no small measure to the collapse of the financial sector in the country, costing the country billions and leading to much misery for entities which became bankrupt and individuals who lost their jobs, savings and lives. Looking at the rule of law, A. V. Dicey, quoting Tocqueville, who was comparing the English, the Americans (USA) and the Swiss—but also incidentally the French—state, "the Swiss do not show at bottom respect for justice, that love of law, that dislike of using force, without which no free nation can exist, which strikes so forcibly in England" (Dicey 1897: 178). The fact that Jamaicans took the retroactive legislation which virtually bankrupted the country, forcing it into receivership, leading to the compromising of various aspects of life, without protest, without even a whimper, and still elected the same government that visited so much misery on the society back into government in 1997 and in 2003, shows that Jamaicans are no better than the Swiss being described by Tocqueville. They are able to be ruled without either care for law or for consequences of illegality.

The overall implication of this is that the rights of members of society are determined by legal rules which are clearly stated, and not by arbitrary dictates or behavior of authorities. In other words, authorities are as much constrained in what they can do or not do as are individual citizens in the society. This is very fundamental to the nature of a civil society, and it is always validated by the possibility of appealing the actions of agencies of state.

The second feature of the rule of law is that it is the rules which are prescribed by the law and no other rules must be applied or enforced in the society. This means that the rules must be known to all and sundry and only those rules which are known by all are to be applied in moderating the actions and behavior of members of society. If any other laws are enforced, they will be *ultra vires*, null and void and of no effect. But critical to this feature is that there are independent and clearly respected institutions for the adjudication of cases, as no punishment can be inflicted on any one unless it has been so prescribed by law and decided by the duly constituted court or similar institution—individuals cannot inflict punishment arbitrarily even if they have such capacity in virtue of wealth or position in society. What this does is to protect the members of society from the chaos that the social contract theorists speak of, where in the state of nature it was war of all against all, and survival of the fittest. By removing the capacity to be litigant, prosecutor and judge in one's own case, the rule of law addresses the temptation for victimization and arbitrariness of actions by the rich, powerful and connected.

The third feature of the rule of law is that disputes about the rules must seem to have been resolved effectively and fairly to the satisfaction of all parties to the dispute, without fear or favor. This is what makes all members of society subject themselves to the dictates of the rules, because they have the confidence that, win or lose, they will have their day in court, and they can count on the fairness of the process and the outcome of the process. The commitment that individual members of society have to the law is derived from the fact that they understand that each person is equal before the law, and the law is no respecter of persons on account of pedigree, wealth, connections or other factors unrelated to the issue at stake (Bewaji 1989). When members of society have this kind of confidence in the laws that govern them, they are able to go to any length to defend the society, to the point of being able to put their own lives on the line for the welfare of members of their society, since they expect no less from other members of society who are equally of the same consciousness.

A fourth feature of the rule of law is that no one is exempt from the jurisdiction of the law, as everyone, insofar as the person lives in society, is bound by the dictates of the law. This is the notion of the government itself not being above the law, and the functionaries of the government are not exempt from the dictates of the law. This provided the protection from impunity and abuse of power, as the state can be brought to justice for actions carried out by functionaries of the state, at great expense to the state and with consequences for state agents.

On the overall, for society to function properly and empower members to realize their utmost potential, the rules that constitute the law must be such that they are properly understood and respected. According to Saunders,

> There is no point in laying rules down in advance unless they operate prospectively, are publicly available, can be understood, are susceptible of obedience, individually and collectively, and are not changed unreasonably often. The application of rules to particular cases must at least be faithful and consistent and probably also rational and fair. Administrators must have neither too little nor too much discretion and they must be accountable for their actions. The body that resolves disputes, typically a court, must be independent of the particular parties and of the other branches of government. This is even more important in a legal system in which other branches may be parties to the dispute (Saunders 2003: 5).

What this means has been better captured by Galligan (2007) when he described the set of ideas on which modern ideas of legal order rests. I would suggest that any Yoruba person would be very familiar with what Saunders was saying above, and how Dicey would have been reflecting accurately the institutionalization of rules and processes in typical Yoruba society. Hence, when Galligan (2007) says of the foundations of modern European society, as follows, it could be said that he was talking effectively of pre-colonial Yoruba society:

> This is loosely described as the *rule of law* which has several meanings, some based on the innate qualities of rules, others linking law to ideas of liberty, democracy, and rights. . . . These ideas have their origin in

> the rule of law, which has the following qualities: first, legal contexts are defined by, infused with, and constrained by legal rules and standards; secondly, certain qualities are built into the rules; and thirdly, the rules are applied by officials according to certain conditions (pp. 253–54).

Now, what we are saying by the rule of law has been understood in all civilized societies from time immemorial. This was formulated by Plato as follows:

> Where the law is subject to some other authority and has none of its own, the collapse of the state, in my view, is not far off; but if law is the master of the government and the government is its slave, then the situation is full of promise and men enjoy all the blessings that the gods shower on a state (Cooper 1997: 1402).

Aristotle deferred to the rule of law, rather than the rule by human beings, because of the attributes we have observed above. And regardless of the variations in the social constructions, most civilizations have embraced the rule of law, which not only protects and the members of society and guarantees their happiness, but also protects the leadership from various forms of insurgencies. Many writers have noted the ways in which the rule of law dictated varieties of democratic practices in many indigenous African societies (Wiredu 1995, Ramose 2002, Bewaji 1987). It is clear that where there is certainty about the expectations and punishment for infractions, the loyalty of members of society can be predicted and order maintained.

In summary, "the rule of law" is a product of a consciousness of the need for human beings to treat each other as human beings which evolves naturally given the innate human capacity for reflective existence and introspective understanding of personhood; thus, for emphasis, it can be said that it is a product of reason, derived from a consciousness of the fact that other human beings are capable of similar, if not identical emotions, feelings, experiences, aspirations, dreams and propensities, such that any abrogation of the humanity of the other would unleash the beast lurking just a little bit below the surface veneer of decorum and civility that respects and cooperates with the other. Thus, the rule of law implies that the following conditions are met or embraced consciously by members of a society:

a. The law is supreme and all persons are subject to the law, irrespective of their positions in society; the law does not make exceptions for persons on account of personal estate or otherwise, and applies irrevocably across the board to all.
b. There is a concept of justice and fairness, where there is the idea that the laws are moral, good and compatible with the interests of members of society and of society;

c. Clear standards and procedures are available to measure conformity and proper redress; further, the laws must not be ambiguous or contradictory, otherwise there would be grounds presented to others to disobey, and more importantly, the law must not be such that it is impossible to either obey or enforce, thereby becoming self-stultifying and void;
d. The law embraces precedence, rather than fiat or arbitrariness, and equality is maintained in the dispensation of justice; thereby ensuring that conformity is easy to appreciate and fiat reduced to the minimum, and such systems that are in place must ensure that the process maintains records and the law must have a long memory, so that persons may not drag out the process to stultify the system;
e. The law is not retrospective, and it is known ahead of time what is prescribed; that is, the laws that bind members of society must be prospective, and known to all in advance, and consequences for infraction clear to all covered by the law;
f. The law makers are constrained and restrained in their capacity to make laws, especially those that will compromise the liberties of members of society are carefully monitored and are restricted to the minimum in their capacity to be modified by organs of the state without reference to the general commonwealth;
g. There is a connection between law and morality, so that the foundations of obedience can be maintained and not force persons to object on moral grounds to immoral laws. Laws are easier to enforce where they have the moral approbation and sympathies of the population over which it will function.

Where these important conditions are not met, civilized humans are not happy to continue to function and may take measures to redress the situation, or to abrogate the untenable legal system, even when such measures border on violence and causes the source of the compromise to humanity to suffer levels of degradation, in the hope that the source of the compromise will become sensitized to the grouse of the victim.

In a very insightful essay on how the culture of the rule of law enabled Africans in the Americas to successfully overthrow the inhuman and evil regimen of slavery to which they were subjected on the plantations, Clarke says,

> There is no way to go directly into this subject and be understood. Western historians and "authorities" on the cultures of people and societies have not, in most cases, accorded the African people a place in their respectful [(*sic*)] commentaries. They have been sparing and often totally reluctant to use the words "history" and "culture" in matters relating to African people. In approaching this subject it is necessary, at least briefly, to establish the fact that African culture is not only part of world culture, but may well be the basis of world culture. It was this

> culture which sustained the Africans during the holocaust of the slave trade and the colonial system that followed. In South and Central America and in the Caribbean Islands, African culture, reborn on alien soil, became the cohesive force and the communication system that helped to send in motion some of the most successful slave revolts in history (Clarke 1973: 79).

Well, now that it has been conceded that the first humans may have existed in the Nile Valley, from whence they dispersed all over the world, it would seem to follow that Clarke is right in suggesting that the first culturally developed humans may have been Africans, such that it was this indomitable sense of personhood and being which made the enslaved Africans abhor the inhuman condition imposed on them, to the point where death was preferable to life under such inhuman condition. And bearing in mind the evidence documenting the Nile Valley civilizations, and recorded in various other volumes—from the Bible to the Greek traveler tales, from the Pyramids to the Congo observatory—it would appear that Africa, having been the seat of the first civilized human settlements, may have found it an inexorable necessity to form civil governments which would cater to the needs of all members of society—indigenous and alien! It is worth reiterating the views expressed at the beginning of chapter 2 that,

> The state of cultural development, and indeed the level of civilization, of any society can be discerned and measured by the evidence of many factors. Some of these factors relate to a) the extent to which there is security of sustenance resources of food, water and energy for members of society, b) the protection of members of society from the devastation of the forces of nature through the development of habitat structures that conduce to good existence, c) the avenues for the expression of the talents and intuitions of members of the society through the arts and crafts, d) minimization of energy expended by members of society in the process of garnering basic means of existence through the use of creative technologies, e) the level of leisure and luxury that members of society are able to enjoy in order to be able to indulge in the arts, plan for their individual demise, make wars on other competing societies and secure dominance for the in-group by contrast to the out-group, f) the development of resources for the care of the sick, the weak and the old and last but not the least, g) the development of and procurement of means for ensuring that institutions, structures, resources and mechanisms are in place for the determination and protection of the rights of members of the society.

While in *Beauty and Culture* (2003: 161) I had explored some of the artistic checks and balances imposed by society on the possibility and proclivities for excess on the part of the rich and powerful, in order that the rights of all may be protected. And in some other essays (Bewaji 2006; 2010) I had explored the nature of the relationship of leadership to law, order, power and accountability in indigenous Yoruba society, making the point that while, similar to the saying in England that "the king can do no wrong," it is indeed canvassed that the king is *Alase, ekeji orisa*—meaning that the king is the one who has a kind of power/authority next in rank only to the divinities or deity—yet there are avenues and built-in structures to curtail abuse of power and authority on the part of the king and his protégés. In any case, while it is often said that there cannot be two rulers in a town, in many Eastern Yoruba towns there are two kings—albeit, one may be ritual/religious and the other secular, one may be military and the other political—and their domains of authority counterbalances the possibility of tyranny and over-ambition.

Scholars are only beginning to pick up the momentum of research agendas formulated by leading Africanist scholars in the middle of the last century, after the genuflecting efforts of Negritudist nationalist politicians have been found wanting. But even then, much of the metaphysical and epistemological foundations of the rebellions in the Americas that made for the abolition of slavery have not been well researched. For example, to what extent were the republicanism and federalism institutions of the African empires and cities responsible for the revolts against slavery in the New World? How much of what is represented as libertarianism in the West is a product of the travels that Europeans made to Africa, observing the freedoms of decent, civilized Africans and their ability to move, trade, and attain personal and collective development unfettered by greed and avarice? Formulated differently, how much of the state-of-nature theories constructed by Hobbes, Locke and Rousseau was a product of the observance of the African civil existence, rather than a product of the harsh, inhuman, temperate environment which makes one human develop an unconscionable hatred for another?

Taiwo (2010) documents the ground-breaking constitutions of the Fanti people of Ghana and the democratic system of the Egba in the nineteenth century, which was comparable to, if it does not surpass similar governance structures that may be found in the same period in European history. I will use the features of the rule of law as they existed in the indigenous Yoruba society as evidence of the highly sophisticated governmental system in various Yoruba cities, towns and villages, before the imposition of colonialism and the transportation of Africans into slavery in the Americas.

The supremacy of law in indigenous Yoruba society is concretized in many ways, and enforced primarily in the fact that everyone is subjected to the dictates of the laws of the society. When the Yoruba proverbs say the "knife does not know its owner" or "fire does not know the person who set it" in relation to law, what is being suggested is that it does not matter whether you are the one who made the law, once it becomes law, it applies without discrimination. For this reason, infractions from whatever quarters are viewed with seriousness and must be punished or expiated before the equilibrium can be restored. The law does not make exceptions for persons on account of personal estate or otherwise, position or challenges, and applies irrevocably across the board to all.

Arrogance of power, impunity and nonaccountability are all frowned upon in Yoruba society, with a view to ensuring that no one can take matters into their own hands, or apply their own notion of justice without regard to consequences for society at large. There have been instances in recent memory when the king has been de-stooled because of abuse of power and misuse of authority. It is this that makes for order and transparency, especially in monarchical structures of governance to have checks and balances, making sure that it is not only the poor who are subject to law, but also the leadership. First, a generation ago, the Olagbegi of Owo was made to abdicate the royal stool and exiled, and within the last few years, the new Deji of Akure has been made to vacate the royal stool on account of actions detrimental to the welfare of Akure city and its people. What this shows unequivocally is the fact that Yoruba people, even while presenting an apparent autocratic system of traditional governance, are averse to dictatorship, authoritarianism and injustice, and is at heart very democratic. In any case the errant elder or superior or king who abuses position must contend not only with the living, but given the ideas of a continuum between the living and the ancestors, they must also bear responsibility for the ire of the ancestors and the gods.

Indigenous Yoruba society has always frowned on injustice, such that even acts of cheating are held to be reprehensible and odious to all members of society. While in the West there is haste to be modern by referring to Christian ethics, deriving from the religion of Christianity, as constituting the foundation of society and life, on the other hand, when Africans make reference to their indigenous religious beliefs and the grounds for the affirmation of their ethical beliefs, especially in regard to the way the ancestors are supposed to be part of the social welfare operators, the Western intellectual is quick to condemn as primitive or backward references to the ancestors for validating the norms and ethos of society. But any society without antecedents and precedents would have a sociojudicial system that would be empty of critical rational legal foundations and meaning.

In this regard, it is clear that there is a concept of justice and/as fairness, in indigenous Yoruba society, where there is the idea that the laws are intertwined with what is moral, good and compatible with the interests of members of society and of society at large; hence when it is said that *omode ko je obi, oun l'agba go j'oye*, they are saying that if you deny anyone anything because of any disadvantage, be it age, gender, status, or other, then you can see that the repercussion would come back. For this reason, human beings must be treated with fairness at all times, even when the target has no ability to defend himself, or herself, against the superior forces arrayed against him or her (Bewaji 2008b).

Even more critical is the sense that the arbiter in any dispute or disagreement must listen carefully to all the persons involved, so that there would be no miscarriage of justice, no rush to conclusions, and no unnecessary harm to persons. In this regard, it is said that it is malicious to listen to one side and pronounce judgment, for *a gb'ejo enikan da, agba ebita*.

As a follow up to the above, care is taken that there is no unnecessary haste in the disposal of cases. This means that a convenient time for the parties involved is found to adjudicate matters, because it is impossible to properly dispense with justice when a party to a dispute is not there—*a a ki fa ori l'ehin olori*.

For the purpose of instilling in youth a proper sense of justice, young people are always allowed to be present when cases are being decided. This is bearing in mind that there may be instances when young people may be excused from a meeting because of the sensitive nature of what is being discussed, or to protect the innocence of the children from exposure to adult issues. The simple reason why young people are respected and allowed to be present is because it is always recognized that the young people of today are the adults of the future—*omode oni, oun l'agba ola*. As a consequence, there is a need to instill in the youth a sense of order, justice and proper understanding of the foundations of cultural existence, so that the society can continue to function properly when they become adults.

In his celebrated essay on how not to compare African thought with Western thought, one of the issues raised by Kwasi Wiredu is the element of rigidity in aspects of life, such that adaptation and change can be very slow. Indeed, there is a virtue as well as vice in this, for if the system does not accommodate new knowledge and adapt to changing environment, then progress may be curtailed; but there are areas where it is a virtue, especially when the demands of the law and justice are clear to everyone and followed to the letter, thereby allowing for certainty of what constitutes proper conduct, what constitutes infraction and what consequences attend either option.

There are various ways in which Yoruba society ensures conformity to lay down standards and procedures. Some are in the way in which actions are required, with proper guidelines, and others relate to what prohibitions, proscriptions and bans are imposed on modes of behavior regarded as antithetical to good order and governance in society. And there are various cadres of behavior, depending on the gravity of consequences for individuals and the group, such that redress, blame, reward and punishment are graduated accordingly. And efforts are not spared to ensure that there are means available to measure conformity and proper redress; further, the laws must not be ambiguous or contradictory, otherwise there would be grounds presented to others to disobey, and more importantly, the law must not be such that it is impossible to either obey or enforce, thereby becoming self-stultifying and void.

In order to have the kinds of civility required of the *omoluabi*, the cultured, urbane and civilized person that society values so much, there is need to ensure that equality is maintained in the dispensation of justice; thereby ensuring that conformity is easy to appreciate and fiat reduced to the minimum, and such systems that are in place must ensure that the process maintains records and the law must have a long memory, so that persons may not drag out the process to stultify the system. In this regard, it takes a highly polished citizenry to appreciate the value of the kinds of respect for self-hood and identity of the individual, such that members of society regard each other primarily as human, deserving of mutual and reciprocal respect and dignity of reference.

There are certain ideas taken as given in the discussion of the rule of law which is not often properly elucidated. This relates to the issues of power, constituted authority and legitimacy. I will briefly paint a backdrop of Yoruba indigenous culture that makes for order.

Power is variously understood, depending on the area of intellectual discourse and interest of the discussant. For our purpose, since we are concerned with social, political and human interaction in relation to needs and ends, we may well just look at the notion of power within the context of law and order, as it relates to human behavior. For this reason we may simply look at "power" as the ability to produce intended effects, or to carry out one's will, on other people or on things. In the case of law, what allows law to lead to order is the coercive power of the law, as embodied in the state's ability to compel obedience. Often this appears like simple coercive force of the state, but this appearance is only because the combined will of the people, which encapsulate into power by way of aggregation, does not seem obvious when disaggregated. But without the combined will of members of society, or if individual units that make up society were to be pulling in opposing directions, without any internal cohesion and agreement, then the power will dissipate and fizzle and be of no use or force whatever.

In chapter 7, we discuss issues of religion, constitution and law and order in Yoruba society, making a distinction between power and authority. In indigenous Yoruba society authority is meaningful only because there is the means of ensuring compliance. Arbitrary exercise of authority cannot be sustained where there exist a culture of unbridled individual freedom and independence, and for this reason care is taken to ensure that only those so vested with power exercise authority. And where there is abuse, misuse or other arbitrary exercise of authority, means of redress are clearly available to the aggrieved. And the legitimacy enjoyed by the authority derives from the laws or constitution which everyone in society recognizes as binding and irrevocable, regardless of who is involved. Ifa tells the story of an indigenous army general who had made a deal with the gods to sacrifice to them if he won the battle, and the agreement turned out to affect the family member of the general; as someone who knows the sanctity of the contract and implications of avoiding obedience to the contract, the terms of the contract had to be fulfilled, whatever the circumstances may be and no matter how painful the consequences may be to the self and loved ones. This sets the example that if the general could be compelled to carry out a contract in this way, even when it was not favorable personally, then lower persons must understand that the law will not make exceptions for them.

This is where the matter of legitimacy is also affected, because when individuals or functionaries of government become arbitrary or selective in the discharge of their duties, they automatically compromise the legitimacy of their portfolio. It is for this reason I had suggested, with regard to the matter of constitute authority, that (1987: 316–17),

> To understand the notion of constituted authority, however, one will have to gain some understanding of what constitutes authority itself, how it relates to the functioning of social organizations and how it differs from other things that may be similar to it. While power can be understood as an ability or capacity to perform an action, it does not enable us to see and understand the locus of power. Power is a potentiality which may be actuated or realized by utilizing it; it may not be utilized, hence remaining dormant. Legal power enables, it confers right and legally "en-capacitates" a person, group or body for the performance of an activity (Bewaji 1987: 316–17).

Further, I had suggested,

> What distinguishes power from authority in contemporary political thought is legitimacy or the concept of right. . . . Authority is far superior to power and carries more weight; it is not simply a "right to," or "ability to" do something, but also "right of" or an "ability of" demanding obedience. Without the notion of authority, power will cease to have legitimacy; it will become naked force (Bewaji 1988: 316).

Yoruba people are a very orderly people and make every effort to ensure that order prevails, because it is within the condition of order that each and every member of society can effectively participate and realize their potential in society. Though the notion of order is often tied to law, this is because it is law that moderates the outer bounds of exercise of human freedom and discretion. It is for this reason I had indicated,

> To say of a society that it is orderly is to say that members of such a society abide by the norms, ethos and conventions of the society. It suggests a state in which the laws governing interpersonal relationships are observed. On the other hand, if a society is disorderly (like contemporary Nigeria and Jamaica), then members of such a society are not usually observant of the rules of behavior that are prescribed, nor are they conscious of the exponential effect of such disobedience.

> Members of such a society would be unruly, each doing his/her own thing his/her own way, regardless of consequences for members and to the society at large. In a state where such anarchic and individualistic behaviours are prevalent, anarchism and chaos may be the end result (Bewaji 1988: 319).

It is against this background that we have to consider the effect of colonialism and military dictatorships on African polities and how these twin evils have caused so much disaster for developmental efforts in Africa.

While Europe was busy theorizing libertarianism, the expeditioners, explorers, brigands, adventurers and traders were busy invading and pervading the territories of Africans and other climes with the most inhuman force ever devised, killing, maiming, raping and destroying with wanton insanity the civilizations of others. The extent to which Europe was busy celebrating human rights, human civilization and human culture, read simply and narrowly as European culture and civilization, has been documented, to show the way and manner in which Europe perverted all senses of decency, justice and humanity in the societies they invaded and colonized. While the contract theorists—Hobbes, Locke and Rousseau—were busy celebrating the foundations of government, the traders, explorers and merchants were busy stealing, raiding and pillaging other climes with wanton impunity. And when the enslaved blacks in various parts of the Americas revolted, they were exterminated with the worst form of brutality unknown to civilized African peoples, who believe that when you have conquered your enemy then aggression should stop, whereas when Europeans conquer their revolting African slaves, they went systematically about the task of killing the vanquished. And there is no better example of this than the systematic and continuing victimization of Haiti, where blacks had defeated all the forces of the European powers in their fight for freedom, only to defeat their oppressors on the field of battle and find themselves enslaved indirectly through treaties which make them impoverished for generations unborn. The consequences of this have been the fact that every natural disaster becomes a human disaster in Haiti. Yet Haitians remain one of the most civilized people in the Western hemisphere.

Greed combined with ignorance to ensure that the colonialists were immune to any form of control, redress, sanction or restraint. This meant that the colonized were compromised in many ways: their confidence in themselves were destroyed; their confidence in the institutions of governance that conduced to order, self-respect and other-respect were so terribly compromised and destroyed such that the humanity of members of society became abridged; when it was found that there existed some external force far superior to the local agencies as instituted by the traditions, with no consequences ever affecting the agents of the external forces, then the primordial affiliation became ruptured; and with the advent of new religions, new power centers and new cultural dynamics that does not recognize the local and indigenous traditions, there was total collapse of the indigenous power base, indigenous authority, indigenous constituted authority and indigenous law and order.

In any case, without any form of final court predicated on indigenous law, authorities, and legitimate foundations, it meant that the whole surrogate local systems became uninhibited shams and charades. This is even more so when there are no means of appealing faulty decisions of the imported common law systems brought with the colonial system, because in the best of circumstances the law does not reflect the sensitivities and sensibilities of the indigenous peoples, nor was it appreciative of the nuances and cultural foundations of social existence in the indigenous communities. A consequence of this then is the fact that foreign standards of right and justice is imposed on the society, and the convoluted idea that one is presumed innocent until proven guilty runs against the intuitive notion of justice, such that the victim now has to incur additional expense in the uncertain search for rectitude for harm done, while the aggressor is left enjoying the fruits of aggression, until the law finally is made to take effect. This is the nightmare that President Muhammadu Buhari is having in his singular effort to reduce, if not totally eradicate, the scourge of corruption from the Nigerian political landscape, where the president of the Senate is hell-bent on maintaining the status quo of uninhibited looting of the Nigerian commonwealth by politicians and their heartless collaborators.

What then happens is the suspicion that indigenous peoples have of the imported colonial common law, bearing in mind that it came with paraphernalia of application and implementation that is often expensive, time consuming and fraught with all kinds of possibilities, including the victim becoming the loser in the end. The standards of evidence, the process of justice and the dispensation of justice in the new colonial society, which has emasculated the indigenous constituted authority and locus of power, all combine to weaken the trust that people have in law, while at the same time creating uncertainties of redress and alienating the most vulnerable members of society—the poor, the women, the elderly, the unemployed and the disabled. This has had the added disadvantage of encouraging various forms of individual or group vigilantism, so that people feel constrained to take laws into their own hands. In another discussion in chapter 5, I mention the fact that the parallel justice systems that is operated in Nigeria and in many other African societies does not conduce to order, justice and progress. The overall implications of these factors on the rule of law in Nigeria and in many other African societies are that there is no respect for the formal system of laws, and people devise strategies to avoid conformity where they can, operate outside of the law if possible or deviate from the obligations they have to obey the law where it conflicts with the traditions and customs of their indigenous background.

At independence, the continuation of the English monarch as the sovereign head of the new African states still continued to compromise the locus of constituted authority, allowing the inheritors of leadership opportunities to behave like their erstwhile colonial sponsors. The effect of that is that there was the replacement of one group of aliens by another group of domestic aliens; these were the new ones described by Fanon as *Black Skins White Masks* or what the Jamaicans call "roast breadfruits" or "coconuts," because they are indeed blacks exteriorly, but they are mentally white—they see themselves as superior to their indigenous compatriots because they have now mastered the ways of speaking, carriage, and oppression of their colonial examples. What was even worse was the ways in which they set about separating themselves from their former age-mates, siblings, families, classmates and societies by building various centers of false privileges called Government Reservation Areas, Officers Clubs, and Recreational Parks for Senior Officers, etc. They give to themselves the same kinds of rights and privileges as the ex-colonial officers, such as going on home leave annually, because they are foreigners, which the new African officers (civil servants) also now take to go to Europe and America annually, not back to their own villages, and these trips are celebrated with fanfare as it conferred new status on the returnee; seeking annual medical check-ups in Europe and America, at government expense, making it unnecessary for them to have reason to develop the local health sector (like when I traveled on the same airplane with former Nigerian president Obasanjo who was going for a medical check-up in the United States of America this year); sending their children to schools in Europe and America (now Ghana) at government expense, as if they were aliens, thereby giving them no reason to develop the local educational infrastructure!

Since the old indigenous constituted authorities and locus of power has shifted, been compromised, undermined and rendered impotent, there now remains a veneer of emptiness in the minds of the people about seeking redress for harm done by agencies of government as well as by members of society. Actually, the many agencies of state have built into the incorporating statutes such clauses that prevent litigations in case they do wrong to the people. The Nigeria Police Force, the Jamaica Constabulary Force and other such law enforcement institutions in ex-colonies were not founded to ensure justice but to keep the blacks in control and in their rightful places, so that they do not begin to pretend to be equals of the colonial masters and mistresses. Directly or indirectly they were empowered to terrorize the populace at will, with little or no possibility of redress (Nwabueze 1973, Owoade 1991: 123–147). Even civil agencies, such as the defunct National Electricity Power Authority (NEPA), which has now become National Power Holding Company

(NPHC) in Nigeria, had the clause which prevented their customers from being able to seek redress in case of damage to equipment resulting from power surges, and other ensuing hazards from faulty power supply.

The value of the rule of law is the consciousness of protection and access to justice which it gives society; when this is compromised and expropriated, then it leaves a vacuum that needs to be filled. The nondomestication of the various elements of the English legal system in Africa constitutes one of the most signal tragedies that colonialism has imposed on African governance institutions and systems. The end result is the factor of impunity, nonaccountability, chaos and disrespect that obtains in many African states today. It is the factor that is responsible for the near anarchy that reigns in many African countries, and it continues to be a singular factor undermining the African capacity for development, breeding in its gory wake horrendous levels of corruption, ineptitude, nepotism, graft, injustice and various forms of vigilantism, terrorism and insurgencies.

It is an open secret that the military often come to power in many countries with claims of:

a. saving their countries from implosion and disintegration;
b. stemming the chaos attendant on the unruliness and indiscipline of the civilian government;
c. correcting the many mistakes of the political process, thereby bringing accountability to governance; and
d. removing waste, ineptitude, corruption, nepotism and graft in public space.

But what happened have been unmitigated disasters for the states in which the military has tasted power. The simple reason for this is that the military are not suited to political power exercise, and when they come to power, finding that the state power is not easy to manage where there are contending opinions, the military resort to what it is most familiar with—command, control and dictatorship. Since to allow for dissension and competition of political authority is to compromise the power they wield, the military become dictators, and the first thing they often do on attaining power is the suspension of the rule of law, through the repeal and abrogation of the constitution of the country and its replacement with decrees and edicts which are never debated by any public agency representing the population.

In most cases, the armies of the various African states started in the same way as the police in these states. They were mainly designed to enforce the law to ensure that the population does not become ungovernable, instead of being emplaced to protect and defend the countries from aggression from the outside. Many of the top brass of the military are trained in Sandhurst in the United Kingdom and Fort Worth in the United States of America. And this may suggest that they are not products of the cultures of the societies they are trained to serve; this probably explains why they behave like enemies of the societies they are supposed to serve and carry on like armies of occupation—defending themselves (esprit des corps) more than standing for truth, justice and fairness.

Coming from a background in which order, justice, morality, accountability and fairness were esteemed virtues to one in which this was totally compromised because the locus of power was exogenous in the time of colonialism meant that there was serious irruption in the governance structure and systems in Africa. When the civilian regimes carried on the same way as their former colonial mentors, showing disregard for the indigenous institutions and not holding themselves accountable to any one, recklessly abusing the trust and power vested in them, it was no wonder that the military, with its access to unmitigated brute force, took over the control of government institutions. But having taken over power, and where they are not challenged by any other group because of their monopoly of force, it was to be expected that they would combine and perfect all the vices of the colonial masters with those of the visionless and irresponsible civilian rulers in the most garrulous and irresponsible manner. Elaigwu (1980: 156) speaks of minimum accountability, but there was absolutely no way of holding the military accountable. Just like the district officers and other expatriate staff of the colonial administration in the colonies, whenever the military functionaries and their appointees messed up their duties, they were recalled by their principals—the colonial office in the case of the district officer and chief of staff in case of the military and recycled elsewhere—and that was the end of the story; there was no need for responsibility, no investigations carried out to determine culpability, no punishments attended misdemeanors. They were like armies of occupation in conquered territories, responsible to no one in the local communities of their occupation and yet demanding respect and forcing themselves on the people even when they are miscreants of the worst order.

The bastardization of the governance structures by both the civilian and military administrations, in the wake of the demise of colonialism, only led to the entrenchment of a culture of nonaccountability, indiscipline and irresponsibility on the part of public functionaries. This has morphed into the perception that government resources belong to no one, and hence could be appropriated anyhow and commandeered for personal use with impunity. While the public functionaries in the United Kingdom and the United States of America drive themselves around to and from work, and on public business, in the Nigerian context the public officers have assigned to them vehicles and drivers, constituting a drain on public resources. This has now matured to the point where wives and children of public officers now have assigned automobiles and drivers, at public expense, and no one sees this as insane.

The first Nigerian republic and the military governments have ingested this culture of impunity, irresponsibility, indiscipline and nonaccountability. But the other two republics that Nigeria has had have now taken it to new levels. While the second republic was so inept and wantonly wasteful, the third republic has become the worst nightmare of Nigerians. They brazenly award to themselves the highest salaries in the whole world, even while it is obvious that Nigeria is a poor, mono-cultural economy, dependent mostly on petroleum products, and the per capita of the general population is abysmally low.

One could not say that it is not lack of education—in the formal sense—that is responsible for this insanity, whereby resources are being squandered without regard to law, while government functionaries are engaging in pedophilia of the worst kind, where individual government functionaries now constitute contract-awarding organs, and where public agents can just sit on the salaries of public servants and expect no consequences. It has become so bad that the population is now totally apathetic and take for granted that there is no government to protect them or to show the way in any manner or form. Resources are annually allocated for various projects and maintenance, the resources vanish without anything being done, only to resurface in personal accounts and projects, such as villas, mansions, universities and foreign accounts, yet there is no redress for the state, and most members of the public have become so used to it that public appointments are celebrated as personal, group, community, and ethnic group blessing; that is as ways of becoming rich and enriching those from one's part of the world, rather than as a call to service! Because of this, all efforts at development are short-circuited by deliberate actions to make sure that the system does not work, and various ingenious devices are concocted to create room for corruption.

Great pains have been taken by intellectuals to distinguish between law and morality. Often the distinction is an easy one to make and easy to understand. For example, if I were your brother, and you find yourself in need of funds to clear some goods at customs, and you come to me for assistance, unless there was a prior written agreement that I give you the funds you require at a certain time, there is nothing compelling me in filial relationship to give you the funds, and there is no way you can compel me to do so. The worst you can do is to conduct a campaign of calumny against me, telling everyone in the community how unkind I was. You could not take me to any law court to compel me to give you the funds.

On the other hand, if I had borrowed the funds from you, and promised to return the funds to you at a certain time but failed to do so, then you could take me to court, and you will be within your right to ask the courts to compel me to make good my promise, failing which my property should be confiscated, sold and proceeds used to redeem my promise. This is a simple way in which law defers from morality.

However, there is a connection between morality and law which is difficult to explain as clearly as this, especially about how law has to assume a moral posture in order to be able to command obedience, and to have legitimacy. Dworkin (1978), in reading Rawls, would have us belief that there is a connection between morality and law, especially as when issues arise with regard to conscience choices, morality becomes important, even though these connections are often difficult to coherently articulate. There is no doubt that this is so, especially as all the human residents of the world become increasingly interconnected and the beliefs and practices of humans in far-off parts of the world may impact the lives of humans in other parts of the world which were never formerly connected. Dworkin uses the examples of homosexuality and pornography, but we may add to these the factor of inept, corrupt, nonaccountable and irresponsible leadership and the moral implications these throw up for human happiness and economic development.

Let us leave the realm of banalities and specifically relate what we mean by bad leadership—that is, unaccountable, corrupt and inept ones—to questions of under-development and ruination of societies. Anyone familiar with the aftermath of the George W. Bush presidency will appreciate the dangers of poor leadership. Bush inherited trillions of dollars of surplus on attaining the presidency of the United States of America, but within a short period of time, due to inept, corrupt and unaccountable actions and profligate expenditures and military adventurism, all the surplus was wiped out, dragging the United States of America into the worst deficit in human history, with attendant consequences of financial melt-down, devaluation of the American dollar from a high of 126 yen to one dollar to a low of eighty yen to one dollar, unemployment figures never seen in America, poverty levels that rank as the worst in developed economies, and a debt burden that is debilitating. Had the consequences been only for America, then it would just have been similar only to what we are used to in banana republics of Africa and Latin America. But this is America, and it is the biggest economy we are talking about. The desperation of America is palpable, even while America still remains the engine of growth for the world. And the reason why George W. Bush was able to get away with it, at least so far, is because American people still *trust* their presidents to be above deliberate mendacity, pettiness, corruption and ineptitude. Now trust imposes moral and legal obligations on leadership, to the extent that it means that the leader is in power for as long as he/she enjoys that trust. The loss of elections by the Republican Party to the Democratic Party in 2008 is evidence of the checks and balances in America.

Relocate the scenario to Africa, and throw in the heritage of colonialism and military dictatorship, then imagine having a series of self-serving, inept, corrupt, mis-educated, unaccountable, and totally irresponsible persons as government functionaries in perpetuity, then you would be able to understand the vicious cycle of underdevelopment to which Africa has been subjected over the last fifty years. While in Yoruba land, an Oba (king) who has abused his position can be checkmated by his council of chiefs, asked to leave the town, requested to commit suicide or de-stooled, in the current dispensation of impunity, there is no such redress for the people over whom the leaders now impose themselves. In the first instance, many of them are not properly brought up in decent families, and where they have a semblance of home training, the idea of prayer to obviate sin, and the idea of academic qualifications as the sole major means of desert of respect, combine to negate the need to understand what moral trust entails. Secondly, when you throw in the idea that public property belongs to no one, and hence can be used as the public officer chooses, then you have a recipe for collective disaster. The worst part of it is that having not been properly steeped in the culture that produced leadership in African history, and being ignorant of that history, they have no sense of scandal, nor do they appreciate how the rest of the world is looking at Africa in the world community. This is what I have described as epistemic deficit.

Let us take some examples from the Nigerian recent history. In the late 1970s, 2.8 billion Naira was misplaced by agents of the government. When there was so much furor the money was returned, and it was alleged that it was not lost, but was deposited into a wrong account—albeit a personal account. The interest on the funds was not returned to the public purse—imagine that sum of money sitting in my account for just two months and how much richer I would have become. But that was a time when public outcry meant something and public functionaries still had moral inclinations. In the 1980s, over eleven billion Naira was missing, under General Ibrahim Badamosi Babangida. Up until today, that money has not been accounted for, no one has been held responsible, and nothing has been done to find the funds, and General Ibrahim Badamosi Babangida is walking a free man and had the ambition of coming back to become president of Nigeria in 2011. The examples we have given does not include the numerous projects like the River Basin Authorities, the Ajaokuta Steel Industries, the Oil Refineries, the death of the Nigeria Airways, the numerous allocations to the failed NEPA, the fact that no roads are properly constructed and maintained, the morgues that constitute our health facilities and the extortionist nature of our law enforcement agencies, more adept at collecting "family support" from transport operators than enforcing law, and the bribe-ridden and corruption-infested civil service that has perfected red tape to extort clients. Yet Nigeria is a country that is richly endowed, and when Tunji Braithwaite formed his "Chop I Chop" political party in the 1970s, people laughed, even though he had reckoned that if the oil revenue were shared annually, each citizen of Nigeria would take home more than US3000 per annum—that is, N450000 per annum, or something in the region of N37500 per month calculated at the current exchange rates of the time. Imagine the exponential multiplication of that over the last forty years, if we had not had the Vagabonds in Power (VIPs) to perpetually condemn Nigeria to under-development. There is no doubt that some would have squandered their patrimony the way our leaders are doing it on our behalf, but more likely many would have done better with their share. In any case, we would not have reason to blame anyone for wasting our patrimony, without our contribution to our impoverishment!

In the 1990s, a minister of government in Jamaica lost over US42 million on a botched project, and the prime minister put it down to youthful exuberance. About the same time, another minister was involved in a project that led to the inability to properly account for over J$1.2 billion, and all that happened was that the minister was asked to resign. And recently another officer of the government charged with distributing donated light bulbs messed up the process and it ended up costing the government hundreds of millions of Jamaica dollars. Though the matter is being investigated, but all manner of red herring, obfuscation and distractions are being put in the way of the trial of the officer, so that he and his confederates can go free. Yet we all see what happens in cases like that or even less in other climes. There was a time when a very popular American senator was sentenced to jail time for misuse of stamp funds by officers in his office and he was to pay his board and lodging in jail, and there was a year when Japan lost three prime ministers in a row over various forms of scandals, while in recent times, many British members of parliament have been in all sorts of troubles because of various abuses of office and public trust. In the case of Africana peoples, the more scandalous the more prayers for success we get, and those who as much as raise issues of corruption are given all kinds of names, and often get assassins sent after them!

In this discussion I have examined the fundamental place that law—the rule of law—holds in orderliness in any society, showing that society is primarily a product of the interpersonal relations which are moderated by morality, norms, rules, regulations and laws. It is the observance of these which allow members of society to function at their highest level. Where these basic demands are not met, it is clear that society cannot function properly, and development, happiness and realization of life possibilities are compromised.

In order to show why Africana societies are developmentally retrogressive in the main, I argue that the absence of proper attention to the rule of law, through leadership's wanton disregard for law and order, cultivated in a culture of impunity and nonaccountability, is to blame for the poor developmental states of African societies. But I trace the source of the culture of indiscipline, impunity, and profligate irresponsibility to colonialism and its exogenous authority system. But I do not indicate that this is all, because even more significant is the mis-education of Africana leadership which inherited the colonial and plantation mentality which sees their societies are ones for which they need not be accountable to, and which they ran like personal fiefdoms, just the same way that the colonial operatives were not accountable to their local communities but to their home governments. In the case of Africana leaders, they are totally unaccountable, having not been properly introduced to indigenous Africana systems of governance and the checks and balances which made for progress and development in indigenous societies before the evil forces of slavery and colonialism. I also examined the place of military dictatorships in the destruction of responsibility, accountability and discipline in public office. I showed that rather than being corrective, the military in African politics have been responsible for entrenching the culture of impunity.

Deriving from this analysis, the only corrective that is immediately suggested is that there is need to re-educate all Africana leaders and aspiring leaders to understand that leadership is service, and that the trust which a leader enjoys is because of a moral contract that leaders are attuned to the huge responsibilities they have for the welfare of their societies, which when properly exercised will lead to the immortalization of their contributions, while used negatively it leads to disasters for the polities and generations of unborn citizens. To this end, it is contended that because to whom much is given, much is expected, the leadership in Africana societies must wake up to their responsibilities to their societies. It is that which has made the difference in Singapore, Malaysia, South Korea, Indonesia, India, Brazil, and it is what is making the difference in Ghana today, why Nigerians are setting up businesses there and sending their children to school there. When we get it right all other issues will be easy to resolve, without bitterness or division, without need for what I call the garrison-ization of the academy or the coronation-ization of discourse, where all we do is listen to a tale told by idiots, full of sound and fury, signifying nothing. In my view, Africana peoples have suffered long enough, not because they have not been properly endowed with natural and intellectual resources, but simply because they have inherited and been saddled with visionless, intellectually deficient leadership. And Africana peoples cannot wait, nor should they be made to continue to wait for what is truly theirs, as human beings—true development for the enhancement of their chances to prosper as human beings.

FOUR

Aspects of Legal Education and Sociopolitical Order in Indigenous Yoruba Society

Indigenous Yoruba society was highly urbanized from as early as 1000 AD, with cities scattered over what is now the West African region. Even with the spread of the Yoruba people across the region (a large geographical area for an ethnic group to occupy even at that time), the Yoruba people maintained a combination of centralized governance and city-state independence, such that all the various individual cities ran their affairs patterned virtually after that of the capital, while at the same time maintaining loyalty and dependence on the central government at the capital of the empire. Yoruba people spoke dialects of the same language, which can be regarded as the variations of the Yoruba language proper spoken at the capital city—Oyo (Johnson 1969). They also shared the same religio-cultural beliefs, expressed in various metaphysical, epistemological, axiological, political, economic and social ideas. Some of the common ideas that made life meaningful in Yoruba society relate to the concepts of Supreme Being (Olodumare) and the divinities (Orisa), Yoruba scripture (*Ifá*), law (*òfin*), moral existence (*ìwà rere*), education and vocation (*ẹkọ* and *isẹ*), dressing (*aso*), beauty (*ewà*), community and filial relations of society (*àjobí* and *àjọgbé*) and more, (Akiwowo 1980). Yoruba people were a highly cultured people with a sense of identity and humanity, derived from their understanding of creation and being in the world. And the Yoruba society developed a clear sense of community.

In this chapter, our interest is focused on the Yoruba indigenous legal system and various mechanisms that were used to propagate the system, so that it was clear that members of society had sophisticated ideas about justice, fairness, legitimacy, orderliness in human affairs, reward and punishment, good governance and more. We noted that Yoruba indigenous culture is both a patriarchal and hierarchical society and that there were moments of excesses and virtual lawlessness in the history of this people (Johnson 1969), but we also note that checks and balances were highly developed to checkmate the predictable weaknesses in human beings when they are entrusted with powers that originally derive from society but which must have a locus for their proper functioning. One intriguing question that begs for an answer relates to how it was possible for a cohesive empire or kingdom to have functioned as early as 1000 AD in Yoruba land, with clear law and order, social, political, economic, administrative, cultural, artistic and religious development in place (Bewaji 2003). This is an issue that is discussed in this chapter, and for which we provide two obvious answers; namely, a) that there was a sophisticated sense of group identity, group belonging and group pride which transmuted into a sense of shared group destiny and survival that every individual strove to protect and defend even at the pain of death, and b) that there was a highly sophisticated educational system which was deployed in the service of Yoruba society at large and in the protection of the individual member of that society through the proper education of members of the leadership group (which were often hereditary as well as democratically accessible to members of society) and the general populace so that rights, duties, obligations and responsibilities were at all times clearly defined with provisions for mediating grey areas where these may arise from time to time.

With regard to the first element in the answers indicated above, a number of factors have served to undermine the sense of belonging. Some of these include the effect of centrifugal wars that were a consequence of weakness or decadence of leadership before colonial misadventure in Yoruba land on the one hand, and also the effect of colonial subjugation of Yoruba society within the structure of the Nigerian state which affected perniciously not just the consciousness of Yoruba identity, but also which served to destroy the group pride in the culture of Yoruba society that individual Yoruba persons would have reserved for his/her ethnic identity. The instruments used to achieve these ends were a) the political powers of the colonial state which became superior to indigenous power structures, b) the religio-metaphysical constructs that accompanied colonialism which denigrated and derogated most pathologically the indigenous religio-metaphysical constructs that served to maintain the indigenous Yoruba polity, and c) the introduction of formal education as the sole purveyor of knowledge, culture and meaning as defined by the colonial powers, thereby creating a new reality about worth, value and existence in the colonized societies of Nigeria.

Clearly, the second issue mentioned above, relating to the Yoruba indigenous educational system, has direct bearing on the first, as our last annotation shows that Western formal education was an instrument for the irruption of social, political, religious, axiological and economic order (among others), which needs careful analysis and understanding for us to be able to see clearly how and why some of the maladies of contemporary Yoruba and Nigeria societies seem to be entrenched and insoluble! It is this last issue, the educational system that sustained the indigenous Yoruba legal system, social order, political order, justice and fairness and others, that is examined in this chapter, with a view to showing that an alien educational system serving an alien legal system, for example, could only produce the kind of social, cultural, political and moral anarchy that reigns supreme in Yoruba land and in Nigeria in the present.

In a recent publication, Oba (2006) rightly lamented the fact that Nigeria at the national level does not have any form of educational structures, formal or informal, in place for the teaching of student lawyers and other judicial functionaries of state, the various customary legal traditions and instruments of the many ethnic communities that make up Nigeria. But this is not all; it is clear that, even more perilously, the various component semi-autonomous states that make up the Federal Republic of Nigeria have not found it either necessary or expedient to develop deliberate structures to educate citizens within their geographic boundaries about the elements of indigenous laws (native laws and customs) of the people of these states. With regard to the first omission, Oba has argued that there is need that this situation be urgently remedied, so that the dissonance arising from the cacophony of legal traditions be comprehended and addressed so that Nigeria can benefit from the law and order that these traditions have to yield to Nigeria (pp. 107–108). In my view, probably charity should begin from home, so that rather than top down, the proper education of the different components of Nigeria with regard to indigenous laws and traditions should start from the base—that is, from the various local communities where these cultural practices form their native laws and customs.

Looking at the characteristics of indigenous legal traditions and judicial systems, Oba (2006) employed the rather condescending and paternalistic colonial-handed-down nomenclature "customary law," which nomenclature is derived from the second-class status of the colonial-system-relegated indigenous legal systems of the colonized, just as they did relegate all other elements of the traditions and cultures of the colonized peoples they abused and oppressed. But more imprudently he (Oba 2006) seemed to accept, without any critical evaluation, the Eurocentric ideas of Holleman and Obilade (1949), that African "customary laws" were "expressed communally," "more concrete than abstract" and "involves emotional or magico-religious thinking rather than rational, causal, unemotional and commercial thinking" (p. 97), by comparison with the position of Elegido (1994) that African indigenous legal systems place "emphasis on reconciliation and compromise; emphasis on general principles; group responsibility; and frequent use of informal enforcement procedures" which one would have thought more rational, given the fact that humans had to live in communities of others with filial and extra-filial relations (p. 97). Oba did not pay attention to the fact that hardly is there any legal system in any part of the world—past or present—that is bereft of the so-called derogatorily applied "emotional or magico-religious thinking" combined with "rational" elements derived from their experiences of nature and human interaction, the first of which Holleman and Obilade would ascribe to African legal traditions and the latter of which they would deny, for there is so much combination of religio-metaphysical ideas and rational elements in English legal tradition as well as its communal foundations and reflexive feedback.

It is clear from the foregoing that Elegido (1994), cited by Oba in the chapter under consideration, seems to appreciate part of the role of law in Yoruba society by far better than Holleman and Obilade (1949). But more importantly, it seems that Oba did not see the connection between the failure of common law in Nigeria as a direct consequence of the dissonance of the parallel judicial systems in Nigeria and the fact that neither do those entrusted with practicing and enforcing the Nigerian-borrowed British legal system formally embraced have any faith in it, as it is alien to them, nor are they respectful of their own indigenous legal systems, as these have never been regarded as "legal systems" properly so-called, either by their educational up-bringing or professional disposition. It is only when our "learned friends" of the legal profession and the esteemed "my lords" of the bench are afforded a critical lesson in indigenous African history and the legal systems which sustained the African civilizations and societies of millennia past and the relationship between law and order and legal education is properly appreciated by those entrusted with the administration of justice in various African societies that the many African societies will begin to see development in the various areas of their existence, similar to the development of their ancestral civilizations that began in Africa.

Nigeria concluded (over the weekends of April 14, 2007, and April 21, 2007) another sham series of elections—these elections were for councilors and chairmen/women into local governments, members of state legislatures, gubernatorial positions, members of the federal House of Representatives, senators into the federal Senate and for the crown jewel of it all, election of the president of the Republic of Nigeria. Many who were not familiar with the history of Nigeria, the deliberate development and emplacement of a class of indigenous colonial overlords over the affairs of Nigeria, to heartlessly and mindlessly ruin the Nigeria state and the different ethnicities and peoples of Nigeria, expected a miracle. But perceptive individuals, who have managed to retain their intellectual sanity in the face of various odds, did not expect such a miracle to happen from a cadre of political impostors who have neither learnt what African history was about, nor do they have any familiarity with their own ethnic histories. Indeed, it would have been a miracle had the crop of predatory parasites called Nigerian leaders provided a different kind of election; that is, if following the example of the greatest "democracy" (the United States of America) in the world had two horribly flawed elections in a row at the beginning of the twenty-first century, Nigeria had had a free and fair election, one would have been left to wonder how a society without any indigenously owned legal system or tradition like Nigeria could have fared better. One thing that did not constitute a serious factor in this last election, however, was the colonial British-falsified demographics which endowed the North with more humans than the naturally more populous South. Quite clearly the people of this country have been so wholesomely degraded that no ideas of ethnicity mattered anymore; what was important was the immediate reward for participating here and now, hence the do or die approach of the contestants and their supporters which translated into election results where polls were not even conducted.

Given the above, it is clear that Africa has been mis-educated to suppose that "education" is no more than classrooms, teachers, syllabuses, examinations, education officers, education budgets, matriculation and convocation ceremonies and certificates (The Republic of Uganda 1992). This minimalist conception of education would not have been that bad had it encompassed even the basics that are necessary for the orderly functioning of society. Thus, when African governments seek to use education to spur development and unity, they did not factor in, on the one hand, the inadequacy of the minimalist concept of education at work, nor, on the other hand, did they learn from the experiences of their own indigenous traditions where formal, informal and nonformal educational systems were blended seamlessly to ensure the development of a rounded citizen living in an ordered society. For example, the government of Uganda says,

> A national policy on education is Government's strategy for achieving some of its objectives with education as a tool. In this context, education has several basic functions: it transmits societies' traditions and cultural heritage, it provides a core curriculum of basic skills on which individual development is based; it provides opportunity to students to study in a wide variety of fields which they find useful and of interest and which are beneficial to society as a whole (1989: 18).

But it is clear that this was not meant by the Ugandan government, for the government neither intended to allow the true culture, heritage and traditions of Ugandans to be taught meaningfully and critically—as recent eruptions of ethnic protest show when government colluded with Asian-descended businesses to sell indigenous tracts of land for farming—nor could emphasis on a utilitarian education be more than partial, as it does not see that humans need to be educated not just for purposes of being productive members of a workforce but to be educated to become rounded members of society as such. Thus, not unexpectedly, the result of education in most colonies and post-colonies in Africa was the production of a) "book people" who live in two mutually incompatible worlds described by Mazrui as cultural captivity and cultural schizophrenia (Mazrui 1978: 13-29); b) Africans, in all walks of life, who look down on their own indigenous traditions, peoples and cultures as inferior, backward, primitive and *worthless*; c) the perpetuation of an untenable but contrived traditional relationship of dependence between the state and society that was in remission through a separation of state and religion in many African societies before the introduction of Islam and Christianity (Johnson 1969); d) the de-moralization, de-socialization and deculturation of education ostensibly to ensure efficiency of skills training; e) the destruction of the indigenous leadership educational traditions of African societies and their replacement with persons suffering from "double consciousness" (Gordon 2006); f) the development of a dependency consciousness, whereby Africa becomes a recipient society rather than an originating one, and g) the deliberate infusion in the psyche of Africans the consciousness of self-hatred and living of lies, whereby African peoples now want more to be European or American rather than African.

Ghana just celebrated sixty years of nominal political independence from the colonial Britain. Ghana was the first African "country," in the modern sense of country, based on the European partition of Africa, to gain such status of freedom, but hardly does anyone remember that at its apogee, the medieval Ghana empire was almost the size of the whole of contemporary western Europe. No one even bothers to find out how such a feat was possible, politically, economically, technologically, scientifically or culturally. No one bothers to examine the legal structures that sustained such a feat. For this reason, we may remind ourselves what the FESTAC 77 showed with regard to the role of Western education in the destruction of Africa:

> In short, modern education is still based on the principles and objectives of the colonial type which aimed at glorifying western culture and creating Africans who would serve the interests of their masters. Furthermore, it tends to create an elitist class.
>
> Because it is individualistic in nature and capitalist in pattern, it does not aim at meeting the needs of the society for which it is directed. The root of the problem in modern education was seen as being that of lack of interaction and adaptation (Amoda 1978b: 192).

It is clear from the foregoing that the current educational structures in Africa could not produce anything better than people who rob their countries' treasuries to stash away in foreign banks, only to turn around and borrow from the countries where they have hidden their national wealth at oppressive interest rates. What these African "leaders" are doing is just "their masters'" bidding. The level of their success at such perfidy determines their successful accession to the elitist class, forgetting that "one rich person in the family of nine other abjectly poor siblings only mean ten poor persons." This is why such "leaders" now do not find it ironic that they have to barricade themselves behind high home fences, armored personal cars and security details, as they cannot move freely in their own societies because of the evils that they have done, which follow them night and day. By pretending that there is growth and development, civilization and national advancement, they have interpreted individualism to mean sophistication; forgetting that "if the rat has no peace, the bird cannot have any peace," because whatever is frightening the rat will one day trouble the bird, *irorun edk, oun ni irorun eye.*

When one now sees the children of the "leaders" of various African societies going to school in Europe and America in luxuries, having hundreds of thousands of pound sterling or euros or American dollars in their many accounts, buying brand new BMWs with cash and throwing parties for all comers as if there will be no tomorrow, it definitely adds up to show why elections are do or die affairs in Africa, as these set of "leaders" have no other means of livelihood except their unaccountable parasitic dependence on state resources for terribly warped life styles. This means that those who have destroyed the educational, medical and financial infrastructures of their own countries serve only the interests of "their masters," by ensuring eternal dependence of their own countries on others, which is the goal of Western mis-education of the colonial—destined to show the native incompetence of the black folk, as well as the intrinsic irrationality of the African mentality. This all adds up to the reality of the contemporary leadership of the peoples of Africa that can only be described as the wasteful, wasted and wasting generations; a set of VIPs (an acronym for "vagabonds in power"), whose only claim to legitimacy is their unscrupulous access to state power to give them capacity for destruction of their societies.

We noted earlier that education in indigenous Yoruba society has been very sophisticated and diversified from ancient times. Educational structures varied from the highly structured—formal—to the diffuse and general—informal—and to the totally unstructured—nonformal. For example, professional guilds were very concerned with training and validity of qualifications of members of their vocations, such that, for example, one does not just become a blacksmith or hunter or diviner or herbalist or farmer overnight without undergoing many years of tutelage and certification through various tests and examinations culminating in rites of passage and proof, to the satisfaction of professionals in the field—of competence at the end of the training. The fact that the Yoruba civilization depended on high specialization and differentiation of labor, duties and responsibilities as members of different societies and as related to the different segments of these societies, show that various relevant educational materials must be devised to meet the requirements of replenishing the stock of skills and personnel required in various domains of existence. This shows that it is most inaccurate to describe the training processes of the young and old in Yoruba society as informal—that is, before the introduction of the Western education—because education in Yoruba society had all the elements of what takes place in a Western schooling system—curriculum, teachers, students, standards of attainment, terminal tests and examinations, certification and induction into cadres of achievement, and regular upgrading of content and visitations by competent leaders in fields to ensure standards are maintained. For this reason, it is clear that knowledge was not only transmitted, but more importantly, traditions and cultures of the society were transmitted from generation to generation. Since our interest in this discussion is not education per se, but education with regard to the legal system and law and order, we will examine various aspects of the educational practices in indigenous Yoruba society with respect specifically to legal systems as it relates to the specific training of the leadership and that of the general populace. This will show that, by and large, the contemporary failure of the state of Nigeria to pay attention to this kind of education (as lamented by Oba), is at the expense of order and development of the country.

The overall purpose of education in indigenous Yoruba society is both for the culture of the mind of the individual member of society so that the individual can become an *Omoluabi*—a well-rounded, hardworking, honest, responsible, respectful and respectable individual—and also, though more importantly, for the individual to be able to meaningfully be a member of society, knowing his/her duties and responsibilities and discharging these without fear or favor in the overall interest of society. For this reason, education, though life long, is benchmarked by important milestones of achievement, the successful completion and mastery of which was recognized and rewarded with elevation to positions of responsibility and respect within society.

Since the purpose of education was not simply to equip the individual with skills which the individual will then use to survive in society, or to be used to terrorize society by making all sorts of demands for compensation, but to ensure that the individual is able to perform with excellence in spheres of specialization as a member of society, it meant that the preparation of the individual was in the interest of all members of society—such that satisfactory completion of a course of study was also the interest of all members of society, and failure was noted against the success of performance or nonperformance of the individual. For this reason, the Yoruba society never left the education of political leadership to chance, as it was clear that the welfare of society cannot be left to providence. Hence, deliberate effort is made to train and educate the members of the political directorate to ensure that they understand that attaining political office is a thing of high responsibility, as the burden of survival and success of society depends on the leader. And the leader recognizes that the whole issue of personal identity, interests, welfare and aspirations must be put in abeyance when these conflict with the interest of the society. And to this extent the leader is made aware that he/she has no life apart from society—and as such must be ready to lay down his/her life for the overall good of the society if there ever be occasion for such sacrifice.

There were various ways in which the leaders were selected or elected or divined, but more important was the hereditary offices in the various communities. But even with this kind of heredity, there were elements of democracy in the final determination of the king or *Ọba* of any town or the *Baálẹ* of any village. According to Johnson (1969),

> The succession as above said is by election from among members of the royal family, of the one considered as the most worthy, age and nearness to the throne being taken into consideration. It might be mentioned in passing that the feelings and acceptance of the denizens of the harem toward the king-elect are often privately ascertained and assured of previously.
>
> In the earliest days, the eldest son naturally succeeded the father, and in order to be educated in all the duties of the kingship which must one day devolve upon him, he was often associated more or less with the father in performing important duties and thereby reigned with his father under the title of AREMO (the heir apparent) having his own official residence near the palace (p. 41).

Apart from the general process of normal upbringing of members of the royal family or ruling group in each community, deliberate effort is made to instill in the elected or selected leader various aspects of the laws, norms, ethos and culture of the society that he will preside over. Johnson (1969) indicated that there is usually a three-month period of intensive education after the selection of the new *Ọba* or king or *Baálẹ* before the coronation of the king (p. 43). This is to ensure that the new ruler has enough time to understand and meditate on the various aspects of the office that he/she was to occupy. Even at this stage, he/she is closely monitored, supervised and facilitated to understand that becoming the *Ọba* means taking on the total identity of the city, town or village at the expense of the self or one's personal family.

There are several highly complicated stages in the final preparation for coronation of the *Ọba*. Even though Johnson describes these as ceremonies, yet it can be seen that they are necessary ingredients in the preparation and education of the new king for the various functions, especially maintaining the integrity of the town and the dispensation of justice with fairness to all and sundry within his/her domain. As detailed by Johnson (1969: 40–78), each night after the election is spent at a different house to master the secrets of the particular part of the city or town, and to understand the traditions that make the town or city what it is. These serve as reminders whenever there are temptations to lapse into self-ingratiating modes which may become destructive to the entire community.

The process of education of the new king is infused with a lot of symbolism and ritual for various reasons. While it is true that the religious may suppose that religion is at the heart of the design of the symbolism and rituals, and while it is true that traditional rulers in Yoruba land also embody elements of the societal spirituality, the fact that, except in the case of *Ọọni Àdìmúlà* of Ife, most of the other kings in Yoruba land, from the most important one and leader/head of all Obas in Yoruba land—the *Alaàfin* of Oyo—to the village heads—*Baálẹ,* there is clear separation of religion and politics, between religion and state and between the sacred and the secular or profane, speaks volumes to the sense of secular justice, practical organization and rationally defensible leadership of the indigenous Yoruba society.

There is division of labor in the process of educating the new king-elect, as he moves from one place of instruction to the other. These range from the initial sacrifice to the ancestors that must be made at *Ọnà-Ìsokùn,* where he resides the first night of his election (Johnson 1969: 42). The second night is spent at the house of *Ọtún-Ìwẹfa,* who is a priest of Sango, for initiation "into the sacerdotal part of his office" (p. 43). Hence,

> The main gateway to the palace being closed at the demise of the King, a private opening is made for him in the outer wall through which he goes in and out of his temporary residence. During this time he remains strictly in private, *learning and practising the style and deportment of a King, and the details of the important duties and functions of his office.* During this period he is dressed in black, and is entitled to use a "cap of state". . . . The affairs of state are at this time conducted by the Basorun (p. 43).

At the end of the *three-month* intensive training period, the coronation finally takes place. This also is in stages, as he must visit various places, shrines and homes to learn various secrets relating to his society, the virtues, norms, mores and ethos relating to each one of them, so that he may continue to maintain the tradition of the society, and lead the society toward progress and development. Some of the places that he must visit include the *Bàrà* or royal mausoleum, the *Ipadí* or the temporary chambers, *Kòso* the shrine of Sango, the shrine of Ogun, the Kobi Aganju and more. A significant part of the process is the opening of *Igbá Ìwà* which helps the people of the domain to "predict" what to expect during the tenure of the new king, and as such prepare the people for the events, good and ill, during the reign of the king.

But the emphasis should not just be concentrated on the education and preparation of the royal personage, as in Yoruba society the king reigns and does not rule. The rule of any Oba is a process and a joint responsibility of the king (Oba) and the council (the Chiefs or Ijoyes). In any case, it is clear that without the proper backing of the Ijoyes, the king cannot carry out anything in the society. This is why the support of the Ijoyes is essential for the effectiveness and fairness of governance. And this probably is why it is said proverbially that *Eti ọba ní'lé, eti oba l'óko, ènìyàn ni í jẹ bẹẹ,* that is literally that "the king's ears reaches the farms and the nooks and crannies of the town is only possible as a consequence of the support of the people through the chiefs," and *Ènìyàn lo wa l'ẹhìn agbọn tí a bu omi si tí kò jò,* that is, "it is because there is a human backing for the basket, that is why it leaks no water poured into it."

Hence, the selection and training of the chiefs and other officials of the state and cities and villages are not any less rigorous. In fact, heredity is important, but where the person who happens to be the heir apparent is regarded as an evil person, such a person may be bypassed for the selection or election of one that is acceptable for the society (Johnson 1969: 41). It is clear that the process of divination of Ifa is also important as a safeguard for the choice of the chiefs, whereby the overall interest of the chiefs is secondary and the Ifa takes into consideration the overall welfare of the entire society. It is significant that, even within the so-called patriarchal cultural system in Yoruba society, there is no discrimination between the sexes in the determination of the council of chiefs, as there are specified offices for male and female in Yoruba land. For this reason equal respect is offered to the occupiers of offices, and even the king cannot push aside office holders on account of gender without facing the wrath of the other members of his council and the entire society. In fact, the position of women is most significant and commands respect on account of the fact that it is the woman that any living human Yoruba first knows intimately before ever getting to meet or know a father! And the leadership of society is not any less respectful of womanhood; it is taboo to disrespect one's source of being.

In many instances it is the case that the various chiefs and leaders are members of various professional guilds or specialized communities within the domain of the Oba. This means that specialized educational instructions fitting the professions and specializations would have been undertaken before they were selected or elected and made chiefs. And in Yoruba society offices are positions of responsibility where holders are expected to put the society before the self or family. This does not mean that office holders lose their individuality or identity, what it means is that apart from being a self, the individual does not hold a personal office designed by the self, hence the individual could not privatize the office and carry on as if the office is personal and private. To this extent, the privilege of holding an office is highly cherished and respected.

Whether one is a king, chief or lay male or female, young or old member of society, or whether one is descended from wealthy or poor parentage, in Yoruba land there is always the expectation that every person in society grow up to be an *Omoluabi*, that is, the total embodiment of the moral, social, cultural, religious and educated manifestation of the best that any human being can aspire to be. This, becoming an *Ọmọlúàbí*, is the first expectation of what being human means, and it is better to be an *Ọmọlúàbí* than to have the greatest material wealth, as *Ìwà l'ewà omo ènìyàn*, that is, "good character is the beauty of a human being," or that matters than being a king or chief or other titled person (Bewaji 2003: 220). To this end, various educational mechanisms and pedagogical materials are deployed formally, informally and nonformally in the preparation of human beings for responsible and respectful living in society (Akiwowo 1980). To complement this, it is always impressed on the individual at every turn that regardless of what finery one may have to wear or jewelry that may adorn one's livery, not having friends, relatives, children and human beings in one's life is worse than plague, for *ènìyàn bo ni l'ára j'asọ lọ;* that is, in literal terms, "human beings, when present, cover one's nakedness more than clothing."

While the instruction in legal systems of societies are carried out in clear terms, so that there will be no ambiguities with respect to right and wrong, good and evil/bad conduct, proper/just or improper/unjust determination of disputes, for the leadership, to reinforce the early education in the traditions of the society, the legal education of the general populace is done in a number of mutually reinforcing ways. Some these include a) direct instruction with regard to elements of dos and don'ts of society, b) storytelling and the arts generally, c) proverbs, d) presence of young and old in the courtyard during the hearing of disputes or during the trying of cases, e) seeing the practical implications of good conduct for individuals through various rewards and through the witness of the suffering of punishment of bad behavior by miscreants in society, f) through the seeing of the consequences of bad behavior for the society as a whole, because of the punishment which all members of society must endure until the wrong has been righted through sacrifice or payment of damages, g) through the pronouncements of the diviners, who are able to diagnose situations and determine the causative factors in the suffering of individuals and of societies, and h) through the witnessing, in extreme cases, the meeting of such extreme situations with reward such as with chieftaincy titles, parcels of land, marriage to young members of royal families, or punishment with excommunication or even death. We now consider these instructional mechanisms seriatim, but briefly, because of constraints of space.

Yoruba society takes seriously the proper upbringing of young ones, so that even with individual proclivities each youth is educated in the traditions, knowledge, religious, social and political ideas that make life meaningful in the society, and understands that it is only through the participation in the group promoting aspects of living together that his/

her own existence is enriched. The initial instruction of young ones with regard to what is expected behavior and behavior not tolerated by persons, families and communities take place at the "breast" of the mother, as mothers communicate with suckling children to ensure that there is clear understanding of these matters. The value of this communication may be down-played now in the era of "formula" feeding of children, and probably this accounts for why there are stark deviations from norms of behavior now witnessed among the youth who never had this kind of intimacy with their mothers.

In addition to this initial training, all members of the family contribute to the raising of each child, because it is recognized that each child becomes adult not as stand-alone atoms, with individualities that derive from a vacuous space, but rather as a child and as an adult, each individual is a representative of the family and clan and community from which he/she takes a name. This factor of taking a name is very critical, because how each individual represents himself has consequences for how the entire family and community is appreciated in society, and to infract the laws or the norms of the community is to bring extreme shame not just to the self, but to the entire family and community; while to be a good person is to bring pride and recognition to the self and to the entire family and community of which one is descended.

After the initial instruction by the mother, male children are further instructed by fathers and males in the community with regard to proper conduct in society, while female children are instructed by mothers and females in the community regarding proper conduct in society. This does not mean that there are no inter-gender instructions or that these are separatist educational modes; what it means is that there is role-modelling and mentoring that assists the youth in having clear connections with adults in society which facilitate the robust sense of belonging that carries the young one through life to develop the feeling of connection with/to others in society, so that each person sees that they have no individual destiny different from the overall welfare of their society. To take seriously the instruction received and embrace them is to have received *eko*, and to rebuff or refuse to take these seriously is to become an *a lài l'ẹkọ*. This is easy for the society to see, as the person will manifest the traits of *omo sá, èkejì ajá*—or literally, "a useless and untrained child or person who is very loose and without culture, and therefore has habits that is next to a street dog without an owner," for such animals bark meaninglessly and such persons have no manners and are disrespectful to adults and seniors, thereby bringing shame and disgrace to themselves and family.

Adeboye Babalola (1973) brought together a total of sixty-five *Alo Ijapa* in two very important volumes documenting various stories in Yoruba culture. In introducing these stories, he says:

> *Anfaani iwe yi po fun awon obi, awon olukoni ati awon akeko. Iwe yi jasi iwe pataki, iwe t'o joju, ti iya tabi baba le maa nawogan lalaale lati ka alo s'etigbo awon ogo were ki nwon to sun. Iwe yi jasi iwe-kika tuntun ti awon olukoni le maa fi ko awon akeko ni ojulowo ede Yoruba. Be e ni ewe, iwe yi je eyi ti awon omo-ile-iwe le ka ni akagbadun funrawon* (p. vii).

This can be rendered literally in English as follows:

> This book has many advantages for parents, teachers and learners. This book is very important and valuable; mothers or fathers can read it to children at bed-time before the children go to sleep. Teachers can use it to teach Yoruba language at school. Also, school children can read the book for their own individual enjoyment and fun.

Babalola only itemized three aspects of the value of story-telling in Yoruba land. Those that he itemized are very important, and the fact that he also did recognize the changes and challenges that face parents and communities in contemporary society in bringing the stories to text is signal. In an age where moonlight evening togetherness for young and old for sharing and learning is becoming a thing of the past, because of various forces of "modernization" such as television, cable networks, computer games, urbanization and attendant conscription of the traditional values of societies to the dustbin of obsolescence, there can be no gainsaying the need for use of new media to get the same educational materials to the children. What may not have happened, however, is the seriousness with which the use of these resource materials may be taken, as many "educated" families now tend to emphasize learning of English and other foreign languages at the expense of Yoruba, as it is believed that it is a mark of up-ward mobility and civilization to be more at home with English than Yoruba as a formal means of communication.

In highlighting the values of his two volumes, he was writing as a literary person who was concerned with whether or not the stories were fun to read and enjoy; he failed to mention the fact that story-telling and the content of the stories played very significant roles in the education and training of young ones in all aspects of norms, morality, rules of behavior of society in years gone by, whereby children sit with adults on moonlit nights and were regaled with stories which had critical bearing on their moral, social, cultural and legal education. Though the stories revolved around the activities of the turtle (*Ìjàpà Tìròkò oko Yánníbo*), there was little doubt about the validity of the ideas represented in the stories, and how failure to observe the important laws of nature and society led to grief for *Ìjàpà*, implying that similar fate may be anticipated for similar infractions of the law of society (Bewaji 2003).

In *Beauty and Culture*, effort was made to examine the various art forms as instruments of education in Yoruba society in particular and in African societies generally (Bewaji 2003). But the issue examined that there was not the relation of story-telling and the arts as instruments for legal education. However, there is no doubt that this form of use was also consciously made in Yoruba pedagogy, as the various art forms are used to respect, reify and reinforce justice in society. For example, *Egúngún* festivals were occasions where various events in society—good and bad—are clearly remarked comically, satirically or openly, so that through the process of catharsis society may undertake a purgatory and cleansing of the evils that such actions and events may bring to the society (Bewaji 2003: 161).

Proverbs (*Òwe*) are very important in the life of Yoruba society (Bewaji 2003: 172). In a society that prides itself on its capacity for highly rational discourse analysis and utilization in the understanding and communication of ideas, proverbs help to capture complex ideas, render them in concise format and communicate these to very telling effect, thereby illuminating issues and resolving disputes. Proverbs constitute a very important instrument of instruction, as it allows students (the young) to reflect on the content of each proverb, subjecting same to multidimensional analysis and interpretation in order to see the implications and relevance of the content to real life. Oladele Balogun in a recent discussion, has highlighted the jurisprudential foundations of many Yoruba proverbs (Balogun 2006). This shows that proverbs constituted a critical element in conflict resolution and justice dispensation in Yoruba society. For our interest here, we simply note that proverbs are educative means of instilling in young and old ideas of justice, fairness and social equity. But competence in Yoruba language is presumed in the use of proverbs, otherwise the meaning of proverbs would be lost to the audience.

So much has been written about the nature, linguistics structure and moral power of proverbs, but it is only recently that attention is being paid to the jurisprudential elements in proverbs in Yoruba society (Balogun 2006). And also the power of proverbs as an educational tool for teaching Yoruba language has been examined (Alaba 1988), but its use specifically in legal education is yet to be fully explored. What we have done here is just to sketch the fact that proverbs constitute a plank in the proper educational preparation of members of society.

As part of the practical aspects of law and order in Yoruba society, there is open access to the mediation mechanisms for arbitration of disputes. In such instances where there is a complaint about anyone or anything in the community, the matter is brought to the attention of the elders, the chiefs or to the Oba in Council. Complaints are openly aired and the two parties to the issue are brought face to face, so as to allow them to state their cases, call witnesses if need be and allow for evidence to be presented for evaluation. Women, children and young people are usually present to witness the proceedings, both as a learning device and as a means of enabling them to see the process at work. Women, children and young people may not participate, except where they are invited to speak as witnesses to matters on hand, because *enu àgbà l'obì ti í gbó,* meaning literally that "the kolanut is ripe and/or mature only in the mouth of the elder when he/she tries/tastes it," as only elders are wise enough to settle serious matters in society. But if children and young people especially are not allowed to be present, then society would forget that *omodé òní, l'àgbà òla,* that is, "the youth of today, grows up necessarily to become tomorrow's adult and elder" and *eyin ní í di àkùko,* meaning that "it is the egg of today that hatches to become the cockerel of tomorrow."

In the same vein, it can be seen that the Yoruba legal system allows for those of lesser pedigree in society to enjoy a level of humanity and equality. Thus, while it is true that for various reasons, and like in virtually all civilizations, there were instances where some members of society were slaves or indentured servants, either as a consequence of captivity in wars against state enemies or as a consequence of indebtedness of the person to the creditor, there is never serious instances where the personhood or humanity of the poor or slave or servant is abrogated in Yoruba society on account of poverty or servitude. The reason the Yoruba legal system uses for this is that *kò sí eni t'ó l'órì méjì, ní to rí ná à bí a se bí erú, bé e la b'omo,* meaning that "no single individual human being has two heads, and it is the same way a free person is born that a slave is born"; and to crown it all, it is often stated that *Àparò kan kò ga jù'kan lo, à fi èyí tó bá g'orí ebè*, that is, one partridge is not taller than another, except for the one that climbs unto a heap!

Even though it may be contended that age commands respect and may be used to "cheat" the young ones, just to show that one is older, it must also be remembered that Yoruba wisdom does not disregard youth, because *omodé gbọn àgbà gbọn, òun la fi dá ilẹ Ife*—that is, "the youth is wise and elder is wise, that is the foundation on which the city of Ife was built"; and further, *ọwọ omodé kò tó pepe, t'àgbàlagbà ò wo akèngbè*, meaning, "while the young child cannot stretch her hand to take something on the high shelf because of shortness of height, equally an elder's hand cannot enter the narrow gourd's mouth because of narrowness of the mouth of the gourd"; hence *omodé kò je obì, òun ni àgbà kò je oyè*, literally translated, this means that "just as the elder may say that the child is too young to eat kola nut, equally the young one whose support is needed for the appointment of the elder as chief may show the chief that she does not fit the status, as she is too disrespectful of youth." As part of the home training and public education of all members of society, emphasis is placed on proper understanding of the need to respect the rights of all members of society, regardless of age, gender, wealth or royalty.

In spite of contemporary debates about the validity of punishment as deterrence to crime, the Yoruba indigenous legal system was in no doubt that when justice is done fairly, regardless of the station of the offender or pedigree or filial affiliation, then rational potential offenders would contemplate the implications of their course of action for themselves, their families and society before embarking on such a course of action. Apart from incarceration and reparation, there is the huge negative odium of scandal that attaches to family names and how such can blight the integrity of the individual forever. This would imply that such grave matters as positions of trust in society—getting a chieftaincy title, getting decent marriage contracts for self and members of one's family, negotiating business contracts—become impossible. Even the mere reference to the name of the person within the context of criminality is enough to do the damage to the future potential of the person and his/her family.

When members of society witness this, knowing that the punishment was meted out judiciously, then it is enough to deter future offenders. And here we would mention the fact that the Yoruba legal system emphasized evidence and witnesses' testimony and the use of precedents in the determination of cases. The net effect of this is that the obligation to speak the truth is taken seriously in all instances, and given the fact that Yoruba depends on each person stating his/her case, without the assistance of intermediaries—people paid to state other persons' cases such as lawyers (*agb'ẹjọ rò*)—it means that care must be taken to present one's case truthfully so that it can be properly adjudicated. But there are instances where cases are so complex that care must be taken in how arbitration takes place, especially in instances relating to disputes between husbands and wives, because what seems to be a dispute to the public may actually be emotional angst which needs no external or third-party mediation beyond the lovers' nest. In this regard, maybe there is similarity here between the English common law practice of not having spouses testify against each other—except in divorce cases—and the Yoruba wisdom of not coming into arguments between spouses.

Finally, the Yoruba indigenous legal system also has within it the aspect of nemesis, such that it is believed that since "what goes around comes around," then even when someone may seem to be getting away with crime, ultimately they pay for their crimes, because *bí ènìyán bá ń yọ ilẹ dà, oun gánnágánná tàbí oun abẹnú a mà a yọ 'ni se*—which means, "if one does evil in secret, one may also suffer punishment in secret," which punishment may be observed by the public without knowing the cause for the suffering. For this reason, it is believed that *ìwà rere l'ẹsọ ènìyàn*—that is, "good character is the best form of protection of the person."

Events in society often serve as educational resources, and for this reason the observant are able to make linkages between human action and development in society. When there are good or bad rainfall seasons leading to good or bad harvests, when there is outbreak of disease, or when there is war and destruction, the knowledgeable in society make the necessary connections and they let members, young and old, to realize what was happening. For this reason, lessons are brought out and members of society are encouraged to continue the good work and to thank the ancestors and Olodumare, or they are asked to repent for their sins, make sacrifices to the ancestors and to the divinities so that the evils may be cleansed from the society.

The people of Yoruba nation are keen on seeing the society develop, and clearly remember periods when Yoruba was not subservient to any other group but were actually leaders of other societies. For this reason, Hubert Ogunde, the playwright and actor, produced plays and music indicating the need for Yoruba people to take a careful introspective look about what has happened to Yoruba land—whereby Yoruba people no longer have unity of purpose and are now being led in some instances by others of lower pedigree. In fact, Johnson (1969) and Abimbola (2006) have suggested that the disunity and retrogression of Yoruba people as a nation may be due to a long-forgotten injustice and curse attendant to it. This has the implication that there is need to placate the soul of the person wronged, so that the injustice can be remedied and the curse lifted. Mythical as this may seem, it is not without precedence in other societies—of which the ancestors of Christianity are remarkable potentates.

What this means is that apart from punishment and reward for individual action and behavior, Yoruba people believe also in collective reward and punishment for injustice and immoral conduct of members of society or of groups in society or even collectively as a society. To determine this and diagnose what course of action is needed, knowledgeable persons in society may be called upon to give their opinions, as these persons are able to inductively and deductively synthesize information and ideas to determine what may be the cause of the events being witnessed in society. On the other hand, it may be a tough issue which cannot be easily broached by individual members of society, even though the proverb in Yoruba says *ọrọ kì í wúwo k'á fi ọbe bùú*, meaning, "no matter how heavy an issue may be, we would not try to dissect it using a knife, we would still require the mouth to split it into various component parts for easy settlement"; when this happens, it may require consultation of the diviners and Ifa, the god of divination. And because of the high regard the process and the outcome of divination enjoys, based on the fact that Ifa never lies and the diviner is not expected to lie, members of society not only rely on the outcome of divination but it also serves as serious avenues for legal and judicial education. We will discuss this separately as follows.

Most discussion of Ifa Literary Corpus and Ifa Divination System sees it in about five ways, as:

a. a body of knowledge that provides information on all aspects of traditional Yoruba life,
b. an academic discipline with a structured course of instruction of students of Ifa, and a medium for the collaboration and exchange of ideas and findings among trainees and specialists,

c. a scriptural text comparable to the Judeo-Christian Bible or Arabic-Islamic Koran,
d. a source of material for the composition of philosophically interesting, novel and profound theories comparable to rationalism, and
e. a literature comparable to Plato's dialogues, Cartesian Mediations, and other classical literary sources which are regarded as intrinsically philosophical in nature (Bewaji 1992: 140–41).

Clearly, these are very useful ways of looking at the divination system of the Yoruba people. But it is inexhaustive, as it does not pay attention to the ways in which Ifa Divination System is an educational resource material for Yoruba people concerning various aspects of life in society and in nature. And it does not pay attention to how Ifa Literary Corpus and the divination system associated with it is also an instrument of/in legal education. Hence, we wish to indicate here that, by and large, legal matters are illuminated by divination, and important lessons are taught to persons who consult Ifa.

It is noteworthy to indicate that there are public occasions when Ifa divination is consulted for specific issues, and the divination system is able to diagnose situations and determine the causative factors in the suffering of individuals and of societies. When this happens, then society and members learn lessons relating to law, justice and democracy.

We have mentioned the neutrality of the Ifa Divination System and the diviners. In fact, like judges in any situation, there must be perfect neutrality of the judges and the judicial process, otherwise those who sit in justice over others and are partial heap curses on themselves. For this reason, the divination system and the agents of the system regard themselves as mere vessels in the service of the greater supernatural powers and for the greater good of society. Regarding themselves as being privileged to serve, they show their transparency and selflessness through the care they take to mediate disputes and pronounce judgments as they are inspired by the ancestors. And since mediating situations is not the privilege of the elder or the King in Council, as anyone in any situation in life may find him or herself called upon to dispense justice, it means that the occasions when one witnesses the application and dispensation of justice is always a learning experience in the judicial system.

Since we have discussed elements of reward and punishment earlier, without considering it mandatory to do a conceptual analysis or clarification of both concepts (as such an effort would have been an unnecessary digression), what is left to highlight here is the fact that there can be no complete judicial system that does not attend to proper understanding of the place of reward and punishment in the scheme of things. In this regard, and with particular reference to how reward and punishment constitute educational and instructional instruments, what we would wish to emphasize is that since humans are capable of reasoning from data to conclusions, it follows that their beliefs and actions can be products of such reasoning and inferences. In this regard, it would be critical to how society conducts business to ensure that there is a clear connection between what is demanded of members of society and what evidence on the ground show as the practical consequences of human behavior in society.

Over the last quarter of a century, the Yoruba society has witnessed some horrendous irruptions in the moral, legal and social fabric of the community, such that there has been a disintegration of *Asuwàdà ènìyàn,* and *Àjobí* translated into *àjogbé* without any form of common destiny being perceived in the structure of human relations. This has served as the worst form of educational mechanism for the young and adults generally. And the payment for this breakdown of the ethos of human cohabitation in society has been the near anarchy that has been let loose on the society—with such scourges as armed robbery, dishonesty in business dealings, various forms of wanton abuse of power, office and position in society and more.

The fact that corruption has crept into all facets of life meant that reward and punishment are also warped and crooked, to the extent that justice has ceased to be an important element of life in society. For this reason, all organs of society, including the religious agencies, have become tainted and affected negatively. The corruption of the judiciary in the contemporary society in Nigeria is one of the most damaging elements contributing to the breakdown of law and order. We could mention the national disgrace of the judicial proclamation of twelve—two-thirds of states of the Federation of Nigeria—in awarding the 1979 election to Shehu Shagari of the PNP. Clearly, when the judicial process is abused so openly, then the legal system is assaulted. If there is no one to defend it from such abuse, then the whole judicial system becomes a sham, and people observe the law more in breach than in obedience, as people tend to live what they experience—regardless of how repugnant it may initially seem to them. And this has been the case in Nigeria for the last quarter of a century or more. Because of this, indigenous Yoruba society ensured that justice was available to all, except in cases where tyrants appropriate the judicial process for selfish ends. But when this happens, Yoruba society understands that *adìe ìrànà ni, kì í se oun à je gbé,* that is, "the fowl used to announce death of a neighbour is not what one will not pay back when we take part in eating it," because we all owe the debt of death to our humanity.

In this discussion we have attempted to provide some insight into the educational system that supported the effectiveness of the indigenous Yoruba legal system. Because of the constraint of space, we have not been able to provide a detailed analysis of the various aspects of the educational structures—the curriculum layout, the pedagogical tools, the certification evaluation mechanisms, and the effective review process for validity and provenance of the system; but we have been able to show that the coherence and cohesiveness of indigenous Yoruba society, which led to the development of an empire and a kingdom, was possible as a consequence of a legal system which was ably supported by an educational system.

It is clear that given the highly organized nature of Yoruba society, it was impossible not to have a highly developed legal system to sustain the level of social, economic, political and cultural advancement. But more importantly, it was important that means be available for mediating differences and for resolving disputes, rewarding commendable behavior and punishing reprehensible action. When these have become accumulated and accepted, they not only facilitate the welfare of individuals in society, young and old, male and female, rich and poor, they also constitute instruments for defending the identity and destiny of individuals and society at large.

We showed that the degrading and eventual virtual disintegration of the Yoruba national cohesion has been a consequence of the decay and destruction of the rules of natural justice, the delegitimation of the rule of law by contrast with the rule of men and the allowance of greed to supplant corporate goals of welfare for all within the ambits of society. This was what was responsible for the destruction of the Oyo Empire, and this has been responsible for the decay that the Yoruba nation has witnessed within the context of the artificial contraption of Nigeria. When charity fails to begin from home, it becomes difficult to demand and receive respect from distant cousins. Hence, we conclude that the whole contraption of the English Common Law on which Nigeria's legal system is constructed is not only insensitive to the culture of the Yoruba nation and people, it is also dissonant with principles of justice that many other ethnic nationalities in Nigeria embrace indigenously. We urge, along with Oba (2006), that there is urgent need to include indigenous legal education in the curriculum of those entrusted with the application of the legal system of Nigeria, but this is not all; there is a great need to synchronize the discordant legal systems in Nigeria as well as in other African societies to respect the indigenous legal systems and facilitate the cultures of the peoples of Africa. It is only when this is done that justice can be seen to have been done, and hence facilitate whatever systems are grafted onto the indigenous foundations of justice in Africa.

FIVE

Parallel Epistemologies, Parallel Justice Systems

There is the presumption that the introduction of the British common law judicial system and practice in the colonized societies was a progressive development for these colonial societies which, by the power of colonial historical revisionism, according to the Europeans, had no civilizations or cultures that befit human societies, until the arrival of the European colonizing savior. The strongest plank of their argument is that the colonized were without any legal system before colonialism, and hence that the colonized were without a civilized system of human rights definition, dispute adjudication, conflict resolution and social equity maintenance mechanisms. Another part of the argument derives from the presumed superiority of the theoretical and practical aspects of the judicial and other accoutrements of the cultures of the colonizing societies—be they British, French, German, Belgian, Portuguese, Spanish or other—this being part of the reason for the possibility of subjugation of the hapless inferior, sub-human and barbaric colonials in the first place. But the survival of the indigenous cultures of the colonized, and the paradoxical envy and scorn with which aspects of the cultural paraphernalia of the colonizer are viewed, is evidence of the need for a more careful reflection on the nature and value of the imposed systems of culture of the colonizing power.

In this chapter, I explore the fundamental reasons for the existence and continued virile survival and vibrancy of parallel indigenous justice systems alongside the British common law in Nigeria since colonization and after almost half a century of independence and deliberate acceptance of the English common law system as the official judicial system for Nigeria. I argue that this survival of these indigenous justice systems among the various nationalities of Nigeria is not intrinsically dependent on the convenience or cost-effectiveness of the indirect rule system which the British colonizer used in administering the country after amalgamation in 1914. I suggest that the survival of these justice systems is a reflection of the divergent foundations of the cultures of these societies from that of the British systems; these foundations include a) metaphysics, b) existential praxis, c) ecological spaces, d) cultural values, e) axiological beliefs, f) religious nexus of existence and, more importantly, g) epistemologies of existence. In this discussion, I will be commenting on all the first six issues prefatorily, but my main interest lies in subjecting the last foundation to careful critical examination, to show that it is the epistemological incommensurability of indigenous and the imported common law legal systems that underwrite the survival of three parallel justice systems in Nigeria, whether under colonial existence or in the post-colony.

The preliminary conclusion that is reached is that the Nigerian legal theory and practice runs three parallel, almost acutely contradictory and schizophrenic life histories, because of the distorted and distorting nature of the colonial experiment on the one hand, and because of the poor capacity of post-colonial Nigerian leadership to appreciate the value of indigenous judicial and legal systems and practices in the face of the practical and theoretical incapacity, alienating disorientation and humiliating insensitivity of the English common legal system bequeathed to Nigeria with regard to the cultural values of the various ethnicities that make up the fabricated entity called Nigeria. This British legacy has failed to advance the course of Nigerian national development or national integration, but it has managed to continue to be an agent of division, perpetuation of inequities and enthronement of injustice because of the adversarial nature of its epistemological, metaphysical, logical, methodological and theoretical underpinnings and the privileging of the capacity of the wealthy to impose his/her wish on society by being able to buy justice while leaving the weak, poor and vulnerable to languish in a limbo of judicial dispossession, desperation and nonexistence.

It is, therefore, not surprising that the recrudescence of the Islamic legal system and practice, in the form of Sharia law, has become rather contentious as an alternative to the British-English common law that the Nigerian Constitution enshrines in the form of notional secularism of the Nigerian nation-state. What is surprising is that a careful examination will show that many indigenous legal systems of Nigeria would not find the Islamic legal system alien to their indigenous cultural jurisprudence, both in its theoretical epistemological, metaphysical as well as humanistic determination to enthrone justice, and are consequently not threatened by it. Thus, politics apart (though politics is what makes everything interesting and destructive in Nigeria and most African societies for that matter), the apparent tripartite (should we say multipartite?) legal systems in Nigeria is a product of the distinctively tripartite (multipartite) legal epistemological and metaphysical traditions that inhabit the contemporary

Nigerian soul. And it is only when clear attention is paid to these diverse foundations of law in Nigeria that cohesive development and growth would be possible.

All human societies construct ideas to help apprehend, explain, codify and transmit what they consider valuable to them. These ideas are at once stable and unstable—stable in the sense that their being known and accepted, used and practiced, transmitted and respected, makes such ideas not only have a utilitarian value on the one hand, but also, on the other hand, invest in the ideas a means of ordering future experiences and determining the patterns of reality that can be had and understood. These ideas could be regarded as the philosophical and cultural foundations of belief and existence in these societies.

In the first instance, all societies would deign to understand and explain reality as a matter of necessity, to imbue life and existence with pertinent communicable meaning. This would lead to ontologies and metaphysics. The theory(ies) of origin(s), being (natural, non-natural and supernatural), space, time (real and unreal), etc. that are so constructed help to give meaning to life, death and beyond in these societies, and they are inured in the experiences, fears, aspirations and fantasies of members of societies (Bewaji 1997).

The metaphysics constructed underwrite many other ideas that society designs to deal with various aspects of reality. Such metaphysics spans the locus of existence of all beings in the universe and the existential praxis they impose on humans as members of in-groups and as members of other groups. The understanding of the diverse ecological spaces brings about numerous ideas about ecosophical relations which in turn underwrite the virtues of ensuring equilibrium of human existence within the universe. Cultural values are never neutral fiats deriving from emptiness; they are products of deliberate and nondeliberate efforts of humans to express and give meaning to existence in a diversity of ways (Abimbola 2006: 97).

The notion of reality and the effort to manage reality leads to axiological beliefs which are regarded as foundations of well-being of humanity as well as means of enrichment of existence in society; be these ethical, aesthetic, scientific, medical, social and political or just merely practical, they are nondiscountable elements of human existence which help to determine the cultural variations of one society vis-à-vis another. Closely allied to these ideas are the fundamental ideas that determine the religious nexus of existence that is constructed in society to express the understanding of the unknown, the unseen and the near but far aspects of our transience (Bewaji 1997).

Thus, all societies have ideas that underpin existence. The societies also develop the logic of meaning and action. And to make these clearly meaningful, epistemologies are developed to manage the ideas and resolve apparent contradictions that may arise within them. The position of epistemology is dual in this guise: on the one hand, epistemology facilitates the understanding of what constitutes knowledge, how it is attained, limits to it, and who can have it; and on the other hand, epistemology consists of the mapping out of foundations of relations in society, making all relations meaningful, stable and humane (Bewaji 2007).

Humans have often taken too seriously the fact that their (human) cultures and societies, no matter how diverse and different, exhibit certain levels of inter-penetrability of ideas. The anthropologists, sociologists and theologians who have studied "other cultures" with the view to determining the presence or absence of civilization in some cultures have had their ignorance exhibited every time they have divined the primitive, barbaric and uncivilized other into existence. One of the remarkable developments of the growth of science and technology in the twentieth century has been the revelation of the weakness of the bogus science of race, racism, and superiority of one society over others. This has had the effect of revealing the real underlining motives behind all expansionist and colonizing tendencies in human interaction; thereby showing that regardless of the pretension to benevolence, all colonial tendencies, be they political, religious, educational, cultural, social and scientific, derive from pure economic and materialist interests of an expansionist and dominating group seeking dominance over another (Bewaji 2006).

The above would imply the need for caution in foisting the ideas and ideals, indeed the philosophies, of one society on other societies, contrary to what all colonizing societies do in the colonies they overpower and rule by force and subterfuge. The dangers of such presumption is clearly shown by the failures of the strategies of domination that have bedeviled Western international relations in the Middle East for the last half century, threatening to lead the whole world into one huge omnicidal conflagration. For example, societies that have organized knowledge and reality on the basis of the singular consciousness of the atomic individual as the sole knower would definitely exhibit tendencies toward individualism, while societies that recognize that no individual knowers make sense of reality except through the cognitive prism constructed and developed by the communal pool of meaning determination would exhibit tendencies toward communitarianism (Akiwowo 1980). This would show why there are no absolute ways of reality determination that does not pay attention to the varieties and variations of meaning and knowledge transmission, as such determinations are never culturally neutral or motive empty (Bewaji 1998).

All knowledge is human. The weakness of Popperian (1972) epistemology without a knowing subject has been shown by Code (1991 and 1995) to be real, as there are no objective knowledge that does not depend on some human interest, human search, and human agency. Whatever the area of knowledge making and determination, be it in art, religion, politics, science, information technology, genetic engineering, economics, life, death or whatever, it would be clear to discerning minds that humans have not been able and will never be able to transcend their humanity in attaining a nonhumanly derived "God's eye view"—untainted, objective and absolute knowledge; there can be no such Archimedean extra-terrestrial perspective that is not infused with human cognitive limitations and interests (Bewaji 2007d).

Descartes, Locke, Hume and Berkeley, Russell, Ayer, among the leaders of modern European scholarship, have crafted what is intrinsically the psychology of the Western person, centering everything around and about the self, the ego consciousness and the individual identity. They have successfully pioneered the making of reality individually self-determined, "knowledge" egocentrically personal, social relations about the individual person, morality ego-located and by extension the domain of the legal individualistic. On the contrary, there are other cultures in which it is insane, arrogant and irresponsible to build all "knowledge," reality, morality, and social constructs around a lone self—a self that never was before society and could never be without society. In these cultures, in their primordial expression, the self has no meaning except as socioculturally constructed. This is why it is meaningful to realistic and intelligent persons from non-European societies when they hear that "*I am, because we are*"; for there can be no *I* had there been no preceding and nurturing *we*—ontologically, epistemologically, psychologically, logically, morally, socially, politically, etc. (Hord and Lee, 1995: 14, and Bewaji 1998).

The foregoing leads us to question the Western construction of knowledge, reality and existence on the basis of atomic selves. The challenge that faces those of us from the margins of the academe is how to effectively contest the perspective that predominates in the world that we inhabit which seeks to impose individualism as the only meaningful understanding of social and cultural relations. How are we who have been regarded as voiceless be able to indicate to the "voiced" that they may be wrong in the supposition that sub-atomic humanity precedes communal humanity? How do we challenge an epistemology that has created the trips to outer space and developed the most effective technologies for human destruction to show that the reasons for the pursuits of failed notions of happiness involve the failed forms of atomistic individual selves they have fabricated? How do we show that the reasons why the Korash Waco debacle, the ENRON fiasco, and the Iraqi dead-end are not accidents of misguided individuals but necessary results of failed intellectual foundations of meaning in deriving real ends to human existence? How do we begin to show that it is no idle conspiracy theory to understand the failures of Africana socioeconomic and political efforts as consequences of attempts to embrace intellectually defunct foundations of social, cultural and political realities?

The first thing we would do well to understand is that we must recognize the *duality of human existence as personal selves and as public selves*, both of which are interdependent, mutually related in the development of the self, social consciousness and knowledge. In this context, we would argue that all "knowledge" is a social construction whose utility exist within the social context. In fact, we must recognize the intrinsic sickness of a personal reality un-reinforced by social, cultural and community realities. This fact is better understood in the process of devising mechanisms for catering to those with eccentric sense of selves and existence. The first port of call in assisting those who would substitute the self for the community is to let them realize that they did not just drop from nowhere—even clones would need gene pools to exist, and these pools would not be without DNA codes that eventually are determinants of their human realities (Bewaji 2007d).

Thus, the epistemological underpinnings of the indigenous legal system are not individualistic or egoistic. They do not originate from either a Cartesian cogito, whose ergo helps to ascertain its sum, or a non-Cartesian sum whose cogito is nonexistent (the empty baggage syndrome preached by the plantation owners in the Americas regarding the humans they have forcibly enslaved) because of some contrived cultural vacuity of intellect. They develop from the wellspring of what Code (1987) describes are "epistemic responsibility," whereby the collective contribution to knowledge making and knowledge validation all conduce to the notion of order, justice, fairness, responsibility, punishment, compensation, and humanity.

This accounts for the fact that the common good may often take precedence over the individual good, as the calculus of rights cannot be effected without adequate attention to the consequences for the overall well-being of society. And the fact that everyone looks out for everyone else means that careful watch is undertaken to ensure that the well-being of the community is not compromised by inveterate pursuit of self-interest. Thus, when it is suspected that someone may be on the verge of doing something that may be detrimental to the welfare of the community, there is no pretense or affectation of "it is not my business," for there is wisdom in the proverb in Yoruba language that "if one's neighbor is eating raw caterpillar, one should do something about it, for the restlessness that will be caused in the night will mean sleeplessness for one that night" (in Yoruba this means *bi ara ile eni ba nje eruku tutu, a ko gbodo d'agunla, nitori here huru re ko ni je a sun l'oru*). For this reason, there is no way one could feign ignorance or keep quiet when one's neighbor sets on a path that will lead to problems for him or herself and all other members of the community as, again the Yoruba saying would have it, "the peace of the rat is the peace of the bird" (*irorun eku, oun ni irorun eye*).

While the epistemological foundations of the English common law is the individual knowing self, who seeks to protect his/her interest against that of others and society, solemnized in the contractarian legacies of Hobbes, Locke and Rousseau; in the case of the indigenous Yoruba legal system that we have enunciated, the epistemic base of law and legitimacy is grounded in the human collective (collectivist) nature of knowledge which is further grounded in the inseparability of the self from the society that gave birth to one, and the impossibility of existence outside of society (Memmi 1965: 83). For this reason, Yoruba people are very suspicious of the legal system of the English common law that allows for the offender to win, through technicalities of law, when clear wrong has been established. As a consequence, most legal issues are not taken to the English courts established under the Nigerian constitutions, for these courts cannot be trusted to do what is right as they are not sensitive to the traditions and understandings of justice that conduce to ethnic harmony.

To enunciate the problem here, let us undertake a thought experiment that makes for the mistrust of the English common law which many in England would not find puzzling at all. Imagine that you are sleeping in your own house and a thief breaks in, but unknown to him or her, there is a broken bottle beneath the window that he/she has just removed to gain access to your house without your invitation. He/she accidentally falls on the broken glass and received a deep cut which incapacitates him. He/she takes you, the house owner, to court for malicious injury to his/her self, and the English common law finds you guilty of negligence or willful injury to your unwanted guest, asking you to pay compensation to your aggressor. Such would never be possible in a sane legal framework, nor would it be comprehensible to any rational human mind.

In the case of the Islamic legal system, the foundations of social relations and cultural expression are rooted in the religion of Islam. For devout Muslims, it is their belief that all aspects of life are covered by various insights from the religion of Islam which, as a way of life, provides rules and regulations for interpersonal relations as well as relations with Allah, the Supreme Being. In this regard, it is clear that apart from the truths established by Allah, human beings are not in any epistemic capacity, for humans are regarded as the "slaves of God"—*eru Olorun*. This dependency on the Supreme Being leads to a clear epistemological vacuum that is filled by the Islamic cleric, who then serves as the bridge between the population and the Supreme Being in all areas of life and facilitates the good order of all relations.

For example, Islamic culture does not permit usury or the acceptance of interest on loans granted to people, because it is believed that those who are comfortable do not seek loans, and if someone were to borrow and is loaded with additional cost, this will make the chances of survival and success of the venture for which the loan is taken more difficult. And also what are regarded as standards of human rights in the West, whereby the victim of a crime becomes the villain, does not arise in Islamic law, for someone who has willfully and maliciously taken another person's life has lost hers and has no human rights that anti-capital punishment advocates can defend.

It is obvious that there are close affinities between indigenous African cultures and Arabic cultures, such that more indigenous Nigerians are more comfortable with the Islamic legal system, even when there are variations noticeable, than they are with English common law that the Nigerian state has formally adopted. This is because the fundamental presuppositions of the indigenous legal system and Islamic legal system are similar, as they derive from a notion of humanity that is not atomistic, by comparison with the English common law system that creates more adversarial relations than reconciliatory relations. Probably this explains why, of the three legal systems, only the indigenous ethnic legal systems of Nigeria do not feel seriously challenged by each other in the way the colonial imported legal system of British common law feel threatened at every turn by the other two legal systems.

Thus, when we carefully look at the dissonance that obtains in Nigerian legal apparatus, we see that the legal framework refuses to work, and by way of protest, most people subvert the English common law, not because they are incapable of obeying laws, but simply because they are reacting to the intellectual assault that the imposition of this foreign legal framework has wrought on their psyche. Every colonization project must be destructive of the intellectual traditions of the colonized to succeed. But that is not the most dangerous part of colonization—the destruction—what is most dangerous is that, with time, the colonized begin to think and act as described by the colonizer. As Memmi (1965) noted,

> Wilfully created and spread by the colonizer, this mythical and degrading portrait ends up by being accepted and lived with to a certain extent by the colonized. It thus acquires a certain amount of reality and contributes to the true portrait of the colonized.
>
> This process is not unknown. It is a hoax. It is common knowledge that the ideology of a governing class is adopted in large measure by the governed classes. Now, every ideology of combat includes as an integral part of itself a conception of the adversary. By agreeing to this ideology, the dominated classes practically confirm the role assigned to them. This explains *inter alia* the relative stability of societies; oppression is tolerated willy-nilly by the oppressed themselves. In colonial relationships, domination is imposed by people upon people but the pattern remains the same. The characterization and role of the colonized occupies a choice place in colonialist ideology; a characterization which is neither true to life, nor in itself incoherent, but necessary and inseparable within that ideology. It is one to which the colonized gives his troubled and partial, but undeniable assent (pp. 87–88).

What is clear from the foregoing is that as colonized peoples, Africans have become persuaded that the portrait of Africans derived from colonization and slavery are true of Africans. This is why politicians in Nigeria would aver that Nigerians are ungovernable, for example. It is also responsible for theologians of African descent who think that there are not proper understanding of the Supreme Being in Africa until their faiths were introduced by the colonizers. But more damaging has been the effect of the destruction of the legal systems, frameworks, and traditions of African societies. This last part has been responsible for the state of lawlessness that prevails in most African states today.

Pre-European colonial indigenous ethnicities in Nigeria had originated and organised their different societies based on their experiences in their different communities, their aspirations for development of their societies and humanity and, hence, their differing notions of what constitutes a good person (young or old, male or female, rich or poor, official or commoner), a good community, a good society and a good world in which humans are able to attain the best possible co-existence with all other things in existence. It is arguable that, universally, where urbanization had taken place among humans beings, urban communities may have always developed more sophisticated systems for ensuring order and welfare of members of society than would have smaller, farming, peasant, herding or hunting-gathering communities, even though both sets of communities belong to the same linguistic, sociocultural ethnicity [what Idowu (2006: 11) would call the social nature of law]. But whatever the level of sophistication, the ends of human existence would clearly remain the same—advancing the goal of human welfare and social cohesion, so that the individual would be able to enjoy an enriched life, free of fear and anxieties and insecurities. To this end, one could find that from one community within the same ethnicity there may be minor or serious variations in practices and traditions, while similarities may abound between different ethnicities given the level of similarity of urbanity or rurality of existential environment; for what is done and/or allowed in one community may be taboo in another, given the kinds of variations in social organization that is being related here.

It is necessary to emphasize the above because African societies, before interface with external societies in the experience of colonialism, had developed highly sophisticated systems of governance—whether within local rural communities, or within highly populous urban cities, or over a wide area of empires or kingdoms. Depending on the ecology, the economy, the environment and the existential circumstances, the societies had developed various rules—moral, social, economic, religious, political and legal—for dealing with various aspects of personal, interpersonal, social, political, cultural, religious and other forms of interaction. In some instances there were variations in expectations from "in-group" members as against the "out-group" other, such that out-group others may be excused from sanctions which luxuries in-group members are not afforded, because they are supposed to know better. Such "ours/theirs" dichotomies are not uncommon, unexpected or unrealistic, as such are the nature of human differentiation of interaction-mediating mechanisms. The realization of these variations and diversities, for enlightened cultures like that of the Yoruba, rather than indicate the inferiority of the other cultures as the colonizing societies would insist, constitute elements of enrichment of human cultures inter-culturally, while at the same time these variations may become conundrums that must be carefully navigated in order to ensure that order, fairness, equity and justice—necessary components in social stability, peace and cohesion—are not compromised in relations with peoples of these other cultures.

It is against this background that we notice, with respect to the indigenous Yoruba societies of West Africa (and this would apply well to other indigenous African societies as well), before interface with the Western legal system (that is, before interface with the colonial system), that the justice system and the judicial theory and practice which governed the justice system which operated indigenously can be viewed as the "traditional Yoruba legal system". It was, and also remains, traditional not just because it was the system that Yoruba society was familiar with and utilized in dealing with members of society, but in the sense of its being "home-grown," being original and domestic (that is, being locally developed), and its being adapted and tuned to the traditions, customs, culture and beliefs and hopes and aspirations of Yoruba people individually and generally. So, the first legal or justice system in Yoruba land, and similarly for most of the more than three hundred distinct ethnicities that make up Nigeria, is what has often been described derogatorily as "native law and custom" (Oba 2006: 95). This system served for thousands of years before European ingress with their totally different legal system on the one hand, and, on the other hand, before the advent of Islam and a not too dissimilar legal system as the indigenous Yoruba legal system.

Crowder (1968: 10) was very accurate in noting, on the part of the colonial European powers, the arrant native ignorance of, and the deliberately greed-induced blinkered incapacity to appreciate the truth about the economic, religious, scientific and cultural sophistication of the various African peoples that the European powers met in various African communities upon their ventures for trade, resources acquisition, and wealth grabbing in the modern period which led to the colonization of Africans, the destruction of their cultures and heritage and the enslavement of masses of peoples of Africa in various plantations in the Western hemisphere. For these reasons it was obvious that deliberate policies were set afoot which only favored the European domination of the African societies, while having the consequences of destroying and by the way resulting in the compromising or retarding the progress of the African indigenous cultural ideas and practices. He (Crowder 1968: 11) also agreed with the position of Casely-Hayford, that "before even the British came into relations with our people, we were a developed people, having our own institutions, having our own ideas of government"

(p. 10). And it would be inconceivable to concede that the Africans had originated civilizations and systems of government without also agreeing that they had systems of conflict adjudication and resolution for the proper maintenance of law and order. The fact that the British found it expedient to use the "indirect rule" system in Nigeria, even though relegating to second-class status the indigenous judicial foundations of social relations, was a serious indictment of the fallacious position of the ignorant Hugh Trevor-Roper who, instead of using his chair at Oxford as an opportunity and means of educating himself, used the same to mis-educate and propagate error on the hapless youths who were unfortunate to have passed through his classrooms, by teaching them that Africa had no history before European interface. The distortion of reality for an ignorant audience has been necessary for colonizing intellectuals to be able to have the support of the gullible masses of their people to back their backward ideologies. This has been repeated so many times in human history, and is not different in the case of the American invasion of Iraq in 2003; a pernicious invasion that has had repercussions for the rest of the world which was impotent in the face of the unjustified and unjustifiable American aggression on an independent society—contrary to United Nations Organization charter-governing relations between countries of the world.

Jean-Paul Sartre was very sincere in describing the way in which the cultures and humanity of the colonized have been subverted by the colonizer. The negation of the personhood of the colonized is the first necessary step that must be taken to ensure that the subject does not begin to see anything good in her tradition and culture, thereby creating a fiat that subsists subterraneanly, objectively and subjectively in self-perpetuity. Just as occurs in the plantations of the Americas, the colonies were to be denied all aspects of human cognition, so that the only source of reality and knowledge, law and order, human affirmation and negation derive from the metropolis of the "mother country." In this regard, Sartre (1974) says in introducing Memmi's *The Colonizer and the Colonized*:

> Conquest occurred through violence, and over-exploitation and oppression necessitate continued violence, so the army is present. There would be no contradiction in that, if terror reigned everywhere in the world, but the colonizer enjoys, in the mother country, democratic rights that the colonialist system refuses to the colonized native. In fact, the colonialist system favors population growth to reduce the cost of labor, and it forbids assimilation of the natives, whose numerical superiority, if they had voting rights, would shatter the system. Colonialism denies human rights to human beings whom it has subdued by violence, and keeps them by force in a state of misery and ignorance that Marx would rightly call a subhuman condition. Racism is ingrained in actions, institutions, and in the nature of the colonialist methods of production and exchange. Political and social regulations

> reinforce one another. Since the native is subhuman, the Declaration of Human Rights does not apply to him; inversely since he has no rights, he is abandoned without protection for in human forces—brought in with the colonialist praxis, engendered every moment by the colonialist apparatus, and sustained by relations of production that define two sorts of individuals—one for whom privilege and humanity are one, who become human beings through exercising his rights; and the other, for whom a denial of rights sanctions misery, chronic hunger, ignorance, or, in general, "subhumanity" (pp. xxiv–xxv).

What is remarkable here is the fact that Sartre sees through the bogey of altruism that is foisted as cover up on the greed that engenders colonization. He is aware that apart from the material and cultural advantage that the colonizer derives from the colonial venture, the only thing that happens to be the lot of the colonized by design is misery, negation and subhumanity. With regard to the existence of indigenous legal systems of the colonized people, a no-person could not have developed any form of legal system, legal codes, legal institutions or legal philosophy. And the fact that there are still legal minds (professionally certified lawyers and legal luminaries) who feel that indigenous African legal theories are nonexistent or where such exist, they are only in myths, proverbs, legends and others show the success of the colonialist experiment. This is to the effect that two hundred years of denial and destruction, subjugation and suppression, exploitation and appropriation has led to the self-effacement of indigenous intellect, finally almost totally obliterating all traces of the greatness of the cultures that developed various civilizations and achievements in various African empires, cities and rural communities, leading to the near total inability of many products of the colonial educational system to see through the ruse of European magnanimity and humanity to the design of the European soul for the total possession of all that is valuable on earth to the utter pauperization of all other human beings around the world.

The fact that the scions of European mis-education in the post-colonies now do the dirty jobs of destroying their indigenous cultures and societies in the name of fostering civilization is enough testimony to the success of the colonial effort. In the typical manner of "his masters' voice" the colonial could only mimic the ways and gesticulations of the white male, thereby affecting an air of civilization in the destructive manner only known to the colonizer. The most pernicious of this has been the fact that in virtually all areas of the humanities, some of our own Africana colleagues still think they are being perspicacious in mouthing the absence of formal discourse of various theoretical disciplines in Africa, including what is being discussed here as African legal theory; thereby suggesting that African civilizations never considered it important to dialogue on such important issues as justice, responsibility, evidence and more.

Oba (2006: 107) has effectively noted the lacuna that existed in the development of indigenous legal systems in Nigeria (and Africa generally by extrapolation). Since the advent of colonization, there has been no investment of educational resources in training of indigenous legal practitioners on the one hand, and on the other the pursuit of research into indigenous legal systems with a view to using such knowledge to inform the process of justice dispensation and development. According to him,

> Legal Education in Nigeria is divided into two parts: the academic aspect as offered in the faculties of law in the universities and the professional aspect as taught in the Nigerian Law School under the auspices of the Council of Legal Education. The most prominent characteristic of legal education in Nigeria is that it is mostly patterned after what obtains in England. Customary and Islamic law do not form part of the basic curriculum at the Universities and at the Nigerian Law School (p. 107).

There are parallels in various other strata of life in Nigeria. When we think of what happens with regard to medical education, religious education, historical education and even the theoria and praxis of education itself, we see that all of them are patterned after an alien and alienating cultural foundations and theoretical modes of existence. The consequence has been the fact that Nigerian medical doctors trained in the formal system are very ignorant of the existence of the indigenous medical system, just as lawyers are ignorant of the indigenous legal system, while theologians (Christians) are near ignorant of indigenous theologies and religions. All of these factors put indigenous intellectual culture at a serious disadvantage, making it seem as if the original pre-colonial African mind was indeed a tabula rasa!

This is where the words of Loomba (1998) become relevant. Writing on the relationship between colonialism and indigenous knowledge, she observed,

> Colonialism reshaped existing structure of human knowledge. No branch of learning was left untouched by the colonial experience. The process was somewhat like the functioning of ideology itself, simultaneously a misrepresentation of reality and its re-ordering. Like ideology, it arose from 'material circumstances' and was 'material in its effect'. A crucial aspect of this process was the gathering and ordering of information about the lands and peoples visited by, and later subject to, the colonial powers. Fifteenth- and sixteenth-century European ventures to Asia, America and Africa were not the first encounters between Europeans and non-Europeans but writings of this period do mark a new way in thinking about, indeed producing, these two categories of people as binary opposites. Travel writing was an important means of producing 'Europe's differentiated conceptions of itself in relation to something it became possible to call "the rest of the world"' (Loomba 1998: 57).

Though one could say that the current world order, in which we now have a unipolar power structure, leaves no room for the survival of militarily weak but resource-endowed societies, as the invasion of Iraq after the deliberate falsification of history of the Arabian world has been effected by the United States of America and the demonization of the Iraqi president, it is clear that all of these are consequences of the same methodology and logic of material control of the other. Contrary to all the thousands of years of Arabian civilization, a new kind of historical revisionism has been afoot which has sought to equate the conduit through which science and civilization reached Europe—that is, Islam—as primitive, retrogressive and anti-civilization, simply because the votaries of this faith refuse to lie down and play dead while the megalomanias in the unipolar world take control of the assets of the Arabian peninsula.

It is about this historical recursive decimal factor that Loomba was writing when she examined how humans have the capacity, when the power is in one's favor to write the other out of existence. She says,

> The definition of civilization and barbarism rest on the production of irreconcilable difference between 'black' and 'white,' self and other. The late medieval European figure of the 'wild man' who lived in forests, on the outer edges of civilization, and was hairy, nude, violent, lacking in moral sense and excessively sensual, expressed all manner of cultural anxieties. . . . Colonialism expanded the contact between Europeans and non-Europeans, generating a flood of images and ideas on an unprecedented scale (pp. 57–58).

It was no wonder that the unknown, the unfamiliar and the strange became the nonexistent, the primitive, the barbaric, and only humanizable to the extent that he or she or it can become European-like. If the stranger has anything different, such cannot count in the face of the European competition—such must be replaced and what is replaced must be destroyed or marked for destruction. This was the fate of the indigenous Nigerian legal system when it interfaced with the British colonial common law—the indigenous legal systems became "native law and custom" which must be superseded whenever there is conflict with the English common law.

What did not occur to the colonizing power was what was to happen to the cultural antecedents of the English common law in the indigenous peoples of Nigeria and Africa. How were they going to deal with the differing intellectual and cultural foundations which underwrite these systems, but which found no means of adjusting to the newly imposed English common law system? There is a parallel here to the failure of the "Shock and Awe" in Iraq, for why a people cling to their culture regardless of the "superiority" of the force that subjugates the self can only be because the meaning-making epistemologies and metaphysics do not often play the same octaves as those emboldened by brute force. And it is not less understandable that the same politicians who would rob and steal their countries' treasuries empty would think twice before stealing monies contributed toward a post office building in their towns or villages. For that matter, it clearly matters that the same politricking rogue who would swear using the Holy Bible would run away when asked to swear by any symbol of Sango—the Yoruba divinity of thunder, or Ogun—the Yoruba divinity of iron.

What is obvious from the foregoing is that the three justice systems come with three epistemological underpinnings which differ in their provenance for the peoples of Nigeria. Because of this difference, their coexistence is not unwarranted, as the majority of the people continue to maintain their allegiance to the indigenous legal systems, even while parading themselves as the formal custodians of the formal English common law judicial system.

One would have expected that in negotiating these three judicial systems contradictions would arise which would create identity crises for individuals and peoples. But wait a minute! There does not seem to be any identity conflicts at all, as the same clergy man who preaches the mass on Sunday finds no problem with visiting his herbalist/diviner on Saturday following to assure himself that all is well with his congregation. This is because he may have embraced the "foreign" religion, but epistemologically, he is still a Yoruba person with cultural and intellectual underpinnings that are ethnically situated.

In the continuing search for meaning in the cacophony of noise surrounding the state of human society in Africa, there is need to step back and look in from the outside—literally. Conspiracy theorists abound in various guises and from various quarters, but such theories have limitations. The extent to which peoples of African descent universally are able to advance the cause of humanity in Africa and its diaspora will be a function of how much dispassionate self-analysis and comprehension can effectively be undertaken. This discussion of "Parallel Epistemologies, Parallel Justice Systems—An Analysis of the Foundations of Three Justice Systems in Nigeria" is an effort along those lines.

We have elicited the grounds for the apparent lawlessness of persons who are otherwise highly obedient to the law; that is, we have attempted to find meaning in the fact that many Nigerians in public sphere who would traditionally not steal from their communities because it would have been regarded as an abomination to the ancestors and their people to do so would not blink twice when misappropriating or embezzling (euphemism for theft) funds that belong to the Nigerian state, because in their perception and judgment, "public money belongs to no one," and hence no consequences will flow from such larceny and perfidy. We also have shown that the root of the disaster that is the Nigerian state can be located in the legal psychosis that inhabit the Nigerian judicial soul;

which derives from the fact that Nigeria is attempting to make work three apparently mutually inconsistent legal frameworks.

These frameworks, we argue, derive from three different epistemologies which are grounded in three different cultural foundations; one of the cultures is affirmed by the Nigerian state as the culture that is legal, valid and acceptable—the English common law framework—the second is accepted by some states of the federation as legal, valid and acceptable—the Islamic legal framework in some states of the northern parts of Nigeria, while the third legal framework is regarded with scant attention, disrespected and often rejected by the Nigerian state as primitive, backward, native and inconsequential even though it is the framework that most Nigerians feel comfortable with, understand and obey—the Native Law and Custom.

It is concluded that effort is needed to give the indigenous legal system of various Nigerian communities, which underwrite their existence and relationship to others and to humanity proper attention and elevation, so that the grounds for obedience to the law not continue to be separated from the intellectual bonds that hold humanity together in society. First, recognition of the validity of indigenous African legal systems will lead to appreciation of cultural self-worth, acceptance of grounds of legitimacy of legal frameworks that bind relations and evoke loyalty to the communal bonds of association. Second, the whys of law and grounds for punishment will be integrated, leading to a clear perception and acceptance of justice, such that infractions would receive not only clear signals of impropriety, but condemnation by all and hence apprehension and punishment rather than the current state where impunity reigns in public office. These are prefatory ground-works that are necessary for proper order and justice to return to Nigeria.

SIX

Human Rights and Law in Indigenous and Contemporary Africa

There has been much talk in recent times about human rights, giving the impression that humanity in previous millennia probably had no ideas of such lofty values, or if they did, these were not on high-priority burners given the perennial concern of humanity in these yonder generations for survival. This kind of inclement appreciation of the conditions of human existence in these previous generations not only bode of the arrogance of contemporary generations, but it reflects akin genuflections of Euro-American hegemonic proclivities for assuming the role of world educators, world civilizers and world developers. Such claims portend a kind of pretension to be the progenitors of human civilization, coming from the root "civil," suggesting that other societies failed to attend to ideals and ideas of human worth.

This is the context in which this historio-philosophical analysis is undertaken to unearth the theoretical and practical foundations of human rights in indigenous Yoruba culture—using Ifa Literary Corpus especially—comparing this with contemporary Nigerian experience in the light of Universal Ideas and Ideals of Human Rights writ large. We display an awareness of the place of economics in the understanding and development of cultures, valuing humanity qua humanity. This means that we see all the paraphernalia of state-craft and culture-craft as indices for measuring the success or failure of humans in society to balance survival with subsistence. It means that even politics, as a human sociocultural contraption, is not to be taken outside of the search for humanity as a locus of rights. These are some of the variables that are critical to the development and perpetuation of any meaningful concept of human rights in any society.

It is argued that Yoruba culture had developed and maintained high standards of human rights, which the contemporary Nigerian state has bastardized as a direct heritage from the Atlantic slave trade, colonialism, post-colonial economics of dependence, religio-educational imposition, and which international hegemonies of domination, colonization, foreign education, globalization and dependence have only further reinforced in a rankly destructive and morbidly pernicious way. This means that critical leadership is essential to the structuring and re-structuring of human rights in any society, and the African and its diaspora contexts are particularly implicated in this search for the development and enthronement of valuable paradigms of humanity and human rights.

In this chapter, therefore, effort is made to explore the epistemological, metaphysical and axiological presuppositions of the concept of "person," "humanity" and "self," as the foundation and locus of rights, either within the construct of the human person as a self in the process of being and existence, or as social construct deriving from the consciousness of the mediation of interaction of persons in a variety of spaces—communal, religious, political, economic, filial and others. It is this exploration, for which precedents are rare, which will illuminate the varieties of "human rights" discourses that interest us today—legal, social, economic.

All civilized societies have ensured some clear formulation of what constitutes human beings. In many instances these formulations are communicated in the form of creation stories or accounts of descent of humans from primordial times. These accounts show their understanding of the nature, meaning, goals, life, death and ultimate reality and end of humanity. What the United Nations did on December 10, 1948, was to bring together diverse ideas from various cultural backgrounds of humanity around the world to formally endorse a set of minimum rights to which humans are entitled, regardless of where they may live in the world. Extracting from the United Nations Charter of Universal Declaration of Human Rights (1948), I take as a fit paraphrase formulation of what may be called universal "human rights" the following, for the purpose of this discussion:

> All human beings are born free and equal in dignity and rights to pursue their happiness and privacy within the ambit of the law of their societies . . . free from discriminations on account of race, colour, sex, language, religion, political or other opinion, national or social origin, property, birth or other status . . . with a right to life, liberty and security of person . . . free from slavery, torture, cruel, inhuman or degrading treatment or punishment . . . free from arbitrary arrest, detention or exile, having access to equal and fair hearing, etc.

There are other ideas in the Declaration which relate to details of the above, as there are thirty articles in the Declaration, but it is clear to me that social, cultural, and other circumstances determine the capacity of societies to enforce, promote and assure whatever rights they may wish and that humans in these societies may claim. The meaning and content of the human rights so determined as above are, I believe, enshrined in the traditions of civilized humans everywhere in the world. What is clear also is that in these societies, humans have articulated the mediation mechanism for dealing with those regarded as outsiders to their societies, without compromising the humanity of such beings. This is not saying that there are not cases in human history in which humans who are not members of the specific society at issue may not be differently treated or regarded, either as less than human or as sub-human.

What we are suggesting here is that human rights as it is formulated in the United Nations Charter brings to the fore the need to have equality of respect and treatment for the humanity of all humans, regardless of whether these are aliens, citizens, friends or foes, male or female, young or old, rich or poor, etc. And humans have these rights just in virtue of being humans, and for no other reasons except based on their humanity.

There is, as is clear from the above, no room for any considerations of whether some rights are positive or negative, whether they are granted by law or by convention, whether they are bestowed by leadership or claimed by the generality of the populace. Human rights are intrinsic to humanity, regardless of race, sex, wealth, position or any other accidental determinants of human circumstance. In the rest of this chapter, I will show that traditional and indigenous Yoruba society clearly understood the universality of human rights, and that traditional leadership undertakes strong measures to ensure that such human rights are enforced, protected and proclaimed in culture, custom and tradition. But I must introduce a caveat here, to the point of showing that while we speak of traditional and indigenous Yoruba culture as having institutional structures to ensure the defense and propagation of human rights, it is not to be taken as simple pandering to nostalgia or engaging in a morbid hankering for things historically stale and past. It is simply indicating that Yoruba indigenous culture, civilization and society recognized and defended human rights, even in the light of occasional instances of abuses, derogation or abridging of rights which can be seen as aberration. The point is to show that human rights is not an alien idea that is being imported with Western scholarship, Western education, Western political institutions that have been embraced in Nigeria, or through the United Nations Universal Declaration of Human Rights. It is also to show that when there are institutional requirements to abrogate rights, these are done with reason, justification and proper attention to the overall good that underwrite such necessity.

The concept of "human rights" is an intriguing one for thinkers from diverse disciplinary backgrounds. A survey of some perspectives would suffice to show this: Our learned friends, lawyers, would wish to claim that they are the ones properly qualified to interpret laws as it relates to rights of persons and entities within a state, but it could be suggested to them that indigenous societies world-wide did have human rights before the practice of law became a professional institution and that without real laws demarcating rights there would be no reason for advocacy one way or the other. The law enforcement agencies—especially the police—would insist that they are the ones entrusted with monitoring the rights of members of society to ensure that they are not infracted, and that infractions are redressed expeditiously. They would have to be reminded that they are messengers to the cause of order in society and not the order itself. Theologians, especially theistic leaders with backgrounds in creationist accounts of origins of the universe, would suppose that since their Deity is the source of all there is, it would follow that Deity is the source of all kinds of rights and hence they, being the ones with the singular competence to say what is in the mind of their Deity, are the ones who should determine what human rights are ordained by Deity. But one could suppose that the existence of Deity probably was a desideratum that humans formulated to cater to needs of humans for the kinds of order that Deity brings where such is postulated. As a result, it could be suggested that human rights are only reified where humans feel this would make protection of these rights more enhanced with the introduction of some superhuman agency. Human rights activists, on the other hand, would insist that the law being the source of rights, they are the ones who monitor the proper or improper application of the law regarding rights of persons and agencies, to ensure the rich and powerful are not able to trample on the law and the rights of persons in society. This would not be out of place, if it is borne in mind that rights does not exist in a vacuum, and that in all societies, agencies have always existed to ensure that rights of persons are protected against the possibility of the rich and powerful abusing the rights of the weak and vulnerable in society. Philosophers would want to indicate that it is their purview to reflect on the origins, nature, ramifications, limitations and other details about human rights. But it would be right to indicate to philosophers that while they often have the capacity to speculate about what may be, without clear societal efforts to understand and emplace rights, there would be little for philosophers to reflect upon. That is, human rights predate philosophical reflection, and as such philosophers are only helping to enhance what already existed. For this reason, it could only be interesting to see how different disciplinary agencies relate to human rights within the context of society, so that through the collaboration and engagement, we would be able to see how human rights are to be further enriched in society.

Thus, whatever the situation may be, what is done here assumes that human rights is serious business in any society and deserves proper understanding, analysis and protection. We also assume that all civilized societies develop infrastructure to determine, ensure, enhance, protect and moderate human rights, be they ancient, medieval, modern or contemporary. It is assumed that part of what it means to be civilized is to be cultured, and to be cultured means, among other things, to be both self- and other-respecting. This implicates that rights must be affirmed and honored, for there to be civilization and culture.

It is clear, as Leslie Stevenson (1973) believes, that the views that a society embraces regarding human nature determines much more about the society's determination of modes of existence. According to Stevenson,

> What is man? This is surely one of the most important questions of all. For so much else depends on our view of human nature. The meaning and purpose of human life, what we ought to do, and what we can hope to achieve—all these are fundamentally affected by whatever we think is the "real" or "true" nature of man. . . . Different views about human nature lead naturally to different conclusions about what we ought to do and how we can do it. . . . Conflicting beliefs about the nature and purpose of human life are often embodied in different ways of life, in political and economic systems, and in educational theory and practice (p. 3).

In my view, Stevenson is right about the connection between the view of human nature and how this impacts how life is organized in society. His concern was with the seven accounts of human nature that he documented in his book, *Seven Theories of Human Nature*. He has as subtitle, "Christianity, Freud, Lorenz, Marx, Sartre, Skinner and Plato." These are quite interesting in themselves as they reflect how the Western traditions have understood human nature, and we would treat each of these theories later when we compare Western accounts of human rights with Yoruba and Nigeria contemporary ideas about human nature. For now, we wish to make the point that the understanding of the nature of the human being in society determines the kinds of rights that are ascribed to the human being in the society. Put differently, what is being indicated is that the conception of the human being—what it is to be a human by comparison with other beings, the nature of the human, the purpose of human life, the ultimate end of human existence—are critical to the kinds of rights that are allowed human beings. That is, we would not be able to understand human rights, except within the context of the religio-metaphysical, epistemological, axiological, socioeconomic, legal, political and other contexts of the construct of human being and human meaning.

Our discussion would have the effect of speaking to the divergences in how human rights have been conceived theoretically and practically in traditional Yoruba culture, how this compares with both the contemporary Nigerian concept of human rights within the context of a multi-ethnic, multi-cultural, multi-religious, multi-legal, hybridized economic, political, educational, social and moral milieu on the one hand, and on the other, with the fluid international paradigms of human rights discourses. In order to properly do this, we would explore aspects of concepts of human being and human nature in these three spheres of human existence so as to bring out clearly their determining effects on human rights.

Two issues could be, and have been, discussed under Yoruba belief concerning Human Being and Human Nature. The first one concerns the ultimate end of the human being in the universe. That is, *what is a human being? Why was s/he made, if s/he were made? What purpose is human life to serve? Does s/he have a destiny (personal/corporate)? If s/he does, what is this?* Most discussions of these issues have been biased toward the last two questions, that is, the question of human destiny. Such discussions does not help us much in understanding the Yoruba concept of human being with direct implication for the question of rights, as we are concerned with here.

The second one concerns the nature of a human as an existent individual person living in a physical-spiritual universe inhabited by others. This second issue has direct bearing on the human rights problem that we are exploring, because it is in the process of interfacing with other humans—near and far—that a definition of the parameters that must moderate the interaction is determined. But most discussions of personhood in Yoruba culture are not concerned with this second issue directly, to see how individuality and being negotiate and are enabled to negotiate existential circumstances in society to become what their destinies implicate, even though it is this second issue that has the most implication for the issue of human rights which is the object of our discussion. We will review some of the literature to see how they help illuminate our discourse here.

Gbadegesin attempted to provide answers to these questions but his answers were directed at the first set of issues; namely, private destiny (personal destiny) and not public destiny (corporate destiny). In fact, apart from Gbadegesin, whose discussion arose within the context of the problem of Ultimate Reality and Meaning, most discussions of the Yoruba concept of person and destiny (as in the works of Abimbola, Makinde, Hallen, Babatunde) are located within the context of personal, private or individual destiny. And this context is further restricted to human existence as a living person in society, starting from his/her choice of birth, span of life, material well-being, moral character, death, and descendants. Under the second heading of discourse the title "Human Personality" is often adopted in place of "Human Destiny." This is because of the erroneous supposition by scholars that both are seldom conceptually separated in the thought of the subject of investigation—the Yoruba person, contrary to what is intuitively clear concerning the differences these two concepts bear on their faces and for critical analysis.

Concerning "destiny," let us first sketch the factors usually highlighted by the scholars mentioned. In this respect *Ori*, literally translated "head" (with a physical equal as the head we visibly see) is the purveyor or bearer of individual destiny. Among the Yoruba, the *Ori* is both physical and metaphysical, as it is counterparted by *Ori-Inu* the inner-head that nobody sees, but is the essential person (man or woman). According to Hallen and Sodipo:

> For the Yoruba the essential elements of the person (eniyan) when in the world are the body (ara), the vital spirit of the body, or soul (emi) and the destiny (Ori) that will determine every significant event during the particular life time. **The concept of "Ori" is an exceedingly complex and fascinating one, and a good deal of literature already exists on the subject but all we need say of it here is that the same spirit (emi) returns to the world in indefinite number of times, each time with a new destiny (Ori) which is consciously, deliberately and freely chosen before being born** (bold emphasis added).

In the same vein, Makinde says:

> The Yoruba also have the concept of a person which, as in Western Philosophy, consists of the mental and physical elements known as soul (emi) and body (ara), with a clear indication as to how each came about. One important difference in the Western and the Yoruba conceptions of a person is the complication the latter introduced to it. Although the Yoruba holds primarily to the dualistic conception of a person as mind and body, there is a third element of a person—ori (inner head)—as the bearer of human destiny. Like the soul or mind, it is spiritual. In its relation to human personality it determines the destiny of man on earth.

For Gbadegesin,

> The combination of body (ara) breathing spirit (emi) and personality spirit (Ori), then constitute the human person in Yoruba thought. The three are important in their own ways and they are complementary. The breathing spirit has to be embodied to exist in the world of man at least; and without it the body is a lifeless figure which cannot make its earthly journey. The Yoruba are dualists in their metaphysical account of man. Ori, however, introduces a third aspect, perhaps unfamiliar to the West, and it seems the most important of the trio as far as the meaning of human existence is concerned.

Abimbola (2006) seems to go beyond the views adumbrated above by positing two major categories—Ori and Ese. Of Ori, he says, "Ori is the principle of material success and actualization in the sense that it embodies each individual's potentialities for success and/or failure on earth" (p. 72). He goes on show the error of Idowu and other scholars of Yoruba religion, regarding the equation of the Yoruba Supreme Being, called Deity by him, to the Christian Supreme Being, God. Then he says, "Ifa poems make a very clear-cut distinction among Ori (the principle of actualization and earthly success or failure), ese (the principle of individual strife and struggle), and Iwa (good character)" (p. 73).

In the above scenario, an explication of the various strands of personhood as thematized by the Yoruba come under three major ontic categories; namely, body (ara), mind (opolo) and soul (emi). From the passages quoted above, it is clear that personhood has been mistakenly considered and interpreted only in the metaphysical sense of destiny. They have assumed a similarity between Western and African (Yoruba) conceptions of a personhood dualism, whereas I have expounded a triadic explanatory model. The need to forge or distill a philosophically profound system from traditional African (Yoruba) thought, I contend, is no justifiable reason to hastily create a parallelism between European (Western) and African philosophies, otherwise, as Abimbola (2006) concedes, one would fall prey to P'Bitek's paradox of intellectual smuggling.

As it turned out from the discussions of the scholars quoted above, it is obvious that what they have brought out is not a Yoruba conception of a human being, but the Yoruba conception of human destiny. That direction of their discussion automatically led them in search of a destiny-bearing substance, *Ori* or inner head, leaving aside the essentially substantive contribution which the human physical outer visible head as the seat of the intellect, introspection, consciousness, feeling, deliberation, choice, willing, decision making, experience, expertise, apprehension, co-ordination and interpretation, memory, etc., on the one hand, and on the other, the implication of critical analysis for the understanding of the nature of human being and human existence, as if to the Yoruba these issues are not relevant or important. Even when Professor Makinde recognizes the importance of the mental, or the mind, in the personality and constitution of the human being, as these would relate to the determination of such states as feeling of pain, happiness, pleasure, joy, desires, hopes, aspirations, vocational fulfillment, economic interests, political ambitions, religious beliefs, emotional gratification, etc., he fails to distill the philosophically profound and interesting consequences of the ideas from the hazy confusion of traditionally, commonsensical folkloricism and mysticism that shrouds his analysis.

Transience is a reality that the Yoruba consider to be both enabling and limiting. Anchorage in mortality provides transitional leverage from one plane of existence and being to another, and it enriches the depth of the living and the pool of ancestral backbone and bondage. While human personal destiny is solely dependent on the "inner head"—*ori*—and good character (iwa) of the person and the destiny it bears, that of humankind and his society depends on the Deity, the divinities, the ancestors, both deified and natural, on the one hand and on the living, their actions and their destinies on the other hand.

What I consider important is the need to separate the mythical human in terms of the metaphysics of destiny from the real human who is the locus of interaction and experiences. For after all the life-force granting and life-course choosing (destiny determination) have been considered, what we have to deal with is the nature of persons and their constitution in society and in the universe. It is here that Barry Hallen is relevant. He saw the need to conceptualize "eniyan" in terms of the Yoruba account of "Who am I?" "What is man?" That is, in terms of a) what I am made of? b) Am I the same person over a period of time? c) What constitutes my identity as a self-conscious, intelligent rational being (in terms of subjectivity in the first person sense) and as a member of a society (in terms of objectivity in third-person terms needing identification or/and re-identification?

Even with the above, and in fairness to Hallen, his concerns were still limited somewhat to destiny, and I have taken liberty to stretch his ideas a little bit to accommodate dealing with how Yoruba sees a human being in society. Finding that the discussions fail to make coherent the theoretical entities postulated, he proffered possible alternatives one can observe that other possibilities are that personal consciousness is a consequence, in simple, additive sense, of ara, emi, ori, etc. Or that personal consciousness is a consequence of the interaction of certain physical spiritual components in a more complex integrated sense. But this is neither said nor hinted at by any of the authors considered here such as Ellis, Farrow, Johnson, Lucas, Bascom, Idowu, Abimbola, and Verger.

Considered as such, it is interesting to sketch personal identity as conceived by the Yoruba. At birth a child receives a name by which she is known throughout life. This singular and simple act identifies and individuates the person. In terms of human beings being human beings, it is clear in Yoruba metaphysics that only human beings have this attribute of having individual names. In fact, it is indicative of the importance of names that every human must be identified by their individual name. In this regard, it is often said that it is because of when one will commit an abomination or deserve praise that one is given a separate name—*tori ojo t'a o ba da oran, la a fi i l'oruko*. And for clear purposes, the Yoruba knows that individuals are bearers of responsibility; hence there can be no collective punishment for infractions of social and moral norms—unlike the biblical deity who punishes the sin of the father on descendants, up to the fourth generation (Exodus).

Another factor is the intellect (mind) and innate (genetic traits) capabilities and propensities of the person, which help to determine and define the skills and place of a person in life. Built into this last one is the self-consciousness of the person grafted on life experiences and memory (*iriri aye* and *ai gbagbe*) which forms the bedrock of consciousness. Mingled with these are the immediate thoughts and consciousness of the person (*ero/ironu*) which predispose persons to actions or thoughts or beliefs. In my view, to suggest that personal identity is defined by *ori* as Gbadegesin, Makinde, Sodipo, Hallen and others have done, when it is obvious that the individual does not gain any access (privileged or otherwise) to the content of *ori* is mistaken and misleading. Also, personal identity cannot be based on either *emi* (considered as spirit life-force) or *ori* because, for the public, the content of these are not available for interpersonal relational identification, recognition, and consideration. This will, also in the end, mean that we cannot construct a theory of "human nature" or "human being" on such substructures as the metaphysical ideas of identity or destiny.

While it is clear that the capacity for consciousness, reflection, experience, feelings, empathy and introspection are peculiar to humans, these are also probably attributes of animals to some degree. However, when these are combined with memory, with reasoning and with willing it seems clear the humans have a special nature that singles them out for special treatment. While all things in nature have and deserve kind treatment, because they all are beings, it is only humans who can be regarded as centers of humanity.

This is clearly brought out in how humans are educated to appreciate humanity, and as such to be fair to each other—whether friend or foe, relative or stranger, acquaintance or foreigner. As such, the principle of humanity as humans demand that the human being receive proper treatment as humans, even when there are disagreements between parties, because *bi a ba n ja, bi ka ku ko*—that is, even when we are fighting, it does not mean we should kill each other. The story of Akara-oogun's father in D. O. Fagunwa's (1950) book *Ogboju Ode Ninu Igbo Irunmale* is instructive in this regard. This story indicates a man married to four wives, the first wife being a witch. The first wife had a quarrel with one of the other wives, and brought the matter to the husband with the hope for support, in a privileged way, of being the first wife. After hearing the two sides to the dispute, the husband gave judgment based on pure merit, and it went against the first wife, who then tried to use witchcraft to kill all but the husband and the first son.

The result was serious consequences for both the husband whose sense of justice was to be fair to all concerned and the first wife who felt that being the first wife conferred privileges which put others at a disadvantage in the end. What is clear here is that the privileged position of the wife was not an indicator of special treatment, nor could the Ara-orun sent to kill the man do the job, as it was reasoned that the man has not really sinned. What this shows is that in Yoruba culture, there is always clear commitment to the cause of justice at all times, compared with what the Bible said about Yahweh in the book of Job.

This is where we now come to the one critical element in the determination of what a human being is in Yoruba culture and thought that has not been fully explicated. This is "character" or *iwa*. We have seen it occur in the explanations of destiny by Abimbola (2006), but this has not been related to a human person as it is conceived existentially and legally. It is clear though that *iwa* makes a person more valuable or less valuable. This is where there is a distinction between the positive *iwa,* also known as *iwa rere* or good *iwa,* and negative *iwa,* also known as *iwa ibaje* or *iwa buburu,* also known as bad *iwa* and evil *iwa.* In *Beauty and Culture* I had discussed how good *iwa* relates to the beauty of a person (beauty of a human being), and consequently positive appreciation of the person as a human being in society, and negative *iwa* would mean people distancing themselves from the person, and consequent negative appreciation of the humanity of the person (Bewaji 2003: 159). But this will be like putting the cart before the horse, in the sense that it would make the understanding of the intrinsic value of humanity, or human being, dependent on a manifested trait which is not genetically or naturally intrinsic to the humanity of the human being.

Thus, while *iwa* adds to the quality of appraisal that an individual garners, it does not determine the humanity of the person, which is the main attraction center for being human. For this reason, *iwa* is indifferent to the nature and being of a human person. But *iwa* plays a significant role in the making and passing off of rights of individuals. What then is the role of *iwa* in the determination of the humanity of a human being and understanding of human nature?

In the first instance, a human being is a moral being. A human being without morality is *eniyan lasan lasan, eniyan sa, ekeji aja* and is no better than an *eranko*—that is, an animal. This implies that the absence of proper culture, moral probity, and good character devalues the humanity of the person to the level of just an ordinary thing, or animal. Such a person is no better than an animal, a plant or a stone, with no volitions, and no self-determination in the proper sense of it. Such a person loses the humanity that being a member of society confers, and which being a human being demands. In some respects such a person would not be a center of respect.

Does this mean that the person has no rights? Would this imply that the person is no longer a human being and could be treated without attention to human nature? Would legal implications follow from such a disposition, such as arrest and incarceration? The answer to these three questions is an emphatic no. This is because, as we have indicated earlier, clearly good character is important for civil participation and realization of all that is the potential of the person in society, and the absence of such good character does not annul the humanity of the person. It does not mean that the person can now be treated as if the person does not exist. It does not mean that others would have no obligations to respect the person's humanity. And it does not mean that the person can be arrested, having not done anything bad or evil, against the law, and be imprisoned.

It may turn out that the person loses some deserts as a consequence of the bad character, or evil ways, but others still would not want to join in the bad ways, as this would lead to total chaos in society. In fact, what may happen is that the person who has a bad character, attitude or who is totally selfish and inconsiderate of others and of nature may not receive proper material or moral support, because *owo to o, lo n mu owo to o o wa,* that is good begets good, and others would be compelled to "do on to you as you do on to others." This means that "character" or moral uprightness and cultural awareness and respectfulness (*omoluabi*) are critically important in determining the rights that appertain to human beings as agents and bearers of humanity, but these are only a part of the right determinants that Yoruba people are traditionally and intellectually conscious of and that they insist on in society.

Going back to our point earlier about naming, it is significant that apart from individuation, which no other thing in nature has, beyond their specie properties, humans have names. The names are, according to Babalola (1967: 11), important markers of individual traditional heritage, circumstance of birth, expectations and inclinations. These are specific to the bearers of the names, and they specifically delineate the person from others. And for the Yoruba, there is a sense in which the names are portentous of future attributes and behavior. Thus, unlike in Western cultures where animal pets are given names, only humans have names. For no animal in the same family can meet another animal of the same family and address the other animal by the human-assigned names as happens with humans. Nor, can a plant do the same, as humans are capable of doing. And animals may have their own codes of behavior within their different kingdoms, yet they are unable to attenuate actions and reactions with critical hermeneutics that indicate the decision making explanatory models.

There is one minor aspect of the above that bears mention. This relates to the need to always properly address persons and things by their proper names. Whether they are humans, animals or plants, the proper address by names is a sign of respect, recognition, access and control—where such is the case (Bewaji 2003: 158ff).

We need to mention a minor point here before closing this sub-section. When Menkiti (2004: 326) speaks of "the stated journey of the individual toward personhood," it is to be understood in the moral maturation sense and not in the sense in which it may suggest that a human is less of a human being unless the person is an adult. Or, even where it would be incomprehensible to look at the factor of humans maturing morally as indicating that there are no moral obligations that humans owe to the moral midget or to the youth in any culture, and the Yoruba society does not discriminate between the infant and the adult when rights are in contest. What may happen is that humans are to be treated according to their desert, and as such while allowances may be made for the accommodation of young folly, this does not mean that their humanity is in any way compromised.

In Yoruba culture and thought, it is clear that all that is in nature deserve respect in virtue of their different natures. This is why the nature of each being determines the kinds of function that they are expected to perform, and the attendant treatment they receive from the other things in nature, including human beings. Often it is emphasized that Yoruba people are a respectful people. This is not misplaced, as proper treatment of things and people implicate the reception of due consequences that is desired from the interaction. This is because the nature of things is such that when treated properly, it would automatically lead to the reward that leads to good consequences.

Also, it does not matter how simple or challenged a being may seem or be, they have their capacity to act out their nature, and should not be underestimated. The numerous stories of *Ijapa* show this clearly. In many instances, *Ijapa* performs feats that are incredible, given its nature. And in other instances, other beings perform feats that are incredible. This would show that it does not matter whether a person is young, old, big, small, male or female, one should not deny the person the rights that are due to them.

Even when there is so much emphasis on community welfare and communal ownership, it is clear that property rights, apportionment of praise or blame, merit of punishment are individually deserving and determined. For, *ki i je ti baba ati omo, ki o ma l'a aala*, that is, even when the father and son farm a plot of land there are still boundaries between what is the father's and what is the son's.

There is a clear recognition of rights for humans in virtue of being human—young, old, male or female. In fact, there is the extension of rights beyond the level of the living to those yet to be born and to those already dead and long buried. That this is the case relates to how conception, pregnancy and birth are treated with due care, respect, deference and protection. The community of humans endeavors to care for the human being in society, as it is recognized that it is only within the community of humans that rights are meaningful. In fact, it is only in relation of humans to other humans that human existence is meaningful and fully actualized. In this regard, effort is made in Yoruba society to ensure that there are no extremes of poverty or indigence, as a consequence of the fact that in Yoruba society all members of society have functions and are engaged meaningfully and productively (Bewaji 2003). This means that in Yoruba society it is the right of each decent, sane and fit person to expect that society cares for them, and in return they are obliged to contribute meaningfully to the existence of society.

While the Yoruba society is a highly structured and apparently hierarchical one, this is only deceptive, and there is a great amount of protection of the weak and vulnerable against the strong, rich and powerful.

The story of *Efunsetan Aniwura, Iyalode Ibadan* is a good reminder of the need for the persons who have made good today to remember that they are humans and that without society their wealth would be naught. Also, the story *Agba lowo meri, Baale Jontolo* clearly shows how persons who are poor today may become leaders and wealthy persons tomorrow, if they apply themselves and remain honest, disciplined and respectful of the laws of the society.

Akiwowo (1983) itemized five main values that guide Yoruba culture in terms of morality, social relations, religious efforts, politics, personal interaction, etc. These are:

a. *Ire aiku* (the value of good health until old age)
b. *Ire owo* (the value of financial security)
c. *Ire oko-aya* (the value of intimate companionship and love, husband and wife)
d. *Ire omo* (the value of parenthood and having good children) and
e. *Ire abori ota* (the value of secured self-actualization) (pp. 13–14)

Whatever one does within the ambit of the social engagement that society promotes, these are values that society must ensure. In doing this, it means that the individual must be facilitated and protected, regardless of the competitiveness of the existential circumstances: "A (Yoruba) human society, therefore, has meaning for its members if and only if these social values are consciously sought as common goals. These five are internalized as *ire gbogbo,* the values belonging to all members of the collectivity; or simply we may call them social values common to all" (Akiwowo 1983: 14).

He uses the concept of sociation deriving from *Ajobi* and *Ajogbe* to consummate the circumstances in which it is best for human beings to realize the rights each human best deserves. And regardless of how distant Yoruba people may be in terms of filial relations, there is quite no doubt that the fact that they all see each other as *Omo Oduduwa* remains a bonding factor which implicate the extension of the equal rights that close relations are to have. For, *Ona lo jin, eru ni baba*—that is, the distance to home may be long/far, yet a slave has a father. Hence, we should not ill treat those who are vulnerable among us, because they are also humans, with feelings, with desires, with thoughts and with identities and destinies. This is borne out by the clearly ambiguous warning that *bi a ba ka eru, inu eru a ba je,* which means that when the story of how the slave became a slave is told to the slave, it may lead to unhappiness or that we should all be careful as we are all still human, and each one of us have weaknesses which when recounted may lead to unhappiness. In other words, it is a warning that we should not indulge in making others unhappy either through our deeds or words.

Abimbola (2006: 65ff) argues, through showing that Yoruba people abhor human sacrifice, that for the Yoruba, life is valuable in itself. The fact that even for sacrifice human life is regarded as sacred would then indicate that any form of violence that involves the death of another human being is an abomination. This factor is further reinforced in various ways in the life and culture of the Yoruba society in traditional times. For example, honest diligence and application is valued as the source of enduring wealth, as the "Catechism" of Yoruba culture would show—*Toju Iwa re*. On this score, we could simply add that it probably is no accident that the BBC Survey of the Happiest Countries in the world showed Nigerians as the happiest people on earth. Why, because it is believed that *Ba o ku ise o tan*, and as the common pidgin English saying ascribed to Lagosians goes—*E go bet, na im no let poor man lef am for Lagos*. This is because human worth does not diminish by poverty or get enhanced by wealth, and the value of the life of the rich is the same as that of the poor, regardless of happenstance of economic situation.

When it comes to the dispensation of justice, it is clear that each individual has a right to be heard, as was clear in the case of Akara-oogun's father earlier mentioned. This means that no case can be determined without hearing the two sides to the case, and each party must be accorded equal hearing and fairness of presentation of the case before the determination of guilt or innocence can be proclaimed. If there is a miscarriage of justice—*ka gb'are fun elebi, ka gb'ebi fun alare*—it could lead to serious consequences for the judge, the person who has been wrongly favored and the society in which this injustice has been committed. In fact, until the situation is redressed, it is believe that various bad things would be happening to all who were a party to the injustice. Because of this, great care is taken to ensure that every case is given due treatment and determined fairly. And it is no wonder that Yoruba people are very suspicious of the English common law system that was imposed on them in the colonial period. It meant that their standards of evidence, standards of truth, requirements of truth of witnesses, and other critical elements of a properly tethered judicature are abrogated and a foreign one imposed. This has facilitated the instances in which gross miscarriages of justice have taken place over inheritance.

What followed is the fact that, apart from the unnecessary expense of having to now retain the services of a third party to a dispute, who have no sympathy, empathy or cultural grounding, in a case, to now argue the case on behalf of the parties in dispute. Given their suspicion that "lawyers are liars," it follows clearly why traditional systems of conflict resolution in the various indigenous quarters continue to have more popularity than the formal judicial system of the Nigerian state.

Apart from this, there is the issue of each person having to be present when their matters are being determined. In the English legal system, this is called the "Habeas Corpus." For the Yoruba, it is clear that *a kii fa ori lehin olori*, or literally it means that "you cannot shave someone's head in their absence." And regardless of how long it may take, the two parties to any situation must be present when matters pertaining to them are being determined. In fact, this has another critical element. Where witness is known to be dishonest, it is clear that they must be made to confront the person about whom they are giving testimony. It is believed that when a liar confronts the person lied about, the story would change, as tradition, custom and Yoruba religion expects that liars are courting the displeasure of the ancestors and the gods.

From the foregoing, we could see that a critical element of the Yoruba judicial system is the system of truth-telling. This requires that each person must swear by the ancestors, the divinities, and filial patrimony—*ajobi*—in order for them to receive credibility. And no one takes these matters lightly; in fact, it has been urged that instead of people swearing by the Bible or the Quran, they should be asked to swear by Sango, Ogun, Yemaja, Osun or other Yoruba deities, especially the politicians who have neither the requisite cultural upbringing nor moral conscience to regard the trust that society reposed in them in the discharge of their offices.

I have had other occasion to repudiate Mbiti's suggestion that older persons cannot do wrong against younger ones (Bewaji 2003). It is clear that though there is great respect for age and experience, this comes with great responsibility for the older ones. It means that for them to deserve the respect of the young, they must reciprocally endeavor to protect the young and treat them with fairness. For, when this is not done, the young may be under no obligation to respect the old—*agba to je aje e wehin, ni yio ru igba e de'le*. This means that in a culture where elders must not carry luggage while junior ones follow, when the elder eats without care for the sustenance of the young, they get to carry their own luggage even when the young one is carrying nothing at all. When we also bear in mind that Yoruba culture does regard youth as important, it is not surprising that it is indicated that the youth of today is tomorrow's elder, and as such the wisdom of youth is valued as much as the wisdom of the adult, because, *omode gbon, agba gbo, ni isedale Ife,* that is, Ile-Ife (the ancestral home of the Yoruba) is founded on the wisdom of the youth and the adult.

Finally, it may be wondered what is the place of gender in the judicial system? Clearly, this may be interesting in an age in which gender equality is seriously important. For the Yoruba, as Oyeronke Oyewumi (1997) has consistently argued, there is no bias against or in favor of any gender; as in fact, Yoruba language does not take care of determine gender in the value of children—for *eni omo sin lo bi mo,* or a person buried by a child is the one who had children. And even though it may seem that there is rigid division of labor and apportionment of privileges in the culture and tradition, because of the patrilineal nature of the society, this is not to be taken to mean that there is no keen interest in the affirmation of the humanity of all genders equally. In fact, the division of labor is blurred by the disregard that takes place when critical matters need to be determined. In such situations it is often said that *ki okunrin ri ejo, ki obinrin pa ejo, k'ejo ma ti lo lo ja ju*, that is, if a male sees a dangerous snake, and a woman kills the snake before it harms any one is not important, what is important is that the snake does not harm anyone or escape to harm people another day!

In this regard, wealth, status, pedigree or other accidental matters does not affect the nature of human rights in Yoruba culture. In fact, a society that facilitates a slave to become the king of a community definitely does not allow for discrimination with regard to the procurement of the rights of persons, as injustice to any one is injustice to all members of society. We will see how the situation has changed in contemporary society, where it seems that justice is now "cash and carry," and the rights that one has is only as meaningful as the resources one has to claim them; as the network of protection of rights in traditional Yoruba society has been ruptured by the new contraption that is the Nigerian judicial system!

From the foregoing, it is clear that human rights is very well enshrined in the culture and tradition and customs of indigenous Yoruba society before colonialism, amalgamation with Nigeria and independence of Nigeria. This fact is not one that is contestable, and elements of religion, politics, morality, economics, social relations confirm this. The various documents of Yoruba culture, from Ifa, to oratures and literatures, to fables and myths all attest to this. We would now look at the experience of human rights in Nigeria for comparison.

There are three factors that would have to be considered in understanding the concept of human rights in Nigeria. The first relates to the diversity of ethnicities of Nigeria as a political arrangement. The second related to the nature of the inherited common law from the British judicial system. The final one relates to the nature of politics, economics and religion in the Nigerian society. These factors all contribute to the nature of what rights are regarded as intrinsic to the human being qua being, and how these are understood and interpreted within the context of the Nigeria state.

We will consider these seriatim. First, we wish to note that the Nigeria state has not succeeded in creating a nation out of the human beings that constitute the demography of the country. While it can be affirmed that each ethnic constituent of Nigeria has its traditions, cultures, religions, social, political, moral and filial beliefs and practices, all of which determine what rights are ascribed to humans qua humans in their societies, the transition from this to a Nigerian indigenous concept of human rights has not taken place in a way which would show that there has been a proper melding of cultures and traditions. What this means is that there has been no transition from the amalgam of different ethnicities and traditions that compose Nigeria to a cohesive one where there is a sense of belonging, a sense of a unifying tradition, a sense of destiny, a sense of love for the humanity of the other simply because of the humanity of the other, that is a transcendence of the identity of otherness to a filial consanguinity that creates sympathy, love and empathy such that the loss of one is the loss of the other, and the happiness and joy of one is the happiness and joy of the other, regardless of the ethnicity of this other or one. Rather, what has happened over the many years, since the accident of colonialism, post-colonialism and independence, has been the distantiation of ethnicities through various centrifugal forces of disassociation. It is against this background, then, that we have to understand the nature of human rights in Nigeria today.

This has to be understood in the context of the fact that the people living within the geographical space known as Nigeria have interacted for thousands of years, trading, intermarrying and relating at various levels, before the colonial period and the contemporary amalgam that is the Nigerian country. Under these circumstances they have borrowed from each other various words, used ideas shared, related to the understanding of each ethnicity with respect, even differed and fought wars, reconciled and co-existed. In the various events and instances of interface, the humanity of each other has not been compromised even when severely assaulted by differences on the utilization and sharing of resources to the extent that, in fact, it could be said that interaction has only served to strengthen the appreciation of the humanity of the other within the context of the humanity of the self. This means that the failure of the Nigeria state to serve as a modern space for the affirmation and enhancement of the humanity of humans within the space of Nigeria is to be accounted for using creative tools of interpretation and analysis beyond the mere fact of the multi-ethnicity of Nigeria state.

It could be raised as an issue in this context what is meant by tradition and to what extent could one speak of the tradition of an entity that only became a reality through the amalgamation of so many differing and different traditions? While this would be an appropriate issue to raise in this discussion, we would simply understand tradition as (any) long established belief, system, custom, culture of doing things, which receive respect in any society. This does not mean that such society is constrained not to do things in different ways in future; it only means that there is deference to established ways of doing things that have worked and serve the members of the society well in the past.

It may also be contested that given the tradition of discourses arising from liberalism and contractarianism and Marxism, rights are often meaningful only in the context of exclusion. That is, rights only make sense in the context of contending claims which cannot all be accommodated given the limitation of the resources for meeting such claims. In other words, those with an adversarial tradition of conflict resolution and dispute settlement would advise that rights are always to be seen as contentions which are intrinsically disruptive. It would also be contended that given that common law foundation of the laws that Nigeria inherited from the British, it would only be meaningful to cash out rights—human or otherwise—against this background. Given the point that we are making in this section, it would be clear that we do not subscribe to the "ours—theirs" dichotomy which underwrite this suggestion. As it would be clear, indigenous Yoruba culture bases rights on the derivation of communitarian existence, and the impossibility of a single atomistic individual to manufacture or develop rights in isolation of others has been discussed in my "The Social Contract Theory" (1998) to make the point that whatever contractarian system is developed could only be meaningful when it is understood that humans have never existed except in organized communities, no matter how few the membership of the community may be.

The second related to the nature of the inherited common law from the British judicial system. I did mention the fact that Yoruba people are often wary of the imposed common law that came with the advent of colonization. This is a product of the clear departure that ensued regarding the rules of natural justice, fairness, rights and evidence from traditional and indigenous cultures of the various ethnicities that constitute the make-up of the Nigeria state. Clearly, the miscegenation of the judicial process and the hybridization of the process of justice, where parasites become more important in the dispensation of justice than the notion of truth, evidence and fact, all led to a clear intellectual and cultural gap between the understanding of rights and justice within the context of the new contraption that is called Nigeria. In consequence, it is clear that while there is a failure to carefully understand the English legal culture, the newly imposed leadership group members, who have little by way of understanding of their own indigenous culture and ethos, then find various creative and destructive ways to upend the notions of rights, justice, fairness and humanity in the Nigeria state. What I mean by leadership ignorance of their indigenous culture is a serious indictment of the leadership. It is clear that their not being properly educated in their own indigenous tradition means the inability to understand the same, which then translates into an inability to appreciate the foundations of one's indigenous culture and by extension, an incurable inability to be sensitive to the fundamental foundations of the cultures of other members of the body politic that is Nigeria. Thus, not being versed in the notions of life, existence, ultimate meaning and being in one's culture meant not being able to see the same in others and consequent insensitivity to the rights deriving from one's culture and from others' cultures. The constant strictures that take place in the Nigerian society are evidence of this problem.

Thus, even though the new contraption called Nigeria is a signatory to the United Nations Universal Declaration of Human Rights, this has not translated into the same kind of understanding of what is meant by rights, where the rights derive from, who are the responsible groups that would ensure these rights are protected, how the infractions of any rights of any one would constitute an infraction of the rights of every individual Nigerian, just like the Yoruba person knows that any unfairness and injustice to the youngest or the weakest Yoruba is an affront to the whole Yoruba people! The absence of what one could call a Nigerian identity, like Yoruba identity, Ibo identity, Efik identity, Fulani identity, Hausa identity or any other similar identity that protects the humanity (rights) of identity token, means to the new leadership that there is no token target of rights, or in the absolute extreme there are no humans to whom the rights to which the state of Nigerian has signed to, any rights that can be conceded. This is curious in deed. But it is not difficult to understand. For the target of what we call human rights must be unambiguous for such human rights to be meaningfully assignable, or for rights to have a clear sense of determination and procurement. While there is something that is called Nigeria, there are no Nigerians. While there is a state that has a demographic structure, there are no identities that match the space called Nigeria. As such, there are no humans who are Nigerians, and hence, in the proper and most meaningful sense, there are no human rights. This accounts for the contempt with which the various leaders and governments have treated Nigerians.

One could look at the clear evidence of the issue from the way in which the various Nigerian leaders (except for the short periods of Muritala Mohammed in the mid-seventies and Idiagbon in the early eighties) treat common property of Nigerians—that is the wealth and resources of Nigeria (including the human capital of Nigeria). Since there are no Nigerians in the same sense in which there are Ibos, Hausas, Efiks, Ibiobios, Kanuris, Fulanis, or Yorubas, it means that what is Nigerian property and wealth belongs to no one, and as such can be taken and used by whoever is in the position of power at any time. If it was understood that there were true Nigerians to whom they are accountable, and who would be offended if they were to abuse their office, and who can hold them to account in the same way that Yoruba Obas were forced to commit suicide or to abdicate the throne, then they would have been more responsible and responsive in their dealings with public resources and human beings in Nigeria.

When we consider the nature of politics, economics and religion in the Nigerian society, we see clearly that what we have observed above is clearly borne out by the nature of leadership and human rights in the contraption that is called Nigeria. There is a distinct sense in which human rights implicate filial relations. It is in this sense that one has to see that there are beneficial relations between persons who relate. This is where there must be a coalescence of *ajobi* and *ajogbe*, so as to ensure that even while we are of different genetic heritages, we still are, as humans, entitled to similar treatment which would make our relating to each other in the same extended space meaningful and rewarding for all the participants in the relationship.

Understanding *ajobi* and *ajogbe* in the sense annotated by Akiwowo, it is interesting to see how his discussion of both impacts the nature of human rights in Nigeria today. It must be remarked that I am bending his discussion to accommodate my analysis of human rights in Nigeria today, and I am sure he may not take umbrage at my effort along these lines, as his understanding of sociology as *atokun* of a society would be quite along the lines that I discuss.

According to Akiwowo (1988),

> In the first place, both *ajobi* and *ajogbe* possess different fractions of sociation. In *ajobi* the magnitude of concord and consensus is ideally very high, because each member is able to link his or her identity to a common source such as the same mother or the same father, or the same father and mother. In this form of sociation, it is possible for individuals who compose it to grow up together and realize their common interests within it (p. 28).

In Yoruba society, it is clear that there is a tracing of the progeny to Oduduwa, and the place of origin as Ile-Ife. This creates a bond of sociation which translates into *ajobi,* regardless of how further away into the past such genealogy and geographically distant habitation may be from Oduduwa and Ile-Ife. This means that all Yoruba see each other as one. And by extension, the humanity of each Yoruba is seen as equal and, as such, inalienable. But this has not translated into *ajogbe* for Nigerians, in the sense that the consanguinity and co-residency that *ajogbe* (p. 18) implies that there be equality of respect for each other, respect for interests, respect for what each other represents and proper determination of the humanity of each other as being connected intrinsically to the extent that one person's pain translates into the pain of the others in the community writ large. In the words of Akiwowo (1983),

> This vast territory which constitutes the legal and physical homeland for a very large collectivity of some two hundred or more language communities is a unity of denumerable sets of *ajobi* who are consciously becoming a self-conscious *ajogbe*. In my mind, what constitute the *ofi* (warp and woof) of the unity are primarily our will to sociate, the several attractive culture configurations of our peoples, and the unestimated resources available to us on and below the earth's surface. . . . Nigeria is truly an affiliation of several *asuwada eniyan*. Inevitably as a growing *ajogbe,* we the people are trying to discover how best to fashion new social ties as we develop new perceptions of the world around us . . . and to give newer definitions of what-is-mine and what-is-yours. Unfortunately we have come to think that the Constitution, as an objectified will-to-associate of us all, which lives in a written form, is sufficient to sustain us as a people. Yet, as we know very well, social life is a moment-to-moment process of sociation of human beings. It is largely subjective. What we need then to sustain the will-to-sociate in addition

> to the Constitution includes internalized appreciation of the worth of human life individualized in our fellow countrymen (p. 28).

What leads to the seeing of humans as humans is not a contraption that is forced together or the paper on which rules and regulations binding behavior are written, whether we choose to call it constitution or not, it does not make a difference. What matters is the sublime respect that each human gives to the other which often derives from shared history, shared culture, share heritage, shared vision of future, shared suffering, shared joys, shared destiny—especially shared destiny as humanity! It is for this reason that no matter how entrenched the fundamental human rights may be in a document called constitution, as Jamaica is attempting to do, it would not matter if social life is based on the individuation of the individual. The individuation of the individual cannot be redressed by an artifice of a social contract as the Western thinkers wish. This is why human rights is only a legal item in the lives of peoples of the West, and this is why it is to be objected to seriously that non-Western cultures embrace the foreign concept of un-contextualized dissociated human rights which relate to nothing in the culture of the peoples on which they are being foisted around the world.

As Akiwowo would have argued, if his interest were to be human rights, the bonds of consanguinity and co-residency is thicker than water, hence human beings who see each other as *alajogbe* know that when there is a breakdown of law and order in any part of the space that they mutually inhabit, it would spell breakdown in the other parts of the space eventually. To prevent this, the members of society as individual and collectively would feel an affront when any member of the society is subjected to treatment that breaches the protocol of human rights that each and every one takes as entitlement, regardless of religion, ethnicity, economic station in life, political affiliation or position in the scheme of things. Whether it is spelled out in detail or only understood as part of the conventions of interaction between various persons and entities in society, human rights would be meaningful, and it would be real under such circumstances. Abuses of rights would be regarded as an affront to all humans in the collectivity, not just to the persons who suffer from such abuse.

Apart from the platitudinous celebration of Human Rights in the United Nations Universal Declaration of Human Rights that we have mentioned at the beginning of this discussion, the various nongovernmental organizations like Human Rights Watch, Civil Liberties Organizations, and various National and International Bar Associations, Ombudsman, etc. around the world, it can be argued that the breakdown of traditional, indigenous, cohesive forces of sociation that Akiwowo mentioned has led to a parlous state of human rights in the international experience, as it is clear that there is nothing and there could be nothing like human rights in an abstract vacuum. For this reason, it makes little sense to waste time debating human rights in the international context except as a conceptual and wishful lightning rod for the rating and berating of governments of developing societies and recalcitrant ones who would not wish to be subject to the rollercoaster of the Western market forces of domination.

Given the breakdown of the methods of enhancing humanity developed in indigenous cultures which derive from ideas about humanity and well-ordered society, it follows that there is need to develop alternative measures for protecting human rights. The market forces are not the right instruments for these, as what they foster are Darwinian proclivities in humanity. As such, the efforts of various agencies to underwrite human rights are basically feeble and incompetent as they are incapacitated by the limitations of economics and entrenched political and religious interests. For one, in international understanding of human rights, human beings are not treated as equal across borders by states and societies, as humans in some societies are not regarded as worthy of defending—as in the case of Jenin in Palestine in 2003 when Israel imposed collective punishment on the city for resisting the occupation of Palestinian lands and refused the fact-finding mission of the United Nations to Jenin or in situations where the United States of America would go to any length to protect a single American anywhere in the world while it does not consider bombing a highly busy market as anything serious as those who would be killed there are mere collateral damages in the effort to help Iraqis embrace civilized culture of democratic governance! For another, there is still so much racism and racialism in international relations, such that some humans are more valuable—whether as migrants in the case of Asians migrating to the United States of America compared with Haitians fleeing poverty or as a plane-load of mercenaries destined to wreak havoc on the political leadership of other poor developing countries of Africa. And this is not strange, because humans have only been able to respect those who they think they stand to gain from, either out of understanding of the superiority of the other or out of necessity of having to relate with respect to the other in order to receive what benefit is expected. Where humans have been able to impose their own superiority of the other, or where the other has failed to show capacity to reciprocate force with greater force and havoc to the potential instigator of violence, rights have always been denied with impunity or with dire consequences to the self.

I wish to place here again my abridged version of the set of formalized rights, together with the implied others not stated, even while admitting the heuristics of our earlier discussion on social contract:

> All human beings are born free and equal in dignity and rights to pursue their happiness and privacy within the ambit of the law of their

> societies . . . free from discriminations on account of race, colour, sex, language, religion, political or other opinion, national or social origin, property, birth or other status . . . with a right to life, liberty and security of person . . . free from slavery, torture, cruel, inhuman or degrading treatment or punishment . . . free from arbitrary arrest, detention or exile, having access to equal and fair hearing, etc.

There can be no rights, meaningful or otherwise, where there are no social, psychological, mythical, religious or economic factors that make such rights important to society. Clearly, international agencies existing on the grounds of being human rights advocates need to rethink their position. There were no dissociated, noninvolved and disinterested human rights advocates in traditional Yoruba societies, as each human in the society was an advocate for human rights, recognizing that the diminution of the rights of one member of my society is the abrogation of my own rights as a human being, yet human rights were defended, protected and enhanced by the collective responsibility and discipline of the consciousness of the fact that any abrogation of the human right of one is tantamount to the abrogation of the collective human rights of all. In various arts, cultural performances and political fora, efforts were made to ensure that human rights were protected. The masquerade in Esa-Oke in Osun State of Nigeria has a sub-set which is called "Saare," and its annual appearance is usually anticipated for its entertainment value as well as its capacity to serve as the moral conscience of the people through its satirical disclosure of the scandals of the rich, the powerful, the poor, the indolent, the promiscuous, the petty thief and more. This annual ritual helps to psychologically and socially cleanse the society of ills that need to be prevented in the community, and also facilitates the process of redress-seeking and mediates friction in society. What the human rights agencies should be doing then is to be advocating that the conditions that make for the abuse of the rights of persons in society be removed. That is, rather than to be advocating for socioeconomic situations which are consequences of the predatory structuring of the social-economic and other conditions of life in Darwinian interaction and interface environments of the contemporary society, which make it possible for international human rights agencies to raise hell ex-post facto for the redress of rights, they need to see that abuses are consequences of systemic dysfunctionality of socioeconomic arrangements of relations of existence in contemporary society and are consequently a result of national and international structuring of reality.

What this means is that we should be well aware that the contemporary world national and international relations of human beings in society is based on a distorted understanding of reality and humanity. We insist that the factors responsible for this are numerous, and these range from the structure of the United Nations Organization itself to the various trade systems imposed by the societies of the North, from educational structures to information systems and their centers of coordination and dissemination around the world, from social and economic to religious and other structures of interaction around the world. The world may encrypt human rights in whatever format they so desire, for as long as things remain the way they are, the conditions for the abuse of human rights would continue to exist in both the rich and the poor societies of the world. Incidentally, the rich and powerful centers in the world today would wish to believe that there are more "human rights" in the world today than one thousand years ago. This paradox is a consequence of the false faith in technology and information-sharing mechanisms. While not being nostalgic, for someone with a Yoruba background, it seems that things are worse today than in the past, especially in terms of society taking serious interest in the protection of the human rights of all members of society.

In most societies of the world, even with the signing of the treaties protecting human rights by governments, it is clear that most humans cannot access genuine human rights. Situations in which small infringements of rights balloon into systematic denudation of collective rights are not difficult to imagine. If you are poor, and you met in an accident in many third world countries due to no fault of yours and when the other party is genuinely at fault (in Nigeria and Jamaica especially), for you to get your rights from either the guilty party or from the insurers may become an impossible thing, like making the camel pass through the eye of the needle. If you have no resources to claim your rights, it does not matter how much international treaties and declarations may say you have such rights, you virtually do not exist, and the best you can do is hope that you minimize your loss and suffer in silence. This was not the case in indigenous traditional societies as a matter of course.

I am here reminded that traditional Yoruba society was not without what may be regarded as institutional injustice, whereby older persons cheat younger persons because of their age, as it is said *ko si oun ta a n fi agba dida se, omode la a fi i re je*. But at the same time, there is the other side which says to the society that *omode oni oun l'agba ola*, that is, the youth of today will be the adult of tomorrow, and hence, while the old have privileges that entitle them to respect, because even though the young may have many clothes, yet the young cannot have as many worn dresses like the adult (*b'omode ba l'aso bi agba, ko le l'akisa bi agba*), yet we must bear in mind that the foundation of the ancient city of Ile-Ife was built on the respect for the wisdom of the young and the old alike—*omode gbon, agba gbon, oun la fi da Ile-Ife*.

What is clear from the discussion of this section is that the dynamics of "human rights" in contemporary societies of the world has become so complicated and variegated that the attempts to simplify the issues, ideas and meanings of the concept are doomed to failure. We also see that while traditional societies of the world had the advantage of approaching human rights from the perspective of their cultural basis of understanding humanity, the cobbling together of diverse ethnicities in many countries today make such univocal understanding impossible. Further, what used to be the moral, social, cultural, metaphysical and epistemological understanding of humanity, which fed into the consciousness of human rights and the protection mechanisms that they were afforded in such societies, have been subjected to critical attenuation by forces beyond the territorial boundaries of the societies. This means that economics, politics, and other human identity factors now play greater roles in determining the existence and access to human rights in most contemporary societies. These factors mean that we need to generate more innovative and realistic concepts of human rights and processes for ensuring that humans everywhere in the world are able to access and enjoy such basic minimum rights as annotated at the beginning of this discussion and at the beginning of this section, as our consciousness of our personal and collective humanity is challenged directly universally by the diminution of the rights of any human being anywhere in the world.

This last point means that the logic of transnational corporations and the current World Trade Organization arrangements that are heavily loaded in the favor of the powerful industrial and technologically advanced societies of the world would have to be overhauled in order for human rights to be universally meaningful. Clearly what Seattle and Cancun showed the power houses of the world was not simple matters relating to trade between the few but powerful haves of the world and the majority poor, powerless have-nots of the world. What is showed clearly is the need for a clear and determined revisitation of the concept of humanity in the global village, and revisiting humanity means paying attention to the interdependence of humanity globally, such that we begin to appreciate that while we may be sanguine in our little corner comfort while the majority are malnourished and impoverished, it is only a matter of time before their abridged humanity becomes our own negated humanity. This is becoming clearer to the intelligent portions of the rich and powerful West, but it will take more than just universal declarations of human rights to persuade the advantaged rulers of the world to facilitate the meaningful realization of the intent of the United Nations Charter on Human Rights.

The discussion in this chapter has suggested that Yoruba indigenous understanding and practice of human rights, even in millennia past and with the discounting for the weakness in nostalgia as a result of the way it leads to a papering over of instances of abuse that may have been grotesque to those who suffered them, is still by far superior to either the Nigeria state understanding and practice or even the universal understanding and practice of human rights. This is not surprising, as our discussion has elicited the factors that make for a better human rights record in any society; namely, understanding of human person, origin of persons, relations between persons (living or dead), relations between persons and nature, relations between persons and the gods, and the factor of human inter-connectivity. We used the ideas of sociation, as discussed by Akiwowo, to show this, and we traced the lack of properly thematized ideas of *ajobi* or *ajogbe* in the world society and in the Nigerian society as a main factor responsible for the parlous state of human rights in Nigeria and in the world. We make it clear that where individuals are powerless—either because of poverty or ethnicity or race or class—to claim rights, and society feels no constraint to facilitate the rights of such persons, then beyond the levels of formalisms of documentation and activism, there can be no real human rights. Thus, we are persuaded that human rights is only minimally a legal issue, it is more an economic, a cultural, a social, a psychological, an epistemological, a metaphysical and a human issue which can only be dealt with when these issues are deliberately addressed meaningfully by all the power brokers of the world.

SEVEN

Traditional Religion, Constituted Authority, Law and Order

There is no doubt that the various indigenous and traditional societies of the world have, at one time or another, been enamored with religion, whether as the solution to the anxieties and uncertainties that confront human beings in these societies, relating to the unpredictability of the forces of nature, or the acts of some human beings engaging in various machinations steeped in apparent or real negative actions aimed at making the lives of other human beings miserable. Under such circumstances, various religions have played very important roles in the validation of constitutional authority structures designed to oversee social stability and the legitimation of governance structures, thereby conducing to interpersonal peace and cooperative existence of members of society in the various communities. Without indulging in the kinds of over-dramatization engaged in by Idowu (1962), claiming that the Yoruba people were in all things religious, it is clearly valid to say that the traditional Yoruba people of West Africa were not an exception in this regard of having their fair share of religiosity, as there is clear evidence in history that they were as religious as other human beings of similar periods in human history, taking measures largely conditioned or moderated by their beliefs in the supersensible universe, and its influence on the material, social, economic and psychological domain of being to ensure that their lives were meaningful and bereft of unnecessary hindrances either from the unpredictable forces of nature or the shenanigans of fellow human beings.

In this chapter, we examine the Yoruba concept of the social contract and how this influenced the constitution of authority, the enactment of law and what constitutes the legal, how order was maintained in indigenous Yoruba society, while making a comparison of this with the present world situation of social, economic and political flux, combined with the extreme insularities that modernity enshrines with its secularity. It is argued that traditional African religions were instruments designed for upholding the welfare of humans in society, especially as a means of obviating the disastrous tendencies innate to human beings toward rank egoism, possessive individualism and destructive materialism. It is suggested that, within the context of African traditional religions, so much of what passes for religion in the contemporary societies, especially as pursued by the two invading Arabian desert religions of Christianity and Islam, would be regarded as alien, nonreligious, against the will of the Supreme Being, and contrary to the wishes of the ancestors; this would have the consequence of consigning these so-called religions into the pantheon of the ungodly.

In carrying out the project of the chapter, we will examine the notion of "traditional" as "indigenous" religions in traditional African societies, even while recognizing that Christianity can be claimed to be "traditional" to Africa, given its long history in Africa before it went to Europe. We will also look at the notion of constituted authority, law and order in these traditional societies, with a view to understanding the ways in which the religious domain coalesces into the secular to ensure that the navigation of the two domains are without friction. This, it is argued, is responsible for the capacity of indigenous societies to draft all aspects of the intellectual, cultural, material and other resources into the project of ensuring that deviance, tyranny, destructive revolution, meaningless insurrection, atheism and other pathologies of individualism are reined in, thereby ensuring the efficacy of built-in checks and balances, which are a consequence of the ontic and epistemic beliefs of members of such societies.

In chapter 1 we examined ideas relating to the beginnings of civil society, especially challenging the orthodoxies of libertarianism and contractarianism, which puts the cart before the horse in order to justify the need for governance in society. In looking at traditional religions, constituted authority, law and order, it is pertinent to say up front that it is difficult to show how the relationship became forged between the constitution of secular authority and the ascription of divine or supernatural powers or legitimacy to the authority so constituted.

What is not in dispute is that the growth of human communities—from simple families, to hamlets, to villages, and to towns, cities and mega-cities—in terms of demographic numbers must have given rise to the need for mechanisms for maintaining peace, order, stability and cohesion. There would have been a need for defense-generating critical defence mass to curtail the capacity of strangers, enemies, wild animals, foreigners and unwelcome groups. This protection responsibility could only be effective if its locus was clearly recognizable, either in the form of being invested in one person acceptable to the community or in a group designated by the community. Speaking about the traditional era, it becomes significant to underscore the fact that during this epoch the frontiers of the sciences were limited and events and disasters were seen in terms of the interaction of the dual domains—the material and the metaphysical. The responsibility for keeping in check the supernatural forces must then be placed in the hands of one individual who shows an unusual capacity to interface with the supernatural realm. He or she was understood to have some channel of communication with the forces and is able to appease the gods when things went wrong. This was the genesis of rulership or monarchy (Oyeneye and Shoremi 1985: 14).

This form of historiography of rulership, akin to the biblical selection of the first king of Israel, when applied to traditional Yoruba society may be tenuous, but what is not contested is the fact that in the ruler so invested with authority there is a confluence of secular and nonsecular powers. The possession of supernatural powers portends secular influence.

But before exploring the relationship which existed between religion and governance in society, especially in indigenous or traditional Yoruba communities, one needs to address some basic issues of methodology adopted for this discussion. Our starting point then concerns the conceptual clarification mentioned above: What do we mean by "traditional" when we speak of Yoruba society? What constitutes "traditional" religion? What is "constituted authority" as provided in traditional Yoruba society, especially in terms of origin and legitimacy? To what extent is it practical to speak of a homogeneous Yoruba society, vis-à-vis governance and constitution of political apparatuses for governance?

These are questions which are germane to the discussion here, and which cannot be glossed without leaving the reader in the dark, especially as there exist ambiguities and some level of vagueness in the concepts we are treating here. Even while intuitively it is possible to understand the meanings of the concepts, yet for intellectual discourses the meanings cannot be taken for granted.

Discussions of religions are often vitiated on the grounds of the questions relating to what to understand by the concept. This is compounded when combined with the concept "traditional," as historical accounts of religion in terms of age may fail to pay attention to the domestication of religions even while externally originated. In this regard, Awolalu and Dopamu had said,

> When we speak of African Traditional Religion we mean the indigenous religion of the Africans. It is the religion that has been handed down from generation to generation by the forebears of the present generation of Africans. It is not a fossil religion (a thing of the past) but a religion that Africans today have made theirs by living it and practicing it. This is a religion that has no written literature, yet is "written" everywhere for those who care to see and read it. It is largely written in

> the people's myths and folktales, in their songs and dances, in their liturgies and shrines, in their proverbs and pithy sayings. It is a religion whose historical founder is neither known nor worshiped, it is a religion that has no zeal for membership drive, yet it offers persistent fascination for Africans young and old (Awolalu and Dopamu 1979:26).

There are a number of issues which need clarification in the foregoing annotation of the nature of traditional religions provided by Awolalu and Dopamu. In the first instance, it is curious that both erudite scholars were patronizing of African traditional religions to the point of being condescending in defending the religious traditions of Africans; thereby suggesting that these religions are not fossil religions. Every religion, it must be emphasized, derives from the tradition of some human community. That being the case, Christianity and Islam derive from the traditions of the Arabian or Middle Eastern desert peoples; by this token it would mean that these two religions are passed down by the forebears of these peoples of the Arabian or Middle Eastern desert region. If we look at the religions of peoples of other geographical parts of the world, such as Hinduism, Buddhism or Taoism, it would be curious to see any indigenous scholar descended from these traditions describe these religions in the same negative manner as the African scholars quoted above are wont to describe the religious traditions of their forebears.

In the second instance, the idea that the African religions are not fossil, that is not being "a thing of the past" simply and not further explaining what is meant leaves the vagueness of the idea unclarified for the reader. All religions that have any tradition at all meet this requirement of being traditional and consequently being passed from generation to generation, consisting of the ways in which humankind in various situations have related to the supernatural, the other-worldly and the mysterious, which are considered relevant for subsequent generations.

This explanation is essential because in the traditional and contemporary societies in which these religions are practiced, these religions have evolved with the development of the societies' various new structures, liturgies, ideologies, metaphysics and doctrines. Various knowledge systems about things and ideas in the universe have been gradually incorporated into the religions in such a way that problems or conflicts are prevented from threatening the internal capacity of the religions to survive; these have impacted the various planes of existence of practicing members of society—be these social, political, economic, cultural and/or artistic. The nonfossilization of traditional religions of Africa in general, and among the Yoruba people for example, is borne out by the popularity of the religions among Africans, even surviving the buffeting it has received from the invading Arabian Desert religions of Christianity and Islam which tolerate no competition for the minds of human beings wherever they travel, as well as surviving the harsh conditions to which they have been subjected when practitioners were hounded into slavery many thousands of miles away from their original homelands. This popularity, acceptance and access is often cloaked in various garbs, either in direct adherence to the religions, as in the Adimula Ifa congregation in Oyo city, or in apostasy, syncretism as in the various versions of the religion among African Diasporas in the United States of America, Brazil, Haiti and others, or the acceptance of more than one religion at a time, which may range from mere flirtation to total prostitution of religious beliefs or the entrenchment of traditional practices in the newly acquired and accepted religions. Evidence of these abound in the various revivalism sects and prosperity gospels preached by Aladura churches in Christianity and charismatic Alfas in Islam in Yoruba land, which does not prevent the leaders of both foreign religions from consulting the traditional religious leaders in the night in secret.

A third issue relates to the type of society in which traditional religions are effectively related to what constitutes constituted authority, law and order. While there are efforts in some societies to emplace secularism as religion, probably because of the need for the state to remain neutral where patronage of religion is critical to fairness, equity and justice, yet political functionaries make every effort to avow their religiosity and how this grounding is responsible for their moral turpitude and capacity for leadership. But when we look at traditional African religions and their relationship to the socioeconomic and political process, our intellectuals are defensive and evasive, probably as a consequence of centuries of attack by Eurocentric scholarship and colonialism which have consigned anything African to the garbage bin of barbarism, primitivism and irrationality. It is in this scenario that we wonder why Awolalu and Dopamu were genuflecting to the point of explaining that African traditional religions are not "fossil," even though in the same breath both of them speak of these religions having no "written literatures." Without engaging in nit-picking, one is baffled by the notion that African traditional religions have no written literatures, as if that precludes it from having valid literatures of their own. If both of them are ignorant of what constitute literature or the use which literature serves in society or the use to which they are put by members of society, this provides no excuse for denigrating African traditional religions.

Further, our critical look at Awolalu and Dopamu's position above is necessary because in the traditional societies in which traditional religions developed and were practiced, we find that such religions have evolved with the development and changes in such societies, embracing new ideas and rejecting ideas that were found to be invalid. Knowledge of realities and existence have been gradually incorporated into the religion and other aspects of life in such a way that problems or conflicts are not generated on the various planes of existence—social, political, economic, practical, aesthetic, cultural and more. The nonfossilization of traditional religions in Africa in general, and among the Yoruba people in particular, is a fact borne out by the popularity of this religion, to the extent that there is so much syncretism and adherence to more than one religious tradition in individuals, families and communities. This popularity and acceptability and access is often cloaked in various garbs, either in direct adherence to the religion, as in Adimula Ifa Congregation in Oyo township, or in apostasy or adherence to more than one religious belief mentioned above, which may range from mere flirtation to total prostitution of religious practices or the entrenchment of traditional liturgies and practices in the newly acquired religions. This is especially true of the domestication of Christianity as is found in the various Aladura sects and Muslim revivalist movements which are very popular on a continental scale.

Apart from these matters, it is important that religious heterogeneity of societies now demand that religion be relegated to secondary status, so that the sensitivities of persons are not affected by the state adopting specific religions, as against the various other religions embraced by other members of society. This is why we noted the effort in some societies to separate the domains of influence of religion from that of politics—even if hypocritically! Thus, many contemporary societies have, by and large, unsuccessfully affected some artificial severance of the relationship between religious, spiritual, supernatural planes from the secular and practical planes, often at grave costs, as the additional leverage that religion offers for social cohesion and stability is often lost in the zeal to be openly orthodox in the new faiths embraced. Whether such a severance is something of positive value to society or not is however a normative matter which is not explored here in detail, because it will not enhance our discussion of the ways in which traditional religions in Africa have been conscripted into the service of social engineering in Africa and elsewhere, but one thing seems certain, and that is the fact that as Africa and Africans search for pathways to development, careful attention to African heritage is important.

Finally, I would wish to disabuse our minds of the unwarranted tendency to think that religion permeated all aspects of life in indigenous African societies, especially if this is meant to negatively reflect a mental state different from what obtains in other parts of the world in similar historical epochs. This does not mean that the various African societies did not have religious beliefs which ground and underwrite the various behavioral and cultural practices of members of society. What we are to be mindful of is the false tendency to see religious explanatory models as totally displacing practical, commonsensical and scientific explanations of events, issues and ideas, as Idowu (1962) and Horton (1993), for example, would suggest without qualification, or as Sodipo (1972), Wiredu (1977) and others, with some philosophical caveat, would have us believe.

The need to examine the relationship between traditional religion, constituted authority, law and order in indigenous, traditional societies in a critical, reflective manner is derived from the tendency to see democracy as something that never existed on the African continent before the Europeans colonized virtually the whole of Africa; even more so there is a tendency to think that there is something wrong with outlining the need for religion to be part of governance structures of societies, especially in the era of globalization, democracy and information communications technological ingress into every facet of life in contemporary society. On the contrary, it is urged here that understanding the relationships between traditional religions and constitutional and governance structures in indigenous societies of Africa would constitute a useful foundation for the emplacement of democratic systems in African societies in the contemporary time. Furthermore, such a study will provide a useful moral for the concretization of the foundations of the future of African polities. The relationship between traditional religions and sociopolitical organization in traditional societies will clearly show how indigenous peoples have adapted to and adapted Christianity and Islam in the negotiation of governance practices in such societies. In this regard, Mbiti (1969) may be right in saying,

> Traditional religions are not preliminary for the individual, but for his community of which he is part. Chapters of African religions are written everywhere in the life of the community, and in traditional society there are no irreligious people. To be human is to belong to the whole community and to do so is participating in the beliefs, ceremonies, rituals and festivals of that community. A person cannot detach himself from the religion of his group, for to do so is to be severed from his roots, his foundation, his context of security, his kinship and the entire group of those who make him aware of his own existence (p. 2).

It is strange how scholars could have construed the above to be implicative of some profound psychological discoveries about the so-called traditional societies. Indeed, one cannot but be amused about the ascription of religion to only traditional societies, as if it is a form of dementia that is not replicated in various contemporary societies. One could substitute appropriate words, such as technology, democracy, music, sex and more for the words beliefs, ceremonies, rituals and festivals, in the above quotation in order to see the validity of the point being made here. Is it possible for any one of us to escape elements of information communications technologies and the bombardment of our spaces with diverse materials regardless of whether we are willing to partake or not? Does that make all contemporary humans believe in the same way in the values, necessities and importance of technologies? Can we then say that all contemporary humans are steeped in technology in the same way, even when they cannot avoid its impact? Or, take the pervasiveness of money in contemporary society—could it then be argued that all persons in all societies of the contemporary world are devoted to the god of money in the same way? What is done in the quotation is to gloss the diverse degrees of avocation of the religious traditions of the various societies by emphasizing only what is obviously the dominant events and attitudes of the dominant members of society, leaving out all the rooms for individuality and difference.

One could make a short digression here. In the days leading up to the 2011 Australian Lawn Tennis Open Tournament, one province of Australia, Queensland, was devastated by flooding of a magnitude not seen in recent memory. If this were to have happened in some African country, this would have totally overshadowed the tournament, to the point that within the reporting and casting of the tournament, references would have been made to the loss of life, suffering and peculiar conditions of the Africans, and the glitz and glamour of the tournament would have been eroded. In a way, it only shows how selective emphasis on aspects of life can be a disservice to the proper understanding of the totality of life—especially of the disempowered other.

Now, these are not points or questions intended to dilute the importance of the role of any of these human intellectual artefacts, even if we are not concerned to reflect on the utilitarian value of these artefacts to different groups within society. On the contrary, what we think should be distilled from the position of Mbiti is not the overly crude ascription of religiosity to traditional Africans but the validity of the factor of religious contributions to orderliness and enforcement of law in traditional societies in Africa, as well as in other societies of the world—whether traditional or modern. There is nothing in the African physiological or psychological make-up which differentiates her religiosity from those of groups from other climes, as is clear from how human beings have related to the unknown, whether it is scientific, religious, medical or otherwise. Hence, the overly religio-philic celebration of the supernatural in African societies is no more than a self-serving effort to entrench a partial modus of understanding of African societies.

There are three basic related concepts to be clarified here which, given proper analysis, will provide a good understanding of how religion is the handmaiden of thoughtful members of society in the process of ordering social relations. The first one is "authority," as presented in the phrase "constituted authority," especially how this relates to the functioning of social organizations and how it differs from other things which may be similar to it. One easy way to understand authority is to look at it as "legal power" or "right," where power here is derived from office or character or prestige a person or body holding power has; but this way of understanding authority is not very informative, as we need to understand "power" and "right" before this notion of authority can be usefully understood.

"Power" can be understood as an ability or capacity to perform an action. In this sense, it is a potentiality which may be actuated or realized by utilizing it; but it may not be utilized, hence remaining merely at the level of latency or dormancy. Legal power enables, it confers right and legally "en-capacitates" a person, group or body for the performance of an activity. Speaking of "power," John Beattie (1964) writes,

> In a very fundamental sense, power is human power, and human power is the ability to produce intended effects, that is, to carry out one's will oneself; on other people, or on things. Since it implies that the end which is brought about is foreseen, the notion of power is essentially teleological. When we say that a man has power we mean that he can do what he wants to do (p. 141).

What distinguishes power from authority, in contemporary political thought, is "legitimacy" or the concept of right which was secondarily introduced in our initial look at authority. Authority is far superior to power and carries more weight, as it is not simply a "right to" or "ability to" do something, but also the "right of" or an "ability of demanding obedience" (Raphael 2003: 66). Without the notion of authority, power will cease to have legitimacy: it will become naked force, and it will lack potency.

Looked at in another setting, we commonly conceive of causes as producing their effects because they have the power to do so. And we tend to think of this power as a kind of latent ability to alter the existing state of things, such as we are aware of in our own psychic experience (Beattie 1964: 140). If, however, the power has no backing, then it would be easily neutralized. The necessary backing for power is the attainment of legitimacy or right. This right constitutes an obligation on the side of others not to obstruct the discharge of power conferred, to obey the person exercising the power. This is why Beattie contrasts "power" with "authority" as follows: "Unlike power, authority implies right; a robber may have power to rob, but he has no authority to do so. And right is a concept, an idea; it may exist in people's minds. It is something that people acknowledge and it exists only in being acknowledged" (Beattie 1964: 141). Also, Bertrand Russell (1977) was considering authority when he said, "The power of the law will illustrate these complexities. The ultimate power of the law is the coercive power of the state. It is characteristic of civilized communities that direct physical coercion . . . (is) the prerogative of the state" (p. 26).

It is because authority is meaningful only if it has the means of ensuring compliance that the issue of legitimacy is so crucial to it. This is the view enunciated by Raphael. In all civilized societies the exercise of authority is seldom arbitrary. Even with the claims to freedoms and liberties that liberal democracies arrogate to members of society, we see that, post-9/11, it is a phenomenon of modern states that governments directly or indirectly control, or have access to, all facets of human life, and this has brought to the fore the need to attempt an assimilation of individual autonomy into state authority or, more accurately, to present state authority as an extension and expression of individual autonomy if individuals are to see themselves as members of a community, society or state in the right sense of it.

It is legitimacy when properly enjoyed by authority that confers proper constitution on governments. If authority is legitimate it means that it has been properly constituted and the people over whom the authority is exercised see that the authority is properly constituted or, if the authority got there by fiat—through the means of a "coup d'état," usurpation or by whatever other means—the authority will seek means or undertake such measures which will legitimize it and endear it to the populace that it governs. Constituted authority is therefore a person or group of persons within society who has been vested with the rights to make decisions, issue orders and apply sanctions in matters affecting themselves and other members of the society (Beattie 1964: 141).

Having looked at the first issue in the discussion here—that is, "constituted authority"—it becomes easier for us to examine the concept of "law." But we want our reader to bear in mind that what we do in this chapter is provide a context-dependent notion of law, because in other chapters in this book, the notion of law is explored in greater detail. Our discussion of law is simply to annotate its relation to the issues of traditional religion, constituted authority and order, in order to see how effective religion is as an instrument in the governance of African societies. In this context, it can be argued that whatever the constituted authority pronounces on matters affecting inter-personal relationships and whatever norms have been recognized formally as guiding or moderating such relationships can be regarded as law. As Beattie says, "When . . . we speak of 'law' and 'social sanction' we are thinking primarily of the behaviour of individual people and of the relationship between them, and of the social factors which by and large, ensure their conformity to the accepted rules of the society" (p. 140).

The implications of this notion of law may mislead if not qualified. In many communities where no defined authority is specifically constituted or apparent it may be supposed that laws will be absent, but no society can survive for any length of time without certain norms, rules and procedures being adhered to in the interest of members, as well as of the corporate survival of community as a whole. This is what Russell intended when he asserted that "society cannot exist without law and order (Russell 1977: 50), and also what Appadorai (1975: 59) referred to about the ordinary sense of law as a body of rules which govern human action.

That such a body of rules may not have originated by a constituted authority in the contemporary sense does not nullify their existence or utility. No matter the origin of such rules, they assist humankind in society to regulate behavior and are often found worthy of preservation, thereby turning them into legal codes over time, and being adopted by modern law-making bodies as part of the constitutions of the societies in which they exist. Thus, in any human community, there will develop set and customary ways of carrying on social activities, which save time and facilitate the avoidance of friction in society. They combine to form written and unwritten codes, enforced by various layers of social organizations, from family to community, from religious to political and other institutions, including the effects of pressure exerted by public opinion. Some of these customs may become so important for general social welfare that stronger measures that mere social influence or public opinion must be brought to bear on those members of society who act in violation of such accepted social standards. In such instances, according to Appadorai (1975),

> Whenever any community . . . undertakes to apply such pressure by fixing a penalty for violation, then such customs cease to be purely social but also political. They become the law of the land. They are virtually commands, ordering or prohibiting certain actions, disobedience to which involves a penalty inflicted by the government (i.e., the constituted authority) (p. 59).

It is usually the coercive powers of the constituted authority which distinguishes laws in states from rules of those other associations or organizations in society. Associations of communities do not have absolute powers of coercion (which covers life and death) which states have and exercise through its organs (Raphael 2003: 32). The complications which civil disobedience, conscientious objection, rule departures, radical protest, etc., pose to such powers and laws are reflections both of the legitimacy of governments, the rightness or justness of laws that are passed by the governments and the fairness or sustainability of the punishments imposed. These are issues examined in other chapters. For our purpose here, we simply wish to indicate the relationship between authority, law and order and traditional religions. This means that we have to take a look now at the third leg of the conceptual matters we indicated earlier—namely, order.

Usually the notion of "order" has always been tied up with that of law; hence the common reference to law and order. This is not accidental. Though law can be separated and discussed, this is rarely the case with order, because order depends on the validity, legitimacy and fairness of the prescriptions of the law. The dictates of the legal codes often determine the norms of behavior and the standards of action in public spaces, especially when these indicate consequences for reward or punishment, for approbation or reprobation, and for that matter when social importance is ascribed to human interaction as a way of laying precedence for peaceful sustenance of order and encouragement of younger ones to strengthen their commitment to community welfare rather than crass individualist emphasis on happiness.

To say of a society that it is orderly is to say that members of such a society recognize and abide by the norms, ethos and conventions of behavior and interaction prevalent in such a society. It suggests a state in which the laws governing interpersonal relationships are observed. On the other hand, if a society is disorderly, then members are not observant of the rules of behavior prescribed, or where they recognize the existence of the rules, they choose, for one reason or the other, to act against the prescription of these rules; and such choices could be on moral, conscientious and principled grounds as noted earlier, so as to force the society to re-evaluate the fundamental ethical and legal principles that underwrite the norms, or they may choose to disobey on selfish grounds if they are sure that the state/society is too weak to enforce the rules that it has in place to ensure good, peaceful and orderly coexistence of members of society. This last scenario is a harbinger of a failed state or state in crises of governance, with tendencies toward social disintegration rather than cohesiveness.

This is where the other component of orderliness of society becomes singularly relevant, as it is the means by which one can easily measure the degree to which constituted authority and the laws emanating from the authority is regarded as legitimate and respected on moral grounds. As it is generally recognized, the reason why laws are necessary is to moderate the conflicts of interest that arise between individuals on personal levels and between individuals and society at the corporate level. While it could be suggested that laws often conflict with individual inclinations and benefits, understood minimally, and that when this happens, the tendency is for individuals (at least, most individuals) to seek means of avoiding (if possible) unpleasant situations or things and consequences of their choices (if they can avoid such consequences). It devolves on society to use its organs to ensure compliance with the laws and norms. Hence the institution of law enforcement agencies have become formalized and empowered through legislation.

Against the background of these minimal conceptual clarifications we may see the relationship between traditional religions in Africa and constituted authority, law and order; this with a clear understanding that apart from simple social factors members of society often resort to various other means to validate the need for respect for authority and the maintenance of law and order. It is in this regard, I suggest, that the deployment of religion becomes relevant in the interest of law and order in society, so as to secure a frictionless interpersonal and communal existence in society, or at least to minimise such friction where they may arise.

Wande Abimbola, one of the foremost exponents of Yoruba culture and religion, identified the structure of authority among the Yoruba people in discussing "The Yoruba Concept of Human Personality." His identification is very useful for our purpose here, even though his concern was other than how religion affects authority, law and order as such. He says one can therefore represent the hierarchical structure of authority on the two planes of existence as follows: Olodumare (Almighty God), Orisa (Divinities), Orun (the realm of the spiritual or heavenly—good and bad places for the departed), Oku Orun (Ancestors), and Oba (King and his chiefs), Baale (Village and Town heads), Baale (Household Heads), Aye (Earth or the real of the material), Agba (Elders) and Omode (Children).

The relationship between the two planes of existence noted above by Abimbola is a very close one, and there is no absolute separation of one from the other. In indigenous Yoruba society (as in most civilized societies), as is clear from the above, there is a clear hierarchy of authority; as a consequence, authority usually does not lie with children or the young, no matter how precocious they may be, and it is an aberration for children to wield and exercise authority in any community. But there are clear exceptions, where, for example, a young person may be empowered by the higher authorities to carry out certain functions, or to exercise certain powers specifically on behalf of the deities or spirits or ancestors. The respect the children receive is then a consequence of the respect that is associated with the powers of which the children are surrogates. This is not in any way suggesting that children do not have respect or value in Yoruba society, rather, it is a function of the structure of order and devolution of authority that determine who constitutes authority and who can exercise power with legitimacy in society.

If, on the other hand, children were to willy-nilly exercise authority and power, it will be evidence of disorderliness of the society, and it will show that the community in which that occurs has no responsible adult who can exercise leadership functions; while precocity is valued in kids, as they will foster growth in intellect and knowledge in the community, if such children fail to recognize their position and respect elders, then it becomes a serious problem that may threaten the orderliness that is valued by members of society. Combined with the instances we have mentioned in the last paragraph, there are also occasions when young people have to perform traditional ritual functions at the death of their parents in virtue of heredity. Also it should be mentioned that our discussion to this point has been gender neutral, because in Yoruba society there is no reason why whatever applies generally to male may not apply to female; even though there are gender roles proscribing functions across gender lines, without exhibiting bias or devaluation of any gender worth—there are certain things that only males are biologically suited for doing such a pregnancy, which belie the whole issue of alternative life-style choices in sexual orientation.

Coming back to the issue of authority and exercise of power by children, and the fact that children are supposed to yield to adult supervision, until they become adults—physiologically and mentally (which combine to build character through acceptance of instruction and moral up-bringing)—may have been responsible for Mbiti's errant suggestion that the elder in the typical African village does not offend those who are younger or under him, and that parents do not offend against their children (Mbiti 1969: 208). The fact that there is a hierarchy of authority does not in any way mean that children have no rights or that those rights can be infringed upon without any repercussion. Even if children cannot redress infringement of their rights themselves, other members of society take steps to redress such abuse of the rights and to restore justice to the aggrieved. This applies to all members of society, and the fact that a person, male or female, young or old, rich or poor, cannot protect herself or himself from infractions of rights does not mean that they have no rights, because society takes steps to ensure that the moral and social equilibrium is maintained. And it is worth noting in this regard that in Yoruba society, members have a concept of intrinsic rightness and wrongness, regardless of praise and reward, commendation, blame and punishment. It is this which underlines the mistake in the statement by Mbiti that "never or rarely does a person or being of higher status do what constitutes an offense against a person of a lower status (for) what is considered evil or offensive (generates) from a lower level to a higher level" (p. 208, parentheses added for clarity).

Oluwole (1984: 14–15) has attempted to elucidate the humanistic aspects and foundations of morality in Yoruba ethics. This effort shows that Mbiti's strange understanding of morality cannot be generalized to all African cultures. For a society where women, the children and the weak have no rights at all would be a most primitive and uncivilized one, and it would not have survived to bring about cultures or civilizations. One would wonder what type of preparation the young were being given to become responsible members of society. And such a society would have difficulty maintaining law and order. To say that children are naturally placed at the lower rung of the responsibility scale is not to suggest that they are any less human, any less deserving of respect as human beings, it simply means that they are recognized as juvenile and in need of facilitation so that they can take their rightful positions when they become adult members of society.

The adults and elders (agba) in the communities are the guardians of the youth and ensure community order, and for this reason it is said, *agba ko si ni ilu, ilu baje, baale ile ku, ile d'ahoro*. There are structures for ensuring the welfare of members of society. This is a task that is naturally placed upon them in virtue of membership of their communities, and no contests are needed as the age-grade system adequately maps the categories to which each member of society belongs—often in order of age, gender, and role in society.

Each household constitutes a unit within a community. In most instances in many African communities, patriarchy is embraced and males head households. This is why the Baale or household head is the father or husband in the home. But when households are bonded by filial relationship, then the eldest male descendant of the founder of the household is the head. This is recognized automatically without this leading to autocracy, as the head knows that he is there in virtue of ancestry and he has responsibility to be upright in all his dealings with the families in the group of households he heads. Consultation is the process by which consent and allegiance is maintained.

However, when numerous households or groups of households come together to form a village or a town, then there arises the need for a formal instance of a leader. In most cases the leader emerges from the household that is the founder of the village or town. The title of the village leader or head is Baale, while that of the town or city is Oba. When growth takes place and the households multiply, then the selection process may become a bit complicated, as it may not be very obvious which among the many individual households laying claims to leadership on account of descending from the same founder should be preferred or should hold sway under the rotation system that is adopted to ensure fairness. This is where here is need for the intervention of spiritual leaders and the divination system. And no positions are filled without consultation of Ifa, the divinity of wisdom in Yoruba society, through the Babalawo—literally translated as the father who holds the secrets of knowledge and future. When the consultation has been properly done, the choice is then acceptable to the gods and to Olodumare, making for legitimacy.

As has been shown here, the determination of constituted authority and the process of identifying who wields power have to receive the sanction of Ifa, even while it is clearly a matter of heredity and descent from the original ancestral founder of the community. This shows the approval of Olorun Olodumare, the Supreme Being among the Yoruba people, backed by the divinities, the ancestors and the numerous spirits which inhabit the unseen world of the supernatural forces. Thus, the constituted authority is derived from a pre-established and accepted tradition. The hierarchy and cooperation is ordained and defended through the traditions of the people, and recourse is often made for the perpetual confirmation of, and the confidence in, this authority through the perennial consultation of Ifa. As Aderibigbe has indicated, the cohesion of the kingdom of Oyo was based upon the homogeneity of origin as well as on a religion which acknowledge a Supreme Being high and in the heavens but too exalted to be approached directly by human beings (a condition which necessitated the intervention of minor gods or orisa), and also that the Oyo authority made use of the time-honored imperial expedient of extolling the powers and divinity of the emperor on state occasions.

Since the authority is sanctioned by powers supposedly beyond human control, it follows that the control exercised by members of society on such authority is limited in scope. This is particularly so if all the tiers of government, that is from the kings to the chiefs, from the Baales to the Baales, as well as the generality of the population, are in agreement concerning the laws that are enacted by them or on courses of action sanctioned for the benefit of society, then there is little chance of disagreement, disobedience or insurrection by those who may not agree with the laws or regulations. But we must not forget that even when it is said that the kings own the land or are next to the divinities, there are checks and balances on the powers they wield and exercise. And the leaders seldom exercise any powers without consultation and consensus.

In this regard, it is clear that in the Yoruba sociopolitical system it shows how power must be exercised in conformity with tradition and when there is excess or transgressions on the part of the leaders and kings, processes are set in motion to curb, curtail and strip such persons of the legitimacy they enjoy in virtue of the recognition by society; apart from this, when the Obas cannot enforce their rule over the community, then it is obvious that the Oba has lost legitimacy. Examples of this are found in Yoruba history as well as in contemporary instances, such as in the case of Olagbegi of Owo and the Deji of Akure—both Obas were made to abdicate their thrones because of misdemeanors and infractions of the cultures and traditions of their kingdoms.

In the pre-colonial era in Yoruba society, it was quite easy to maintain law and order, because each adult member of society and household have a high sense of moral existence and respect for constituted authority, law and order and treated with utter contempt any action, behavior or activity that would undermine this social cohesion. This is the reason why the kinds of individualist angst that led to the development of existentialism in Europe was somewhat absent in many traditional African societies. This is not suggesting that there are no challenges to personhood, identity and choices, especially moral choices. But because members of society are socialized to understand that as members of society, their existence and accomplishment of their goals cannot be separated from the overall good health of society, it thereby minimizes the negative aspects of modernism without compromising the humanity of the individual (Bewaji 2004b).

There are various categories of infractions against the law and commensurate punishment or redress that are provided. Perhaps it is because members of society take extra care to be law-abiding that life was safe and free in Yoruba society. Law breaking is not an individual thing; it is equally a reflection of/on the family of the law-breaker, her household, community, village, town and lineage from which the individual comes and was raised. The shamefulness of such tendencies is reflected in the treatment of such criminals by way of sanctions and ostracism.

Given the consciousness of what is right and what is wrong, and discrimination by members of society against aberrant members of society, the leaders, the chiefs and the Obas have an easy task administering law and order in society. However, their tasks of leading the society are further simplified because of the consciousness of two other components of social engineering. The first one is the consciousness of the presence of supernatural watchdogs of the interest of the society—namely the ancestors, the spirits, the gods and above all, Olodumare, who does not brook any form of criminality. Thus, any action that goes against the dictates of the constituted authority is feared; as the supernatural forces are always near to reckon such acts against the offenders. The second is the consciousness of the certainty of reprimand and punishment, which is often serious and severe; hence the deliberate effort to ensure that one is never caught on the wrong side of the law, even when there is no one to witness the infraction or to hold one accountable.

Now the combination of the secular maintenance of law and order under the body of the unwritten constitution and the reinforcement by the supernatural forces ensure that there is obedience of the constituted authority and a proper preservation of law and order. Ifa is always consulted when abnormal occurrences take place in society, but it is supposed that such occurrences must have causes deriving from the behavior of members of society or a function of the displeasure of supernatural forces arising from actions or inactions of members of society in upholding the rules, regulations and laws of society. Such infractions must be redressed in order to bring back order and social balance in the society.

What is obvious from the foregoing is an apparent coalescence of the secular and the supernatural forces to ensure that constituted authority, law and order are observed and obeyed in Yoruba society. The importance of religion, however, has been overstated by Idowu, especially when he stated that the real keynote of the life of the Yoruba is neither in their noble ancestry nor in the past deeds of their heroes. The keynote of their life is their religion. In all things, they are religious. Religion forms the foundation and the all-governing principle of life for time and further that Orisha-nla is the supreme owner of Kabiyesi, His (royal) Majesty here on earth.

The gratuitousness of this superficial analysis of Yoruba life is derived from a need to over-reach in search for means of spreading the foreign religion of Christianity and infusing religion into all aspects of life by emphasizing the cementing function of religion when it comes to making for cohesive social existence and explanation of extra-ordinary events, as if Yoruba people are any different from human beings from other parts of the world—in the sense of searching for answers to problems and propounding supernatural causes for those that happen to be beyond their practical comprehension. Hence, when Yoruba proclaim that the first king, Oduduwa, descended directly from the divinities sent by Olodumare to create the earth, they also provide a balance suggesting that when we call on the dead at a distance, it is a hidden living person who answers, and that when a masquerade is pursuing you to flog you, you must continue to run, because as the living person is tiring, so also is the ancestor tiring (Bewaji 2003). Thus, when Abimbola says that the major Yoruba kings are believed to be directly descended from Oduduwa, the great mythical ancestor of the Yoruba, he was reflecting the fundamental historical values which Yoruba people place on their king, even though such kings were made by humans. They therefore have divine authority. The Oba (king) is assisted by a paraphernalia of town and village heads known as Baale. The Baale takes decisions with the approval of household adults who are known as Agba. In this hierarchical order, children and young people occupy the lowest position. They have no authority whatsoever, and if they die before they become adults they cannot be come ancestors.

So what is clear from the foregoing is that there is an obvious support system designed by Yoruba people for the sustenance of law and order in society. As a consequence of this relationship, each individual sees the law as designed for his/her protection and hence they subscribe to the dictates of the law. No single Oba or village head would wish to preside over an ungovernable community or over the liquidation of the community, because such events are recorded for posterity as having been brought about by the activities of recalcitrant persons in society. Also important is the fact that members of the ruling groups are aware of the fact that it is through the orderliness of society that the ruler benefits.

Given the above, one may ask the question how crime management is conducted in Yoruba society. As we noted earlier, there are various categories of crime, but some are regarded as ordinary, while others are serious. The ordinary crimes could be related to controlling fighting, theft, lying, and rumor-mongering. These may be regarded as civil matters, while others are more serious and could affect the stability and survival of society itself.

With regard to those crimes which do not threaten the existence of society, they may be dealt with at the family level, village level, or town level. Persons found guilty of such crimes are usually punished with the imposition of fines or being forced to labor on community projects or those of their victims in reparation/restitution for the loss caused.

However, in the case of the more serious crimes, these must be treated with seriousness because they threaten the existence of society if uncurbed. As we noted earlier they may bring about anarchy and insurrection in society. We will mention some of these again, and emphasize the fact that they are against the community and the traditions of the society as a whole. They include armed robbery, witchcraft, bad or evil magic, arson, murder, deviance, atheism, tyranny, revolution, insurrection and more. Because of the nature of these crimes, it is necessary to bring in the gods either as witnesses of the expiation of the infractions and the punishment meted out, or as the medium by which the aggrieved could seek redress to his/her satisfaction.

In extreme cases, if the matter is considered to be such that it threatens the existence of the society, the offender is excommunicated from the community, while the family from which he/she came is required to perform sacrifices to the appropriate ancestors and divinities in order to restore the balance that was destabilized. And members of the society continue to view the action as most odious to the living and the dead, as well as to Olodumare, believing that there is a kind of direct connection between the negative things that happen in the society and the deeds.

The question may now arise as to the moral, social, political relationships between traditional religions, constituted authority, law and order in contemporary society—say Nigeria. While there is the drum of secularism and modernism being beaten all around the world and the emphasis is on democracy, it must be recognized that all societies of the world still relate to their traditional institutions and cultures as the foundations underwriting the survival of society. In this regard, a basic principle that is underlined here is that Yoruba culture, religions and indigenous institutions served as the foundations for law and order, arising from the recognition of their capacity as the groundswell of the legitimacy of the authorities that governed the society. Contemporary situations where foreign religions, which derive from foreign cultures, are now being imposed on the grounds of law and order may be responsible for the dysfunctional legal systems that fail to conduce to good order and which lead social dissonance in Nigeria and other African societies today.

The overall implication of the analysis we have attempted here is that there is a need to see in traditional religions, cultures, beliefs and practices of indigenous societies the resources which constitute critical factors in providing the cementing factors for law, order and good governance in society. While on the face of it, religion may be seen as being concerned with the supersensible order, deriving from mystical forces and dependent on metaphysical explanations for validity, clearly the leadership of the Yoruba society were never in doubt that human beings contribute in no small measure to the continued survival of the religions, and that the religions contribute immensely to the survival of society. Without the mutual benefit derived by/from religion by members of society and the religion, there is no doubt that the utilitarian value of the religion will vanish and the religion itself will be threatened with death. This is why it is an imperative that one's religion must serve one's interest or leave one alone—as in the saying, *orisa bo o le gbe mi, se mi bo o se ba mi*! Some of these issues are further discussed in other parts of this book, showing how it is necessary to ground the well-being of African societies in the indigenous knowledge systems and consciousness of the peoples, otherwise courting lawlessness and disorderliness, as we see in various aspects of life in Africa today.

EIGHT

Social Ethics, Law and Development

What we do in this chapter is to characterize and elaborate the reality of, and the warrant for, the incipient feeling of despondency that has engulfed the academic branch of philosophy called ethics or moral philosophy in recent time, driving ethical philosophers from normative and prescriptive philosophizing to, first, critical, analytical and speculative ethics and, second, into the region of applied and meta-ethical philosophizing in the West, thereby making informed and intellectual on-lookers suspicious and disinterested in the labors of moral philosophers, as neither traditional ethics nor its new off-spring, applied ethics, have transcended the defects of a puerile theoria and praxis, indeed a defective intellectual practice. This is the feeling that ethics and moral philosophy—whether in its traditional form or in its specialized, applied form—is a worthless exercise in self-delusion on the part of scholars who indulge in them, as centuries of Western scholarship in these directions have not succeeded in equipping humanity, in the West and in those societies that have decided to ape the West, with the mental and intellectual facility to be morally upright human beings, or even to try out, in practice, some of the intellectual results of such philosophers, as one would, for example, try out the results of critical thinking in areas such as the legal profession and philosophy with children, economic principles in real-life situations, even if it may not often lead to success.

In fact, the inability of Western philosophers to determine the purview of ethics and its nature constitute an indictment of their prevarication while social order and interpersonal trust disintegrates. I argue that the fate that has befallen ethics as an academic discipline in the West is not an accident. It is a necessary development or progression. I identify the separation of moral theory from moral practice, on the one hand, and on the other, the professionalistic insulation of the philosophical enterprise as culprits responsible for the sorry pass to which ethics and moral philosophy has found itself in.

I conclude, *salva analycitatem*, pace Quine, by comparing Western and African ethical and moral practical and intellectual perspectives, showing that the Western separation of reality, truth, fact and purpose from the ethical foundations of society constitutes the creeping foundation of the decadence being experienced in Western society and similarly, African societies where Western academic and intellectual moral or ethical philosophical traditions of an insulated discourse, separated from real-life experiences of human beings from whom the problems are meaningful, have been most effectively embraced, and are showing similar dissipation of the cohesive cements of social fabric. In this regard, the chapter concludes with a moral that the issue of intellectual relevance is not simply creating highfalutin dialogues about concepts and ideas, rather that it is high time that Western philosophers wake up to their responsibility to humanity by making their discourses realistic and applicable to members of the societies they inhabit.

The ominous words of Peter Singer (1986), introducing his anthology, *Applied Ethics*, is significant in many respects and could be regarded as a very good entrée to a discussion of the checkered history of ethics and moral philosophy in the West. Let me take the liberty of quoting these words here for perspective. He says, just about a decade and a half ago, that, "to an observer of moral philosophy in the twentieth century, the most striking development of the past twenty years would not be any advancement in our theoretical understanding of the subject, nor would it be the acceptance of any particular ideas about right and wrong. It would, rather, be the revival of an entire department of the subject: applied ethics" (p. 1).

While the developments of the last thirty-five or so years in the area of applied ethics have been nominally significant, one wonders why this intellectual development has not translated into better practice or, better still, into morally informed actions, decisions, beliefs, and dispositions to behave. It may be instructive to suggest that the recent preoccupation with applied ethics that Singer sees as probably a welcome "striking development" is no accident. First is the impatience with the direction that philosophy took in the West in the preceding almost three quarters of the twentieth century before Singer wrote the quoted words, with its travails in positivism, linguistic analytic hairsplitting, and recursive flirtations with amoralism, nihilism and agnosticism. Second is the increasing and increased professionalization of the philosophical enterprise, at once isolating and insulating the issues of discourse from reality and from life experiences of humans and equally succeeding in devising an insular dialogue and correspondence among a distracted and irrelevant membership of an academe in danger of ceding their places to a festering and festooning mercantilism and militialism and fascism of various genres unless they succeed in recreating themselves and become "relevant" to something. And third, but not the least, is the so-called reflexivity of the philosophical predilection toward self-appraisal, self-critique and introspective disciplinary assessment. The American Philosophical Association's disclaimer about holding any employment promises to new entrants into the philosophical discipline in the latter part of the last century is instructive in this respect.

Bernard Williams (1972) is equally critical of the emptiness of contemporary moral philosophy of the analytical and linguistic type. According to him, contemporary moral philosophy has found an original way of being boring, which is by not discussing moral issues at all. Or, rather, it is not so much that a style of moral philosophy has been evolved which cuts the connection with moral issues altogether—that, if it were possible, would have the interest of being remarkable; but the desire to reduce revealed moral commitment to a minimum and to use moral arguments in the role of being uncontentiously illustrative leaves an impression that all the important issues are off the page, somewhere, and that great caution and imagination have been used in letting tiny corners of them appear (p. 10).

While he struggled to remedy the situation by being relevant to immediate moral issues of society, it is still clear that, as an introduction to an insulated discourse, his efforts were destined for little influence on contemporary moral philosophy. This was not an unpredictable fate, as, in the first place, try as he did, his effort operated within the shackles of the tradition that he so ably lamented, and, in the second place, his audacity was encumbered by the limitations of thousands of years of philosophical distancing from the society that produced it. As a consequence, a reading of Williams (even his chapter of "What is morality about"), like a reading of many (if not all) other contemporary moral philosophy texts (including J. L. Mackie's 1977 *Ethics—Inventing Right and Wrong*) bears little or no concrete behavioral guides for interested members of Western society.

His and Mackie's failed, but gallant, efforts fall in the same category as that of Kurt Baier and Kai Nelson. These are moral philosophers who felt that the distance between Western ethical philosophizing and life was too large, and used a combination of intuitive and common sense arguments, after the manner of G. E. Moore before them, to salvage the parlous situation. The effort did not yield desired results mainly because Western academic philosophical tradition has been too far gone in the direction of philosophical disorientation. Consequently, interest shifted into more practical and more pressing new diversions. This is what accounts for the novelty of Peter Singer's *Applied Ethics* and Gary Percesepe's anthology in applied ethics (1995), *Introduction to Ethics—Personal and Social Responsibility in a Diverse World.* The efforts in this new direction have somehow been overshadowed by the importance of what R. M. Hare (1952) has represented in contemporary moral philosophy. Hare has no illusion about his task, and could not imagine how others could have been misled into other ideas of their task. For him, "Ethics, as I conceive it, is the logical study of the language of morals" (p. v).

Thus, applied ethics, like applied mathematics, applied physics, applied chemistry and applied religion—liberation theology!—and many other applied this and that have a novelty about them, an intrigue and a certain scientific panache that one immediately expects something new and different. In the case of the many other "applieds," there probably is an intrinsic justification for their epithet as, in actual fact; they seem to be applying the epistemic, methodological, analytical and theoretical gains of their progeny to new issues and problems, thereby facilitating the solution of wide ranges of theoretical and practical problems. While in the case of ethics the fact that there are no similarly decided epistemic, methodological, analytical and theoretical gains, that no issues are settled regarding even the subject-matter of what is to be applied itself, constitute a preliminary setback.

Before the twentieth century, thinkers have followed different intellectual inclinations in deciding the question what ethics itself is all about. Probably the move away from the Socratic practice of not being directly concerned with the question "What is ethics?" but rather with, for example, "What is virtue?" "What is justice?" "What is duty?" "What is happiness?" and more, is largely responsible for the state of ethical philosophy in the West today. When Socrates and his contemporaries perused the questions mentioned above, his interest was not purely academic as the interest of his masters before him were not, but he and his society were concerned with how we (humans) should actually live in society and, ultimately, his life was an example of how he believed a moral life should be lived. But once we started the disciplinary hiatus about "what is ethics?" leading off into meta-ethical considerations, coming back to reconnect with the core concerns of the philosophical discussions of ethics and morality in society became a difficulty. In fact, some would argue that the central issue and the greatest challenge in moral philosophy consist in determining the purview of ethics as a discipline.

The inability of moral philosophers to agree on the subject matter of their discourse is, however, not strange. Some have indicated that ethics is concerned with answering the questions relating to whether certain actions are morally permitted, forbidden or obligatory. According to Alston and Brandt (1974), for example,

> "Ethics" is basically concerned with investigating the grounds or basis for answering such questions. The philosopher's job is to find some defensible general principles that can be applied to any particular situations that arise, general principles that will indicate what we need to determine about the particular situation in order to answer the specific questions that arise there (pp. 122–23).

He and other philosophers were not sure, however, which was more fundamental, whether it was normative ethics in the sense stated above, or meta-ethics, in the sense of "the interpretation of ethical terms and judgements, and with the methodology of normative ethics, i.e., with how one can rationally assess ethical judgements" (p. 123).

Their dilemma may be better understood as a necessary consequence of the heritage of Western scholarship—the pull and push between the need for a commitment to either of the normative tradition and the analytic tradition, creating an intellectual soul troubled incessantly by the challenge of the noncognitivism as represented by mainstream logical positivism (Ayer 1936).

We may observe here, in order to get to immediate grips with the primary issue involved, that the question "What is ethics?" is very similar to the question "What is morality?" but different from the related question "What is ethical?" or "What is moral?" The last is an ambiguous question which could be asking for a universal but unrealistic determination of what is right, good, appropriate, acceptable, virtuous, edifying, pleasing, wanted, etc., in general, while at the same time, it could be a context-specific request for a guide as to what is right, good, appropriate, acceptable, etc. in this or that particular situation of decision making and action or expectation of action by self and others.

To answer the first part of this question, it could be said that what is moral or ethical is what God ordains (Divine Law approach), what society approves (culture, norms, tradition and conventions as the basis of morality), what our reason dictates (variants of deontologism, intuitionism and moral point of view cum common sense approach), what brings pleasure (hedonistic approach), what conduces to our happiness or the happiness of others (versions of eudemonia, altruism, utilitarianism and teleologism), doing to others what one would wish others to do to oneself (Golden Rule and/or categorical imperative), and more. The theories that these positions have spurned will be mentioned presently, but for now, we will simply note these as some of the historical answers in Western philosophical scholarship to the question we have raised above, but it is useful to bear in mind that even categorizing all the responses neatly has not been an easy task. In this regard, I will be using two categories, one most recent category by Almeder, which is very useful but inexhaustive, and another one which consists of my own attempt to synthesize Western and non-Western answers to the question raised.

Robert Almeder (2000), in *Human Happiness and Morality*, one of the most serious recent contributions to moral philosophy, annotates eight major ethical traditions in Western philosophical scholarship. These are ethical egoism, egoistic hedonism, act utilitarianism, rule utilitarianism, ethical relativism, Kantianism, ethical intuitionism and theologism (p. 25). Clearly his categories, useful guides as they are for further discussion, are not exhaustive, as they do not encompass responses by altruists or amoralists.

In virtually all societies various justifications and grounds have been advanced to support different types of moral prescriptions and values. These grounds can be (and have been) systematized into ethical arguments and theories. Some of the most popular ethical theories (or moral theories) in Western philosophical scholarship are *ethical relativism* which suggests that moral rightness or wrongness vary from society to society, from context to context (contextualism) and from culture to culture, and this theory has often been derived from cultural relativism. This derivation is not necessary though, as we should be able to separate cultural differences from ethical principles—difficult though this may be! Ethical Subjectivism is a version of ethical relativism which makes individual attitude the determinant of right and wrong, as no objective moral standards are acknowledged by the subjectivist: forms of ethical subjectivism have been emotivism, egoism, amoralism and versions of intuitionism. Another theory is Divine Command Theory, the view that God has ordained behavioral laws for persons and that the Ten Commandments or the Golden Rule of the Sermon on the Mount found in the Holy Bible (or equivalents found in other similar scriptures) is the basic law that should govern human interaction and relationships. A version of this is Natural Law theory that nature ordains right and wrong and humans only discern them. We may simply mention other theories for notice, as our argument does not stand or fall as a consequence of proper or improper annotation of all the Western ethical theories; these are various versions of Consequentialism—Psychological Egoism, Ethical Egoism, Utilitarianism—on the one hand, and, on the other hand, various versions of Nonconsequentialism—Categorical Imperative, and the Moral Point of View arising from rationality of persons.

In a serious sense, the answers identified above are clear, indirect attempts to understand moral behavior in society, that is, to identify how the question "What is moral?" has been answered by members of society, in spite of disclaimers to the contrary by ethical philosophers as they struggle to avoid being embroiled in the exigencies of human daily existence. Thus, what seems to be an analysis is actually a post mortem of ethical ideas that govern behavior. This has the consequence of helping us to understand morality in a sense, but it leaves to the person or group the onerous task of determining how to arrive at the specifications implied in these answers as a proper guide to his/her or group for action. On the one hand, if one finds oneself in positions or situations where there is a need to determine what is moral, one could look at the various aspects of each context, situation first, and second examine the implications or consequences of acting one way or the other for self and for others, and, on the basis of these considerations, determine what is the best course of action to undertake. This is the question "How do I determine which is the right thing to do?" in this situation. But this is not the same question as "What makes right acts right and wrong acts wrong?" If we conflate these two questions, we may be misled into searching in the wrong direction for speculative answers to practical questions.

On the other hand, when the question, "What is morality?" is asked, we get a feeling that more than merely determining what to do in a specific situation is required. More, in the sense of a need to not only identify what is right, good, duty, obligatory, required, etc., but also in the sense of a need to analyze the moral ideas, statements and beliefs of self, people, society and human actors and also determine the grounds, the foundations, the origins and the bases of the judgments we make on them, the principles and theories we use to establish them, and their implications for our beliefs and actions as rational beings. This last activity has been regarded in some quarters (especially, the analytic tradition of English language philosophy championed by R. M. Hare) as the primary object of study of the academic branch of philosophy called *ethics* or *moral philosophy*. In this approach, the ethical philosopher abdicates the responsibility to get involved for both escapist and prudential reasons—escapist as the philosopher claims not to have any special means of helping his society determine what is the proper and moral thing to do in circumstances of their daily existence, and would not want to be expected to be a better human being on account of being a moral philosopher, hence insisting prudentially that he/she was merely being realistically modest out of necessity, because his/her vocation does not confer on him/her a divine spectator status.

Even this understanding of morality is not incapable, if care is not taken, of being confused with another sense, where it could be asked "What is the morality of a group or society?" This is the sense in which there is a request for what are the moral beliefs of a person or group or society. This is a descriptive sense of morality—more in the area of moral anthropology than in the area of critical ethics or, for that matter, moral philosophy. It must be indicated that as this appears unseemly on the face of it, it is an exercise not totally without merit, especially when there is need to understand the logic of the behavior of a person, group or society, and on the basis of such understanding develop a predictive capacity, a cooperative or interactive foundation and an analytic premise for further study.

Morality, or ethics, in the most interesting sense, is not simply analytic, that is, conceptual analysis for purely intellectual exposition of meanings of ethical terms, and as such merely an academic exercise, but normative and prescriptive. It seeks to determine what actions are right, why they are right and enjoin people in similar existential, sociological, physiological and psychological circumstances to so act, as they prescribe norms or rules of action and forms of behavior in claiming to determine right, as against wrong, barring other conditions that may have overriding values which serve to attenuate the rightness of the action or mode of behavior prescribed originally by morality or ethics.

While the idea expressed here may give the impression that we are concerned with the general question "Why are right acts right?" that is, "What property does right acts have which wrong acts fail to have?" this type of interpretation will only be partially right. The position that comes out clearly, which makes the secondary questions formulated above difficult to answer, arise from the ambiguity of the question. The question is general and particular—general in the simple sense that it requests for the common feature of all right acts, and particular in the sense that no such universal "righting" feature can be discovered which then becomes applicable to all actions of the same genre. We note this problem in order to indicate the mutability of simple questions and the care that must be taken in order not to think that while one is answering one implied question that the other implied question has been answered. Repetitive as some of the things we have said above may appear, it would seem necessary in order that the pitfalls they represent be avoided in the same manner in which many other ethical traditions have avoided the unnecessary obfuscation that logic-chopping and concept analysis have entailed.

In this regard, we seriously ask the follow-up question: Why do we need norms or moral rules or regulations for action? This is a question to which we (and to which people in various societies) can (and have) easily give (given) intuitive answers: that norms are necessary to ensure, enhance and protect peace, harmony, happiness, and the good life in the face of conflicting claims we, as human beings, make against each other in the process of interaction in private and public domains, and especially in the light of the limitations imposed by economic exigencies and scarcity of resources for meeting the needs of humans contiguously situated in the shrinking space encompassed by society. It could also be (and have, by some thinkers, been) suggested that we did not need the norms and then go forward to simply create them ourselves, but that we were found to need them and hence we find the norms already there instituted by nature and enforced by God. Or we may even say that human society derives norms from the needs for survival of the species or self-interest in the face of competition with other sentient beings.

Whatever answer we give, it is important to recognize that norms are there and they regulate life. But it is not all the norms that we feel persuaded or compelled to obey as some norms are seen as patently wrong. The crux of the matter then becomes separating the good from the bad, and instituting good ones in the place of the bad ones. The task of delineating the good from the bad is a critical, analytic and at times speculative one which properly devolves on the moral philosophy. This is not saying that the moral philosophy has a special divination mechanism, but in virtue of his/her training, it is clear that philosophers cannot morally disavow this obligation they owe to society. This was what Socrates recognized, which contemporary moral philosophers fail to embrace. They seem to shy from the responsibility under the pretext that they have no special capacity to legislate for humanity, forgetting that they are not called upon to legislate for humanity.

In the personal domain, on the one hand, we have what can be regarded as private or personal morality; and in public life, we have public morality. Private morality deals with personal and interpersonal relationships, regulating the domain of mutual expectations of behavior which are shared. In this area there are no enforceable sanctions. If, for example, you are my brother and needed assistance and asked me for a loan of five hundred dollars and I refuse to grant you the loan, there is no recourse for compelling me to give you the loan. In this regard, it also follows that if I give you the loan, I do so only out of generosity and love or sibling obligation, not because I am under any legal obligation to give the loan. You may say that I was mean not to give the loan, but not that I broke any law.

On the other hand, in public life, people ascribe rights, duties, and obligations which guide expectations. The clergy, the political leader, the banker, the insurance officer, the farmer, the medical doctor, the nurse, the pharmacist, the genetic engineer, the nuclear scientist, the teacher, the cleaner in the office, the security services, etc. all have duties, obligations, rights, etc., which they acquire in virtue of the positions they occupy in society. Legal enforcement is usually instituted to ensure compliance with and discharge of these public requirements. Without the legal backing and requirement of obedience of many of these duties and obligations it is almost certain that they will be observed in breach than in compliance as a lot of them place unpleasantries on the persons required to fulfil their demands.

In studying ethics and morality, as an academic discipline in Western cultures of the Anglo-European tradition, we try to identify, understand, and critically analyze the moral concepts and moral principles that individuals and people live by or are expected to live by, act and operate by in society. We find that there are certain features of moral statements and principles in general that have been identified within the philosophical branch of ethics that are worth noting. These are, first, that there is a prescritivity to ethical statements and concepts as ethical injunctions and concepts are value laden and, hence, prescribe norms that are, or are not, supposed to be action-guiding; second, ethical statements are supposed to have intrinsic universalizability, giving the issue to which it applies (in context), thereby leaving no room for exceptions and, hence, having a law-like nature; third, the overridingness of moral principles suggest that moral principles take precedence over other types of considerations such as convenience of the agent, prudential considerations by agent, legal dictates, filial commitments, aesthetic inclinations and more; fourth, that there is an intrinsic public nature of moral principles, as moral principles are publicly acknowledged, otherwise they would be self-defeating; fifth, that moral principles have a natural practicability about them, that is, moral principles must be workable if every one were to follow them as the basis of action without engendering contradictory consequences; and sixth, that moral principles must be rational in the sense of having the most reasonable explanation or justification. This last needs immediate clarification, because the other conditions we have listed constitute possible considerations of rationality. But what is here intended is that it must be possible to rationally defend an ethical statement, either by adducing evidence from practical consequences, the intuitions that ground it, or by appealing to the internal coherence of the belief system within which it originates and, at other times, to the external sources from which such principles derive their meaning and authority.

Morality and ethics in Western and non-Western societies have similar importance in that human social and interpersonal behavior issue from necessity relate to other members of society to attain goals that are conducive to well-being and happiness of agents. In all societies the concept of right and wrong are determined by perceptions of what constitute the good life and well-being of persons on the one hand and general good and well-being of society on the other. The divergences in the moral prescriptions between Western and non-Western societies are largely due to variations in cultural traditions, ecological, sociological and other existential differences. Scholarship on ethics and moral philosophy in Western and non-Western societies have also been reflective of the perspectives that the different societies have developed and emphasized. In Western, Anglo-American philosophical tradition, the emphasis has been on individuality, the person, the *ergo*, as the cynosure of existence and essence, the point of identity and identification, the primus of reflection and reflectivity, while reflexively the retrospective projections limit and are limited to, and by, the welfare of the individual. Consequently, in Western societies, of the Anglo-American philosophical tradition, while the philosophers may have been under the impression that they were seriously developing theoretical ideas on morality with universal applicability and validity, they were propounding and expounding theoretical webs enunciating ethical prescriptions from individual perspective and focus, with limited and limiting application to the cultures that bred them, which ultimately gave them perspective, orientation, outlook and meaning.

The fact that these philosophers have misconceived their jobs and the value of the products of their intellectual reflections by becoming infatuated with the possibility of conceptually interesting but realistically valueless abstractions, belie the universal utilitarian importance of their efforts. It may be retorted that philosophy and philosophers are not bothered by the demand for relevance, but this type of reply only begs the question at issue. If philosophy was not expected to be practical or relevant, what is logic all about? Why methodology or epistemology and, in our direct interest area, why *applied ethics*? And, if philosophy can afford the rarefied and stratospheric excursus in irrelevance, why the lamentation about the parlous job market for graduates in philosophy by the most prestigious and largest professional philosophical organization in the world, APA? It may therefore, *eo ipso*, be interesting to indicate the point of departure of ethics and ethical reflections in other intellectual traditions, with the probable insight being provided into the situation of early childhood education and corporate sense of community that is prevalent in Western (especially in the United States of America) societies today.

In non-Western societies (specifically in African societies) and in the philosophical reflections relating to morality in these societies there are certain desiderata that determine the orientation of discourse. At the pain of being accused of ethnophilosophizing, I will attempt an illumination of perspectives that need careful consideration, both for the sake of understanding the wellspring of morality in Africa (and parts thereof) and for an appreciation and better analysis of the foundations of such morality. The value of the consciousness of the possibility of the charge of engaging in an ethnophilosophical exercise is that it reduces the circumscription of the writer to the cocoon of indifference in the face of ethical and cultural imperialism, bringing along with it all the terrible consequences of infant homicide, adult dementia characterized by shooting sprees, and other ills lamented by Westerners, about the direction their society takes or seems to be inexorably taking in the next century.

In this regard, one can boldly affirm that the wellspring of morality and ethics (moral reflections, prescription and analysis) in African societies are a balance of individual well-being and social (communal, community, corporate) well-being. What, it may be asked, is meant by this? My response is to look at the norm-generating foundation of human interaction in society. The first critical and most important part is this: What moral, social and personal obligation has a person to the self? The conceptualization and appreciation of this imposes certain norms of behavior on self as agent, as a being, as an individual, and as a human (that is, as a member of a specie), by contrast with being a beast. Here the primary obligation that a self has at the age of maturity, adulthood, and competence—a progressive reality that one gradually attains—is self-preservation, self-definition, self-actualization, self-projection and ultimately, self-perpetuation. Before this, however, the society—meaning family and community and nation—take on the responsibility of protection, caring, nurturing and social, cultural, ethical, political, religious and other necessary developments of the infant and the young.

The second critical part of the moral equation is this: What obligation has a person to his/her community and society? By this I do not want to be understood to indulge in unnecessary abstraction, as obligation to society, to others, and to community is as concrete as the obligation one owes to the self. The definition of this obligation is crucial to the consciousness of the self as a person and as well as the sense of community that empowers the individual and that gives the individual the support mechanism for coping with the exigencies of life. We need to say a little more on this score, because on this revolves the whole issue of moral emphasis in society.

It is not unusual to get the impression that African cultures extol the virtues of community, that moral obligations are primarily social before becoming individual, that communal factors often take precedence over individual rights or interests, that morality is predicated on a religious superstructure, that the episteme of otherness is weighted unduly heavily against the sense of self requirements in African societies, etc. These, when meant as a negative appreciation of and as derogatory commentaries on the moral universe in which Africans live, are based on improper reflection on the cognitive orientation that helps to fashion the moral and social fabric in African societies. Consider the idea that each person is a representative of himself and herself as well as his/her family. This has the implication that you as an agent not only consider the course of action you plan to embark upon as to how it affects you personally—what are the benefits of pleasure, satisfaction, upliftment, approbation, pain and more, that the action will bode for you as the agent? You are also enjoined to be seriously mindful of how this plan of action impacts your family by way of direct consequences and by way of reflection on how your family is subsequently perceived in its community. In this regard, it is important to understand that you have a personality and your family has a "personality." What we mean by this is that a certain tradition of excellence and image have been laid by your ancestors, grandparents and parents which you are expected not to tarnish, even while you pursue seriously your goals of happiness and survival.

The above is easily understood when we bear in mind the at once limited diversity and diversification and equal complexity of society, community and relationships in many African societies of the past and of the present. In situations like these, persons are conscious of the family name, family tradition and family image. Attainment of the age of consent, and progressively, attainment of independence from one's immediate family, brings with it grave responsibilities that are at once liberating, fulfilling, and equally confining. Individuals are morally obliged to take into consideration such matters because, when positions of responsibility are being considered in the community, when offices are being filled, when spouses are being selected and when interests are being protected, those whose family names have been soiled on account of the immoral behavior of their son or daughter loses out. The ostracism and pariah insignia that this bestows will tarry for generations and will not be diminished by sudden bursts of good work on the part of one or a few members of such families. It is interesting that individuals may acquire skills of trade and competence in specialties that are critical to community and family survival, but if the individual does not get the moral orientation right, or belongs to a family of untrustworthy persons, these skills are wasted as they would not find patronage and fulfillment within the environment in which it matters most, the social context of one's community.

The third and final critical question is this: What is the responsibility of the community or society to the person and to itself? This is a very serious and all important question. It may seem that morality is a personal thing first and foremost. This is only partially true from the African perspective. The artificial separation of individual moral responsibility from that of society, creating a cleavage of moral disparity constitutes a superficial discourse. It is obvious that the context in which the moral obligations arise is the interactive one, the social milieu in which contestations for scarce resources in the environment are undertaken, but it is not only resources in the environment that are scarce, the human requirements and resources of love, patronage, recognition, pity, compassion, association, competition and more are also scarce, and require deliberate efforts of persons and community to generate enough and to distribute fairly and equitably in order for these to go round all members of society. Here lies the crux of the moral responsibility of society to its members and to itself. And this fact is represented in numerous ideas of relationships in African societies.

Appiah (1992: 17) notes a common factor that leads to moral solidarity in African diaspora—the factor of being seen by others as belonging to a common race, blackness! This type of solidarity is awkward. This is because it does not quite translate into a proper perception of moral rights, duties and obligations in the sense noted in the previous paragraph—a proper sense of belonging to a community, a shared sense of common origin and history, a shared sense of common destiny, a shared sense of investment in common welfare and a shared expectation of cooperation and collaboration in forging a common front against all perils (natural and supernatural).

What happens here is the dislocation of the sense of moral solidarity by the relocation into an alien environment forcibly brought about by slavery and years of residency in disjointed social circumstances where community cohesion has been transcended by the demands of possessive individualism and have consequently created serious infractions on the moral fabric nurtured only in the cauldron of a clear sense of belonging. As it were, the grounding of the statement "I am, because we are" (Gbadegesin 1991a: 66), has been negated in the African Diaspora, as in its place has been firmly planted a perceptions of a festering "ours—theirs" dichotomy. It is only where there is a perceived relationship between the survival of the self and that of community, generated through responsible sense of community and morally cultured leadership, that the grounds of individual moral obligations are clear to understand and duties easy to perceive and execute. For Gbadegesin,

> From this it follows that there need not be any tension between individuality and community since it is possible for an individual to freely give up his/her own perceived interest for the survival of the community. But in giving up one's interest thus, one is also sure that the community will not disown one and that one's well-being will be its concern. . . . The idea of individual rights, based on a conception of individuals as atoms, is therefore bound to be foreign to this system. For community is founded on notions of intrinsic and enduring relationships among its members (pp. 66–67).

If we shift gears a bit, we will understand the full meaning of the above reflections immediately. The suggestion that Africans are "in all things religious" (Bolaji Idowu [1962], John Mbiti, J. O. Awolalu and other African theologian scholars and their Western mentors such as G. E. Parrinder, S. S. Rattray, A. B. Ellis and their accomplices) and that religion is the basis, the groundswell, the validation of morality misses the relationship between religion and morality. They fail to understand what makes religion important in African life—the welfare of the person and that of society, not an abstract other. This is why many reflective students of morality in Africa will easily relate to Wiredu's position that the basis of morality (a universal in all societies, even if what is moral is not universally the same in all societies [vide his *Cultural Universals and Particulars* 1996]) in Africa is human welfare. He says,

> It has often been said that our traditional outlook was intensely humanistic. It seems to me that, as far as the basis of the traditional ethic is concerned, this claim is abundantly justified. Traditional thinking about the foundations of morality is refreshingly nonsupernaturalistic. *Not that one can find in traditional sources elaborate theories of humanism.* But anyone who reflects on our traditional ways of speaking about morality is bound to be struck by the preoccupation with human welfare: What is morally good is what befits a human being; it is what is decent for a man—what brings dignity, respect, contentment, prosperity, joy, to man and his community. And what is morally bad is what brings misery, misfortune, and disgrace. Of course, immoral conduct is held to be hateful to God, the Supreme Being, and even to the lesser gods. But the thought is not that something is good because God approves of it but rather that God approves of it because it is good in the first place—a distinction which, as Socrates noted in the context of a different culture, does not come easily to every pious mind (1996: 6).

It is noteworthy that I have italicized a sentence of Wiredu's words above to bring attention to my dissent with the sentence. Wiredu claims that it is not the case that African sources will show elaborate reflections on the humanistic foundation of ethics. This is inaccurate, as the Yoruba Ifa reflects serious effort to show the basis of ethics as the concern for human welfare and community well-being (Gbadegesin 1991a: 5). This point is not considered a serious issue here and will not be pursued further, rather we will return to the strand of our discourse which evidences the humanistic foundation of ethics in Africa. This can be made more evident when we bring to light the interrelationship between ethics and other relationships and their perception and discussion in African societies.

In *Art, Outrage and Dialogue*, Wole Soyinka (1988) laments the tendency in American society for a self-destructive and socially disintegrative inclination in the notion of individuality which makes the foundations of morality tenuous and subservient to considerations of the ego. In the chapter "Between Self and System" (pp. 61–85), he pays attention to this particular dislocation of intellectual and artistic focus in American materialism and a self-destructive journalistic system. For him there can be little separation, if any at all, between the ends of art and the ends of ethics. This is not unexpected as in the Yoruba thought system there is an inseparable integration between ethics and all aspects of life, and there is often a description of that which is moral or ethical as that which is beautiful or pleasing to human artistic sensibilities, that is, as that which is aesthetically pleasing. Roland Abiodun (1983) dilates on this relationship between beauty and character, concluding that both are inseparable in Yoruba moral reflection and philosophies of art and ethics as to have one and lack the other is to have an incomplete intellectual and practical essence. Thus, Wiredu's views are in tandem with the important relationship being discussed here; that is, that a humanist ethics is central to African culture. He says,

> There is an aesthetic strain in our traditional ethical thought that is worthy of special mention in this connection. As noted already, what is good is conceived to be what is fitting . . ., what is fitting is what is beautiful. . . . There are, indeed, aesthetic analogies in the moral language of other cultures. But aesthetic analogies are taken much more seriously and have more extensive moral relevance in our traditional though (1980: 6).

After considering the third issue we cannot but provide a reflective analysis of the other components of the moral philosophy of many African societies. This is an aspect that has not been very popular and to which scant attention, if any, has been paid by scholars in the past, and because of this there is very little material to go by, either by way of reference or for critical analysis. This is the fourth key question that we need to ask and answer: What is the relationship between the self, the community and the environment? Or, what is the moral responsibility that humans and his/her society owe to the universe, the environment and to nature? This question is not taken lightly in African moral discourse. The reason for this is the fact that the universe is the habitation of human beings, and the manner in which humans dwell in it determines whether it is favorably disposed to the continued survival of humans and other living things in it. In nature can be found the diversity that makes existence interesting, and the sustenance of the interesting nature of this universe is a human obligation, moral and otherwise. Part of the moral obligation that many African societies are convinced that humans owe to the universe stems from the unity of existence, as they often make little distinction between the various realms of existence, which to then constitute one continuous whole. For the distinctions animate-inanimate, material-immaterial, real-unreal, natural-supernatural, being-nonbeing, etc., are too artificial and are encumbrances to the proper understanding of what there is. Such distinctions also warrant the possibility of disrespect for other things in nature apart from humans, and constitute a disincentive to proper study and understanding of reality. The possibilities of transition from one domain of existence to another are both exhilarating and humbling in the extreme. It is exhilarating in the sense that the oneness of the self with nature and the universe constitutes a locus of moral responsibility between the continuum of humanity—from the unborn, to the living, to the dead who become ancestors and to the pool of heritage from which the society takes its ultimate sense.

One may wonder now how the ancients knew about genes and genetic factors in the determination of self. It took Western science centuries to know about genes, cellular unity of nature, transmission of life from one generation to the other, etc. Things like genes and their indicators of character, for being, for health, for life, the holomovement, all forms of spaces and their dimensions, the relationship between wellness and happiness, the curative power of natural herbs and the contribution of positive thinking to success and happiness and more. These are ideas long known to many African societies and long used in the interest of members of society and selves. It is remarkable that the continuity of life in society is often ignored, and the effects of past on present and future downplayed. These we have often done at our peril, but the proper moral person realizes the warrant of goodness on account of what conduces to the good of the self, the society as well as what one's ancestors approve of. What is being urged here is the ultimate moral responsibility that humans assume for the equilibrium of nature, such that all aspects of life and living must be balanced, and children are taught environmental ethics from the cradle.

While the ancestors may be invoked as the sanction for the ethics of environmental care, it is obvious in the writing of many African philosophers and in the Scripture of Yoruba religion, for example, that the foundations of morality and moral philosophy is the human person, not any esoteric, supernatural origin. In consequence, the maintenance of the ethos of good life and the perpetuation of the norms of healthy human relationships may be said to be desired by the gods or the Supreme Being and the ancestors for mainly pragmatic and didactic reasons, the basic fact is that it is the pursuance of human good, which informed members of society are aware of, which moderates the moral foundations of interaction. And as Wiredu indicated, "A rule of conduct is not a moral rule unless its nonexistence or reversal would bring about the collapse of human community," but more importantly the absence of rules, the uncontrolled usage of resources, the disregard for the environment threatens also the collapse of the balance of the ecosystem.

The final aspect of the moral equation in society that needs to be emphasized is the religious aspect. This may be aptly formulated as the question: What is the moral relationship between humans, society and the supernatural? In another the same question may be formulated from a different perspective, thus: What moral obligations do humans owe to the supernatural and what moral obligations do the supernatural owe to the individual and to his/her society? To answer this question clearly may lead us into the conundrums of religion, and a digression into such matters may, at this stage of this chapter, not necessarily enrich the discourse a whit. What will be indicated here briefly is the simple trajectory of the obvious relation of institutionalized religion and organized society. In this regard, religion is both an instrument of cohesion and a factor of order, bringing to the fore the creative genius of members of society, while at the same time constituting a probable stifle to the common people's freedoms. In essence, it is being suggested here that religion developed out of human necessity and served the human need for knowledge, support and curiosity. The injunctions of morality related to religion in the African environment has been found to issue from humanistic considerations, whence there is the important and often untainted knowledge by the initiated concerning the nature of values in general in society that, in Wiredu's words, relating the Akan axiological reflection, thus:

> The first axiom of all Akan axiological thinking is that man or woman is the measure of all value. . . . And every Akan maxim about the specifically moral values that I know, explicitly or implicitly, postulates the harmonization of interests as the means, and the securing of human well-being as the end, of all moral endeavours.
>
> The circles of obligations, rights, and privileges which radiated from the center of household relations of kinship to the larger circumferences of lineages and clan affinities provided a natural school for training in the practice of sympathetic impartiality which, in its most generalized form, is the root of all moral virtue (1997: 65).

Therefore, the invocation of the Supreme Being, the divinities, the ancestors and other forces in moral matters is mainly to lend legitimacy through an already available reinforcement mechanism to what is often taken for granted as incontestable. Being morally upright is not as much a matter of pleasing the supernatural forces as it is promoting human welfare. It is in this regard that the skepticism of the Yoruba people pertaining to the place of religion and the supernatural forces in morality becomes clear to understand. Patronage of the deities is not as much in the interest of the deities as it is in the interest of the people, and when one deity fails to support society, members of society feel no special bond of attachment which can prevent the severance of the relationship.

Having arrived at this stage of our discourse, it is clear that morality and moral discourse has followed divergent paths in Western and African societies. What is even more curious is the element of insularity that the philosophers have infused into Western ethical discourse by contrast with the practicality, pragmatism and relevance of African ethical discourse. The ideas of right and wrong are not discussed in abstract in African intellectual reflections, but they are made relevant to social and human needs of members of society.

There are a number of related concepts used in the assessment of behavior in Yoruba ethical reasoning. In Yoruba philosophical discourse, ethics relates to the norms that govern human behavior on the one hand, and societal—community behavior, and the behavior of the supernatural beings in their relationship with humans on the other. Ethics is not an abstraction, without content. And as the above suggests, it is not only humans, as selves, that have to be ethical. In Yoruba language, ethical behavior and morally approved conduct is *iwa rere, iwa pele, iwa irele, iwa tutu,* or *iwa omoluabi*. A morally upright person, who exhibits the character of good behavior, such as honesty, respect for self, of elders and for others, decency, helpfulness and more, is *oniwa rere, onirele, oniwa tutu, oniwa pele, Omoluabi*. Such persons are highly valued and respected in Yoruba society. And in reality they get rewarded by society in various ways for their goodness, kindness and uprightness.

Let us get beyond the mere naming of what constitutes moral concepts in Yoruba ethics and deal in concrete with real issues. There is some abstruseness to Yoruba ethical reflection that is very intriguing and at the same time revealing. Types or forms of behavior are not just lumped together and characterized as good or bad. Such generic description is insensitive to the nuanced nature of ethics in society, because it leads to ambiguities and superfluities—even superficialities of interpretation. Probably this has been part of the disastrous academic situation imposed on Western ethical discourse by academies of the analytic tradition. For failing to get to grips with the real meaning of morality as it is lived in society could inhibit proper analysis by distanced academics.

The first concept that I want to examine here is *ese* or sin. This concept has gained much currency in religious discourse because of the influx of Christian ethics into many African societies. This is not suggesting that it was absent originally from the lexicon of Yoruba people, contrary to Bolaji Idowu (1962: 148). Nor is there any insinuation that there was a theology of sin. Rather, the point at issue here is the fact that the general category that covers all sins in Yoruba language is *ese* or sin, but there are various types of sins and various forms of sin, meaning that it is not only religious infractions against the Supreme Being, the deities, and the ancestors that constitute sin, but that infractions against the supernatural forces are *ese* because these infractions were primarily against fellow human beings, hence, they constitute sin. This fact alone dictates that while a person may have done wrong, it does not necessarily follow that the person has sinned, if sin is understood in the purely Christocentric sense. One may say anecdotally here that probably the reason for the disintegration of the moral fabric in Nigerian polity is a consequence of the substitution of an alien concept of right and wrong for the indigenous ideas of morality, thus having the implication that those infractions of behavior against fellow humans are no longer regarded as sins because sins are now only possible against God, Allah, Olodumare, Chukwu or Osanobuwa—depending on each person's religion.

While all categories of wrong behavior against persons and the supernatural beings are sins, there are other important sub-categories of sin that are useful insights into Yoruba moral philosophy. This is where one can deal with *eewo, aimo, egbin, abuku, aleebu, ibaje, aidaa,* among others. I will briefly discuss some of these concepts before concluding the chapter. The reason why I will not discuss all of them is mainly because the chapter has become rather extended in length because of the necessity to properly position the discussion meaningfully outside the context of the limited tradition of Western moral philosophy without being conversely guilty of the ethnophilosophical disparagement. This has been like being caught between a rock and a hard place—if you do, you are condemned, and if you don't, you are condemned.

This concept has a dual aspect. It is often translated as *tabu* by theologian writers on African religions in their attempt to understand Yoruba beliefs. *Tabu* or *eewo* in this sense relates to things prohibited by the Supreme Being, the divinities and the ancestors. However, there is the more secular meaning of *eewo* or *tabu* which relates to morality *simpliciter*. *Eewo,* conceived in this sense, means things that are wrong to do and for which sanctions are incurred. When one says "sanctions," this is not to be construed as meaning punishment formally enforced as in legal punishment. It may be in the form of simply losing stature, status or face in the community, whereas in the religious sense, some atonement or sacrifice has to be made to assuage the unseen forces that may have been offended.

It is important to note here *eewo,* in the secular moral sense that I am adverting to originate from various grounds with practical and commonsensical orientation. Even the religious sense of it still redounds to the humanistic perspective, as it is mostly promulgated in the interest of good conduct and interpersonal interaction in society. Such serious wrongs as stealing, adultery, poaching other people's livestock, destruction of other people's property or public property and more, are regarded as serious offenses that must be expiated by punishment, retribution, reparation and atonement.

We are not to confuse *eewo* with *ofin*. *Ofin* in Yoruba language is "law," and it is often backed up by the coercive power of the state, and so not to be confused with *eewo*. What is clear is that while *eewo* in secular life may not draw the legal force, persons suffer variously for committing *eewo* as an act, and where it is a form of ingestible material, they suffer physiological disorders for eating *eewo* (this is often allergic reactions to some foods which are probably mistaken in Yoruba communities for punishment for social or interpersonal infractions, but this even provides a practical insight into the Yoruba conception of *eewo*). In many cases the moral suasion of ostracism, disrespect and odium engages the agent to be more forthright and morally sensitive in the future.

Literally this concept translates as "blemish." In Yoruba understanding of morality, to act against the moral expectation is to exhibit a moral blemish on one's character. It is to have a moral dislocation. We may understand this more properly by looking at the analogy of food products. A good tuber of yam will not have cuts, rotten parts, or other signs of spoilage. When this happens, it constitutes *abuku* to the original good state of the yam. When this happens to the yam, its value is diminished and, usually, such yam cannot be taken to the market for sale but must be consumed domestically; when taken to the market at all, it must be sold at prices less than real value. So also human beings with moral blemish are deformed by the blemish, and will be shy, as a consequence, to raise his/her head in public to pontificate on matters of community affairs. In fact, to have such blemish is to be unworthy of gathering with peers, holding responsible offices in community, representing the family or community in public domain and more.

One thing is a recurring factor in the Yoruba analysis that we are attempting to understand here, and this is the fact that there is a great sense of history. What is meant here is the fact that character is developed with the input of virtually all persons living in proximate situation to the growing child, and the child developing a personality, a character is closely monitored and guided, without being conscripted into anonymity. But once the character is formed or patterns of behavior developed, the good traits are lauded and the bad ones are reproached, but the pattern or character is often noted and goes into referencing on the individual, even beyond immediate issues of recognition. A person may have done something bad in a distant past, or a member of his/her family may have been the one responsible for the act (even when the person has died), probably the agent may have forgotten the act and many other members of the community may also have forgotten, but it takes only someone with a good memory and sense of history to bring the *abuku* to the attention of people, and the person's desires may be thwarted. This is the more reason why individuals are ever conscious of the need to always protect their moral integrity from blemishes that may forever spot their character and integrity in their societies. Another word one may find in the moral language of the Yoruba people that has the same meaning as *abuku* is *abawon*. The two words are often used as synonyms, and the analysis provided for one applies to the understanding of the other.

There is a duality to this word in terms of meaning that must be understood here. There is the epistemic aspect of *aimo*, meaning "lack of knowledge" or "absence of knowledge" (Hallen and Sodipo 1986). This is the consequence of using different intonation marks on the letters in the word. But *aimo* in the epistemic sense could lead to moral infractions in the ethical sense that is of interest to us. When the tone marks are changed the word *aimo* becomes moral uncleanliness, or dirtiness. In this same sense *aimo* is very close to the blemish or *abuku* that we examined just now, but the difference is that the nature of *aimo* is that it is understood not to be skin deep, and is easier to expiate and be rid of than the one that become *moliki* to the body or nature of the agent—habitual.

There are so many things that may create *aimo* for a person; some of them are small, some big. The importance of these minor and major acts can be cumulative, and their effect in the value one attaches to self and self-concept real. What is urged is often that one be mindful of one's actions so that one does not unnecessarily antagonize others or perpetrate injury to other's emotions and person unintentionally.

Now, it may be asked whether *aimo* does not properly relate to how clean or dirty one's dress is. We will not make heavy weather of the fact that the same word is used to describe a dirty dress, because the proper understanding of the moral language, indeed Yoruba language in general, reveals that the same word, depending on the context, could have more than one single meaning. *Aimo* applied to dress would mean being spotted or being dirty, while when applied to moral being it would mean not being upright in one way or another, and consequently having done some wrong for which blame is appropriate.

Egbin is the word for which polar ideas are attributable. In the one sense, the height of beauty is characterized by the similarity between the person or thing and a beautiful animal by the name *egbin*. On the other hand, when an act is despicable and odious to the senses, capable literally of causing nausea, it is said to be *egbin*. As to be expected, what changes, and which create the polarity is the change in the tone marks on the letters in the word.

In the moral meaning of *egbin*, it is clear that Yoruba have annotated degrees of moral decadence that members are cautioned against. Children are brought up with a clear sense of differentiation of all these ills in character, and as they mature they imbibe the virtues of good behavior, while desisting from those acts which paint them in negative light among their peers and community.

Other concepts that space does not permit us to discuss here, but which we mentioned are *aleebu*, *ibaje*, and *aidaa*. The three of them are related to what we have discussed in a variety of ways. *Aleebu* and *ibaje* are related to *abuku*, while *aidaa* is related to *aimo*, except the latter is more easily seen in behavior, while *aidaa* may be concealed to the unwary, only to come to the surface when critical situations arise and people are expected to stand up and be counted. In fact, it may merit mentioning here that acts that are described as bad or less than good do not merely relate to requirements to do, but relate to the manner of carriage in society, ability to keep peer confidence, discretion and more. These are clearly factors that are seriously viewed in judgements of character and evaluation of family members, and in the determination of responsibility in the community and in the wider society at large. And it would be strange to see adults in the Yoruba community not being aware of all the aspects of personal and public morality noted here.

Clearly it may be said that what we refer to as moral concepts are practical nuances of right and wrong conduct. This will only in part be accurate, as morality in most civilized societies does not start and end with mere notions of right and wrong, totally dissociated from the emotions and feelings of members of society. What makes moral dictates so strong is not the mere rationality of the grounds for their determination. What gives moral ideas the imperativeness of their purports is the fact that persons and communities feel that infractions of their demands are constitutive of serious challenges to survival, existence and perpetuation of life and culture. And a sense of outrage is not a logically distillable consequence of acts, it is a combination of many factors which are not materially quantifiable but whose nonobservance may lead to disasters of monumental proportions.

Our discussion in this chapter has attempted to understand the nature of ethics and ethical philosophy in the West and in Africa (as an example of non-Western society). We have suggested that the dichotomy between ethics and practical life in the West is a function of the distorted understanding of the task of moral philosophy in the West and the obligation inherent in philosophizing. It has been argued that the abstraction of philosophy from reality and the atomization of the individual self in the West are twain destructive elements in the Western moral fabric which non-Western societies need to watch out for in the desire to be part of the global environment. We conclude that morality in the most relevant sense is the attempt to understand good, bad, right, wrong, conducts in society and enable youth and future generations to properly integrate into society and world community. Our examination of Yoruba moral philosophy, using the different concepts of analysis of ethics in the Yoruba language, enabled us to see the clear distinction between ethical discourse in Africa and the West.

The nature of ethics in Africa may be obliquely described as humanistic. If care is not taken to clarify what is intended, it may be asked: Why so much human disaster in Africa? That is, why is there so much leadership disorientation and attendant socioeconomic catastrophe? The proper understanding of the fundamental factors that lead to the situation as is deeper than what a cursory glance can unravel. Suffice to simply say that the majority of the leadership crises experienced today is a consequence of a breakdown in the indigenous moral education process attendant upon the adoption of alien culture, alien ethos of politics, alien ethos of business, alien legal apparatuses and more. When this failure is coupled with the fact that the first set of people to be exposed to Western education were mostly the rejects in families because of the innate suspicion of foreign education and distrust of the Westerner's system of end justifies means, it becomes clear that the leadership disaster current on the continent is predictable and unavoidable.

NINE

Law, Order, Èṣù and Liminality in the Yoruba Legal System

Any discussion of Yoruba religion cannot ignore the profound metaphysic and episteme that undergird the cultural ethos and politics of the pre-colonial indigenous Yoruba society. While the combined intrusion and insurgency of the twin innately destructive Arabian peninsula religions of Christianity and Islam have greatly devalued the devotion and commitment of Yoruba people individually and collectively in Nigeria and world-wide to the inheritance of religio-philosophical and intellectual greatness of their fore-bears, it must be acknowledged that those of Yoruba descent who remain sane enough will hardly dispute the ways in which Yoruba culture had moderated well-ordered existence in Yoruba communities, even at the most challenging times of internecine wars and social upheavals brought about by the slave trade, homegrown schisms and the colonial experience of the British (where life was "nasty, British and short"), and what can be described as the colonialism of the current contraption that is the Nigerian state (where life is now "nasty, Nigerian and short")! Indeed, nostalgia apart, it is undeniably clear that life in Yoruba land in what we know as modern-day Nigeria is now many centuries regressed into primordial pre-medieval barbarity, beneath what many generations of living Yoruba individuals can remember having ever experienced, to the point where near absolute anarchy now rules the land, survival of the jungle-fittest reigns supreme, disorderliness and irresponsibility becomes glorious pastimes of all and sundry, sense of moderation in abeyance, total disregard for the value of ethnic and personal responsibility is the norm, appreciation of good name or image in short supply, little or no regard for the other humans has become prevalent and disregard for what is scandalous becomes the way of life as religion, politics and social mores are now subservient to the almighty Naira exchange mechanism that has taken over our existence.

That Yoruba indigenous society was a highly sophisticated one, with layers of spaces, tropes of relationships, and arenas of discourses that were highly fluid, presenting often interesting paradoxes and ambiguities of meaning, interpolative mediation of realities and confounding the uninitiated with abstruse interpretive mechanisms which facilitate meaning in both numerical and qualitative ways (Zaslavsky 1999). The nature of the pre-colonial indigenous Yoruba cosmos and the natural and contrived spaces of interaction—secular as well as sacred, cultural as well as natural, political as well as economic, social as well as practical, etc—all presented challenges of apprehension, understanding, interpretation, management and utilization, for the purpose of deriving a well-ordered society. Many cultural and intellectual artifacts have been developed in Yoruba culture, from religion to science, from mathematics to pharmacology, from language to music, from orature to dance, from the literary arts to gymnastic performances, from architecture to sculpture, from nutritional dietary habits to social graces, from education to politics, from moral norms to reward and punishment mechanisms, and from clothing to formal modes of action in special areas of existence; just to mention a few (Bewaji 2003). All of these tropes and avenues were capable of generating conundrums that needed special intellectual development, careful moral guidance, and patient attention to navigate. Because of the sophistication and complexities of Yoruba life, existence and culture, there were various checks and balances, moderators and clarifiers of ideas, issues and problems; but there were also various ways of muddling, compounding and confounding ideas, issues and problems, depending on what one's interests and goals are.

It is in the last instance mentioned above that we look at the elements of religion, language, social interactions, relationships and culture as liminal tropes in our present reflection on the nature of social, economic, religious, political and cultural leadership of Yoruba society in what is often described as the pre-colonial era. There are heuristic and hermeneutic devices in Yoruba culture, and there are methodologies that have been tested and proven to sustain life and culture in Yoruba society, which facilitate order, conflict mediation, excess mitigation, power limitation, justice and fairness in all aspects of life. At the intersection of these tropes of liminality, it is suggested, is Èṣù, who as a divinity charged with the ultimate responsibility for ensuring justice and fairness, responsibility and accountability, and who is always found insisting on clarity, faithfulness and righteousness of individuals, social groups, leadership, even the divinities and ultimately, the Supreme Deity, who is the overall being, beyond whom there is no other, but who is not beyond reining in by Èṣù; while at the same time, conniving and conspiring to confound, confuse and destabilize the paths of the unwary, the wayward, the greedy and the criminally minded, all with a view to challenging members of society to live to higher moral standards demanded by living members of society, the ancestors, the divinities and the Supreme Being (Bewaji 1998).

Now, our examination departs from extant discussion of the place of Èṣù in Yoruba cosmography and the limitations of religio-cultural, philosophically literal analyses of his role in Yoruba ontology, psychology, and epistemological apprehension of reality and constitute a critical (skeptical and diachronic) effort to provide an enabling stricture for us to appreciate the powers of epistemic and metaphysical constructions of Yoruba discourse, dialogue and communication as layered and nuanced tools for the clear purpose of establishing and maintaining social, political and cultural equilibrium, order and peace in Yoruba society, and how Èṣù stands vanguard in this process. In order to do this, we ask, and answer, a number of questions: Why is the home of Èṣù at the crossroads or outside of the home or shrine? Why are the divinities in Yoruba religion unable to become laws unto themselves? Why does Olodumare not dispose of Èṣù, even when Èṣù becomes a cross in Olodumare's throat—compelling Olodumare to do justice, rather than injustice? To what extent is Èṣù responsible for the epistemic veracity and veridicality in Yoruba knowledge systems? Why is it that our politicians and civil functionaries are averse to swearing or taking the oath with the indigenous symbols like Ogun's Iron, Ose of Sango, Ase of Èṣù?

The questions we raise and the responses that are provided in this chapter must be situated against the background of how law and order, punishment and reward as well as responsibility for justice are conceived in indigenous Yoruba society before the advent of Europe in Africa. In Western societies a number of symbols and practices are used to reinforce the legal traditions such as swearing before a judge using the Holy Bible or the national flag and a prison system to remove criminals from society. Law enforcement personnel wear special clothing bearing the crest of the government as a symbol of authority. Even more significantly, the judicial system collaborated with an incarceration prison system for depriving miscreants of their freedom. The complexities of these matters are cemented by a modern system of policing, trial and punishment which range from fines to incarceration and even capital punishment.

In indigenous Yoruba society these were clearly incorporated in the form of mechanisms to ensure and enhance public order, justice and fairness. Layers of clearly recognizable metaphysical tropes and judicial procedures are in place to ensure justice is done. In this chapter we enumerate the factors of symbolism and liminality of Èṣù in the preservation of justice in Yoruba society, noting that punishment in fines, excommunication, community service and even capital punishment are all incorporated. From the trust in the judges who are expected to be impartial, to the recognition of the severe dangers in false testimony or witnessing, to the meticulous following through of the judgment, it is clear that Yoruba people had perfected the jurisprudential system to ensure transparency and fairness in the dispensation of justice. Clearly, the role of Èṣù in this process cannot be undervalued, and this is what is considered in this chapter.

One of the pioneer Yoruba scholars, of whom very little is known, is Pastor E. M. Lijadu, who made it a point of duty to study Yoruba religion, culture, psychology and science in order to be able to meaningfully utilize the knowledge in the Christian prosyletization process among the Yoruba people. He was errorneuosly never in any doubt that Christian religion was superior to Yoruba religion, even though his reasons for so believing is very dubious and often contradictorily deriving from the arrogance of someone who has now embraced the belief and value system of colonizers. While annotating many parallels between Yoruba religion and Christian religion, it is only by appreciating the pains to which he went to show how deeply philosophical, moral and religious Yoruba people are, and how invaluable are the moral foundations of Yoruba society, that one will understand the insights which he has generated in Yoruba philosophy of religion scholarship. In his theological efforts, he encouraged other Christian theologians who want to be successful to do likewise, making the effort to understand indigenous culture, value system and religion as, in so doing, they will enrich their teaching by being privy to the sociocultural, economic, intellectual and psychological foundations of behavious, fears, aims, aspirations, dreams and, indeed, all aspects of life of the target prospective converts. The reverend was not happy with the way in which his colleagues were conducting the spread of Christianity, not making progress, and not appreciating why they were failing; for this reason, it was, in his view, imperative to change the approach so as to be able to convince the "heathens" about the errancy of their beliefs, and consequently the need to come to acceptance of the Christian belief system.

It is noteworthy that Pastor E. M. Lijadu produced the first book on Ifa in 1898, indicating the fact that it (Ifa) is the Yoruba divination system, as well as showing that it is a divinity and finally that the knowledge system enshrined in Ifa constitute the foundation and repository of most, if not all, religious ideas, speculations and reflections in Yoruba society. Even while his ideas and conclusions about Yoruba religion and systems of worship were mostly parternalistic, it was clear that Lijadu recognized the value of such system as constitutive of the fundamental presuppositions of life in Yoruba society; this was a fact that enabled him to respect the system, while being able to positively use such understanding and respect as the prop on which conversion and sustenance of conversion was to be constructed. He says:

> Li enu awon baba-nla wa li a ba oro ogbon yi pe, "Eniti o ba wipe, Olorun ko si, oluware paapaa ni ko si". Nje a le wipe ogbon ati ero

> wiwa Olorun ni ipile isin li okan enia gbogbo? Sugbon bi ko ti si isin kan ti o pe laini ohun meta wonyi ninu, . . . (1) Imo Olorun otito, (2) Ifihan oro Olorun otito, ati (3) Emi ododo ninu isin. Mo ngbiyanju ninu iwe yi lati gba ona meteta wonyi fihan bi isin ti a ba lowo awon baba wa ti kuna to (1898, 8).

I will render this in literal translation as follows:

> We inherited the following words of wisdom from our ancestors, that "Whoever says the Supreme Being (God) does not exist, it is he himself/herself who does not exist". It could be inquired that the wisdom and the curiosity for seeking the Supreme Being is the foundation of worship in all human heart? But as there can be not true worship without the following three features, (1) Knowledge of the true Supreme Being, (2) Revelation of the true Supreme Being, and (3) Truth in worship or true worship. I will try in this book to use these three features to show how sound the religious beliefs of our ancestors are.

This was different from the colonizer's opinion that Africans had no religion or concept of Supreme Being. However, in the pages of the book, it is clear that Pastor Lijadu was ambivalent, often confused, even paradoxical, in his understanding of the nature of the beliefs of Yoruba people, the place of the divinities and their understanding of the Supreme Being—God—in Yoruba philosophy of religion. While, on the one hand, he was clear that Yoruba had comparative beliefs, theology and philosophy of religion, which may even be superior to the Arabian desert-derived Christian and Islamic religions, one of which he now has to promote; on the other hand, he was determined to show that the beliefs of the Yoruba people regarding God and the divinities were misguided, wrong and inferior. While recognizing that Yahweh, the Jewish deity, saw nothing wrong in consulting the hosts of heaven at the beginning of creation, he saw the consultation which Olodumare makes of Ifa as demeaning of the supremacy of the Supreme Being!

Since this effort is not concerned with a general analysis of the work of Lijadu as a general one concerned with Yoruba religion, we will not engage in such a general analysis. Why we begin our discussion with his effort is because even at that early stage it was clear how confused the "educated" Yoruba were concerning the religion, culture and philosophy of their forebears and how these have traditionally enabled Yoruba society to be the advanced civilization that it was before the ingress of European colonisation. For this reason we will look at the segments of the work which had direct bearing on the place of the Yoruba divinity, Èṣù, in the overall social, moral, aesthetic, religious, cultural and other aspects of Yoruba life. It is my hope that by teasing out certain elements that have been ignored in Yoruba culture, we would be able to see part of what accounts for the general morass that afflicts Yoruba society, Nigeria and many African societies in contemporary times.

Traditional Yoruba scholarship on Yoruba religions and culture is very rich and, since the time of Michael Crowder to Lijadu and contemporary times, scholars have been interested in understanding the various divinities in Yoruba religion for various reasons. Some of the reasons relate to understanding of the Yoruba universe, ethics, aesthetics, culture, social and political terrains, and not the least, the avenues of entertainment and play. But apart from some rather brave investigators from the literary, languages and artistic directions, very few scholars from the disciplines of political science and philosophy take seriously the challenge of understanding Èşù.

Instead of seeing what Wole Soyinka has described as the liminal role of Èşù in the general sociocultural, ethical, political, economic, epistemic and metaphysical constructs of Yoruba, Lijadu agrees with other scholars of Yoruba religion to see Èşù as existing primarily in the ways in which Yoruba people, shorn of religious syncretism, see the divinity; that is, as a divinity, indeed, as a personage among the Yoruba divinities, who, it can be said, nobody loves and nobody hates (can hate); while, at the same time, seeing in Èşù that Jewish-Christian persona of the Demon, Devil, Satan or Lucifer and the Arab Islamic Shaitan, who is typically understood in Arabian psychologically divisive bi-polar terminolgy as the opposite of the Supreme Being God and the supreme good denoted by positive. But operating within the Yoruba traditional religious philosophy, where there is no absolute evil or absolute good, where all things are capable of enabling both good and evil, one is therefore minded to ask, what is the basis of interpretation of Èşù as Satan? Could it be what P'Bitek called intellectual smuggling—clothing African deities in borrowed garments in order to destroy them—by the converts to Christianity who try to make sense of their own culture in the language of their convert religion? Or was it a genuine misunderstanding, borne of ignorance of the Yoruba philosophy of religion and with no relation to a deliberate falsification of the belief system of Yoruba people (since most of them were probably not properly schooled in their indigenous culture before they were converted to the new religions of the colonial masters)?

More fundamentally, on the intellectual aspect engendering and enabling the growth, evolution and adaptation of Yoruba ideas relating religion to Yoruba experiences over time, how effective has what appears to be the deliberate falsificaiton of Yoruba religious beliefs, the iconography of their deities and axiology, been contributory to the deliberate, pernicious and debilitatig epistemicide of Yoruba philosophy, philosophy of religion and attention to such liminal constructs as Èşù in Yoruba media of social, cultural, political, moral and other modes of existence by Western adventurers, colonizers and neo-coloizers with the conivance of their indigenous converts to the two most destructive religions originating from the Arabian Desert? These are questions to which Lijadu had no answer directly, but to which his pieoneering effort is indicative of how he would have answered. And one would have expected the erudite scholars who have followed in his stead, such as Idowu, Awolalu, Dopamu, Kayode, etc., to have transcended the narrow confines of his initial effort to rigorously discuss Èṣù.

What is even more damning is the aura of fear that has been generated around Èṣù, deriving from the Christo-Islamocentric renditions of the Yoruba divinity Èṣù as Lucifer/Satan/Demon/Shaitan, such that efforts to see how Yoruba understand the divinity is shrouded in prohibition, courtship with evil, rapport with disaster and more. Even while researching this chapter, very few colleagues were willing to discuss Èṣù at all, as they all seem to be intimidated by the Arabian culture of polarities, where even entertaining any thoughts about Èṣù is like courting the wrath of God. It is almost as if these colleagues, who are otherwise very intelligent scholars with numerous publications which have been groundbreaking, are scared stiff at the mention of word or name Èṣù, unable to transcend the opprobrium heaped on this divinity by Christianity and Islam. Some even wondered why the interest in Èṣù? Is it a way of encouraging demonology, or Devil worship?

For me, this is beyond my comprehension, because it seems as if certain intellectual discourses are prohibited *ab initio*, without any rational consideration to understand why it is prohibited. On the other hand, to banish the investigation of certain areas is to continue to allow the said area to mystify and fester on falsehood and half-truths. And this makes one to wonder whether effectively the disconnection between the living conditions of Yoruba peoples in contemporary times and yonder years has been a consequence of the disconnect that is mentioned here; namely the abandonment of the indigenous Yoruba intellectual traditions, religions, moral beliefs, principles of leadership and instruments of social control and sustenance.

Could the malaise in Yoruba life be a function of the deliberate destruction of Yoruba knowledge systems by the forces of colonization, Christianity, Islam and globalization—what has been described as epistemicide (Bewaji 2012)? To what extent is the absence of any standards of right, goodness, excellence and uprightness in contemporary Yoruba consciousness a function of this deliberate destruction and bastardization of Yoruba knowledge systems? How adequate are the borrowed cultural icons, myths and alien cultures originating from the Arabian Desert of primordial violence and polarisms for the development of lives in other more clement, more civil and less polar and divisive environments? Could it be that the historical factors of the Arabian life, which was necessitated by one very small ethnicity claiming all that is good for itself on account of a tribal deity necessitate the understanding of everything in terms of absolutes in order to survive—a zero-sum nihilism? Should African peoples not now start to look closely at the limitations of these borrowed cultures and the negative impacts they have on lives in Africa, as a way of engineering order and development in society? While now understanding that, maybe, the mythologies and mysticisms of our forebears have been useful for their times, would our times need to evolve our own adaptations of their beliefs to make progress beyond what they have achieved? Could the concept of Èṣù then be likened to the American "Big Brother," who is constantly watching you? Could we then become more liberated and civilized and developed on account of our understanding of Èṣù agency as a necessary element in the orientation of errant persons to curb their excesses and live moderated lives with other-regarding thoughts and actions? While persons living in the United States of America are appreciative of the long arm of the law, and the apparent eternity of the memory of the law, it helps them to keep in check the human tendency toward taking advantage of the weak and vulnerable. We will dilate on this phenomenon and the concept of the rule of law in the English legal tradition shortly.

Discussions of Yoruba divinities have often been based on religious and linguistics interests. Even those who have proclaimed an interest in philosophical understanding of African religions have not been able to transcend the parochial foundations of religiosity that determines their initial effort, as in Idowu, Mbiti, Dopamu, Awolalu and other efforts. The works of Oha, Adeleke and other recent discussions of Èṣù have evidenced a bias that is more in tune with traditional annotations of Èṣù, or as clear efforts at post-modernist interpretations, deriving from literary interests based on the desire to portray Èṣù not as agency but as model of externally derived action.

Hence, our effort in this discussion will not be addressed to how Lijadu understood Yoruba theology, religion and philosophy of religion, except insofar as this contributes to the project of understanding how one of the divinities in Yoruba religion contibuted to the overall picture of sociocultural, political, economic and other facets of well-ordered society, that conduced to the level of civilization the Yoruba society enjoyed before the interface with Europeans. Subsequently, in what follows, we will read Lijadu and other authors to answer the questions:

a. What is the basis of the theological interpretation of Èṣù as Satan?
b. Could it be what P'Bitek called intellectual smuggling—clothing African deities in borrowed garments in order to destroy them?
c. Or was it a genuine misunderstanding, arising from ignorance of Yoruba culture and religion, with no relation to a deliberate falsification of the belief system of Yoruba people?
d. To what extent can the phenomenon of Èṣù be a cultural foundation for the development of knowledge, science and morality in Yoruba society?
e. What has Yoruba society lost through the convoluted translation of Èṣù as Satan, to wit the element of nonmoral behavior, absence of a

sense of proportion and personal/family image and social probity (by comparison with Japanese entry into modernity on its own cultural terms, through the retention of the culture of Japan to undergird human interaction and social relations)?

Adeleke's (2005, 11–31) essay, "Even the Gods Are Fools," is a very problematic piece. In my view, what the essay was aimed at showing was the fact that (a) the divinities in Yoruba religion were not averse to anthropocentric features, (b) the divinities related to each other just like humans and hence have interaction issues, frictions, and need conflict resolution methodologies that restore order and harmony, (c) the divinities have weaknesses and strengths which can be emphasized or exploited, (d) the divinities are not beyond tricks and exploitation by each other, either as tests of intellectual capacity or as means of showing each other's limitations and (e) the divinities being capable of being fooled makes them vulnerable. But the author made it seem as if the person playing the trick, the prank (that is, fooling the other) is as foolish and the victim of the prank or trick or joke. This, in my opinion, defeats the howler in the title which seems to suggest that the gods are fools!

The three deities (Osun, Èṣù and Orunmila) that Adeleke examines and the "folly" exhibited by them does not seem, in my view, to show them as fools. In the case of Osun, it clearly shows, as he says, the creativity of Osun in solving her problem within a matrimonial polyginous context, while Oba was shown as intellectually uncritical, in the sense that she accepted the advice of Osun unreflectively. For, if Oba had been reflective, she would have wondered what it would have been like for the guests of their husband to find a human ear in their soup, or how many times one would have had to cut and cook one's ear in order to continue to make the soup. Thus, if anything, it was Oba who was the fool, not Osun (15–18).

In the case of Èṣù, there was no evidence that Èṣù did anything wrong. In the Yoruba society where there was some gender-based division of labor, it was the women who went to the market to trade, while the men did other chores for the family. For this reason, it made sense that when Èṣù had a goat to sell, he should implore the women (Oya, Osun and Yemoja), who were apparently friends and who shared stalls, to help him sell the goat; on the understanding that for their troubles they would receive half the proceeds of the sale to share. That the women sold the goat, gave ten cowries to Èṣù and had difficulty sharing their ten cowries was not the fault of Èṣù at all, nor is this attributable to any trick from Èṣù. In Yoruba land, there are cultural traditions for sharing things—seniority in age, seniority in marital status, or other social and religious status could have come play. That the women quarelled on their share was a product of their weak reflectivity and inability to hark to Yoruba tradition. Hence, how Èṣù resolved their conflict for them, which was by burying the extra cowrie shell, was creative and intellectualy reflective of Yoruba culture of giving thanks to the ancestors who made our possibility possible in the first instance (18–23).

As for the case of Orunmila, it is not beyond comprehension that in Yoruba religion, the reason why Orunmila is regarded as the wise one is because of his power of observation and ability to remember things. Consequently, what we find here does not seem to hold up the discussion of Adeleke about the tricksterhood of Orunmila, thereby making him a fool. At the most, one can surmise that Orunmila displays an uncanny ability to observe the nature of things, their behavior and also relate things to each other in order to draw the inferences which follow therefrom. That the other divinities fail miserably in this is not the fault of Orunmila, nor can we determine, just as it was impossible to do with the example of Èṣù earlier, that he had any negative motive of explointing the weakness of his co-divinities for personal gain. On the one hand, in all human socieites, one finds that those with the observation capacity are responsible for teaching others and civilizing society. On the other hand, Orunmila could have patented his knowledge and used it at the expense of his society, if he were from an egocentrically greedy society of the Western genre. The fact that he did not do this, but rather made light of the shortage of knowledge of his co-divinities, shows that everyone can marvel at the knowledge of Orunmila, while learning from him and becoming better persons (23–29).

What do we get from these narratives? Clearly, it seems that the social millieu of interaction is one fraught with all kinds of connundrums. Some of these are competitive, some are moral and some are cognitive. But as Wiredu (2004) argued concerning the Akan conceptual scheme about truth, there is always the element of virtue involved in all aspects of Yoruba social, cultural and moral interaction. For this reason, even competition must never become extreme, which is the reason why Oba and Osun suffered consequences of their interactive friction. Èṣù clearly challenged the women to think, become knowledgeable in the tradtions that gave them birth, and appreciate even the mathematical oddity of sharing even numbers among odd agents, hence showing that negotiations of relations must moderate human claims and interests. There is no element of destructiveness or divisiveness in Èṣù's relations in this instance, as in most other naratives that concern him; giving the lie to the absolute translation of Èṣù as Satan or Shaitan!

What is even more interesting is that we do not see any form of perfidy on the part of Èṣù. While Èṣù could have exploited the situation of the women, taken the extra cowrie shell and added it to his own, he would do no such thing, because a contract is a contract! Thus, Èṣù keeps his bargain, but leaves the three women satisfied that none of them has been exploited by the other. Clearly, we see that Èṣù does not stand for theft, larceny, intellectual or material expolitation of the weakness of anyone. To that extent, it is clear that contemporary society has a lot to learn from the traditional religions of our ancestors—because profiting from the weakness of others, from one's vantage position of power, knowledge, religious office or other is totally anathemical to the culture of Yoruba people.

Societies evolve various cultural artifacts and technologies to survive in the face of environmental experiences. But it is the deliberate efforts of members of society to hone and develop the best practices, based on what experiences teach; learning to improve on weaknesses and to strengthen those that work, which leads to the growth of peoples. For this reason, I consider the critical elements of societal development to be dependent on leadership. I have been attempting to discern the various aspects of leadership which when put together have enabled societies to become dominant or to become mendicant. In other forums I have looked at the cultural fabrications of society which conduce to harmony in society—these being art, ethics, music, agriculture, science and technology and more (Bewaji 2003). As we have indicated earlier, it would not be possible to discuss religion in detail; rather, we will only look at the element of Yoruba religious divinity of Ѐṣù in relation to leadership in society, with a view to showing that Ѐṣù is a necessary divinity for the maintenance of law and order in Yoruba society.

But it may be asked, why do I consider Yoruba religion and its appreciation of Ѐṣù as a divinity to be important in leadership discourse for the development of Yoruba society in particular, and similarly other Africana societies in general? This is a pertinent question, especially as most of our societies make serious pretense of separating religion from political, formal, governmental aspects of life, and more seriously, since Ѐṣù is almost a no-go area for intellectual discussion in Yoruba society given the opprobrium heaped on Ѐṣù upon his association with biblical Lucifer or Satan and Islamic Shaitan. In post-colonial Africa, we are often regarded as ether developing or under-developing (advancing or not advancing) to the extent that we make a show of separating our religion (religious beliefs and practices) from our socioeconomic and political lives (ideologies and practical economic decisions). We also tend to think, though erroneously, that the countries of the West that we try to blindly emulate have been able to develop to the extent they have been able to separate the state from religion, as they make every effort to show this kind of separation as being a necessary component of their humanism, development and civilization. On closer examination, one would see in all aspects of life the tentacles of religion—both in pre-colonial and in post-colonial Nigeria and in the various other societies of the West which we unreflectively aspire to be like. Curiously it has become an issue that various inscriptions of biblical passages have been found on weapons manufactured in the United States of America and used in Afghanistan, Iraq and sold to New Zealand. Now, let me clearly state that I am not here to say whether this is a good thing or a bad thing. My interest is purely critical, metaphysical, epistemological, ethical and political—exhibiting the elements of indigenous Yoruba religion in the ways of our existence, and allowing all of us to then stand back and take a look for ourselves to see if what we see in the mirror as what we now parade as our humanity in a very depraved way is an edifying picture of ourselves or a despicable parody of our humanity that we have created deliberately to our utter self-destruction.

But our concern here is with Yoruba religion, and hence, our focus will be on Yoruba religion in the ways the divinity Èşù is understood and appropriated for social order, accountability and responsibility; especially our interest in how religion may have helped the human being in indigenous Yoruba pre-colonial society to master reality and gain control over the apparently intractable and often intransigent complexities of social, political and economic existence. Now, we need not interpret what I am suggesting here to be another celebration of the religiosity of humanity—like Idowu (1962) would have us believe that human beings are in all things religious. Human beings, in my opinion, are not any more religious than they are sexual, gregarious, social, political, economic, or even any other such thing. Religion is an artifact like any other, created for the interest and benefit of human beings.

It can be seen that in Yoruba society, like in other human societies, there are three main categories of persons involved in the various religions, once the visions have encrusted and congealed into some fixed doctrine. These are, in the contemporary language of theology and religious studies, the missionaries, the theologians and the rank and file believers. One of the portals on which religion survives is institutionalization of the various structures, paraphernalia and edifices that assist in the control mechanism that it must have. For this reason, various cadres of parasitic wayfarers are developed and maintained. For this reason, when institutionalization becomes consolidated, the first and second categories of persons in religion are merged, determining the institutional structures that define, distinguish, bear and perpetuate the religion. While the last category are often humble enough to admit the limitations of their understanding of the tenets, visions and *numens* of the religion; they are the bedrock or bulwark of religious faith and, in some instances they are the willing and unwilling victims, instruments and perpetrators of fundamentalism and fanaticism, as they are often called upon to undertake the funding and feuding over religion, on the one hand, while on the other, when they are allowed to have little room for self-reflection over the items and basis of their faith, they are often more intolerant of divergences of other beliefs from their accepted ones.

The above relates more to the imported religions of Christianity and Islam. In my view, it can be argued that if there was no Islam in the wilderness of Arabia, one would have had to be invented, to serve as the antidote to Judaism and its offspring, the Christian religion in the Arabian Desert and its claims which were totally unconscionable and destructive of peace, justice, harmony and good order in the region. For it would have been unimaginable that the myth of the chosen people and the promised land could have been allowed by all those affected to succeed without contestation, thereby allowing one very minor member of a larger human family in the region to take over the heritage of other members of the same large family of Arabs (of which Jews are a member)! It is for this reason that wherever these too sibling religions have met, they have continued their quarrel over land and the scarce resources which they started from the desolate desert region of their birth, taking down the paths of destruction societies that have had no religious wars in their ancestry!

For literary scholars, attention is concentrated on the various accounts of why Èṣù does not live in groves, homes, or other kind of confinement like the other divinities. The explanations range from sociological, political to literary. In this regard, it is often indicated that because of some incestuous behavior of Èṣù in his dealings with women and with other divinities, he was banished from the abode of the other divinities to live outside of the home or to live at the crossroads. Some would suggest that Èṣù outwitted himself and suffered the fate of the perfidious, while others yet would say that it was the cantankerous attitude of Èṣù that destined him for the vagabondery that he suffers. And yet others will say it was because Èṣù was the gatekeeper, the untiring watchman over the heavens and the earth, which accounts for no homestead containing him. In this regard, Obododima Oha's (2008) essay "The Èṣù Paradigm in the Semiotics of Identity and Community" represents one of the most critical and incisive discussion of the persona, the mythology and the semiotics of Èṣù; his goal was to account for the apparently confusing understanding of Èṣù. Weaving together many narratives from a diversity of Yoruba communities across the globe, he was able to show why Èṣù defies univocal appreciation—partly due to Èṣù and partly due to the efforts of Yoruba believers to provide an understanding that would help them manage their relationship with the divinities, their world and society.

While these theories and explanatory models may simply be informative as handles on myths (semiotics), constructs to explain perplexing religious and literary ideas, which are intrinsically meaningful, it is clear that even these myths are compatible with totally discrepant philosophical interpretations, like the one I posit here. In my view, the banishment of Èṣù to the outside of the home or to living at the crossroads does not in any way antagonize the idea that Èṣù at his worst was a better friend than many would have us belief. For in all of these instances, there is nowhere that Èṣù could be said to abdicate responsibility, treat with others treacherously, renege on a promise, or fail to face the consequences of his beliefs, actions or behavior, which would be hard to say of other divinities.

There is nowhere it could be suggested that Èṣù asked that his action be exonerated on account of being one of the first three divinities (Adeleke 2005, 26–27). And when his tricks backfire and come back to haunt him, he accepted the repercussion with equanimity, looking for no scapegoat nor searching for an alibi for his apparent folly (Oha 2008, 299)! It is obvious that Èṣù could not be controlled, bribed, harassed or intimidated by any one—including by Olodumare, the Supreme Being. He enforces the law, as it should be enforced, and does not allow for personal friendships, allegiances or interest to dominate what is regarded as right, truth, justice or good order in society and in the heavens.

A persona such as Èṣù's is not usually a popular one, nor is such a persona a very much tolerated one, because of the nature of living organisms and their perception of what constitutes their interests. In the case of the divinities who were very much like human beings, it was clear that they were easily affected by the foibles of human beings, and they would not be able to live up to the high expectations of their offices and positions relative to God, each other and to humanity and other beings. When Èṣù then demands that what is right is done, that the truth must be told, and that persons be accountable at all times, humans look for ways of evading responsibility. Since Èṣù does not make excuses, and would not give a blind eye to demands, it is clear that cohabitation with other people will be well-nigh impossible.

What Èṣù encapsulates is simply, in my view, the symbolism of the law in civilized societies. "The law is an ass," is a popular saying in Western democracies, but this only means that when you work with the law, the law can be made to work with you. Differently expressed, this could mean that if you understand the system you live under and live within the bounds of the system, you can be sure that the system will work for you. However, if you try to play smart, holier than thou or beyond the confines of the law that is when you find out that you are entrapped by the law. However, being an ass means that human beings can manipulate the law to take advantage of the loopholes in the law, if they are able to get a good lawyer, without social conscience (i.e., EFCC vs. Saraki/Agabi), who is able to argue their case in front of the judge or jury. It is this phenomenon of the law, as introduced with colonialism, that the Yoruba people are very suspicious of. What this means is that if you are caught stealing a goat, your lawyer could easily argue that you had no intention of stealing the goat; you were only playing with the goat! Another analogy that I would wish to use with regard to Yoruba appreciation of Èṣù as a divinity is simply "Big Brother" in the consciousness of citizens of the United States of America.

Human societies have to deal with varieties of unpredictabilities—natural and humanly contrived. In the process there has to be care taken to not be too rigid, without being too flexible at the same time, as either extreme can be exploited to the utter detriment of society. In the United

States of America and other European democracies, one of the means of sustaining the civil society and protect the weak and vulnerable is for the law, that is "Big Brother," to have a very long memory, be impartial, and often very attentive. This is the notion of the rule of law in these societies. This is often assumed to be nonexistent in colonial societies erroneously, because the colonial masters fail to understand what made for sophisticated civilizations to have happened in these societies, as well as their lack of care to grant these societies a modicum of intellectual respect. Going back to the nature of humans in society, we find that because of these attributes, human errantry must be held in check through various mechanisms. And for this reason, persons who otherwise would have been renegades and destructive are prevented from such anti-social behavior, because they are aware that temporarily they may seem to get away with their misbehavior, but they cannot permanently escape retribution.

One clear thing, for external observers of the American judicial system, is the fact that the law has a long memory, a very long reach, and targets the well-being of society as the overall goal of law. Justice then is the end to which every event tends. In so doing, there is a disincentive to disobedience of the law, but when such happens, there is also an acknowledgement of the need to accept the consequences of actions as necessary. When it is said that "Big Brother is watching you," what is meant is that you are not able to escape the long arms of the law, and that no matter who you are, what your achievements are, or what your status in life may be, you are subject to the law of the land. To that extent, it does not matter that you were not observed when you committed an offence, or that you were well connected; what matters is that the judicial process triumphs at last in most cases, and for that reason, there is trust in the law, there is respect for the law, there is support for the law, as a system, as a practice, and as a means to the end of harmony in society—control is only incidental to the end of the law; what matters most is that members of society see themselves as being amenable to the law of the land. "Big Brother" ensures this inexorable end!

In the United States of America many resources are deployed to ensure that the law is obeyed. With the advent of various technological advancements, these are also made to serve the end of law, to ensure that even sophisticated cheats in wrestling and the Olympics are discovered, using more sophisticated resources to detect their ploys. And there is no instance in which financial resources are denied the prosecution of the end of law, even when there is financial recession. The security of life and property under the American flag is guaranteed, regardless of where in the world the American may be! This facilitates compliance and minimizes perfidy of persons. And when it is not enough deterrence, then the law takes its course and punishes the one who breaches the law.

Now, it may be argued that this is the façade that is presented to the world, that the American system is a corrupt as any other in the world, or that the dispensation of justice is skewed against blacks, thereby creating various other issues of injustice. While I will not deny the force of these arguments, this does not detract from the position advanced here that what matters most is that members of society have the perception that the law of the land will (does) work for them. It may well be a myth, and it may well be just perception, with no reality underpinning it, yet in human relations, just the belief and the perception that it is near impossible to get away with crime is all that is needed to ensure compliance.

I am using Èşù in the same liminal role in this discussion. Probably the whole construction is a myth. Probably humans would have to transcend such myths in contemporary iconoclastic society where globalization is the order of the day. And even more significant, doing a philosophical anthropology of justice, noting the place of Èşù in the order of politics, economics, social relations, etc., cannot be anything bad, especially if the goal is developing indigenous mechanisms for ensuring that members of Yoruba, and Nigerian, society obey the law. For in the end what is clear about the nature and character of Èşù is that one should be sure that justice will be served. It does not matter what personal relationship one may have with the law, when one breaks the law, one should expect the law to take its due course. This is why people would rather stay far from the law. In the Yoruba case, it is best to keep Èşù at arm's length, because he can be trusted to tell on you, make sure you suffer consequences for your action, and not defend you when you are wrong.

And in an environment of extreme human frailty, it is understandable that both the divinities and humans would recognize the nature of Èşù: you cannot live in too close a proximity with him, and you cannot live in too distant a location from him (Oha 2008, 304). Èşù is needed to take care of the various odds and ends of interactional relations of society, but he is feared because he does not look away even at the most insignificant of issues. The way this is presented is through the pathway of Èşù being the bearer of sacrifices to the various deities and Olodumare; but more significantly the fact that Èşù exacts his fair share of sacrifices while in the process of delivering the same, for he must be propitiated in every sacrifice before it is offered to the various divinities and ancestors.

Thus while most authors would dub Èşù as the trickster or prankster, none has been able to show that Èşù acts beyond the propriety of his powers. And when occasionally he gets carried away, he is the first one to judge himself in the harshest of ways (Oha 2008, 306). This would show that the impartiality of Èşù surpasses even that of Olodumare, who could be compassionate when there is need to stand firm, while Èşù will remain rigid and immutable, once it comes to the question of justice, fairness and truth (Abimbola). The ways in which those who represent justice and truth are supposed to be insulated from the foibles of lesser mortals in contemporary society does reflect what the Yoruba people were trying to achieve in the nature and persona of Èṣù. But it is clear that humans in society need more that a version of probity in order to continue to maintain order in society. For this reason, the persona of Èṣù is most volatile and "unpredictable" (he is unyielding to temptations like the other deities), hence the benign ostracism that is foisted on him by making him reside a distance away from humans and deities—irrespective of the fact that none of them could do without his help on a daily basis, and he getting a fair share of whatever is presented to the deities and Olodumare!

This is a question that is interesting and also curious. In most religions, the gods are beyond reproach, and stake their powers on their inviolability. This is not the case in Yoruba society, as the gods' support depends on their performance with regard to the welfare of their devotees. For it is said in moments of skepticism and challenge that *Orisa bo o le gbe mi, se mi bo o ti ba mi,* meaning that "if the gods cannot enhance my existence, leave me as you met me". This shows that the Yoruba people, while appearing to be very deeply religious, never lose sight of the purpose of the religiosity—enhancement of human existence.

And as noted earlier, some of the divinities in Yoruba religion were spiritual beings who also once lived as human beings. They were also supposed to have had human characteristics, which meant that they were subject to the limitations of human beings. However, they were capable of navigating two planes of existence—the natural and the supernatural. They were very powerful, and had varieties of devotees and followers. This phenomenon meant that they could do whatever they wished and enjoyed some level of impunity. However, they were closely watched, observed and monitored by Èṣù, such that they always had to be on their toes, holding themselves to higher standards and being held to such standards as are supposed to be befitting the divinities.

Those of them who became head-strong, obdurate and uncontrollable were tamed by Èṣù, who would use his deftness with words, observation of weaknesses of these divinities and the responsibility expected of the overall police officer, to ensure that the divinities maintained their high office, responsibility and uprightness in their dealings with each other and with humans. The fact that Èṣù could not be bribed also reinforced the respect that everyone held him, and it meant that he was able to enforce the law.

One of the remarkable elements of Yoruba religion that is human empowering is the centrality of human agency and knowledge. While there is no doubt about the hierarchical structure of Yoruba cosmos, the hierarchies are not absolute. There is always movement vertically and laterally between domains, thereby providing checks and balances. For example, the fact that Olodumare never pretends to have endless, total, incorrigible knowledge is significant. To that extent, it means that Olodumare must have consultations with Ifa (Orunmila) and make sacrifices to his own Ori like the other beings. Lijadu thinks that this was a gross mistake on the part of the Yoruba people, regarding their understanding of the Supreme Being, but I consider this to be a most sophisticated apprehension of the nature of the Supreme Being; for this makes meaningful the various paradoxes, dilemmas, incongruities and dissonance in the world, without having to engage in faulty theodicy or scapegoat search for some nonexistent alibi for the weaknesses of the Supreme Being (Lijadu 1972, 19). So, if Olodumare can be subject to such cognitive or epistemic limitations, if Olodumare needs to offer sacrifices to his Ori, it would follow that the divinities would also be subject to limitations. This is one of the outcomes of the test that Orunmila sets for the divinities by way of brain-twisters in Adeleke's essay (2005). But more significant is the fact that when Olodumare consults the divination systems, he must follow through whatever prescription is made by the diviner. Consequently, Olodumare sets examples in obedience, humility and respect for all the other divinities, and by so doing, sets examples for the divinities and humans in transparency and accountability, so that no one is above the law, nor beyond the prescriptions of morality, obedience to laws of nature and subject to the controls necessary for the necessity of good order and respect for all members of the population, especially the weak and vulnerable in the society. To that extent, there is interdependence between the various beings vis-à-vis the nature of their accountability and responsibility. But should any one of them resist the prescription of Ifa, refuse to make the sacrifice prescribed, it is the responsibility of Èṣù to ensure that the divinity or even Olodumare encounters the hardship that is necessitated by the disobedience—friendship, colleagueship or whatever relationships apart! For persons not familiar with Yoruba culture, this may seem rather dangerous, as it may be interpreted as placing Èṣù above Olodumare in the scheme of things. This, however, is a misperception that will not be addressed here, due to the narrow remit of this effort.

Students of cultures often indulge in unwitting and unconscious comparative effort. When there is hybridity and syncretism, the nature of the comparison may take on sublime and covert structures. The era of anthropological and theological superiority has been eclipsed by the new wave of globalization and multiculturalism, but this has not dampened the severity and persistence of religious comparisons and "one faith is better than the other" syndrome. But having survived the age of denial, negation, bastardization, epistemicide and rejection, African religions and cultures are now faced with a more benign and insidious age brought about by the destructive consequences of the deliberate, conscientious and persistent epistemicide that we noted earlier. This means that when the beliefs of African societies differ from the beliefs of Arabian and European origins, which Africans have come across and are compelled to embrace because of slavery and colonialism, the African beliefs are treated or regarded as inferior and deserving only of destruction; this putatively fabricated but nonexistent "inferiority" is used as the basis for the compulsion of converts to the two warring Arabian religions as reason to destroy the indigenous African religions and join the warring Arabian religions.

Bearing in mind then that Yoruba culture does not acknowledge absolute divisions, such that members of the same family could belong to different religions, celebrate with each other at the times of the festivities of the different religions, and never see any threat on account of belonging to different religions, given their knowledge that religion is only as good as it is able to deliver service to human beings, it would then follow that the question of Olodumare needing to destroy Èṣù would not arise, for Èṣù does not pose any threat to Olodumare; on the contrary, the existence and good health of Èṣù is necessary for the effectiveness of Olodumare's agenda in the universe. Èṣù never aspired to world domination; actually Èṣù could not harbor such pretensions, given self-consciousness on his part that he is not the Supreme Being. This is very unlike the Christian Lucifer or Satan or Demon. To that extent, those who make sacrifices to Èṣù do so understanding the necessity of making offerings to him so that he could deliver their major sacrifices to the proper destinations. It is in this regard also that the tenuous identification of Èṣù with Satan must be rejected outright.

But as I have argued (Bewaji 1997), there is no reason why ideas of religion must be homogenous across cultures, nor why humans in all parts of the world must devise identical creation stories to explain where everything started from and how. For this reason, the fact that Yoruba people do not see Èṣù as competing with Olodumare or even attempting to ruin the perfect work of Olodumare does not mean Yoruba people do not understand the nature of the Supreme Being!

Given the above, it means that Èṣù does not constitute a problem for Olodumare. In fact, the existence of Èṣù is necessary for the perfection of the work of Olodumare, as for the Yoruba, it is inconceivable for there to be a universe without either Olodumare or Èṣù or any of the other divinities. Consequently, there is no reason why humans should constitute themselves into a salvation army with Olodumare to vanquish Èṣù. And it is important to note that of the Ajoguns in the world, Èṣù is not listed among them; but contrary to that, the efforts of Èṣù, when fairness, truth, justice and accountability is observed, is necessary for the restoration of health, order and justice in society.

What we are saying is that there are no absolute polarities in the Yoruba world to warrant a need for Olodumare to undertake the destruction of Èṣù. Since this kind of enmity does not originate at a primordial level, nor is there competition for spheres of dominance between Olodumare and Èṣù, there is no need for the kinds of agnosticism, atheism and skepticism that pervade theistic Christianity. Scholars who have not been able to transcend the "either/or" of their new religions must exercise caution in the ascriptions of powers to Èṣù. And in the end, there would have to be better appreciation of Yoruba culture and religion to understand why there was constant collaboration between the deities, the ancestors and human beings in Yoruba cosmos.

In all aspects of reflective life in Yoruba society, whether it is about simple and mundane matters, or it is about serious social, political, economic, religious, cultural, scientific and technological matters, one important element that Yoruba culture emphasizes is "ooto"—truth. To make this clear to all Yoruba children, stories are told of the various ways in which human society and individuals have been affected for good or ill on account of the truth being spoken or not. Under this kind of arrangement, the tenuousness of what you call rhetoric or sophistry is clarified. And the attainment of "imo"—knowledge—is determined through the apprehension of "ooto," such that when "ooto" has not yet been attained, "iwadi" must continue. The continuation of "iwadi"—research or investigation—is not idle, and must be diligently done, with responsibility and determination (Hallen and Sodipo 1986).

An epistemology constricted by this pursuit of "ooto" therefore has built-in skepticism, which at all times make "iwadi" an open affair (Bewaji 2007d). Critical interrogation of sources to eliminate "iro"—lies or false tales—or "awiso"—hearsay—is undertaken, thereby making it possible to entertain all matters pertaining to the matter on hand. These considerations may be purely theoretical or they may involve investigations of an empirical nature. But one could not rush to judgement without adequately responsibly attending to information that is to be had from all sides to the issue.

Now, it may be asked: What is the role of Èṣù in this epistemic exercise? Clearly, from the deliberations we have undertaken so far, it would be obvious that Èṣù serves a dual role: a) as a protagonist for "imo," thereby pointing in the various directions in which "imo" can be attained and ensuring due diligence in the search for "imo"; and b) as an antagonist, creating the critical doubts that are necessary to prevent complacency, fake certainty, or peremptory acceptance of any appearance of truth without having exhausted all the possible relevance evidence. To this end, it is clear that only "ooto" is acceptable to the Yoruba people, and those who are known for telling "ooto," regardless of the consequences are highly valued in society, and are often entrusted with matters that have grave value to society (Bewaji 2003, 2007d).

The feature of Èṣù which we have observed about truthfulness and veracity of testimony also bind the diviners—Orunmila, Ifa and all followers—who have the obligation of making consultations on behalf of their clients. In the first instance, because of the ubiquity of Èṣù, the diviner cannot but tell the truth after making a consultation. If he/she is confused, then he/she must appease Èşù to facilitate clarity of his vision into the message of Ifa. Secondly, for interpretations of ideas through the process of divination, the variations of possible interpretations and their nuances must be laid before Èşù to ask for direction so that errors may be eliminated. Finally, the diviners are usually not the richest members of their communities, because their knowledge and service is not something they can profit from, lest they incur the ire of Èşù. It is always understood that Èşù does not condone cheating, lies, exploitation or any other form of oppression of the needy, the poor or the afflicted. If they contravene this key element of their oath, similar to the one contemporary doctors swear to, then they must face the wrath of Èşù, which is not something any one, human or ancestors, divinities or even Olodumare could look forward to with happiness. In the next section we look more closely at this critical nature, clarifying and interpretative aspect of Yoruba beliefs with regard to Èşù.

As it were, Professor Oha's (2008) celebration of the punishment of Èşù's incestuous indiscretions, eloquently on display through a larger-than-life phallus on the sculpture of Èşù, and Abimbola's (1968) annotation of the fact that Èşù had to be searching for his phallus, after having been punished for some indiscretion, both show the attention that Yoruba thinkers pay to the need for balance in society. As we have noted, humans, primitive, medieval or modern, live by myths. These myths may be religious, purely nonreligiously metaphysical, political, scientific or otherwise. This was well noted by R. G. Collingwood (1940) in his discussion of the metaphysical presuppositions of the sciences—and I assume each age has a scientific epoch underwritten by these presuppositions. As a consequence, the leadership of the Yoruba knowledge system, political and cultural life, economic and epistemological developments was well aware of the need to utilize the ideas which are understandable to members of society to develop and sustain the Yoruba civilization.

Thus, while it is not the intention of this discussion to ask our intellectuals and leaders to remain ossified at the level of puerile nostalgia, hankering over a dead and buried past, the important lesson that we need to begin to learn as a people is that our knowledge systems which have been destroyed, denied, devalued and written off need to be excavated, analyzed and where there are useful ideas, beliefs, and episteme, we must harness these for the development of our societies and our posterity. If the moguls of Japanese businesses go to their ancestral shrines at the beginning of each year to make sacrifices and to pray for guidance and protection, yet they have the second largest economy—at least for now—in the world, and a most sophisticated society technologically, if the inauguration of the presidents of the United States of America is presaged by prayer to the Christian God as guide for the new president, if every opening of the Parliament in the UK brings the bishop of the Church of England to the joint sitting of both houses of parliament for prayers and in the process still make room for that evidence of the decadent relic of British past—the queen—to present the speech from the throne, then there is no reason why the facilities of our culture, which were deliberately pilloried, vilified, undermined and destroyed for the overall colonization and domination of our lives, our minds, our resources and our existence, cannot now be revisited as a means of understanding, if only that, why Yoruba civilization remains one of the most sophisticated in the world, and why urbanization was a phenomenon that Yoruba people cherished and developed, with all its dangers, challenges and potentialities.

While on the subject matter of the past being dead and buried, it is interesting to note that part of human experience that never allows it to be dead and buried is the past. The past has a way of repeating itself, resurfacing at the least opportunity, re-emerging when least expected, of simply not going away, and as a consequence determining our understanding of ourselves, controlling the phenomenologies of our being in the world, and underwriting the possibilities that await society and peoples, given the location of the past and the activities that take place in the present.

Students of political science, political philosophy and governance may already be chaffing at the whole business of resuscitating Èşù. The worry here is ill conceived for a number of reasons. In the first instance, when we discussed the role of "Big Brother" in American sociopolitical and judicial life and culture, what we meant was the way in which the idea was signal in ensuring that human errant proclivities are minimized, because, regardless of how high and mighty you are, or whether the action for which you are being held accountable was committed thirty years ago, there are aspects of law and justice that are not subject to "statutes of limitation," which ensure that human beings can have trust in law, governance and security. This was why the citizens of the United States of America continue to value the presidency and the federalist presidential system of government, with its checks and balances of political directorate, not just to rein in individuals with criminal proclivities, in spite of the experience of the citizens over eight years of misrule by George Bush after the years of Bill Clinton in the White House.

In this British system of governance, ostensibly inherited by the various British Commonwealth countries, "the rule of law" is the equivalent of the United States of America's "Big Brother". Students of law would tell us that the rule of law supersedes all other matters when it comes to adjudicating between individuals and individuals, individuals and groups, individuals and communities, individuals and the state, and by extension, the relations between the various other strata of society, in their interaction, thereby defining rights, duties and obligations under the law. The question of justice is only meaningful under the arrangement provided by discernible statutes and legal codes which moderate human interaction in society.

Given the above, one could argue that these are myths deliberately created for the good order of the United States of America and the United Kingdom. But putting it this way will be unsophisticated, pedestrian and uninteresting, because, having been conquered physically, having had our knowledge systems destroyed (epistemicide), having had our metaphysical constructs destroyed—through the destruction of our religious thoughts, our theology and our belief systems—what one may call "ontologicide," having accepted that we, blacks, Africans, and peoples of color, were inferior, having made it our responsibility to as much as possible become like the monsters who have conquered us, we became partners in the destruction of our culture, our knowledge systems, our political traditions, our religions and the theologies on which they were built, and everything valuable in our culture was negated deliberately, and we now have to start from the middle of nowhere—*orita meta*!

Now, how can we complain that everything is wrong with us? How can we fail to understand that our lives have been taken over by foreign gods, who have no sympathies for us, who probably do not understand us and our peculiar needs? How can gods devised in the inclement, perilous, and desolate Arabian Desert, whose only mode of existence is war, destruction, polarization, theft, deceit, dislocation of peoples, and genocide as means to ends, now be the way in which humans in Yoruba society, Nigeria and Africa are now going to find development, civilization and growth? These are questions that are very clearly easy to answer, if we pay attention to the discussion in this chapter, and the role Èşù played in the Yoruba knowledge system, society, economics, literatures, politics, morality, and culture generally. Consider the idea of "orita meta" alluded to above and how it can confuse a stranger to a place. Without a proper roadmap and direction, it is quite easy for the stranger to get lost; and in the context of Yoruba society, given the fact that Èşù stands watch at the cross-roads, getting lost is hardly an option to those who have been good persons, who have paid their dues to society through honesty, moral probity, truthfulness and clear "Omoluabi" (Bewaji 2003). In fact, if forces beyond the wayfarer were to want to mislead the traveler at the cross-roads, Èşù will intercede to ensure that such effort come to naught!

One may illustrate this with what happened to Orunmila at Ilawe, when the people of the town ganged up against Orunmila, asking how he was going to pass through or where he was going to stay in Ilawe. It was Èşù, who directed Orunmila as to what to do. Now, it is clear that Abimbola's (2008) tropes of appreciating Yoruba religion would pride Orunmila with knowledge through Ifa, but such rigid hierarchical approximations may not be totally valid, because one could then ask, "How did Orunmila not forecast the imminent danger at Ilawe?" such that Èşù now had to come to the rescue. The clear answer, in my view, is that there are no absolutes in Yoruba culture: no absolutes of power, no absolutes of wealth, no absolutes of poverty (actually traditional Yoruba culture had no idea of *homelessness* and destitution), no absolutes of knowledge, no absolutes of beauty (as the story of the divinity who challenged Olodumare to a dress match, but who could not surpass even what the chameleon would show), and more critically, no absolute of intellectual creative or destructive ability; thereby removing the problem of theodicy from Yoruba religion and the universe (Bewaji 1997), but more importantly reducing the cravings for regressive individualism and egoism that makes for the development of pernicious capitalism. For if knowledge is derivative (derived from those who have lived before one, those who have raised one, the numerous sources of ideas that contribute to one's development), then the issue of patent, copyright, and absolute property ownership becomes unacceptable (Bewaji 2007b); hence no one can claim absolute access, denying every other human access, through the acquiring of some title, certificate or other documentation.

The clear signal from what has been detailed above is that Yoruba culture would be a better foundation for Yoruba society. The idea of Christianity and the system of governance (polarizing political democratic culture) and an adversarial legal system (where the thief is not allowed to accept guilt but has to be proven guilty) that came with it, which is alien to Yoruba people (leading to disdain they have in local communities of Yoruba land for "common law" in Nigeria and the way it often gives acquittal to the criminal while punishing the innocent (Bewaji 2008b) and many Nigerians, making them reticent in seeking justice within the formal system. The fact that the Christian God "is slow to anger and quick to forgive" does not help matters. For in human affairs, as shown by "Big Brother" and "the rule of law," the law must not only have a long memory, it must have a long reach, and its application must be known to be certain, dispassionate, without fear or favor. The combination of an alien judicial system enshrined in the common law (which presumes the thief innocent till proven guilty) and the idea of "grace" in Christianity (whereby all your sins you have committed in your lifetime and those you are yet to commit before you die have been forgiven *ab initio*, making it possible to have a phenomenon like Olusegun Obasanjo who proclaimed his "born again" status at every turn in spite of the recklessness with which state resources were being squandered everywhere under his leadership) makes a mockery of justice.

On the other hand, it is very strange for many reflective Yoruba people how it is possible for any religion to strictly police interpersonal relationships, imposing serious sanctions for infractions such as adultery, theft, cheating, lying, etc., while at the same having nothing to say to the grand larceny of public resources or the expatriation of public funds to foreign lands to maintain huge balances when the country from which the resources are derived suffer infrastructural and industrial decadence. Since Islam is a religion of peace and justice, one would have expected that it would have made it irreligious, hence punishable with the vengeance of Allah, to commit the numerous atrocities which Muslims have committed in leadership positions in Nigeria since independence. This means that Islam does not have the answer to the problems of leadership of Nigeria, and hence cannot be relied on to do justice to the most vulnerable and poor in society. In any case, one of the pillars of Islam is Sakat—giving of alms—which means that there must be the poor and destitute in Islamic society, otherwise who is to receive alms if everyone were meaningfully engaged and able to fend for themselves? As indicated earlier, Yoruba society abhors idleness, indolence and poverty, and as a consequence the idea of being a beggar is alien to Yoruba culture.

Clearly the two Arabian Desert religions of Christianity and Islam see nothing wrong with the situation of inequality and state plunder, and this means that there is some strangeness in the beliefs they portend for society. But since religion in indigenous Yoruba society is a means to the end of human welfare, and since the two religions here mentioned represent superior force to various parts of Nigeria, this may explain why Yoruba people and Nigerians embrace both religions in large numbers. In any case, anyone familiar with what happens under the auspices of the two religions will understand that much is farcical while the genuine ones may look rather ordinary, poor and on the struggling lane, like the masses of the people they refuse to rip off!

On another note, it is clear that most Nigerian sociopolitical and economic leadership are hiding behind the two Arabian Desert religions to perpetrate wanton destruction on the poor, ignorant, weak and vulnerable in society. For if they had subscribed to the indigenous religio-metaphysical beliefs, it would have been impossible for them to get away with their robbery of the public treasury. And it would have been unacceptable to the indigenous divinities, ancestors, and the Supreme Being to steal from the poor in order to give Sakat or to make those obscene contributions to the churches and mosques! Definitely Èṣù would have none of it, and all of them individually and collectively would have to reckon with retribution directly from Èṣù. Worse would have been their fate to be stealing from their communities and taking it to foreign lands to lodge in numbered accounts, as there is nowhere immune to the reach of Èṣù, as *bi eniyan ba n yo ile da, oun abenu a ma a yo won se*; that is, if one should be doing evil in secret, evil things will be happening to them without outsiders knowing where they are emanating from.

Things are not facilitated by the fact that there is an insanely corrupt law-enforcement system, which intractably frustrates the cause of justice. While the Yoruba culture judicial system placed premium on truth, fact and social harmony, the common law assumes a different stance, giving more latitude to the wealthy in the procurement of justice—as if it is a commodity. The role of the police of today is totally different from that of Èşù—while the current police system is decadent and anti-society, Èşù was never amenable to any efforts at bribery, intimidation, bias or other forms of misdemeanor. Where Èşù errs, he is the first to discover himself and apply the same punishment (Oha 2008 and Adeleke 2005) to himself in the presence of every one, and abiding by the consequences of his action, without attempting to frame anyone, shift blame or retard and pervert the cause of justice.

Now, Abimbola (2006) made the point that Èşù was the custodian of Ase—the seal of realization of whatever is intended. For this reason, Èşù has grave responsibility indeed. Being aware of this position imposes on him the need to always be mindful of his associations, his pronouncements, his behavior and to constantly be re-evaluating all aspects of his own life—for as custodian of Ase, it does not mean that he is beyond the reach of Ase, or that he could abuse it without dire consequences to him. For readers who may need a mythological parallel in governance in today's world, we could talk of the United States of America's presidential seal! This seal, once applied, on the signature of the president of the United States of America, to the jointly passed legislation, emanating from the House of Representatives and the Senate, become law, and as such become applicable across the land of the United States of America.

What the above clearly demonstrate is that in Yoruba culture, the idea of the seal of authority or power was necessary in the daily ordering of society. To that extent, each king in the community represents the Orisha of the community, and obtains and retains Ase as a consequence of such representation. This devolves great responsibility on the king, just as on Èşù. For this reason all persons who find themselves in a position of power must take such power with serious responsibility, because neither Èşù, nor a king, nor a Babalawo, nor an Onisegun can escape justice for the abuse of Ase. There are no ways of escaping judgement—as even Èşù was made to apply the same justice that applies to other persons to himself (Adeleke 2005).

As I have said repeatedly, the goal of this chapter is not to say Yoruba people must all go back to Yoruba traditional religion. If that were the goal, it would have been obviously still-born. Also, it is not about Èşù as a divinity *simpliciter*, for I am not the most knowledgeable in the Yoruba religion to be able to make prescriptions about Èşù to the Yoruba people at home and in the Diaspora. That kind of effort will be most ludicrous, especially in the light of my having been brought up in the Apostolic Church, and the fact that elements of Christian beliefs will have been evident to a careful reader of this chapter, in spite of my effort to remain dispassionate in understanding Yoruba religion! Further, my interest would clearly have been seen to be directed at not a condemnation or praise of any religion as such, except to do a critical, epistemological, metaphysical analysis of Èşù, thereby showing the ways in which Èşù serves literary, cultural, political, economic, epistemic and other clarifying roles, making issues clearer in the end (even while appearing to befuddle to the uninitiated), helping society to maintain balance, ensuring justice and determining that there is accountability and responsibility in all who live in society—rich, poor, male, female, young, old, clergy (diviner), laity, etc.

Given the above, as a Yoruba-descended person and a Nigerian who as a student of philosophy has been engaged over the last decade in developing what I regard as the necessary foundations of Africana leadership philosophy, and being tired of the perennial problems of poor governance, poverty in the midst of plenty, nonaccountability of leadership since independence from United Kingdom, it devolves on me and others who take the problems of Nigeria very seriously to search for realistic solutions to them. What I attempt then is to go beyond mere lamentation of the numerous problems, to see if within our cultural background we would be able to find ideas that may make for better sociopolitical and economic leadership. Even the various denominations of the various religions that have captured the imagination of the poor and needy members of society, who have become captives to their messages of hope, can learn from Yoruba indigenous religion and the notion of accountability, truthfulness, nonexploitation and responsibility to humans, the ancestors, the divinities and the Supreme Being. The type of obscene wealth that those in leadership of the religions have accumulated, from the extortionist messages and demands they make of the poor membership, who are threatened with damnation and hellfire if they would not empty their poor pockets into the collection till, would diminish, as they would now have Èṣù inexorably on their back, ensuring that justice, restitution and retribution are dispensed without fear or favor—and with no hopes of forgiveness of deliberate sins either in the here or now, or in any future dispensation beyond the grave (if such were to exist).

However, it may be wondered: How is this proposition of liminal Èṣù going to be practicable in our contemporary Yoruba society and in Nigeria? This seems to be the easiest part of the problem, because all human societies live on symbolism—national flag, national anthem, national seal, national heroes, etc. Bringing back to society a most important element of Yoruba indigenous religion, tradition and culture such as Èṣù would not be difficult at all. Since we have clearly shown that Èṣù is not the Christian Lucifer, Satan or Demon and the Islamic Shaitan, this liberates the symbolism of Èṣù for strategic, phenomenological, social, political, cultural, and other uses. It means that we find in our culture that which we could not obtain otherwise from the alien cultures and religions which have served to divide and militate against our development for the last many centuries. And there are many ways of doing this, of which I will recommend the following:

a. In the process of swearing in of officers at all levels of government in Yoruba land, there should be a verse of the oath which should say that Èṣù should stand witness to the proceedings of the day;
b. The various Yoruba states should encrust Èṣù symbol into the seals of their states. This would have the effect of ensuring that everyone who enter the hallowed halls of government in Yoruba land is in the presence of Èṣù, and unavoidably accountable to Èṣù, Olodumare, the ancestors and the people;
c. All the local governments in Yoruba land should also have seals with the symbol of Èṣù clearly encrusted into it. In fact, the presence of Èṣù is to be invoked upon the conclusion of any deliberation;
d. In strategically visible locations at the entrance to Parliament and other public institutions—especially courts of justice—the symbol of Èṣù should be placed. In fact, if this is done, maybe that industry which had become moribund—palm oil—will come back, as we would have the obligation to occasionally put some oil on Èṣù (anyone who abuses this contractual obligation will always know he/she has Èṣù to deal with); and finally
e. All schools in Yoruba land, from elementary to tertiary, should begin to teach our children about the religion of our ancestors—along with whatever religions of the founders of such schools. This will ensure that there is appreciation of the place of religion and symbolism in society. This will help also to cement in them the spirit of accountability, responsibility and respect for others and for society.

These are suggestions that clearly help locate the seat of power in the Yoruba culture directly. There will be resistance from various sources—not least from the beneficiaries of the current decadent system of governance that we have, but also from Christians and Muslims alike. This resistance is to be expected. But what is the alternative that we have? If we look at the various symbols of state in various countries, we will see various residues of mythologies of the societies in question ingrained in money, seal, anthem, flag, etc. These are accorded due respect, including the idea of royalty, while for so long the indigenous traditions have been trampled wantonly. Probably it is no wonder that Èṣù has refused to endorse all the wrongs we have been perpetrating against each other, against society, against the ancestors, against the divinities, and against Olodumare—hence making it difficult for Yoruba land to prosper!

TEN

Culture, Property Rights and Risk Management in African Development

The whole universe is like one huge society, with contemporary human society within it being a society in which there is unavoidable mutual interdependence of all humans and other sentient beings that inhabit the universe. The rich need the poor to survive, and the poor need the rich to continue to exist. The technologically advanced need the technologically backward to continue to maximize the benefits of technology and the technologically stunted need the technologically advanced to have a psychological feeling of being a part of humanity, through their attachment to the outward appearances of the age and being relevant to the new age of information consumption and manipulation. The "Christian" need the "other" (non-Christian) in order to have a point of contrast, and the non-Christian needs a religio-metaphysical point of departure from the Christian in order to justify not being a Christian—whether fanatically or otherwise. The scientifically hi-tech "civilized" person and her society needs the scientifically under-privileged in order to be able to continue the supremacy of science, while at the same time pretending that scientific knowledge and technology is open and accessible to everyone who dare wish to attain the nirvana that it promises; yet science is, metaphysically and realistically, as closed a knowledge area as any in the esoteric mysteries of various reclusive orders in the world. There is even a sense in which the ecosphere is one in which animals, plants, and even the so-called inanimate objects need each other for the systemic continuance of the general equilibrium that sustains the multiverse. This is why it is important to pay attention to the extinction of plants, animals, and the depletion of sources of energies—be they fossil or otherwise.

But there is a distrust of each other that pervades the souls of the polar identities and mentalities of the interdependent entities that we have mentioned above, to the extent that the actions of any agency may have dire consequences for other unrelated agents in the multiverse. This is because, intrinsically, in the one instance those who derive advantage from particular positions and institutions will do everything possible to maintain the advantage, while wondering why those who are outside of the rim (or "loop," as Americans will say) want so desperately to have the advantage. While on the other side, those who are at the wrong end of things, be they human or nonhuman—knowledge, information, wealth, piety, power, etc.—would do all that is possible to have a piece of the action, including even death, and in many instances, cause the destabilization of the equilibrium, when parties fail to observe the necessary mutual respect patterns that make for equilibrium!

In this chapter, I explore aspects of the question of risk in research, indicating that the fact that there is no homogenous understanding of ethics or morality among human players in the world arena accounts for the lack of uniform understanding of research ethics and knowledge risks attendant on the pursuit and attainment of knowledge. This provides a leverage for the challenging of the dis-configured global system (as sanctified by the WTO, UN, and other international multilateral organizations of the world) of the pursuit of knowledge, ownership of knowledge, dissemination of knowledge and utilization of knowledge—all of which is intrinsically geared toward the accumulation of the material resources to facilitate the opulent lives of those who have the transient advantage of power and influence, to the detriment of the majority have-nots.

The discussion is undertaken under the following section headings: First there is a section where I briefly indicate my misgiving with the structure of international mapping of intellectual property rights, its organization and its application in a global world market. This is followed by the sections on knowledge, research, ethics and risk. A final concluding section harnesses the points contained in the chapter, making suggestions regarding how the various research and knowledge pursuance and accumulation risks identified can be mitigated. It is the opinion of this writer that research needs deliberate effort and support in order to ensure that the potential for knowledge and use of knowledge in the South is not compromised at the expense of the collective survival of peoples of these societies.

In 2002 there was the staging of the FIFA Football World Cup in Japan and South Korea. Before the staging, there was the frenzy of international animal rights, friends of the earth and other environmental awareness organizations in the West staging all kinds of protest around the capitals of the global economic power houses. They were canvassing that the peoples of the Pacific kill a particular animal for food (an ethnic delicacy of the region) in a particular way that was "inhumane." Because of this, these animal rights advocacy organizations asked the whole world to boycott the FIFA Football World Cup, to pressure the peoples of this region to stop killing this animal in this way. A lot of furor was generated from this particular campaign. At the end of the day, the World Cup went ahead, and humanity did not get whipped into acquiescence with regard to the demands of one narrow "holier than thou" segment of the human race to see the world only through the visual prism of the advocacy groups on this matter.

Let it not be indicated that this writer endorses cruelty to any living being—whether human or otherwise. It is clear that there is a cycle of life in which things must prey on each other for survival and balancing of the equilibrium of existence—and those who proclaim vegetarian life-styles are not exempt here. In this regard, it is the view of this writer that where possible, the minimum of pain must be the goal. But this is not the real issue. The real issue is the effort of a group to constitute themselves into the totality of humanity and impose their own standards and perception of morality as *the* morality on the world. If the standards were uniformly applied to all aspects of human existence, then there would be no problem. When, on the other hand, animal rights advocates condemn some humans for doing "harm" to their prey, one wonders whether the consumption of any living thing is not intrinsically harmful to the consumed—whether plant, animal or neither. This would suggest that if the animal rights advocates do not like *how Koreans and Japanese kill dogs for food*, for example, they should be able to say this without imposing their own cultural views on the rest of the world, while right under their elongated noses their own kith and kin mete out extreme cruelty and wickedness of the highest unimaginable kind to another living thing for sport—that is, *sport fishing*, which is carried out on real-time television beamed to all of humanity, whereby a fish is hooked, suffering excruciating pain in the process, dragged up to the boat, examined, measured, and released back into the sea! I guess the proponents of this would say that there was no intrinsic harm done to the fish, as it is released back into its habitat in the final analysis. But the issue is whether any human would like to experience the hook in her/his upper jaw or palate even for a few seconds—not to mention the many minutes that it takes to drag the fish to the boat or to the fisher-person for viewing, measurement and depraved self-adulation, and eventual release into the sea.

The relevance of the above is simply to show how some humans in some climes take it upon themselves to be the determiners of rights, justice, morality and virtue for the rest of humanity. And this also indicates how peoples of the world are often asked to join discourses as they are posed (such as feminism and gender), as if such discourses are culturally neutral; that is, as if the discourses have universally agreed-upon underlining presuppositions, universally agreeable benefits or utilitarian values, universally approved parameters and universally valid/validating structure of evidence, justification and conclusion-deriving mechanisms. The issue, then, of research ethics is one of those issues that humanity, globally, are enjoined to engage in a rather univocal manner, with no room for proper interrogation of the various factors that are relevant to proper analysis of the issues.

What we are suggesting is that the issue of research ethics is not different from the issue of cruelty to animals, environmental protection, child labor, female circumcision, polygamy, transient monogamy, homosexuality, feminism, etc., where humanity are being compelled to adopt the perspective of one segment of humanity, and all other perspectives are being coerced into submission and nonexistence. The issue of research ethics is often posed against the background of the purported "universal" values regarding property rights, such that the historically circumscribed rights deriving from a Lockean perspective, whereby ownership is a product of effort or exertion plus creative intellect, regardless of the *status quo ante,* prior to the point of right ascription—vide the problems related to land in Botswana, Palestine, South Africa, and Zimbabwe (Bewaji 2008a). This is posed against the background of who registers an idea, patents it, and gets a title to it, rather than as in the collective wisdom of humans in a collectivity, where the knowledge resided *ab origin.*

What this means is that, regardless of how a person or group originally acquired ownership of an item or material, whether intellectual, spiritual or psychological, in this case an idea—just like land—once the person or group is in "possession" of the item or material, and is able to register his/her or group name to the item or material, then any subsequent access to or use of the item or material by the rest of humanity must respect, acknowledge or pay homage (materially and otherwise) to the so-called "original" owner(s) of the item or material. This is the skewed logic of international agreements on intellectual property rights that currently is employed by and sanctioned by the powers that rule the world today. And we, who are on the margins of capitalist systems of thought and economy, are not allowed to critically analyse the fundamental presuppositions of this so-called Eurocentric, self-serving, "self-evident" logic of ownership!

As we will see clearly in this discussion of risk in research, our inference is based on the structure of reality that endorsed the entrenchment of contemporary international power structures, power relations and perpetuation of the status quo of wealth acquisition, wealth ownership, wealth creation and wealth utilization under capitalism. This is the first big risk—the risk of asking prohibited questions, the risk of trying to find out whose perspectives determine the agenda for discourse of research ethics and the risk entailed in being a fringe researcher, with no entrenched capacity to make a difference to discourse. I am saying then that before we begin to debate risk in research, the first issue that cries out for clear analysis is the structure of intellectual property in the world. Our discussion in the following sections, going behind the issue of research ethics to understand the nature of knowledge, ethics, and research, will bear this out clearly as our investigation unfolds.

Attainment, utilization, hoarding, and even monopoly of "knowledge" and practically useful "information," have always been serious desires of humans in all epochs and ages in history, and because of these factors understanding "knowledge" as a concept and as an instrument of success, control of existence and dominance over nature and other human beings have been serious pre-occupations of the reflective members and those desirous of power among peoples of all civilized societies from time immemorial, becoming a subject of great intellectual, theoretical, practical, material, cultural and technological investment (Bewaji 2007d). For this reason, it is critical that all developing societies (read poor, dependent, and neo-colonial societies) must take interest in the ownership, appropriation and utilization of all sorts of knowledge and technologies that are necessary for their sustenance and development. Not doing this is tantamount to a swan song of disaster and perpetual poverty.

It could be argued that the concern of humanity with knowledge is simply because, in most traditional and among contemporary societies, it can be said that "knowledge" has been the major factor that has separated the haves from the have-nots. It is the main basis for the control that exists between peoples and individuals. It is that main item on the menu that enables groups to gain control over other groups. "Knowledge" is at the centre of success or failure. "Knowledge" is the crucial element in all domains of life—be it practical or theoretical. And in an increasingly pernicious and destructively competitive Darwinian world of survival of the richest, there can be no separation of "knowledge" from the wellspring of human realities—namely life, death, pain, hunger, wealth, failure, heaven, hell, planetary mappings and trips, exegesis, love and hate, death, happiness, and whatever we want to become, plus and inclusive of the process of becoming or extinction; everything depends on the presence or absence of "knowledge!" This is a simple issue which implicates the fact and need for each society to deliberately orchestrate the search for knowledge in ways suitable to their epistemic, intellectual and practical requirements and agendas, bearing in mind that no epistemology is utilitarianly neutral. And when we consider the fact that having natural resources is no guarantee of welfare, wealth, development or advancement if this is not combined with the knowledge of how, technological competence to manipulate the resources to yield positive results for the benefit of humanity and intellectually sound policies. In other words, Nigeria, for example, has so much natural resources which has not benefited the majority population that lives within its borders but became a stumbling block in the path of progress and human welfare of Nigerians, while there are other countries without half of the resources of Nigeria which has higher per capita income, better life expectancy, better conditions of living, greater access to better life-enhancing infrastructural facilities, higher levels of awareness of human rights, etc. (Bewaji 2007d).

Clearly, in a very competitive world, where individual and group or corporate survival depends on how much of scarce resources a person, a group and a people can single-mindedly commandeer, especially where less than one-third of humanity consumes more than 60 percent of the wealth of the world, humans have moved away from a life in which conscience and morality (whatever we may regard that to be in a hetero-cultural world) counts (if ever there was such a time in history when conscience counted, going by the accounts of pernicious genocidal wars documented in the Bible), to one in which knowledge or the appearance of having it (pretence to it) counts for existence or extinction—you either have it or you don't, as the deception that took place on a global scale in the intelligence the United States of America used to canvass the invasion of Iraq in 2003 shows. Fools allied to knowledge (or the appearance of knowledge) can order the wise to do their foolish bidding, and the wise allied to a poverty of knowledge (ignorance) can only gape and pray in vain that the fool will come to a realization of the poor taste and demerit of the course of their action—a pipe dream which the Yoruba clearly realized when formulating the wise saying that *ki ile to pa osika, oun gan na gan na yi o ti baje*—meaning literally that "before nemesis catches up with the wicked, very important and critical things would have been destroyed!"

In the contemporary world, it is safe to say that if you have knowledge (or can pretend to have it) or appear to have knowledge, all other things shall and will be added unto you, but if you lack knowledge or appear to lack knowledge, you may as well pack all your things into a basket and do the only rational thing for your kind—commit individual or group suicide by allowing the ones with knowledge to exploit and expropriate you and to continue to rule over you. For what are you worth when you do not understand the technical issues that are used to determine your modes of existence, or when you buy an equipment which you do not understand, cannot maintain and whose blueprint in is the capital of your greatest foe? If you are perpetually a mendicant, with your palm always open below the thrust of the hands of your benefactors, how could you dictate what happens within your borders, when you go to bed, when you wake up or when and whether you can mate with your spouse or not?

It is clear that so much for the "civilization," with the advances in information and communications technologies which have made the world to become a huge global village, the ideals of liberalism that governs the centres of Western powers, the disappearance of cold-war ideological divides in the world, and the confederation of nations under the aegis of the much vaunted United Nations, have not combined to make any difference to the human nature, the callousness of the human instincts and the venality of human brazenness in taking from the poor to give to the rich and idle. The world we live in has not become any more clement than that of the ancestors of humans one hundred thousand years ago (those ape-like "imbeciles" foraging eternally for survival and immediate sustenance), nor are we any better than our ancestors of about 5,500 years ago, when some people in some climes got it into their heads that their deranged god had ordained that they should wipe out another people entirely, because these people stand in the way of their economic and physical survival (thereby perpetrating the first recorded case of ethnic cleansing or genocide in human history), nor does it become any more clement today when some people can sit somewhere and decide that they need to get rid of the leaders of another people, society or country because the leader of that people, society or country are no longer in their good books as these leaders are determined not to allow them to gain unimpaired access to the natural resources of that country; or so that the international conglomerates can label products expired and get them destroyed as unfit for human consumption while half the world population hunger and thirst for crumbs from these tables and die in abject poverty because of the non-level playing field which the capturing of knowledge in some quarters have yielded, where some are paid farm subsidies to fatten cows or to not grow some crops for ethanol and others are told their cows cannot have similar subsidies or that even those crops that they have produced cannot be bought at their economic cost/value because they lack the knowledge necessary to matter and hence they are not the chosen people to benefit from the largesse of the knowledgeable powerful (Bewaji 2004).

Many questions then become immediately and critically compelling. What is knowledge? What can we know? How can we know? Who can know? Why do we need to know? What is the use of knowing? What is the use of knowledge and ignorance? Are we ever certain of anything or should we be content with belief? Do we really need certainty? What is certainty? When is (some) justification enough for claims to knowledge? Is knowledge time, age, sex, religion, location dependent? Is indubitable knowledge ever attainable? Is knowledge relative to context or is knowledge absolute and eternal? What is truth? How is truth related to what is known? How is it related to the knower? Is truth subjective or objective (Bewaji 2007d)?

On another plane, there are other sets of questions which directly relate to our discussion here, especially with regard to science, technology, development, information manipulation and access. Some of these are listed here. Does science give knowledge or only probable truth? What does knowledge confer, which ignorance denies? Is it better to know than to merely believe? Or, again, should we be content with belief and never bother trying to attain knowledge? When we talk about the knowledge age (often confused with information age), what do we mean? Are there some kinds of knowledge—like nuclear knowledge and technology—that only a few races, peoples, geo-political zones (like Israel, Australia, India, Pakistan, Brazil, the United States of America, Britain, Russia, Japan, China, France and Germany) could (should) access, because of right of birth, color (melanin density endowment), ideological and religious persuasion, cultural achievements, technological achievement or economic superiority, which others (such as Iran, Nigeria, and North Korea) cannot and should not have because of their religious and ideological proclivities? Are technological competence or scientific information and knowledge transparently accessible to all humanity or only to the select "real" humans who define what constitute humanity? Or should we even say that all knowledge is relative, and as such those who control the power centres of the world today only appear to have knowledge, whereas they really do not have infallible and eternal knowledge—which only the omniscient God has? Would it be reasonable for those who have borne the brunt of burden of human survival not to ever bother to find out why is it that they are always being called to make more sacrifices only with the promise of some recompense in the afterlife? What if there is no afterlife—would their sacrifices have been in vain? Why could they not get a piece of the action here and still a bigger piece of the action in the afterlife—would anything be wrong with that if they live their lives according to the injunctions of their deities?

Yet there are other sets of issues, after we have raised those above, that need to be investigated, which poignantly relate to what we mean and understand by ethics and risk in research. These are clearly important and include the following. Why are some persons called experts and others not? What exactly do they (experts) have, which others (non-experts) lack? What is the responsibility of the human knower in the process of knowing, in representing knowledge, in justifying knowledge and in communicating knowledge? Why must experts only come from one geopolitical zone? Is this epistemic responsibility absolute, relative, transferable, permanent, local or non-local? How much of the responsibility is shared by humans with other humans as members of a sentient knowing group? Is knowledge inherently coded into human genes, such that humans are naturally endowed with certain basic cognitions unless they are challenged in some way to prevent the manifestations of these pre-ordained human cognitions? Are there some genetic evolutionary patterns which epistemologically separate humans from other animals in the universe as knowing agents? Why is it that only the "experts" from some select geo-political zones of the world receive the recognition and patronage of others around the world, and where there are betters from other societies they do not receive notice, much less recognition? Does this not seem to be a form of conspiratorial in-breeding that keeps the knowledge and the reward for the knowledge within the enclosure of the privileged domain? Why is it that the very brilliant ideas created by southern intellect cannot be discerned to come from the South, and where they do, then need a northern echo to receive attention and acclaim? Why does any intellectual from some big institution have to validate the "kangaroo" way of carrying children when for millennia many West African parents (fathers and mothers) have known this and carried their babies that way? These are some of the many questions which we must confront when we discuss issues about knowledge, information development, utilization, research, ethics, research ethics in a global environment and risks involved in the various aspects of the search for and use of knowledge in the contemporary societies of today.

It is compulsory for human beings who are aware of the benefits of knowledge then to seek knowledge. But seeking knowledge itself is not enough; knowledge must be sought in a coherent, methodologically robust, scientifically responsible and humanistically sustainable manner. It is imperative for institutions devoted to the development of knowledge, documentation, preservation and dissemination of knowledge to see that too many times science and technology, knowledge and the intellect are not allowed free rein to be creative, imaginative and investigative. Thus, there is clear need then to see that knowledge comes shackled by various constraints and strings from various sources, and that deliberate efforts need to be made to unshackle, unfetter and un-tether knowledge and information, so that the potential of our peoples, societies, communities and other subaltern sub-worlds can be unleashed. This is where research comes in, and this is where various considerations must be factored into the process and method of developing and accessing knowledge. Against this background I will briefly consider the nature and understanding of "research," as a concept and as a practice.

Many textbooks in the sciences, the social sciences, and even in the humanities have been devoted to detailing what is meant by "research" as a concept and as a practice within the various disciplines of interest to the writers of the books. The goals of these write-ups are often to facilitate practitioners within these domains in the business of providing information for the proper determination of what constitute creation and testing of knowledge in these disciplines. Some of these write-ups even facilitate the interested student in practicing the process of research in the disciplines of choice, making it possible for them to become experts, consultants and leaders of opinion in their areas of choice. But in developing perspectives on research in the diverse disciplinary backgrounds, there is always some element of vagueness and/or ambiguity in the assumption that what we are talking about—research—is a homogenous concept across the board. Consider what would constitute research into the determination of what the Christian God would want a Christian to do to enter heaven, by comparison with research into what would determine the existence of human settlement in the Kgalagardi Desert in the year 5,000 BC! Or, if we wonder what would constitute critical and robust research into determining the melting temperature of titanium, by comparison with careful and meaningful research into what would happen to lifestyles, consciousness and behavioral patterns of people of an inner-city community if they were to be relocated into a plush upper-income housing situation as compensation for hundreds of years of unjust dumping of garbage in their previous living environment? These are serious questions that cannot be determined by fiat.

At a more fundamental level, there is the issue of competence. Who is competent to conduct research? Does competence confer any more validity on research? Or is it pedigree that confers respect on research? These are issues which bear on the nature, content and provenance of research, beyond the simple aspect of the validity of research conducted itself. And there are all kinds of reasons for determining the responses one way or another beyond the mere questions of science of the research. We will have time to look at these issues later; for now, we simply want to understand what is meant by "research."

"Research" is a careful, detailed, rigorous, critical and deliberate investigation of, looking at, analysis of, an issue, phenomena or object, in order to develop, increase, document or apply knowledge about the object of research. Research is about finding out the "truth" about what is investigated. It is predicated on the principle that "truth" is important, deserving of discovery, and worthy of the risk, effort and investment of resources that are expended in making the discovery and documentation. Research takes place in practical as well as in theoretical and quasi-practical or theoretical domains. Research feeds on the needs and resources of society. No society has ever survived nor could ever have survived without research, no matter how we now retrospectively describe some societies as primitive or traditional. And since humans are naturally curious, in virtue of the evolution of our cognitive and cerebral mechanisms, it means that humans in all epochs and climes undertook research, either to meet their curiosity or for the purpose of engineering survival. And since the needs for research, the resources for research, the technological capacities of researchers and the ends of research are diverse, it means that the types of research, the process and the degrees of simplicity and sophistication of research would also vary proportionately as these factors varied—ranging from very simple ones, for example, about what co-presence of factors make particular planting periods more productive than others, to what kinds of climatic conditions are to be found on Venus and Mars.

One of the marks of human advancement, development, civilization and cultural improvement has been the awareness of the critical position of research to the simplification of tasks, documentation of good practices, and reproduction of good or best practices, prevention of unwanted consequences of events, actions and happenstances of nature. Even in such matters where the benefits of research are not immediately evident, it is often accepted that no knowledge is lost or a waste, hence research is valued for its own sake. Under such circumstances, especially technologically driven societies value, treasure and protect those among them with that capacity and talent for research, endowing them with the facilities and resources that would make the use of their special talent, skill and capacity to be used for the benefit of society. But one of the marks of underdevelopment in many of subaltern contemporary societies is the disproportionate investment in consumption materials which have little or no further benefit for humankind than their satisfaction of the inveterate desire of members of society for ostentation at the expense of investment in research, education and development of the intellectual capacity of members of society. This has been the foundation of the vicious cycle of poverty, which leads inevitably to the dependency of such societies on those societies who have deliberately invested in the development, discovery and harnessing of knowledge, through carefully planned and implemented research policies.

One signal point contained in the last paragraph deserves noting. This relates to the fact that research may be an end in itself. Clearly knowledge is an end in itself for societies that can afford this luxury. Hence, the great investments in exploring the external extremities of the universe may be made by societies that can afford such a luxury of investigating things that may not seem to have immediate utilitarian potential for humans. Now, this does not mean that the knowledge derived from such investigations have no immediate relevance to human existence, but for societies that are busy trying to survive various curable diseases and human-induced poverties, justifying investment in the sexual behavior of slugs may not constitute a priority! As a result of this, serious "ethical" issues may arise about how meaningful, useful and relevant research is to be understood, and how to allocate the scarce resources available between the competing priorities in poor economies. I deliberately put in quotes "ethical" here, because of the relativity of what constitutes useful expenditure of scarce resources. And also because of the need to understand that the failure of leadership to see the relevance of particular investment in research and development of institutional infrastructures to facilitate a research need not be because of critical ethical dilemmas regarding proper use of resources but a product, in many cases, of leadership intellectual myopia. At a glance, this immediately puts in clear relief the reasons why our institutional hierarchies suffer from cognitive lethargy and intellectual inertia, thereby making research a handmaiden of sycophancy, crass cronyism and glorification of mediocrity.

Frantz Fanon (2001) clearly understood this, in another domain, when he railed on the dangers that myopic leadership are incapable of seeing, understanding or avoiding in relation to how they go about constructing systems that only serve their ego trips and megalomaniac sense of grandiosity in public life. Strangely, what he says is also applicable to how intellectual opportunists conduct their understanding of leadership in the academia. He says,

> As we see it, the national bourgeoisie of certain under-developed countries has learned nothing from the books. If they had looked closer at the Latin American countries they doubtless would have recognized the dangers which threaten them. We may thus conclude that this bourgeoisie in miniature that thrusts itself into the forefront is condemned to mark time, accomplishing nothing. In under-developed countries the bourgeois phase is impossibly arid. Certainly, there is a police dictatorship and a profiteering caste, but the construction of an elaborate bourgeois society seems to be condemned to failure. The ranks of decked-out profiteers whose grasping hands scrape up the bank-notes from a poverty-stricken country will sooner or later be men of straw in the hands of the army, cleverly handled by foreign experts. In this way the former mother country practices indirect government, both by the bourgeoisie that it upholds and also by the national army led by its experts, an army that pins down the people down, immobilizing and terrorizing them (Fanon 2001: 140).

Clearly what Fanon has said above has become true over and over again in most societies that have experienced slavery, emancipation, colonialism, neo-colonialism and post-colonialism. In the academy this has not been any different, as research is constricted by factors other than academic interest, but political and psychological myopia of leadership which does not believe that there can be other truths other than those championed from the colonial metropoles, forgetting that part of the risks that must be borne relate to daring to create new and different tropes of comprehending reality, managing reality and advancing reality. The creative imagination of humanity must not be shackled by limiting the intellect in this way, hence one can say with Lewis Gordon and Jane Gordon (2006) that *not only the master's tools* are needed to deal with reality and to own the reality of human existence on the fringes.

In *Pedagogy of the Oppressed*, Paulo Freire (2003) detailed so many factors that reinforce the poverty and underdevelopment of the oppressed peoples of the world. Two of these factors are first, the authoritarianism of the home and school in the education of the young ones, which ensure that they (the young) are conscripted into perpetual incapacity for self-realization as thinkers and creators of ideas, tolerating mediocrity, glorifying corruption and reifying criminals to heroes and heroines; and second the fact that this system of education, a culture of intellectual nihilism and incapacity, only breeds a human that is afraid of freedom, independence and who is intrinsically incapable of severing the umbilical cord of coloniality (Freire 2003: 154ff), one who lives in existential limbo with crises of being and identity gnawing away at the fundamental basis of their consciousness.

These factors lead to the fear of research, the fear of scholarship, the fear of transcending the limitations of intellect imposed exogenously from the power centres of the Breton Woods and the Paris Club; and this goes even up to the highest levels of intellectual, academic and educational development of peoples of the developing societies, to the extent that everything is done to short-circuit research, either through the under-funding of research, or through neglect and the deliberate creation of road-blocks in the paths of the researchers, or through the alienation of researches which seem to challenge the received dogmas that come from the metropolitan "masters" institutions of learning. It is as if there is a fear of daring, a fear of trying to know, a fear of even trying to be different, and a fear of wanting to move up in life as a group. It is as if there is a self-fulfilling destiny of backwardness that must not be redressed. This translates into a carefully orchestrated and deliberate effort to ensure that critical thinking is prevented, so that there will for ever be dependence on foreign experts—who are in most cases the second- or third-rate minds of their societies, but who are regarded as better than the very best that the indigenous peoples of the developing societies have produced, thereby reifying technicians into engineers and hiring rejects of other societies as professors, while our own great minds are coloured into nonexistence by the accident of their melanin endowment. The manifestation of the phobia for developing the intellect to think critically is evident in the ways in which we fail to provide institutional support for disciplines that teach critical thinking and philosophical reflection, as in the case of the University of the West Indies family of campuses, that could stimulate our young to research and reflect upon their condition and how they got to the sorry passes they are in.

The ominous words of Peter Singer (1986), introducing his anthology, *Applied Ethics*, is significant in many respects and could be regarded as a very good entrée to a discussion of the chequered history of ethics and moral philosophy in the West. Let me take the liberty of quoting these words here for perspective. He says, just two decades ago, that

> to an observer of moral philosophy in the twentieth century, the most striking development of the past twenty years would not be any advancement in our theoretical understanding of the subject, nor would it be the acceptance of any particular ideas about right and wrong. It would, rather, be the revival of an entire department of the subject: applied ethics (Singer 1986: 1).

While the developments of the last thirty-five or so years in the area of applied ethics have been nominally significant, one wonders why this intellectual development has not translated into better practice or, better still, into morally informed actions, decisions, beliefs, and dispositions to behave in Western societies that have prided themselves of being bastions on civilization, advancement, development and humanity *per excel-*

lence. It may be instructive to suggest that the recent preoccupation with applied ethics that Singer sees as probably a welcome "striking development" itself is no accident. First, it could be argued, is the impatience with the direction that philosophy took in the West in the preceding almost three-quarters of the twentieth century before Singer wrote the quoted words, with its travails in positivism, linguistic analytic hair-splitting, and recursive flirtations with amoralism, recrudescent existentialism, unabashed individualism, inveterate and pernicious capitalism, rank nihilism and shameless agnosticism. Second is the increasing and increased professionalization of the philosophical enterprise, at once isolating and insulating the issues of discourse from reality and from life experiences of humans and equally succeeding in devising an insular dialogue and correspondence among a distracted and irrelevant membership of an academe in danger of ceding their places to a festering and festooning mercantilism, militarism and militialism and fascism of various genres, unless they succeed in recreating themselves and become "relevant" to something (Bewaji 2003). And third, but not the least, is the so-called reflexivity of the philosophical predilection toward self-appraisal, self-critique, introspective disciplinary assessment and consequent self-effacement in the face of challenges from paranoid conservatives on the extreme right and standardless liberals on the extreme left—making the coast almost clear to a Trump in the White House.

Bernard Williams (1972) is equally critical of the emptiness of contemporary moral philosophy of the analytical and linguistic types. According to him,

> Contemporary moral philosophy has found an original way of being boring, which is by not discussing moral issues at all. Or, rather, it is not so much that a style of moral philosophy has been evolved which cuts the connection with moral issues altogether—that, if it were possible, would have the interest of being remarkable; but the desire to reduce revealed moral commitment to a minimum and to use moral arguments in the role of being uncontentiously illustrative leaves an impression that all the important issues are off the page, somewhere, and that great caution and imagination have been used in letting tiny corners of them appear (p. 10).

While he struggled to remedy the situation by being relevant to immediate moral issues of society, it is still clear that, as an introduction to an insulated discourse, his efforts were destined to be of little influence on contemporary moral philosophy practiced by his compatriots in the hallowed halls of the intellectual philosophical infamy. This was not an unpredictable fate, as, in the first place, try as he did, his effort operated within the shackles of the tradition that he so ably lamented, and, in the second place, his audacity was encumbered by the limitations of thousands of years of philosophical distancing from the society that produced it. As a consequence, a reading of Williams (even his chapter of "What Is Morality About"), like a reading of many (if not all) other contemporary moral philosophy texts (including J. L. Mackie's 1977 *Ethics—Inventing Right and Wrong*) bears little or no concrete behavioural guides for interested members of Western society.

His and Mackie's failed, but gallant efforts fall in the same category as that of Kurt Baier and Kai Nelson. These are moral philosophers who felt that the distance between Western ethical philosophizing and life was too large, and used a combination of intuitive and common sense arguments, after the manner of G. E. Moore before them, to salvage the parlous situation. The effort did not yield desired results mainly because Western academic philosophical tradition has been too far gone in the direction of philosophical disorientation. Consequently, interest shifted into more practical and more pressing new diversions. This is what accounts for the novelty of Peter Singer's *Applied Ethics* and Gary Percesepe's anthology in applied ethics (1995), *Introduction to Ethics—Personal and Social Responsibility in a Diverse World.* The efforts in this new direction have somehow been overshadowed by the importance of what R. M. Hare (1952) has represented in contemporary moral philosophy. Hare has no illusion about his task, and could not imagine how others could have been misled into other ideas of their task. For him, "Ethics, as I conceive it, is the logical study of the language of morals" (p. v).

Thus, applied ethics, like applied mathematics, applied physics, applied chemistry and applied religion—liberation theology!—and many other applied this and that, have a novelty about them, an intrigue and a certain scientific panache, that one immediately expects something new and different. In the case of the many other "applieds," there probably is an intrinsic justification for their epithet as, in actual fact; they seem to be applying the epistemic, metaphysical, methodological, analytical and theoretical gains of their progeny to new issues and problems, thereby facilitating the solution of wide ranges of theoretical and practical problems. While in the case of ethics, the fact that there are no similarly decided epistemic, metaphysical, methodological, analytical and theoretical gains, that no issues are settled regarding even the subject matter of what is to be applied itself constitute a preliminary setback.

Before the twentieth century, thinkers have followed different intellectual inclinations in deciding the question what ethics itself is all about. Probably the move away from the Socratic practice of not being directly concerned with the question "What is ethics?" but rather with, for example, "What is virtue?" "What is justice?" "What is duty?" "What is happiness?" etc., is largely responsible for the state of ethical philosophy in the West today. When Socrates and his contemporaries perused the questions mentioned above, his interest was not purely academic as the interest of his masters before him was not, but he and his society were concerned with how we (humans) should actually live in society and, ultimately, his life was an example of how he believed a moral life should be lived. But once we started the disciplinary hiatus about "what is ethics?" leading off into meta-ethical considerations, coming back to reconnect with the core concerns of the philosophical discussions of ethics and morality in Western "civilized" society became a difficulty that has not been overcome. In fact, some would argue that the central issue and the greatest challenge in moral philosophy consist in determining the purview of ethics as a discipline; that is, in tethering ethics or moral philosophy, in a way that would make it relevant to the lives of humans and to the decisional exigencies of real actors in the face of choice-making.

The inability of moral philosophers to agree on the subject matter of their discourse is, however, not strange. Some have indicated that ethics is concerned with answering the questions relating to whether certain actions are morally permitted, forbidden or obligatory. According to Alston and Brandt (1974), for example,

> "Ethics" is basically concerned with investigating the grounds or basis for answering such questions. The philosopher's job is to find some defensible general principles that can be applied to any particular situations that arise, general principles that will indicate what we need to determine about the particular situation in order to answer the specific questions that arise there (pp. 122–23).

They and other erudite philosophers were not sure, however, which was more fundamental, whether it was normative ethics in the sense stated above, or meta-ethics, in the sense of "the interpretation of ethical terms and judgements, and with the methodology of normative ethics, i.e., with how one can rationally assess ethical judgements" (p. 123).

Their dilemma may be better understood as a necessary consequence of the heritage of Western scholarship—the pull and push between the need for a commitment to either the normative tradition or the analytic tradition, creating an intellectual soul troubled incessantly by the challenge of the non-cognitivism as represented by mainstream logical positivism (Ayer 1936).

Having paid due attention to these matters, and having remarked the weakness of the Western intellectual understanding of morality outside of the marketplace, one can boldly affirm, even at the pain of contradiction by those who may wish to argue otherwise, that the wellspring of morality and ethics (moral reflections, prescription and analysis) originally in most other civilized societies (in African, Asia, before Socrates and the Industrial Revolution) are a balance of individual well-being and social (communal, community, corporate) well-being. What, it may be asked, is meant by this? My response is to look at the norm-generating foundation of human interaction in civilized society.

The first critical and most important part is this: What moral, social and personal obligation has a person to the self, as an acting being, with agency, in a community of others? The conceptualization and appreciation of this imposes certain norms of behavior on self as agent, as a being, as an individual, and as a human (that is, as a member of a specie), by contrast with being a beast (which beastliness may incidentally be what extreme individualism panders to in Western societies). Here the primary obligation that a self has, whether before or at the age of maturity, adulthood, and competence—a progressive reality that one gradually attains—is self-preservation, self-definition, self-identity, self-apprehension, self-appreciation, self-actualization, self-projection and, ultimately, self-perpetuation (through procreation, which may be part of why human survival as a species makes homosexuality an unnatural sexual orientation). Before this, however, the society—meaning family and community and nation—take on the responsibility of protection, caring, nurturing and social, cultural, ethical, political, religious and other necessary developments of the infant and the young (Bewaji 1998, 2003).

The second critical part of the moral equation is this: What obligation has a person to his/her community and society? By this I do not want to be understood to indulge in unnecessary obfuscation or pedantic abstraction, as duty or obligation to society, to others, and to community is as concrete as the obligation one owes to the self. The definition of this obligation is crucial to the consciousness of the self as a person and as well as the sense of community that empowers the individual and that gives the individual the support mechanism for coping with the exigencies of life. We will need to say a little more on this score presently, because on this revolves the whole issue of moral emphasis in society (Bewaji 2004).

The third and final critical question is this: What is the responsibility of the community or society to the person and to itself? This is very serious and all-important question. It may seem that morality is a personal thing first and foremost. This is only partially true from the perspective of any society, whether Western, Eastern, African or African Diaspora. The artificial intellectual separation of individual moral responsibility from that of society, creating a cleavage of moral disparity, constitutes a superficial discourse. It is obvious that the context in which the moral obligations arise is the interactive one, the social milieu in which contestations for scarce resources in the environment (as economists suggest) are undertaken, but it is not only resources in the environment that are scarce, the human requirements and resources of love, trust, patronage, recognition, pity, compassion, association, competition, etc., are also scarce and require deliberate efforts of persons and community to generate enough and distribution of, fairly and equitably, in order for these to go round all members of society (Fukuyama 1995). Here lies the crux of the moral responsibility of society to its members and to itself. And this fact is represented in numerous ideas of relationships in all societies, benchmarked in various ideologies and systems of sociopolitical and economic patterns of development.

Encapsulated in the three obligations that we have itemized above are the needs for humans and societies to negotiate the various loci of interaction that take place in every daily existence. To this end, humans have to incorporate in their existence various identity packages which implicate moral issues and engender decision-making demands. As Sen (2006) suggested, the fact that humans, especially adults, have to embody a complex combination of identities at various existential junctures indicate that moral issues are never easy, random, nor inchoate. We would hasten to add that humans are actors as parents, husbands, wives, sons, daughters, friends, teachers, doctors, researchers, etc. These are combined with other identity constructs that are related to gender, religious affiliations, ethnicities, sub-racial textures, etc. These only take place meaningfully within the context of inter-textual regeneration of trusts, as Fukuyama (1995) would argue. When the trust capital is mutually accumulated and respected, all the identities and actions deriving from interactivity of humans are mediated seamlessly with little or no friction taking place in society.

Clearly this does not mean that there are no anxieties relating to human behavior or the anticipation of behavior on the part of others. This is where humans are called upon to negotiate various forms of risks—whether these are natural, non-natural, human or nonhuman in origin. To this end, there is a critical need to investigate how the moral demands of human interaction are purveyors of risks, and whether these risks are any different for researchers or persons who devote their working lives to the generation and organization of knowledge.

Judith Jarvis Thomson (1986), in *Rights, Restitution and Risk,* explored various forms of risks to human beings as agents, with moral obligations to self, to others and to society. But the discussion did not illuminate the concept or nature of risk that underpin intrinsically the discussion of risk, as the annotation of what constitute high or low risk is not without ambiguities of the circumstances of action and implications of action. For this reason, it is useful to indicate what is understood by "risk," and how researchers have to live with, avoid, deal with or negotiate the various risks that attend their research lives and efforts. Thus, for the understanding of "risk" in this discussion we would mean such "hazard," "danger," "chance of loss, failure, injury, unfortunate consequence, mishap, abuse or error" that may attend an action or inaction on the part of the agent.

Those who may wish to trivialize the concept may latch onto the fact that it is very wide in scope to indicate that there is risk therefore in every aspect of human life. They may even suggest the fact that since "choking death" is one of the highest causes of death in society suffering from an epidemic of obesity like the United States of America shows that eating is a risky business! Or that it is not any less risky flying than taking a walk in the park, as the risks are calculable and the probability of danger in either instance can be worked out by statisticians. In either case, I would argue, such baloney would fail to understand the special nature of risks that we have in mind when we say researchers have the potential and real risks that make the performance of their chosen vocations very daunting. We will now indicate some of the risks, some of which are endogenous to the nature of research, but some also exogenous.

To understand the point at issue here, let us take two "hypothetical" cases (hypothetical because they are mere intellectual thought experiments) to illustrate what we have in view, without referencing any real-life experiences of researchers. A student had to conduct research among the indigenous people of a country on a socioreligious issue and proceeds to develop the research materials as adequately as she believes need to be done. She travels to the venue of research and begins in earnest, without paying attention to the sensitivities of authority and power relations in the society that is the terrain of the research. Word gets to the power base, and the student is stopped dead in her tracks. Research cannot proceed, she is evicted if the power base is generous or she is abducted and tortured to death if the power base is facetious and sinister! Clearly, attention to power relations and authority bases play a significant role in the moderation and navigation of research.

In a second case, a researcher is interested in researching the experiences of the indigenous peoples of a particular society, especially as this relates to government, religious institutions and society at large. After using extant materials relating to the research, proceeding to conduct a critical analysis, and sends the material to the sponsoring agency for publication, receives a warning from the reviewer, who happens to be affiliated to one of the parties involved to desist from the research, as there has not been proper application for license to conduct the research. The researcher finds a way around this by carefully indicating to the agent provocateur that the research was not an anthropological, sociological or archaeological one, but a critical re-examination of what the state agencies have put in the public domain. By doing this, the research is able to circumvent authority and power.

These are just two instances in which researchers may run serious risk in the conduct of investigation to develop or appreciate knowledge. The roadblocks to research could come from various sources, constituting risks to the person and work of the researcher. And if the researcher should persist, such persistence could be critical to the survival of the researcher as a person, on the one hand; while, on the other hand, playing ball (cooperating) with the agencies of censorship could lead to the compromising of truth, knowledge and everything that rides on these two critical elements of human intellectual culture.

There are other ways in which authoritarianism and power manifest themselves in conscripting researcher's interests and existence. It is not without reason that Iran is in the spotlight for trying to enrich uranium, as the spread of the nuclear technology around the world is not simply a matter of protecting humanity from nuclear omnicide, it is about the threat that this poses to the monopoly that some societies hold over the use of terror, control of resources and imposition of conditions of master-servant relations on humans from other climes, through internationally distended institutional frameworks for the maintenance of inequalities in the world.

Another serious risk related to this for researchers is the racketeering that takes place in what is the now known as copyrights laws that govern international businesses around the world. If a bright researcher from a backwater developing subaltern country should come up with some vaccine to cure HIV and AIDS tomorrow, such research would receive no support and would be run down, the procedure debunked and ridiculed, since it is not coming from the multinational pharmaceutical companies that control knowledge and wealth in the industry of health.

What is most distressing is that the indigenous knowledge of the world is being taken by the multinational power-broking industries (especially pharmaceutical companies) without any compensation to the indigenous peoples, patented and then resold to the indigenous peoples and other peoples around the world at great profit. Under such circumstances, researchers from the global South are privated and expropriated from their cultural knowledge, and intimidated into silence where the right to such knowledge is concerned. The risk here relates to the Yoruba words of wisdom which cautions that *b'owo eni o ba i te ku ida, a i i bere iku to pa baba eni*—that is, if one is not in a position of strength, one dare not ask how one's father died! This is a serious risk which is peculiar to Southern researchers in how they are treated by a perfectly networked Western-dominated international capitalist system that reduces to nullity the intellectual efforts of researchers from the South.

Metropolitanism is a risk that is palpable in societies that have experienced slavery, colonialism and conquest. It is a risk deriving from the penchant to adore whatever originates from the corridors of the centres of power and domination, as there is always the belief that success has many relatives while failure is a loner! What is being suggested here is that researchers in dependent societies lose the audacity to be creative, and look instead to the centres of political power and economic and technological domination of the world for intellectual and academic support and leadership. They fail to value the indigenous intellect of their own, and would seldom hire the best of their own minds and researchers, while preferring to hire and worship the mediocre by-products of the external former colonizing and enslaving societies, thereby continuing the perpetuation of control and dependency when there is no need to do so. This is what accounts for the dependence on external experts to study indigenous issues and problems in many post-slavery and post-colonial societies, with the attendant risk that indigenous and local researchers actually hardly get the kinds of exposure, confidence and trust they need to develop their skills, help their societies to progress and make progress in liberating their societies from being eternal appendages to imperial metropoles.

What this means is that on the one hand, most local researchers, who are actually first rate, because of lack of patronage chose to work outside of their countries of origin. This is what is a first leg of a brain drain which benefits the dominant metropoles, at the expense of the subaltern societies of the world. But on the other hand, there is the warped logic by which Southern societies negotiate loans from international and external national agencies, and hire second-rate agents of the lending organization, or locally bred but externally based traitors to their own societies, to perform the feasibility and other jobs related to the jobs they are borrowing to execute, while their own indigenous researchers are side-tracked without patronage that would help them in the long run to master their trades, only for their governments to turn to them to fix attendant problems arising from the undomesticated application of the international one-size-fits-all solutions and prescriptions of the foreign experts.

The risk I have characterized as institutionalism is multi-faceted. But I will highlight only two aspects of the risk to the researcher. In the investigation of the origins and structures of human evolution, civilization, culture and development the place of established orthodoxies seem to have been permanently etched in stone. The efforts of Diop, Clarke, Van Sertima, Asante, and others are simply ignored, unacknowledged, pilloried and vilified. Those who take interest in their effort cannot get tenure in esteemed traditional departments of institutions of the various democratic, civilized and cultured societies of the West. Even when those they have paid to conduct counter researches to nullify the results of the research of these scholars have come back with confirmation of the original works of these rejected cornerstones of human history, culture, civilization, philosophy, art and science, there is still deliberate, conspiratorial and despicable disregard for the efforts and products of these intellectuals in the global academy. This is clearly a part of what Thomas Kuhn has shown about the reticence of science to accommodate change, openness and transparency. In the process of pursuing research, researchers from the South risk being called all kinds of names, while mediocre researchers from the North (Western countries) gain all kinds of fanciful fame and recognition for repeating what the Southern researchers have known and proclaimed, without anyone ever acknowledging them.

On a closer-to-home consideration, based on (b) above, the indigenous hankering for what is "foreign" only helps to facilitate the dislocation of the integrity of the local researchers, as the efforts of the local researchers need the validation of the institutional structures that only serve to perpetuate control, domination and dependency. This can only constitute a psychological and intellectual problem for the local researcher, which need not be the case.

Many researchers are unable to understand that research is a painstaking, slow to mature and even hard to reward effort. In some instances there are all kinds of pressures that the researcher must withstand in order to allow only the truth to come out. Where there is an improper balance of the duties that we examined earlier to the self, to others and to society, then the researcher runs serious risk of fabricating results to please sponsors or to gain instant fame and garner economically gratifying success. The case of genetic engineering in South Korea is fresh in mind here. But in even poorer countries where there are survival issues, researchers could create all kinds of fictitious data to support the views that their donor agencies are interested in. Even among elite researchers, there is always the risk, as in the fabrication of evidence of "Weapons of Mass Destruction" in Iraq, by the messengers of the United States of America's oil and war establishments to justify the invasion of a country that was only one-third under the pre-invasion Iraqi authorities in 2003, and people in Western societies wonder why Arabs hate us.

Researchers are (should be) investigators of truth (under normal circumstances). In political and cultural matters, they are unwanted thorns in the flesh of the rich and powerful. They constitute the conscience of society, and have responsibility to ensure that the civilizations which previous generations have built are not destroyed by megalomaniacs parading as leaders. It is this pursuit of truth which often makes researchers run afoul of the myopic leadership in autocratic states. And for this reason, one of the elements of a poorly led society is the prevalence of ignorance, which is a good tool for the perpetual deception of the people and the festering of rank religiosity, fanaticism and superstition. Where there is ignorance, it is not true that "you can only fool all the people some of the time, and you cannot fool all the people all of the time," as you can fool fools as many times as you care, and they will never wise up to your tricks, as Nicolo Machiavelli was able to annotate. If the majority of the people are ignorant, you definitely have a large pool of hooligans to keep the few that may be knowledgeable under control—or you may even be able facilitate their emigration, if they find the oppressive environment you have created intolerable for their existence (the phenomenon of brain drain). Researchers under such conditions are usually the enemies of the oppressive regimes and are mortally in danger of physical and mental abuse.

Recently there was the outbreak of avian flu in Asia. Many of the researchers who were trying to gather the information necessary for analysis and development of cures were infected and they died. Thus, because of having to work with certain resources, instruments and reagents, it is possible for researchers to be in serious danger for their own physical and mental welfare. Apart from this, there are researches that have to be conducted in environments that are dangerous—whether in farther externalities of out of space or in the deep recesses of the bowels of the earth. These researchers carry with them extreme dangers and risks, which even the best prevention may not totally assuage.

Media practitioners and forensic investigators of various kinds—from criminal investigators to financial investigators of greedy humans—encounter various research risks that call for serious personal and group survival decisions, with considerable moral implications. Should they pursue the truth even at the expense of their own health and welfare? Or should they follow the popular dictum of "she, who pays the piper, dictates the tune"? Whatever the decisions that they take, the risks may become even more pronounced, having implications for others beyond the confines of the researcher's purview.

Researchers have to brave various situations to carry out their trade. In contemporary science, medicine and technology, there are various situations that carry with them cultural, emotional, and religious sentiments which make researchers targets of abuse, recriminations and attacks. For example, animal rights activists are canvassing for the abolition of the use of animals for testing drugs, and many researchers are put under various kinds of emotional and mental pressures related to these demands. What these animal rights groups fail to consider is the question of what other testing alternatives are available for the provision of necessary drugs for human treatment and cure. In any case, it probably never occurs to them that complaining about the abuses of the process is not the same as total ban of process.

What this example shows is that there are not easy solutions to the moral dilemmas relating to researches that further the growth of knowledge and development of humans in the world. Even more significant are the moral challenges that are faced in some not so easy to justify investigations, such as going to the extremities of space to understand life on other planets. Also, researchers in genetic engineering are constantly pressured to forgo embryonic research related to cloning, stem cell and other techniques that may have untold advantages for the treatment of various diseases in the future. This is not to talk of the pressure relating to the threat that those who conduct some research are destined for hell, where such decisions are left to cultural deities and not taken in hand by fanatics who bomb out homes of known researchers and their laboratories! It is clear that researchers have to be secretive about what they are doing today, as it was in the past that many researchers were tied up at the stake and burnt alive as they were believed to be trying to investigate the work of God.

The point made above automatically leads to the point that is mentioned here. This relates to how researchers often become distanced from their object of study. This is especially critical where the object is also a subject and there is the risk of inattention to the subjectivity of the object.

There is a popular saying in anthropological researches that the "foreigner has eyes, but cannot see; the foreigner has ears, but cannot hear" (Hallen and Sodipo 1986). This is a consequence of the fact that the problems of cultural relativism and various forms of ethnocentrism may militate against proper understanding of the object/subject of study. This risk may lead to the vitiation of the results of research, as the tendency is there to impose the points of view that one has inherited, like cultural spectacles, on the seeing that takes place in the process of investigation of the object/subject of research. It is against this background that phenomenological methods of investigation have been developed, but they risk the possibility of over-immersion and thus the compromising of scholar distance.

The risks here noted are related to the inability of researchers to acknowledge error, seeking to validate the position already taken even in the face of mistakes that are evident in the evidence on the one hand, while on the other there may be intrinsic interest of members of the profession or cognate disciplines not to want a specific researcher to prosper, as this would mean the elevation of the research at the expense of the competitors. The risks involved may be subtle, but it may also become overt and dangerously compromising of health, probity of research and career opportunities. This is even more pronounced where there is competition for positions that have resource allocation or power. These competitions may lead to the creation of bottlenecks for progressive researchers, rather than for the threatened persons seeking to improve their own effort and resume in order to advance and be recognized. Furthermore, there is the possibility that the competition may deteriorate to open jealousy, whereby researchers cease being researchers and become political animals, fighting for scarce benefits and spoils from superiors!

Research is a necessary activity for the advancement, recording and preservation of human society, culture and civilization. Yet there is so much risk attending research. Most of the risk deals mostly with respect to researchers' capacity, conduct, interests and outcomes, while in most cases the fruit of successful research is usually for the whole of humanity. We have indicated clearly in this chapter that the practice in which indigenous knowledge systems have been taken over by ungrateful, scavenging and predatory international conglomerates is more the norm than accident given the lopsided nature of the international movement of resources and power relations globally, but this is with a view to indicating that research can be misused and abused from various quarters, including by those who conduct such research. This shows that the playing field is never level, where knowledge and intellectual property is concerned.

In this final chapter, we have primarily shown that risks of research are in most cases avoidable, since they are largely humanly contrived for one reason or another, as they arise from quarters where there are critical interests to be protected that the truth not be known, either because of ignorance on the part of the agents of repression and suppression of knowledge, as happened to scientists in Europe at the advent of the Scientific Revolution when many of them were tied up and burnt at the stake for "preaching" ideas which contradicted the orthodoxies of the day; or in other instances, out of the need to cover up the deeds and/or misdeeds of the powerful in society, or to continue to perpetuate the subjugation, subjection, appropriation, expropriation, oppression and repression of other people whose interests are never regarded as worthy of any form of defense (even in societies that pride itself on openness, democracy, etc.), as happens when governments ban publication of some information that they deem to be harmful to public "good."

This shows that there is always a clear connection between the concepts of property rights, knowledge, research, ethics and risk, which need to be carefully understood, especially for those who must operate from the margins of capitalist structures of economic development in third world societies. While the situation may appear gloomy, there are clear means of rectification, to lift the societies of the South out of dependency. Some of the suggestions already implied in this chapter include visionary and transparent socioeconomic and political leadership, attuned to the historical backgrounds of their societies and intent on ensuring that their societies constitute the best place for the enhancement of life of indigenous humans individually and collectively, rather than forcing members of such societies to migrate to climes where their capacity to contribute to development is mostly undervalued.

Also, it has been argued that it is imperative that legal and moral frameworks undergirding research as well as the research agendas within the developing societies be endogenously developed and funded. This will ensure first that these researches are directed at solving critical problems within the society, and even more importantly, secondly, that the external pressures of funding agencies with no sympathies for indigenous sensitivities encapsulated in the indigenous cultures will be minimized. Following on is the need for researchers to respect the objects of their research, whether as things in nature or as potentially cognitive subjects with capabilities for feelings, beliefs and opinions. This issue relates to both matters of respect, honesty and appreciation of others, as beings and as sources of information essential for the success of research.

One final point must be made. This relates to how copyrights have become bogies to the world, as instruments for the oppression and subjugation of others, rather than simply as moral tools for truthful recording of who did what, where and when, on the one hand, and for the protection of effort for those who have toiled to contribute to the knowledge systems of the world as well as to advance in the welfare of humanity through such toils. This has been the case with various drugs, for the treatment of serious diseases, which have been used to hold various proportions of the world population to ransom. Governments and researchers must not compromise humanity for profit, no matter how tempting the lucre of profit may seem or even the fact that the capacity of the victims for redress is minuscule.

Conclusion

There has always been the tendency, on the part of those ignorant or with superficial understanding of the social, political, cultural and religious institutions of Africa, to suggest that the indigenous leadership style of most African societies was individualistic, autocratic, dictatorial, or tyrannical simply because symbolically the locus of power revolved around specific individuals, families or small groups of persons in the different communities. What is even more depressing is the fact that if a scholar were to attempt a historical analysis of governance in Africa, expounding the philosophical and theoretical foundations of indigenous governance traditions, and suggesting that the weakness of contemporary African embrace of imported institutional structures of governance that have no metaphysical, epistemological and axiological foundations in the African consciousness, then one is accused of engaging in ethnophilosophical scholarship. What we easily forget is the multiple standards that pervade scholarship as it is done in the contemporary world. Whereas it is not regarded as ethnophilosophy for scholars to hark to Greek origin of what is regarded in the West as "democracy", or the fact that all of humanity are required to join in reading Plato, Aristotle, A. V. Dicey, John Locke, Thomas Hobbes, J-J Rousseau, and many African intellectuals are erudite when they quote verbatim from *Merchant of Venice* or *Macbeth*, any effort to understand the historicity and philosophical foundations of their own indigenous societies are scoffed at and denigrated as ethnohistorical or ethnophilosophical or ethnopolitical or ethnosociological or ethnotheological or ethnomathematical and, consequently, backward looking. To compound these problems for Africa, Africans are foresworn from swearing by their own ancestors.

Let us consider this point a little more. When the Arabs found that they would be permanently lost if they did not create an antidote to the influence of Hebrewisms and Semitism on their lives, they would be permanently compromised, they developed and evolved the approximation of the theologies of the Old Testament and fast-forwarded the ideas it enshrines as the work of the Prophet. But do not forget that there is close affinity between the Old Testament itself and the Egyptian traditions, which it only acknowledged in passing as the demonic group which enslaved the good people of God and would not allow them to leave to serve "the" only god. This kind of predicament is what I have described as epistemicide (Bewaji 2012). But the consequences of epistemicide is multifarious, and only certain elements of these consequences have been expounded in this book, to show that the indigenous African philosophy of law emphasized the rule of law, and was person-affirming while at the same time group-protecting.

Recently a colleague from another ethnic group in Africa wondered aloud why it is that Yoruba people are ever proud of Yoruba culture; such that if you examine wherever Yoruba people have migrated they have carried with them their culture and regardless of persecution or lapse of time, retentions of Yoruba traditions remain strong—albeit varied. He used the examples of the Haitian Revolution, which preceded the contractarian ideas of the Europeans, and which according to him was a product of the urbane cultural traditions of Yoruba captives on the island of Hispaniola. He also mentioned the effects of Yoruba culture in Brazil and other Latin American countries as well as in the southern part of the United States of America, where Orisha metastasized in various forms—from Voudou to Zango to Obaluaye to Oricha, etc. Even more significant is the fact that the Yoruba language has survived the efforts of the enslavers to totally strip the enslaved Africans of every vestige of their indigenous culture. Well, I was not able to explain these obvious facts to my colleague, except to say that it seemed to me that it is not only Yorubas, but what happened in the case of the Yoruba enslaved and migrants is that they have evolved a sense of humanity, a recognition of the personhood of every human, regardless of temporary challenges or vicissitudes; even slavery was not something that could rid you of your humanity, because contrary to European primitivism which makes it possible to see other human beings as chattel or objects of possession, the Yoruba people understand that *ona lo ji, eru ni baba*. They are ever conscious that stations of life may mean temporary disadvantage, yet those who are blessed or who find themselves in positions of power today must remember that some who were in such positions before and who abused these positions have been reduced to nothing when the tables were turned. This is why it is fundamental to recognize that since you cannot know what tomorrow will bring, the only good thing is to do good; whatever station or position you find yourself, you are required to use it to benefit not only yourself but for the benefit of those around you.

When we started this conclusion with the idea of how repugnant it is in most indigenous African societies for individuals to arrogate to themselves absolute power or authority, it may be wondered how one could rationalize monarchical systems as anything but totalitarian or authoritarian? But such a question would miss the entire point, because it would take appearance as reality: it would suggest that the respect and authority that the individual who occupies a position exercises is either absolute or not derived from the community over which it is exercised. In Yoruba society there is high respect, for example, for age and elders. This is not because it is not recognized that some elders are buffoons or stupid or unworthy of respect. The respect that is accorded the older person is one that derives from collective investiture of those before us respect, so that we may also get respect. Having given the respect, it is then the responsibility of the older person to show that the respect is deserved. Should the person fail to respect the young person in return, then it means that the elder has not respected himself and whatever happens to him would be what he has brought upon himself. A simple way of illustrating that is when it is indicated that *agba t'o je a je i w'eyin, oun ni yio ru'gba e de'le*. For the elders to deserve the respect which the ancestors would be pleased with, the elders must show that they deserve it.

Equally, when the king or queen or chief is respected, it is not the individual who is respected; it is the collective membership of the society, the community, the ancestors and the institution symbolized or represented in him or her that is being respected. The respect that is accorded the monarch is a reflection of the individual respect that each member of the society deserves, and that is why any member of the society would take umbrage at any disrespect that may be shown to the locus of the communal respect as such. Human society, instead of moving away from symbolism, as some would want us to believe, as primitive or backward, has found new ways of shoring up symbols in new packages and investing them with even more power. Anybody listening to CNN or BBC would easily recognize this, if an objective analysis is done—especially when reports of the various activities of the American president or the British prime minister are reported. It often gives the impression of a larger-than-life individual, who merely happens to be the occupier of the White House at that time in human history. But when the same is done with the president of North Korea or the Iranian prime minister, snide remarks of dictatorship pervade the air, as if symbolism has suddenly changed—except for the power of reportage which is abused in the instance of denigration of the leadership of these other countries.

In any case, Yoruba are aware that *eti oba ni'le, eti oba l'oko, eniyan lo n je be e*, because, at the end of the day, *eniyan lo wa l'ehin agbon ti a fi bu omi si ti ko jo*. Any leader who should fail to understand this will find out very quickly that *igbati itakun ba ja, owo a te okere l'oko*. For the fact that one enjoys the collective protection of members of the society, this is the reason why one is able to boast that one is someone important in the gathering of others, because *agbajo owo la fi n so aya; igi eyokan ki i da igbo se*. The society, therefore, owes the obligation to maintain its traditions; for as a colleague once suggested, when any group or people alienates its own traditions and embraces the traditions of others, which it ill understands, then its destruction as a corporate body has commenced. This is part of the tragedy that is Africa, where we swear by the religions, political traditions, cultures, technologies and even humanities of others, at the expense of our own, consequently floating incommunicado like drunken layabouts in the seas of ignorance of our identities.

One of the other attendant tragedies of our collective experience is the way in which African scholars have bought into all forms of fallacies: that Africans have no indigenous traditions for documenting ideas, no religions, no histories, no ancestors worthy of veneration or any sociopolitical traditions, etc. Having accepted these fallacies, we have become susceptible to the importation of all kinds of dehumanizing traditions from all parts of the world, to the detriment of our collective and individual humanity; thereby compromising our capacity for agency, self-respect and other protecting—even when the other happens to be a foreigner, a vulnerable poor or physically or mentally challenged. In the true nature of the new ideas we have embraced, we have become rather callous to the point where nothing matters to us again with regard to issues of legacy, posterity or even our own long-term interest; thus we have no qualms borrowing money in the name of our countries, sharing the money in the hotel rooms of our foreign friends and keeping the money in numbered accounts for ourselves while expecting our countries to pay back in many multiples to the lenders. At the end of the day, what we simply forget is that *eni to se n nkan t'enikan o se ri, oju re a ri n nkan t'enikan ko ri ri*; such that when terrible things begin to happen to those who behave this way, people somehow forget that they are reaping the just rewards of their evil deeds against their societies.

In short, what we have done in this book is to begin the process of encouraging restitution for the injustices we have done to our indigenous African traditions and knowledge systems, which accounts for the collective disarray that has become the lot of Africa today—whereby a continent that is so blessed has remained the mendicant doormat of the rest of humanity. The fact that we seem to have no collective or individual shame is evidence that we have become collective bastards of humanity—beasts of no nation! By exploring various issues relating to indigenous African philosophy of law, the rule of law, the institutions which make for development of civilizations in Africa and the building of ancient cities and empires, and in the process showing how law and order, or what may be regarded as well-ordered societies, flourished in traditional Africa in millennia past, we have shown that there is a serious way of showing the current crop of vagabonds in power (VIPs) that they are there today as transient occupiers of the offices they hold, as some have held similar offices before them, they definitely will be gone tomorrow, either because humans have a shelf life and expiry dates or because they are booted out—which the fool in them may wish to interpret literally as an impossibility because, in their idiocy and imbecility, they will say they will still be around to torment the rest of their compatriots, contrary to my "prediction" beyond the next twenty-four hours!

Of course, it could be argued, as Babagana Kingibe did when challenged, that "Rome was not built in a day"! This would assume that we should wait, because a hundred years in the life of a nation is just like the twinkle of an eye, forgetting that the it is possible that a mad leadership could do so much harm to humanity in eight years (George W. Bush) which may take more than one hundred years to undo—as humanity has learnt from the collusion of Bush and Blair to create the mayhem that has sundered the rest of humanity's direction for the next hundred years after the criminal invasion of Iraq under false pretences—weapons of mass destruction. This also confirms what the Yoruba understand that *ki ile to pa osika, n nka pataki (gannaganna) a ti baje*. The reason they say that is because they are aware that there are humans who would do such things, shielding themselves under veils of communal protection, but they should not forget that *oba to je ti ilu toro, oruko re ko ni pare, eyi to je ti ilu tu ka, oruko re na a ko ni pare*. The problem in the case of Africa is more complicated, because it seems, as in the case of Nigeria, redemption has been elusive—the only thing that has been constant has been a cacophony of bad governance—no respite for the poor from the persistent, primitive, decadent and destructive bad leadership. As this author told Kingibe on that fateful evening, "Yes indeed, Rome was not built in a day, but people incrementally built Rome, with resources stolen from various parts of the world, while we, Africans, have only been persistently tearing apart our own Rome, to build other people's Rome"! If we were to ever begin to build our own Rome, then posterity will smile upon us and say that we were not permanently jinxed, as some of us were humans, regardless of what out detractors may have said about our humanity. It is this humanity, denied, reaffirmed and now being denied by our own, in a fashion not totally dissimilar to the way Negritude and Hegel did, that needs to be confirmed through not just words but action of everyone who may find himself in a position of power, authority or influence. This is where the challenge lies; it is the challenge that has been consistently denied, which leads one to say that it is a truism that *bi ina o tan l'aso, eje o le tan le eekanna*. When you compound that with the self-replicative potential of decadence in all aspects of life, then you will understand that *egbirin ote, ba a ti n pa kan l'okan nru*. What then is the option? To give up? To persevere? Or to soldier on? Well, for some of us, even in the face of what appears to be a collective malady of leadership, it seems there is catharsis in expressing the obvious; for it is the only way of representing for posterity the fact that *gbogbo wa o sun ko, ori si ibikan na a*. There were some of us who were aware of where the "rain started beating us" and would do what we can to ensure that "rain does not beat our posterity" in the same way, if we can assure that!

Imagine a situation where a Blair heads a commission for Africa, or where a Sarkozy could say that without Africa, where would France be? Why is it impossible for African leaders to be aware that there is no possibility of Euro-American generosity toward the continent, because *ife ti a fe adie ko koja pipa je*? What would account for the absolute stupidity of Africa to sell the best land in Africa to China only to receive a donation of the headquarters of the symbol of the organization of African Union as gift from China? Does it not smack of condescension and extreme paternalism that any society would be so kind that it would offer without strings the symbol of the freedom of its vassal? Yet our so-called leaders can only quarrel over who would be the Secretary of the African Union for one year, without even having the capacity to say, what is one year in the life of a continent that we should squabble endlessly? The fact of the matter is, Africa has lost its soul to Europe and the rest of the world, and there is no amount of fake religious replacement that will help liberate Africa if Africans will not retrace their steps back to the point of the displacement of our humanity to exhume and excavate whatever is left of it and begin to have confidence in its capacity to begin the salvific journey to our future.

For me I make no apologies in this regard with the effort to derive African institutional structures of law and order from indigenous African historic efforts. Those who wish may call it ethno-philosophy of law or whatever. The same happened to African art, African science, African mathematics and African technologies—when they were stolen and improved, they became universal ideas. When Africans then want to have authentic capacity to use these same ideas that were originated from Africa, they are told that there is no way any geo-political or cultural zone could have geo-epistemic or geo-metaphysical ideas which are not dependent on the universal (which was originally African). The whole experience of Iran with regard to nuclear technology easily comes to mind as example. While only the absolute ignoramus will not recognize the role of Islam in the transmission of science and civilization to primitive Europe, yet Iranians are no longer human enough to be able to live in peace with their neighbors the moment they have nuclear technology. The point made by Soyinka (1988) regarding Negritude is instructive here; it seems a kind of disease infects the oppressed to the point where she/he would like to show magnanimity to the oppressor by praying for his redemption. And while he closes his eyes to pray, the oppressor continues to plunder the physical, economic, social, cultural and spiritual resources of the oppressed. This explains why the Jews have resolved that the Jesus syndrome of turning the left cheek to someone who has smote you on the right is an impossibility; why Africans continue to go back for more whipping is a strange kind of mentality—even inventing more cruel whips to put in the hand of the oppressor not just for oneself but for one's progeny!

At times I have often wondered if there was not something intrinsically, genetically or compulsively wrong with black leadership; well, this is being unnecessarily guarded, what I was going to say, along with what many feel but find politically incorrect to say is whether or not blacks are naturally inferior to other peoples, given the fact that there is not a single African country that can be said to be doing well, nor an African population that is not at the bottom of the Human Development Index—largely! I know that this would play into the gallery of the racist Euro-American establishment and would fit the agenda of the French, especially, who believe that Africa must be chaperoned in every respect, so that maybe in the distant future when they are left to fend for themselves, they would have become slightly matured at taking care of their own affairs—no longer having the French treasury as the central bank for the so-called former colonies. As ludicrous as this suggestion may sound, it is not farfetched given the behavior of many black leaders—especially in the way in which they seek external solutions to indigenously African problems, and in the manner in which they would rather trust the half-baked technicians from Europe and America rather than the engineers from Africa who probably taught the technicians when they were in Europe and America in the first place. But the general incompetence and malady of underdevelopment that afflict Africa seems to make these ideas a recurring decimal in the way in which issues must be theorized and understood. Had it not been because of the efforts of African scholars who unearthed various documents and scientific data (linguistic, archaeological, geological, etc.) which show the African origin of culture, civilization, science, mathematics, etc., one would have been left with no alternative, given the megalomaniac behavior of generations of African vampires in government—to conclude nothing else but the genetic incapacity of African peoples.

It is against this background that what we did in this book becomes especially relevant to the paradox of development in Africa. Given the weakness of the educational stratum that infuses our leadership with diffidence and singular incapacity, we need to creatively reflect on our historical antecedents in order to find resources to channel our future potentials for development. It is in this regard that our discussion of the nature of governance, based on a compact of the people with each other and represented by their leaders, become essential. Africa could not have developed empires and civilizations in years gone by if the leaders behaved like occupation forces that the current generation of political parasites have become over their own people, and with little capacity for retrospective analysis of the fate of those who did similar things before them—like Eyadema, Bokassa, Mobutu, Kerekou, Babangida, Abacha or Idi Amin or other such desperadoes whose only legacies are the impoverishment of their societies.

The fact that various institutions have survived colonization and run parallel to the imported European systems of governance which is working very poorly in Africa is evidence of the need to investigate and incorporate into governance structures tested and proven mechanisms which have served these societies for millennia in the past. And the importance of an institutionally focused development, rather than either authoritarian- or charismatic-inflected systems which would only be detrimental to the overall development of the African societies, seem to suggest what Wiredu calls consensual politics, in place of the trust-destroying, graft-encouraging winner takes all, and losers suffer adversarial and divisive systems of judiciary and politics which only succeeds in creating divisions between members of various hetero-cultural, hetero-religious and hetero-ethnic societies which the Europeans have cobbled together to form states in contemporary Africa.

That most African society has become lawless, bribe-taking, and graft-consuming societies is a disgrace to the African tradition and humanity. The various checks and balances which guided and protected every member of such societies have been undermined, and in its place have been introduced systems which facilitate fraud, deception and deliberate misdirection of resources. The fact that impunity and no consequences have attended any of these infractions of public trust, and the new religions only preach confession of sins at any time before death, and where punishment does not seem to be observable to others (because it happens posthumously) means that there is a tendency on the part of the miscreant to assume that they have truly gotten away with the pain they have inflicted on the population. While this may be wrong and inaccurate, the fact that the immediate connection of the African ancestors to the suffering the evildoers undergo suggests that the deterrence mechanism that was basic to African indigenous sociopolitical institutions have been compromised. With such compromise comes all kinds of dangers, especially the danger that more persons are drawn into the web of destruction of the societies which they are supposed to develop. This is the kind of issue that was treated in chapters dealing with the rule of law and the epistemological foundations of law in African societies in the context of the imported jurisprudence which depends on the means of the victim to procure justice—instead of society ensuring the interest of the victim to be protected as a necessity to ensure justice being done (i.e., Sasaki vs. the people of Nigeria, EFCC).

Another important development that must be emphasized is the fact that the international dimension of relationships is discussed. This has to do with how societies must treat with the knowledge systems that are important for their survival, be it those that are generated by members of the society itself or those which are to be acquired from others. In the case of those which are generated locally, there is need to protect the individual or group ownership of such knowledge from the scavenging activities of international predators. There have been instances in the past when discoveries were made by poor members of African societies, while these ideas were stolen in broad daylight only to become the basis of unequal exchange with the societies where the ideas were stolen. It seems that Africana leadership are too busy feathering their own nests at the expense of the societies which placed them in the positions of leadership.

Even more significant is the behavior of African leaders when they interface with peoples of other climes—affecting genuflections of subservience, and become almost inaudible, while accepting whatever fake adulations are heaped on them while their own societies are being robbed to the bone. Examples of this abound, with a Nigerian president pointing to praise from American president as evidence of good performance, while his Minister of Finance originated a pernicious policy of deregulation of the oils sector even while presiding over the worst regime of corruption and looting of public resources in the history of Nigeria, only to turn around and use nonperformance as the springboard for aspiration to a presidency of the World Bank. It would just seem as if Nigerian leaders suspect that other leaders of other countries are daft and ignorant of the shenanigans of themselves or probably, sharing in the destructive loot of Nigerian resources, they think they will be compensated even more from Western coffers!

In the final analysis, it is argued that the crises of confidence that Africa suffers is a direct result of the decadence of the management style of African leaders which has only been capable of producing underdevelopment and poverty on a continent-wide scale. This crises has deflated the identity aspirations of many African youth who queue up overnight in the front of embassies of other countries, with the aim of emigrating or who have to cross the Sahara Desert without navigational equipment and die horrible deaths, or who crowd into rudderless boats to cross the Mediterranean Sea only to capsize and perish like ordinary cargo or who take to terrorism in the names of some demented ideas which have no relation to reality as in the Boko Haram (a group which paradoxically use the products of Boko knowledge to oppose the benefits of Boko), where ignorance of the poor messengers of death they send to kill constitute the only thing they could articulate.

Given the place of knowledge in contemporary society, it is urged that Africa needs to invest in human capital. This is the only way of preventing communal suicide on the part of black people universally, and this investment in education will be resisted by the West, as they have always done through the imposition of various forms of pernicious measures related to trade, finance and technological support. Consider the fact that when the United States of America was faced with the financial meltdown in 2007, the government bailed out the businesses arguing they were too big to fail and sent checks to members of the public, while if the same had happened to a black country, the receivers from IMF and World Bank would have descended on the country with austerity measures and conditionalities which only further complicates the conditions of the societies in question and deepens the poverty and debt crisis being faced.

What this means, in clear terms, is that there is no free lunch in the world, and to expect otherwise is to continue to court disaster. The consequence of failure to follow the honorable path of development can only continue to mean dependence. A look at what India, Brazil and China (and to a lesser extent, in spite of the festooning crisis of the land, Republic of South Africa) have accomplished in recent years should serve as lessons to the rest of Africa. Self-reliance, introspective institutional development and investment in human resources must be the prongs on which black development can grow—but this must be based on the rule of law and the indigenous legal traditions of Africa which are sensitive to the cultures and sensitivities of African communities. This is the challenge thrown out for investigation in this effort.

Bibliography

Abimbola, K. *Yoruba Culture: A Philosophical Account*. Birmingham: Iroko Academic Publishers, 2006.

Abimbola, W. *Awon Oju Odu Mereerindinlogun*. Oxford: Oxford University Press, 1978.

———. *Ijinle ohun enu Ifa* 1. Glasgow, UK: Aim Press, 1968.

———. *Ifa: An Exposition of Ifa Literary Corpus*. Ibadan, Nigeria: Oxford University Press, 1976.

———. "Ifa as a Body of Knowledge and as an Academic Discipline." *Journal of Cultures and Ideas* (University of Ife, Ile-Ife, Nigeria) (1983): 1–11.

———. *Ijinle ohun enu Ifa* 2. Oxford: Oxford University Press, 1987.

Abiodun, R. "Identity and the Artistic Process in the Yoruba Aesthetic Concept of Iwa." *Journal of Cultures and Ideas* 1, no. 1 (1983): 13–30.

Abrahams, R. D. *African Folktales*. New York: Pantheon Books, 1983.

Achebe, C. *Anthills of the Savannah*. Oxford: Heinemann, 1987.

———. *Arrow of God*. New York: Anchor Books, 1989.

———. *Hopes and Impediments*. New York: Anchor Books, 1989.

———. *Things Fall Apart*. Oxford: Macmillan, 1958.

———. *The Trouble with Nigeria*. Enugu, Nigeria: Fourth Dimension Publishing Co., 1983.

Adams, M. "African Visual Art from an Art Historical Perspective." *The African Studies Review* 32, no. 2 (1989): 55–103.

Adams, M. and C. Mayhew. *Publish It Not: the Middle East Cover-up*. New YOrk: Longman, 1975.

Ade-Ajayi, J. F. and I. Espie, eds., *A Thousand Years of West African History*. London: Thomas Nelson, 1979.

Adeleke, D. A. "Even the Gods are Fools." In *Orita—Ibadan Journal of Religious Studies* XXVII, nos. 1 and 2 (2005): 11–31.

Adeniyi, O. R. *Introduction to Philosophy and Logic*. Lagos, Nigeria: Newsletters Limited, 2004.

Adepoju, O. *Ironu Akewi*. Ibadan, Nigeria: Onibonoje Press, 1972.

Adler, M. J. *Ten Philosophical Mistakes*. New York: Macmillan, 1985.

Afolabi, N. ed., *Toyin Falola: The Man, The Mask, The Muse*. Durham, NC: Carolina Academic Press, 2010.

Ahmad, I. et al. *World Cultures: A Global Mosaic*. Englewood Cliffs, NJ: Prentice Hall, 1996.

Aigbodioh, J. A. "Imperatives of Human Knowledge Illustrated with Epistemological Conceptions in African Thought." *Ibadan Journal of Humanistic Studies*, no 7 (October 1997).

Aiyejina, F. and P. Morgan. *Caribbean Literature in a Global Context*. San Juan, Trinidad and Tobago, 2006.

Ajayi, J. F. A. *A Thousand Years of West African History*. Ibadan, Nigeria: Ibadan University Press, 1965.

Ajayi, S. A. ed., *African Culture and Civilization*. Ibadan, Nigeria: Atlantis Books, 2005.

Ake, C. *Democracy and Development in Africa*. Washington, DC: Brookings Institute.

———. *Social Science as Imperialism*. Ibadan, Nigeria: Ibadan University Press, 2009.

Akinkugbe, O. O. *Swirling Currents, Swollen Streams*. Ibadan, Nigeria: Spectrum Books Ltd., 1996.

Akinrinade, S. et al. eds., *The Humanities, Nationalism and Democracy*. Ile-Ife, Nigeria: Faculty of Arts, Obafemi Awolowo University, 2006.

———. *Locating the Local in the Global: Voices on a Globalized Nigeria*. Ile-Ife, Nigeria: Faculty of Arts, Obafemi Awolowo University, 2004.

———. *Rethinking the Humanities in Africa*. Ile-Ife, Nigeria: Faculty of Arts, Obafemi Awolowo University, 2007.

Akinyemi, A. B. et al. *Readings on Federalism*. Lagos, Nigeria: Nigerian Institute of International Affairs, 1980.

Akiola, A. "Who Needs the Past." *Ibadan Journal of Humanistic Studies*, no. 1 (August 1981).

Akiwowo, A. *Ajobi and Ajogbe: Variations on the Theme of Sociation*. Ile-Ife, Nigeria: University of Ife Press, 1983.

———. "Sociology in Africa Today." *Current Sociology* 28 (1980): 2.

———. "Understanding Interpretive Sociology in the Light of the *Oriki* of Orunmila" *Journal of Cultures and Ideas* 1: 139–57.

———. and O. Morakinyo, "The Yoruba Ontology of Personality and Motivation." In *Journal of Social and Biological Structures* 4 (1981): 19–28.

Akurgal, E. *The Art of Greece: Its Origins in the Mediterranean and the Near East*. Ithaca, NY: Crown Publishers, 1968.

Alaba, I. O. "Virtue is Knowledge—Illustrations from Yoruba Life and Thoughts." In C. S. Momoh, Abdai Mohammed, Chieduzie Ogbalue eds. Religion and Morality Lagos: CBAAC/NARETO, ch. 7, 198.

Alcoff, L. M., ed., *Epistemology: The Big Questions*. Malden, MA: Blackwell Publishers, 1998.

Aldred, C. *Egyptian Art*. London: Thames and Hudson, 1996.

Alleyne, M. *Roots of Jamaican Culture*. London: Pluto Press, 1989.

Almeder, R. *Harmless Naturalism*. Chicago, IL: Open Court, 1998.

———. *Human Happiness and Morality*. Lanham, MD: Rowman & Littlefield, 2000.

Alston, W. and R. Brandt, eds., *Problems of Philosophy: Introductory Readings*. New York: Allyn and Bacon, 1974.

Altham, J. E. J. *The Logic of Plurality*. London: Methuen, 1971.

Aluko, T. M. *One Man, One Wife*. Ibadan, Nigeria: Heinmann, 1967.

Amanze, J. N. *African Traditional Religions and Culture in Botswana*. Gaborone, Botswana: Pula Press, 2002.

———. *African Traditional Religions in Malawi*. Blantyre, Malawi: Christian Literature Association of Malawi, 2002.

———. *Biblical Studies, Theology, Religion and Philosophy*. Eldoret, Kenya: ZAPF Chancery, 2010.

Amoda, M. *Black World Development*. Proceedings of 1977 FESTAC. Lagos, Nigeria: Nigeria Magazine, 1978b.

———. *Festac Colloquium and Black World Development*. Lagos, Nigeria: Nigeria Magazine, 1978a.

Andah, B. W. *African Development in Cultural Perspective*. Ibadan, Nigeria: Department of Archaeology and Anthropology, University of Ibadan, 1982.

Anyanwu, K. C. "The Problem of Method in African Philosophy." *The Substance of African Philosophy*. Edited by C. S. Momoh. Auchi, Nigeria: African Philosophy Publications, 1989.

Apel, K-O. *Charles S. Peirce: From Pragmatism to Pragmaticism*. New Jersey: Humanities Press, 1995.

Appadorai, A. *The Substance of Politics* London: Oxford University, 1975.

Appiah, K. A. *In My Father's House: Africa in the Philosophy of Culture*. New York: Oxford University Press, 1992.

Appiah, K. and A. Gutmann. *Color Conscious*. Princeton, NJ: Princeton University Press, 1996.

Appleby, J. L. Hunt and Margaret Jacob. *Telling the Truth about History*. New York: W. W. Norton and Company, 1994.

Arendt, H. *The Human Condition*. Chicago, IL: Chicago University Press, 1958.
Aristotle. *On Man in the Universe*. New York: The Classics Club, 1943.
Arnott, K. *African Myths and Legends*. Oxford: Oxford University Press, 1994.
Aromolaran, O. *Akomolede Ijinle Yoruba*. Lagos, Nigeria: Macmillan, 1976.
Aronson, G. *Creating Facts*. New York: Kegan Paul International, 1987.
Arthur, J. and W. H. Shaw. *Readings in the Philosophy of Law*. Upper Saddle, NJ: Prentice Hall, 2006.
Asante, M. K. *Kemet, Afrocentricity and Knowledge*. Trenton, NJ: Africa World Press, 1990.
Asante, M. K. and K. W. Asante. *African Culture*. Trenton, NJ: Africa World Press, 1990.
Asiegbe, M. F. and J. A. Agbakoba. *Philosophy and Praxis in Africa*. Ibadan, Nigeria: Hope Publications, 2006.
Asiwaju, A. I. ed., *Partitioned Africans: Ethnic Relations across Africa's International Boundaries 1884–1984*. London: C. Hurst and Co. and Lagos, Nigeria: University of Lagos Press, 1985.
Audi, R. *The Structure of Justification*. Cambridge: Cambridge University Press, 1993.
Aune, B. *Metaphysics: The Elements*. Minneapolis, MN: University of Minnesota Press, 1998.
Awolalu, J. O. and P. A. Dopamu. *West African Traditional Religions*. Ibadan, Nigeria: Onibon-Oje Press, 1979.
Awolowo, O. *Path to People's Constitution*. Lagos, Nigeria: CDHR, 2000.
———. *The People's Republic*. Ibadan, Nigeria: Oxford University Press, 1968.
———. *The Problems of Africa*. London: Macmillan, 1977.
Ayodele-Bamisaye, O. *What Is Man, That We Should Educate Him?* Ibadan, Nigeria: University of Ibadan, 2009.
Ayer, A. J. *Language, Truth and Logic*. New York: Dover Books, 1936.
———. *Philosophy in the Twentieth Century*. New York: Vintage Books, 1984.
———. *Probability and Evidence*. London: Macmillan, 1972.
Azad M. A. K. *History of Philosophy—Eastern and Western*. Long Beach: Long Beach Publications, 1987.
Babalola, Adeboye. *Akojopo Alo Ijapa—Apa Keji*. Ibadan, Nigeria: Oxford University Press, 1973.
———. *Akojopo Alo Ijapa—Apa Kinni*. Ibadan, Nigeria: Oxford University PRess, 1973.
———. *Awon Oriki Orile*, London: Collins, 1967.
Babawale, T. et al., eds., *Teaching and Propagating African and Diaspora History and Culture*. Lagos, Nigeria: Concept Publications, 2009.
Babawale, T. and A. Alao. *Global African Spirituality, Social Capital and Self-reliance in Africa*. Lagos, Nigeria: Malthouse Press Ltd., 2008.
Babbitt, Susan and Sue Campbell, eds., *Racism and Philosophy*. Ithaca, NY: Cornell University Press, 1999.
Bahm, A. J. *Epistemology*. Albuquerque: World Books, 1995.
Balde, A. "Black Civilization and Language." In J. O. Okpaku et al., eds., *The Arts and Civilization of Black and African Peoples* 4, (1986).
Balogun, D. A. et al. *Principles and Practice of Education*. Lagos, Nigeria: Macmillan Publishers, 1981.
Balogun, O. *The Tragic Years*. Benin City, Nigeria: Ethiope Publishing Co., 1973.
———. "A Jurisprudential Analysis of Yoruba Proverbs." In *Cambrian Law Review* 37, (2006).
Bamgbose, A. *The Novels of D. O. Fagunwa*. Benin City, Nigeria: Ethiopia, 1974.
Bamikole, L. O. *Essays in Comparative Philosophy*. Lagos, Nigeria: Majab Publishers, 2002.
Barnes, A. *Seeing Through Self-deception*. Cambridge: Cambridge University Press, 1997.
Barthes, R. *Mythologies*. New York: Transaction Publishers, 1972.
Beattie, J. *Other Cultures*. New York: Free Press. 1964
Beckford, G. et al. eds., *A Caribbean Reader on Development*. Kingston, Jamaica: Friedrich Ebert Stiftung, 1987.

Beckford, G. L. *Persistent Poverty*. Kingston, Jamaica: University of the West Indies Press, 1999.
Bell, R. *Understanding African Philosophy*. New York: Routledge, 2002.
———. *Rethinking Justice*. Lanham, MD: Rowman & Littlefield, 2006.
Bello, A. G. A. "Rationality, Myth and Philosophy." In *Ibadan Journal of Humanistic Studies* 1, (August 1981).
Bender, J. W. and H. G. Blocker, eds., *Contemporary Philosophy of Art*. Englewood Cliffs, NJ: Prentice Hall, 1993.
Ben-Jochanan, Y. A. A. *Black Man of the Nile*. Baltimore, MD: Black Classic Press, 1989.
———. and J. H. Clarke. *New Dimensions in African History*. New Jersey: Africa World Press, 1991.
Berghe, P. L. van den. *Race and Racism—A Comparative Perspective*. New York: John Wiley & Sons, 1978.
Bergquist, C., ed., *Labor in the Capitalist World-Economy*. London: Sage Publications, 1984.
Berlin, I. *Concepts and Categories*. Oxford: Oxford University Press, 1980.
Berlinski, D. *Black Mischief*. New York: Harcourt, Brace, Jovanovich, 1988.
Bernal, M. *Black Athena*. New Jersey: Rutgers University Press, 1987.
Bernecker, S. and F. Dretske. *Knowledge: Readings in Contemporary Epistemology*. Oxford: Oxford University Press, 2000.
Bertalanfy, L. von. *Robots, Man and Minds*. New York: George Braziller, 1967.
Best, C. *Roots to Popular Culture*. London: Macmillan, 2001.
Bewaji, J. A. I., Adebola Adebileje and Rotimi Omosulu, eds., *Introduction to Philosophy and Logic*. Ede, Nigeria: Directorate of General Studies, Redeemer's University, Ede. 2014
Bewaji, J. A. I., and Imafidon, E., eds., *Ontologized Ethics—New Essays in African Meta-Ethics*. Lanham, MD: Lexington Books, 2013.
Bewaji, J. A. I. "African Aesthetics" (A—29). In *A Companion to Aesthetics*. Edited by Stephen Davies et al. New York: Blackwell Publishing, 2009a.
———. "African Beliefs." In Oyeneye and Soremi, eds., *Nigerian Life and Culture*. Ago-Iwoye, Nigeria: 1985, 307-360.
———. "African Philosophy: Some Comments." In *The Nigerian Journal of Philosophy* 3, nos. 1 & 2 (1983): 70-83.
———. "Art and Consciousness—Future Pasts and Past Futures of Identity Crises." In Tunde Babawale and Akin Alao, eds., *Global African Spirituality, Social Capital and Self-reliance in Africa*. Lagos, Nigeria: Malthouse Press Ltd., 2008b.
———. "Arts, Memory and Identity." In Tunde Babawale et al., eds., *Pan-Africanism, and the Integration of Continental Africa and Diaspora Africa*. Lagos, Nigeria: CBAAC, 2011.
———. *Beauty and Culture—Perspectives in Black Aesthetics*. Ibadan, Nigeria: Spectrum Books Ltd., 2003.
———. *Black Aesthetics—Beauty and Culture: An Introduction to African and African Diaspora Philosophy of Art*. Trenton, NY: Africa World Press. 2013.
———. "The Certain, the Evident, and the Problem of Criterion in the Philosophy of Roderick M. Chisholm." In *The Philosophy of Roderick M. Chisholm. Library of Living Philosophers* 25. Edited by Lewis E. Hahn. Chicago, IL: Open Court Publishers, 1997, 587-608.
———. "The Church, the Land, the Government and Ethics—An Analysis of the Church Position on Basarwa Eco-relocation in Botswana." In Nkomazana, Fidelis and Laurel Lanner, eds., *Aspects of History of the Church in Botswana*. Pietermaritzburg, South Africa: Cluster Publications Ltd., 2007c.
———. "A Critical Analysis of the Philosophical Status of Yoruba Ifa Literary Corpus." *Weiner Reihe* VI, (1992): 142-155.
———. "Critical Comments on Pearce, African Philosophy and the Sociological Thesis." *Philosophy of the Social Sciences* 25, no. 1 (1995): 99-119.

———. "Culture, Poverty, and Civil Society: A Critical Analysis of Aspects of Leadership in Africa and its Diaspora," in Akinrinade, Sola, et al., eds., *The Humanities, Nationalism, and Democracy*. Ile Ife, Nigeria: Faculty of Arts, Obafemi Awolowo University, 2006, 54–86.
———. "Education and Society—Requiem for Western Education in Africana Societies to Transcend Platocracy, Coloniality and Neocoloniality." In *Teaching and Propagating African and Diaspora History and Culture*, eds., Tunde Babawale et al. Lagos, Nigeria: CBAAC and Concept Publications Ltd., 2009b.
———. "Empiricism versus Pragmatism: Truth versus Results," *Indian Philosophical Quarterly* XX, no. 3, (1993): 203-242.
———. "Ethics and Morality—Critical Exploration of Western and African and Diaspora Intellectual and Practical Perspectives." In Noel Cowell, ed., *Ethical Perspectives for Caribbean Business*. Kingston, Jamaica: Arawak Press Ltd., 2007b.
———. "Ethics and Morality in Yoruba Culture." In Kwasi Wiredu, ed., *A Companion to African Philosophy*, New York: Basil Blackwell Press, 2004, 396-403.
———. "Ifa: A Yoruba Epistemology?" In *Proceedings of Faclty of Arts Seminar on Yoruba Folklore*, Ago-Iwoye: Ogun State University, Ago-Iwoye, ch. 8, 1987.
———. *An Introduction to the Theory of Knowledge—A Pluricultural Approach*. Ibadan, Nigeria: Hope Publications. 2007d.
———. "Language, Culture, Science, Technology and Philosophy." In *African Philosophy—Journal on African Philosophy*. http://www.africanphilosophy.com/afphil/vol.1.1/bewaji.html 2002.
______. *Narratives of Struggle—the Philosophy and Politics of Development*. Durham, NC: Carolina Academic Press, 2012.
———. "Neugebauer's Critical Note on Ethno-philosophy in the Philosophical Discourse in Africa: Some Remarks." In *Quest: Philosophical Discussions* V, no 1 (1991): 95-103.
———. "Olodumare: God in Yoruba Belief and the Problem of Evil." In *African Studies Quarterly* 4 (Electronic Journal), 1998.
———. "Philosophy in History and History of Philosophy as Academic Politics." In Liubava Moreva, ed., *UNESCO International Readings on Theory, History and Philosophy of Culture* 18: *Differentiation and Integration of World Views—Philosophical and Religious Experience*. Moscow, 2004.
———. "Philosophy, Cultures and Errors of Ontogenesis: Challenges, Opportunities and Dangers" in Roxanne Burton, et al. eds., *Conversations in Philosophy: Crossing the Boundaries*. Cambridge: Cambridge Scholars Publishing, 2008a.
———. "The Politics of Philosophy as History of Culture." In Tunde Babawale, ed., *The Place of Research and Studies in the Development of African and the African Diaspora*. Lagos, Nigeria: Concept Publications Ltd., 2007a.
———. "Toyin Falola and (African) History: A Critical Perspective" in *Toyin Falola—The Man, The Mask, The Muse*. Niyi Afolabi, ed., Durham, NC: Carolina Academic Press, 2010.
———. "Traditional Religions, Constituted Authority, Law and Order: The Yoruba Perspective." In Momoh, C. S., C. O. Onikepe and Victor Chukwulozie, eds., *Nigerian Studies in Religious Tolerance*. Vol. 3. Lagos, Nigeria: Centre for Black and African Arts and Civilization, 1989, 311–331.
———. "Truth and Ethics in African Philosophy: A Reply to Emmanuel Eze." *Quest: Philosophical Discussions* VIII, 1 (1994): 76-89.
Bewaji, M. B. *Ogede* . Unpublished NCE dissertation at Oyo State College of Education, Ilesa, Nigeria: 1983.
———. *Essentials of Information Skills*. Kingston, Jamaica: The University Printery. 2002.
Bhabha, H. K. *The Location of Culture*. London: Routledge, 1994.
Bird, G. *William James*. London: Routledge, 1986.
Blackburn, R. *Overthrow of Colonial Slavery 1776–1848*. London: Verso, 1990.
Blakey, T. D. et al., eds., *Religion in Africa*. London: James Currey, 1994.
Boahen, A. et al. *Topics in West African History* . Essex, UK: Longman, 1986.

Bodunrin, P. O., ed., *Philosophy in Africa*. Ile-Ife, Nigeria: University of Ife Press, 1985.
———. *Plato and His Contemporaries on the Possibility of Falsehood*. Ph.D. Thesis, University of Minnesota, 1971.
Bogues, A. *Black Heretics, Black Prophets*. New York: Routledge, 2003.
Braine, D. *The Human Person*. Notre Dame, IN: University of Notre Dame Press, 1992.
Braithwaite, R. B. *Scientific Explanation*. Cambridge: Cambridge University Press, 1968.
Brathwaite, E. *The Arrivants*. Oxford: Oxford University Press, 1973.
Brettler, M. Z. *How to Read the Bible*. Philadelphia, PA: The Jewish Publication Society, 1995.
Broad, C. D. *Scientific Thought*. New York: International University Press, Inc., 1958.
Brody, B. A. *Readings in the Philosophy of Religion*. Englewood Cliffs, NJ: Prentice Hall, 1992.
Brophy, A. L. *Reparations: Pro and Con*. Oxford: Oxford University Press, 2006.
Brown, S. *The Art of Kamau Brathwaite*. Mid Glamorgan, Wales: Seren, 1995.
Brubaker, J. O. *Understanding People*. Wheaton, IL: Evangelical Teacher Training Association, 1984.
Buber, M. *I and Thou*. New York: Charles Scribner's Sons, 1958.
Buchler, J., ed., *The Philosophical Writings of Peirce*. New York: Dover Publications, 1955.
Budge, W. *The Egyptian Sudan*. Vols. 1–2, London: Kegan, Trench. 1907.
Butcher, H. J. *Human Intelligence—Its Nature and Assessment*. London: Methuen, 1968.
Calvocoressi, P. *Independent Africa and the World*. London: Longman, 1985.
Campbell, N. R. *Foundations of Science*. New York: Dover Books, 1957.
Camus, A. *The Stranger*. New York: Vintage Books, 1946.
Carpenter, R. *Discontinuity in Greek Civilization*. Cambridge: Cambridge University Press, 1966.
Carroll, N. *Philosophy of Art*. New York: Routledge, 1999.
Cassam, Q. *Self-Knowledge*. Oxford: Oxford University Press, 1994.
Cassirer, E. *An Essay on Man*. New York: Charles Scribner's Sons, 1969.
Castro, F. *The World Economic and Social Crisis*. Havana, Cuba: Publishing Office of the Council of State, 1983.
Cato, C. E. *Philosophy and Ordinary Language*. Urbana, Chicago, IL: University of Illinois Press, 1970.
Cesaire, A. *The Collected Poetry*. Berkeley, CA: University of California Press, 1983.
Chambers, I. *Border Dialogues: Journeys in Postmodernity*. London: Routledge, 1990.
Chambliss, J. J. *Educational Theory as Theory of Conduct*. New York: SUNY Press, 1987.
Chapman, A. J. and D. M. Jones, eds., *Models of Man*. Leicester, UK: The British Psychology Society, 1981.
Chapman, C. *Whose Promised Land?* Oxford: Lion Publishing, 1983.
Chevannes, B. *Betwixt and Between*. Kingston, Jamaica: Ian Randle Publishers, 2006.
——— *What We Sow, and What We Reap*. Kingston, Jamaica: Grace Kennedy Foundation, 1999.
Chude-Sokei, L. *Dr. Satan's Echo Chamber: Reggae, Technology and the Diaspora Process*. Bob Marley Lecture, University of the West Indies, Mona Campus, Institute of Caribbean Studies (Reggae Studies Unit), 1997.
Church, F. J. *Plato*. Indianapolis: Bobbs Merrill, 1980.
Churchland, P. M. *Matter and Consciousness*. Cambridge, MA: MIT Press, 1990.
Christie, P. *Language in Jamaica*. Kingston, Jamaica: Arawak Press, 2003.
Clark, E. and H. Richardson. *Women and Religion*. New York: Harper & Row, 1977.
Clark. M. *Nietzsche on Truth and Philosophy*. New York: Cambridge University Press, 1990.
Clarke, J. H. "Slave Revolt in the Caribbean," in *Black World*. New York: Johnson Publishing, 1973(Feb.), Vol. XXII, no. 4.
Clarke, J. H., ed., *New Dimensions in African History*. Trenton, NJ: Africa World Press, 1991.
Coates, J., ed., *Language and Gender: A Reader*. Oxford: Blackwell, 1998.

Coetzee, P. H. and A. P. J. Roux, eds., *The African Philosophy Reader*. New York: Routledge, 1998.
Code, L. *Ecological Thinking*. Oxford: Oxford University Press, 2006.
———. *Epistemic Responsibility*. Hanover and London: University of New England Press, 1987.
———. *Rhetorical Spaces*. New York: Routledge, 1995.
———. *What Can She Know?* Ithaca, NY: Cornell University Press, 1991.
Cohen, L. J. *The Diversity of Meaning*. London: Methuen and Co., 1966.
Cohen, M. R. and E. Nagel. *An Introduction to Logic and Scientific Method*. London: Routledge and Kegan Paul Ltd., 1964.
Coke, F-M. *Intersections*. Leeds, UK: Peepal Tree Press Ltd., 2010.
Collingwood, R. G. *An Essay on Metaphysics*. London: Oxford University Press, 1940.
———. *The Idea of Nature*. New York: Oxford University Press, 1960.
———. *Speculum Mentis or The Map of Knowledge*. Oxford: The Clarendon Press, 1946.
Collini, S., ed., *J. S. Mill on Liberty and Other Essays*. Cambridge: Cambridge University Press, 1991.
Collins, A. W. *Thought and Nature: Studies in Rationalist Philosophy*. Notre Dame, IN: University of Notre Dame Press, 1985.
Collins, J. C. *The Apocalyptic Imagination*. New York: Cross Road Publishing Company, 1992.
Congar, Y. *The Meaning of Tradition*. New York: Hawthorn Books, 1964.
Conrad, J. *Under Western Eyes*. Oxford: Oxford University Press, 1983.
Conradie, F., L. F. Teffo and J. E. Nel, eds., *Africa*. Sovenga, South Africa: University of the North Press, 1994.
Cooper, A. *The Hanging of Angelique*. Toronto, Canada: HarperCollins Publishers, 2006.
Cooper, D. E., ed., *Aesthetics: The Classic Readings*. Oxford: Blackwell, 1997.
Copleston, R. *A History of Philosophy*. Vol. 1. Great Britain: Continuum, 1993.
———. *A History of Philosophy*. Vol. 6. *Modern Philosophy: Kant*. New York: Image Books, 1964.
Cowell, N. et al., eds., *Ethical Perspectives for Caribbean Business*. Kingston, Jamaica: Arawak Publications, 2007.
Cox, C. *Nietzsche*. Berkeley, CA: University of California Press, 1999.
Craig, D., ed., *Education in the West Indies*. Kingston, Jamaica: ISER, 1996.
Crowder, M. *West Africa Under Colonial Rule*. London: Hutchinson, 1968.
Dapila, F. N. *The Role of Theology in the New South Africa*. Roma, Lesotho: Department of Theology and Religious Studies, 1998.
Davidson, B. *Africa in History*. New York: Simon & Schuster, 1995.
———. *The Black Man's Burden: Africa and the Curse of Nation State*. New York: Random House, 1992.
Davies, S. *Definitions of Art*. Ithaca, NY: Cornell University Press, 1991.
Davies, S. et. al., eds., *A Companion to Aesthetics*. West Sussex, UK: Blackwell, 2009.
Davis, P. *God and the New Physics*. New York: Simon & Schuster, 1994.
de Anda, D., ed., *Controversial Issues in Multiculturalism*. Boston, MA: Allyn & Bacon, 1997.
De Chardin, T. *The Phenomenon of Man*. London: Harper & Row, 1961.
De Georg, R. *Business Ethics*. Englewood Cliffs, NJ: Prentice Hall, 1995.
Delaney, C. F. *Science, Knowledge and Mind*. Notre Dame, IN: University of Notre Dame Press, 1993.
Desai, V. and R. B. Potter, eds., *The Companion to Development Studies*. London: Hodder Education, 2008.
DeVito, J. *The Psychology of Speech and Language: An Introduction to Psycholinguistics*. Washington, DC: Random House, 1970.
Devitt, M. and K. Sterelny. *Language and Reality*. Oxford: Blackwell, 1986.
Dicey, A. V. *Introduction to the Study of the Law of the Constitution*. London: McMillan and Co. (5th ed. 1897) [1885].
Dicken, P. *Global Shift*. London: Paul Chapman Publishing Co., 1999.

Diop, C. A. *Civilization or Barbarism*. Chicago, IL: Lawrence Hill Books, 1991.
———. *The Cultural Unity of Black Africa*. Chicago, IL: Third World Press, 1990.
Dixon, B. R. et al. *A Handbook of Social Science Research*. Oxford: Oxford University Press, 1991.
Dopamu, P. A. *Esu: the Invisible Foe of Man*. Ijebu-Ode, Nigeria: Shebiotimo Publications, 1986.
Dostoevsky, F. *Notes from the Underground*. New York: Vintage Books, 1993.
Doxtader, E. and C. Villa-Vicencio, eds., *To Repair the Irreparable*. Claremont, South Africa: David Philip, 2004.
Du Bois, W. E. B. *The Soul of Black Folks*. New York: Vintage Press, 1990.
Dubos, R. *Man Adapting*. New Haven, CT: Yale University Press, 1980.
Durant, Will. *Our Oriental Heritage*. New York: MJF Books, 1953.
Dworkin, Ronald. *Taking Rights Seriously* Cambridge, MA: Harvard University Press, 1978.
Eastman, R., ed., *The Ways of Religion*. New York: Oxford University Press, 1999.
Eckert, P. and S. McConnell-Ginet. *Language and Gender*. Cambridge: Cambridge University Press, 2003.
Edie, J. et al., eds., *Russian Philosophy* Vol. II and III. New Cork: Quadrangle Books, 1965.
Edwards, J. *When Race Counts* . London: Routledge, 1995.
Edwards, N. "Derek Walcott: The Poetics of Two Margins." In *Mississippi Review*, 1996. 24, no. 3.
Ekwuazi, H. *Creating the Screen Image*. Lagos, Nigeria: Kraft Books Ltd., 1991.
Eliade, M. *Man and the Sacred*. New York: Harper & Row Publishers, 1974.
Elaigwu, I. "The Military and the State Building: Federal-State Relations in Nigeria's Military Federalism 1966–1976." In A. Akinyemi, P. Cole, and W. Ofonogoro, eds., *Readings on Federalism* Lagos: N.I.I.A. 1980, 155–81.
Elegido, I. M. *Jurisprudence: A Textbook for Nigerian Students*. Ibadan, Nigeria: Spectrum Law Pub., 1994.
Elkins, S. M. *Slavery: A Problem in American Institutional and Intellectual Life*. Chicago, IL: University of Chicago Press, 1962.
Ellis, B. *Rational Belief Systems*. Oxford: Blackwell, 1979.
Emecheta, B. *Double Yoke*. New York: George Braziller, 1983.
Esan, O. *Esin Atiroja*. Ibadan, Nigeria: Oxford University Press, 1966.
Etuk, U. *Religion and Cultural Identity*. Ibadan, Nigeria: Hope Publications, 2002.
Evans, A. *Critique of Patriarchal Reason*. San Francisco, CA: White Crane Press, 1997.
Evans, G. and F. McDowell, eds., *Truth and Meaning*. Oxford: Clarendon Press, 1976.
Evans-Prichard, E. E. *Nuer Religion*. Oxford: Oxford University Press, 1956.
———. *Witchcraft, Oracles and Magic among the Azande*. Oxford: Clarendon Press, 1937.
Eze, E. C. *Race and the Enlightenment*. Oxford: Blackwell Publishers, 1997.
Fadahunsi, A. *Philosophy and Society*. Ibadan, Nigeria: Hope Publications, 1999.
Fadahunsi, A. and O. Oladipo, eds., *Philosophy and the African Prospect: Selected Essays of Professor J. Olubi Sodipo*. Ibadan, Nigeria: Hope Publications, 2006.
Fagunwa. D. O. *Adiitu Olodumare*. Lagos, Nigeria: Nelson, 1964.
———. *Igbo Olodumare*. Lagos, Nigeria: Nelson, 1949.
———. *Ireke Onibudo*. London: Nelson, 1965.
———. *Irinkerindo Ninu Igbo Elegbeje*. Lagos, Nigeria: Nelson, 1961.
———. *Ogboju Ode ninu Igbo Irunmale*. Lagos, Nigeria: Nelson, 1950.
Falola, T. and C. Jennings. *Africanizing Knowledge: African Studies across the Disciplines*. New Brunswick, NJ: Transaction Publishers, 2002.
Falola, T. and M. D. Childs, eds., *The Yoruba Diaspora in the Atlantic World*. Bloomington, IN: Indiana University Press, 2004.
Falola, T. *African Historiography: Essays in Honor of Jacob Ade Ajayi*. Essex: Longman Group, 1993.
———. ed., *Britain and Nigeria: Exploitation or Development*. London: Zed Books Ltd., 1987.

———. *Colonial Africa, 1885–1939.* Durham, NC: Carolina Academic Press, 2002.
———. *The History of Nigeria.* Westport, CT: Greenwood Press, 1999.
———. *The Power of African Cultures.* New York: University of Rochester Press, 2003.
Falola, T. and J. O. Ihonvbere. *Nigeria and the International Capitalist System.* Boulder, CO: The University of Denver Press, 1988.
Fanon, F. *Black Skin White Masks.* New York: Grove Weidenfeld, 1967.
———. *The Wretched of the Earth.* London: Penguin, 2001.
Feder, E. K. et al., eds., *A Passion for Wisdom.* Upper Saddle, NJ: Prentice Hall, 2004.
Ferguson, A. *An Essay on the History of Civil Society.* Edited by Fania Oz-Salzberge. Cambridge: Cambridge University Press, 1995.
Festenstein, M. and M. Kenny. *Political Ideologies.* Oxford: Oxford University Press, 2005.
Finch, C. "The African Background of Medical Science." In I. V. Sertima, ed., *Blacks in Science.* 1986, 127-39.
Fine, A. *The Shaky Game: Einstein, Realism and the Quantum Theory.* Chicago, IL: The University of Chicago Press, 1988.
Fingarette, H. *Self-Deception.* London: Routledge, 1969.
Fiorenza, E. S. *Bread Not Stone.* Boston, MA: Beacon Press, 1984.
Foucault, M. *Discipline and Punish.* New York: Vintage Press, 1995.
———. *The History of Sexuality.* New York: Vintage Books, 1980.
Frankfurt, H. G. *Demons, Dreamers and Madmen.* Indianapolis, IN: Bobbs-Merrill, 1969.
Fraser, N. *Unruly Practices.* Minneapolis,MN: University of Minnesota Press, 1991.
Freire, P. *Pedagogy of the Oppressed.* New York: Continuum, 2003.
Freud, S. *New Introductory Lectures on Psychoanalysis.* London: Hogarth Press, 1964.
Friend, J. W. and J. K. Feibleman. *What Science Really Means.* London: Allen & Unwin, 1937.
Fromm, E. *Beyond the Chains of Illusion.* London: Abacus Books, 1962.
———. *Escape From Freedom.* New York: Avon Books, 1941.
———. and R. Xirau. *The Nature of Man.* London: Macmillan, 1969.
Fukuyama, F. *Trust.* New York: Simon & Schuster, 1995.
Gadamer, H-G. *Truth and Method.* New York: Continuum Press, 1993.
Gaie, J. B. R. et al. *God.* Gaborone, Botswana: Department of Theology and Religious Studies, 2001.
———. and S. K. Mmolai. *The Concept of Botho and HIV?AIDS in Botswana.* Eldoret, Kenya: Zapf Chancery, 2007.
Galgut, E. "Poetic Faith and Prosaic Concerns: A Defense of 'Suspension of Belief.'" In *South African Journal of Philosophy* 21, no. 3, (2002): 190–199.
Galligan, D. J. *Law in Modern Society.* Oxford: Oxford University Press. 2007
Garvey, A. J. and U. E. U. Essien-Udom, eds., *More Philosophy and Opinions of Marcus Garvey.* London: Frank Cass, 1977.
Gaskin, J. C. A. *Varieties of Unbelief.* London: Macmillan, 1989.
Gates, H. L. Jr. *Colored People.* New York: Vintage Books, 1994.
———. "A Final Act for the Debate Over Reparations" *New York Times*, 23 April 2010, sec. A27.
———. *The Signifying Monkey.* New York: Oxford University Press, 1988.
Gbadegesin, S. *African Philosophy—Traditional Yoruba Philosophy and Contemporary Realities.* New York: Peter Lang, 1991.
———. *The Politicization of Society During Nigeria's Second Republic, 1979–1983.* Lewiston, NY: Edwin Mellen Press, 1991.
Gellner, E. *The Legitimation of Belief.* London: Cambridge University Press, 1979.
Germond, P and S. de Gruchy, eds., *Aliens in the Household of God.* Cape Town, South Africa: David Philip, 1997.
Giere, R. N. *Explaining Science: A Cognitive Approach.* Chicago, IL: University of Chicago Press, 1990.
Gifforf, A. *The Passionate Advocate.* Kingston, Jamaica: Arawak Publications, 2007.

Gissendanner, J. M., ed., *Proceedings of the Towson State University Multidisciplinary Conference on the Scholarship and Creativity of African Americans*. Towson, MD: Towson State University, 1996.
Glaude, E. S. *In a Shade of Blue*. Chicago, IL: University of Chicago Press, 1968.
Goesta, A. *The Ancient History of Palestine*. New York: Fortress Press, 1993.
Goodman, N. *Fact, Fiction and Forecast*. Cambridge, MA: Harvard University Press, 1955.
Goody, J. *The Domestication of the Savage Mind*. Cambridge: Cambridge University Press, 1977.
———. *Technology, Tradition and the State in Africa*. London: Hutchinson University Library for Africa, 1980.
Gordon, L. R. and J. A. Gordon. *Not Only The Master's Tools*. London: Paradigm Publishers, 2006.
Gordon, L. R. *Bad Faith and Antiblack Racism*. New Jersey: Humanities Press, 1995.
———. *Disciplinary Decadence*. Boulder, CO: Paradigm Publishers, 2006.
———. *Existence in Black*. New York: Routledge, 1997.
———. *Existentia Africana*. New York: Routledge, 2000.
———. *Her Majesty's Other Children*. Lanham, MD: Rowman & Littlefield, 1997.
———. *An Introduction to Africana Philosophy*. Cambridge: Cambridge University Press, 2008
Gould, J. A., ed., *Classic Philosophical Questions*. Englewood Cliffs, NJ: Prentice Hall, 1994.
Graham, G. *Philosophy of Mind*. Malden, MA: Blackwell, 1998.
Green, E. H. H. *Ideologies of Conservatism*. Oxford: Oxford University Press, 2002.
Green, J. E. *Race, Class and Gender in the Future of the Caribbean*. Kingston, Jamaica: ISER, 1993.
Griffiths, A. P., ed., *Knowledge and Belief*. London: Oxford University Press, 1970.
Grondin, J. *Introduction to Philosophical Hermeneutics*. New Haven, CT: Yale University Press, 1994.
Grugeon, E. and P. Walden, eds., *Literature and Learning*. London: Open University Books, 1983.
Gunn, G. *Beyond Solidarity*. Chicago, IL: University of Chicago Press, 2001.
Gutterplan, S. *Mind and Language*. Oxford: Oxford University Press, 1975.
Gyekye, K. *An Essay on African Philosophical Thought*. Cambridge: Cambridge University Press, 1987.
Habermas, J. *Knowledge and Human Interests*. London: Heinmann, 1975.
Hales, S. D. *Relativism and the Foundations of Philosophy*. Cambridge, MA: The MIT Press, 2006.
Hallen, B. *The Good, the Bad and the Beautiful*. Bloomington, IN: Indiana University Press, 2000.
Hallen, B. and J. O. Sodipo. *Knowledge, Belief and Witchcraft*. London: Ethnographica, 1986.
Hallman, D. G. *Ecotheology*. New York: Orbis Books, 1994.
Hamlyn, D. W. *A History of Western Philosophy*. Cambridge: Cambridge University Press, 1987.
Hampshire, S. *Thought and Action*. London: Chatto and Windus, 1959.
Hanfling, O., ed., *Life and Meaning*. Oxford: Blackwell, 1988.
———. *The Quest for Meaning*. Oxford: Blackwell, 1988.
Haralambos, M. and M. Holborn. *Sociology: Themes and Perspectives*. London: Collins Educational, 1991.
Harding, O. G. *Near Death Experience: A Holographic Explanation*. Kingston, Jamaica: LMH Publishing Ltd., 2006.
Hare, R. M. *The Language of Morals*. Oxford: Oxford University Press, 1952.
Hare, W. *In Defense of Open-mindedness*. Kingston, Canada: McGill-Queen's University Press, 1985.

Hare, W. and J. P. Portelli, eds., *Philosophy of Education: Introductory Readings*. Calgary, Alberta, Canada: Detselig Enterprises Ltd., 1988.
Harriott, A. *Organized Crime and Politics in Jamaica*. Kingston, Jamaica: Canoe Press, 2008.
Harris, J. E. *Africans and their History*. New York: Mentor Books, 1987.
Harrison, B. *An Introduction to the Philosophy of Language*. London: Macmillan, 1979.
Hart, K., ed., *Women and the Sexual Division of Labour in the Caribbean*. Kingston, Jamaica: Canoe Press, 1996.
Hart, H. L. A. *The Concept of Law*. Oxford: Oxford University Press, 1961.
———. *Punishment and Responsibility*. Oxford: Clarendon Press, 1968.
Harry, O. G., ed., *Caribbean Journal of Education: Language Use and the Jamaican Educational System*. Kingston, Jamaica: School of Education, UWI Mona, 2007.
Healey, R. *The Philosophy of Quantum Mechanics*. New York: Cambridge University Press, 1990.
Hempel, C. G. *Aspects of Scientific Explanation*. New York: The Free Press, 1965.
Henry, P. *Caliban's Reason*. New York: Routledge, 2000.
Hill, R. A. *Marcus Garvey: Life and Lessons*. Los Angeles, CA: University of California Press, 1987.
Hofstadter, G. *I Am a Strange Loop*. New York: Basic Books, 2007.
Holleman, J. F. "An Anthropological Approach to Bantu Law." In *African Law and Legal Theory*. Edited by G. R. Woodman and A. O. Obilade. New York: New York University Press. 1995.
Hollis, M. and S. Lukes, eds., *Rationality and Relativism*. Oxford: Blackwell Press, 1982.
Holm, J., ed., *Worship*. London: Pinter Publishers, 1994.
Hord, F. L. and Jonathan S. Lee., eds., *I Am Because We Are*. Amherst, MA: University of Massachusetts Press, 1995.
Horner, C. and E. Westacott. *Thinking Through Philosophy*. Cambridge: Cambridge University Press, 2000.
Hornsby, J. and G. Longworth. *Reading Philosophy of Language*. Malden, MA: Blackwell Publishing Inc., 2006.
Horton, R. *Patterns of Thought in Africa and the West*. Cambridge: Cambridge University Press, 1993.
Hountondji, P. *African Philosophy: Myth and Reality*. Bloomington, IN: Indiana University Press, 1983.
Hume, D. *Dialogues Concerning Natural Religion*. New York: Macmillan, 1978.
———. *Enquiries Concerning Human Understanding*. Oxford: Clarendon Press, 1902.
———. *A Treatise of Human Nature*. Oxford: Clarendon Press, 1978.
Hunt, R. and J. Shelly. *Computers and Commonsense*. New York: Prentice Hall, 1988.
Hurston, Z. N. *Their Eyes Were Watching God*. New York: Harper Perennial, 2006.
Hutton, C. *The Logic and Historical Significance of the Haitian Revolution & the Cosmological Roots of Haitian Freedom*. Kingston, Jamaica: Arawak Press, 2005.
Idowu, B. *Olodumare: God in Yoruba Belief*. London: Longman, 1962.
Idowu, William. "African Jurisprudence and the Reconciliation Theory of Law." In *Cambrian Law Review*, 2006: 37.
Ihonvbere, J. O. *Towards a New Constutionalism in Africa*. London: CDD Occasional Papers, 2000.
Inglis, F. *Cultural Studies*. Cambridge: Blackwell, 1994.
Inikori, J. E. *Slavery and the Rise of Capitalism*. Elsa Govia Memorial Lecture, Kingston: University of the West Indies, 1991.
Irele, Dipo. "Essentially Contested Concepts and the Question of Rationality in Traditional African Thought." In *Ibadan Journal of Humanistic Studies*, no. 7 (October 1997).
Isichei, Elizabeth. *History of West Africa since 1800*. London: Macmillan, 1977.
Isola, A. *Aye Ye Won Tan*. Ibadan, Nigeria: DB Martos Press, 2009.
Jahn, J. *Muntu*. New York: Grove Weidenfeld, 1961.
James, C. L. R. *The Black Jacobins*. London: Penguin Books, 1980.

———. *Beyond a Boundary*. London: Yellow Jersey Press, 2005.
James, G. G. M. *The Stolen Legacy*. New York: Philosophical Library, 1954.
Johnson, S. *The History of the Yorubas*. Lagos, Nigeria: CSS Bookshops, 1969.
Jones, E. D. *The Writing of Wole Soyinka*. London: Heinemann Educational Books Inc., 1973.
Jung, C. G. *The Development of Personality*. New York: Routledge, 1934.
Kamera, W. D., E. Kezilahabi and M. R. Besha. "The Sociocultural and Economic Factors in Developing a National Language: The Case of Kiswahili in Tanzania." In Okpaku. et al., eds., *The Arts and Civilization of Black and African Peoples* 4, (1986): 123–39.
Kant, I. *Prolegomenon to Any Future Metaphysics*. New York: Macmillan, 1987.
Karenga, M. *The Book of Coming Forth by Day*. Los Angeles, CA: University of Sankore Press, 1990.
Keita, L. D. "Pearce's 'African Philosophy and the Sociological Thesis': A Response." In *Philosophy of the Social Sciences*, 24 (1994): 192–203.
Kerr, M. *Personality and Conflict in Jamaica*. London: Collins, 1963.
Khunn, T. S. *The Structure of Scientific Revolutions*. Chicago, IL: Chicago University Press, 1962.
Kierkegaard, S. *Either/Or*. New York: Harper Torchbooks, 1987.
Kinni-Olusayin, E. "The Arts as Communication." In *Ibadan Journal of Humanistic Studies*, no. 1 (August 1981).
Kirby, K. M. *Indifferent Boundaries*. New York: The Guilford Press, 1996.
Ki-Zerbo, J. *General History of Africa I: Methodology and African Prehistory*. James Currey. 1990.
Kleinig, J. *Philosophical Issues in Education*. London: Croom Helm, 1982.
Klemke, E. D. *The Meaning of Life*. New York: Oxford University Press. 2000.
———. et al., eds., *Introductory Readings in the Philosophy of Science*. New York: Prometheus Books, 1998.
Knitter, P. F. *No Other Name?* New York: Orbis Books, 1986.
Kolak, B. and R. Martin. *Self and Identity*. New York: Macmillan, 1991.
Kornblith, H. *Inductive Inference and Its Natural Ground*. Cambridge: MIT Press, 1993.
Korner, S., ed., *Observation and Interpretation*. New York: Academic Press, 1957.
Kresse, K. *Philosophising in Mombasa*. London: Edinburgh University Press, 2007.
Kuusi, P. *This World of Man*. Oxford: Pergamon Press Ltd., 1985.
Laine, L. *On the Fringes of Sport*. Sankt Augustin, Germany: Academia Verlag, 1993.
Lakatos, I. and A. Musgrave, eds., *Criticism and the Growth of Knowledge*. Cambridge: Cambridge University Press, 1970.
Lawson, W. A. *Religion and Race: African and European Roots in Conflict, A Jamaican Testament*. New York: Peter Lang, 1996.
Lefkowitz, M. *Not Out of Africa*. New York: Basic Books, 1996.
Lefkowitz, M. R. and G. M. Rogers, eds., *Black Athena Revisited*. Chapel Hill, NC: University of North Carolina Press, 1996.
Leo-Rhynie, E. *The Jamaican Family: Continuity and Change*. Kingston, Jamaica: Grace Kennedy Foundation, 1993.
Levy, H. *They Cry Respect*. Kingston, Jamaica: UWI Center for Population, Community and Social Change, 2001.
Levy-Bruhl, L. *Les Fonctions Mentales dans les Societes Inferieures*. Paris: Alcan, 1910.
Lewicki, P. *Nonconscious Social Information Processing*. Orlando, FL: Academic Press Inc., 1986.
Lewis, G. K. *Main Currents in Caribbean Thought*. Baltimore, MD: John Hopkins University Press, 1987.
Lewis, L. J. *Society, Schools and Progress in Nigeria*. London: Pergamon Press, 1965.
Lewis, R. C. *Walter Rodney's Intellectual and Political Thought*. Kingston, Jamaica: University of the West Indies Press, 1998.
Lewis, R. and P. Bryan. *Garvey: His Work and Impact*. New Jersey: Africa World Press, 1994.

Lijadu, E. M. *Ifa*. Ado-Ekiti, Nigeria: Omolayo Press, 1972.
Little, R. and M. Smith, eds., *Perspectives on World Politics*. London: Routledge, 1991.
Locke, J. *An Essay Concerning Human Understanding*. Edited by J. W. Yolton. London: Dent and Sons Ltd., 1990.
Loomba, A. *Colonialism/Postcolonialism*. London: Routledge, 1998.
Lubac, H. De. *Teilhard Explained*. New York: Paulist Press Deus Books, 1968.
Lumpkin, B. "Africa in the Mainstream of Mathematics History." In I. Van Sertima, ed., *Blacks in Science*. 1991, 101–102.
Macdonald, J. *Calling a Halt to Mindless Change*. New York: American Management Association International, 1997.
Magdoff, H. *The Age of Imperialism*. New York: Monthly Review Press, 1969.
Magubane, B. M. *The Ties That Bind: African-American Consciousness of Africa*. New Jersey: Africa World Press, 1994.
Makinde, M. A. *African Philosophy, Culture and Traditional Medicine*. Athens, OH: Ohio University Press, 1988.
———. "Immortality of the Soul and the Yoruba Theory of Seven Heaven." In *Journal of Cultures and Ideas*. University of Ife, Ile-Ife, Nigeria: 1983, 31–59.
Mannheim, K. *Ideology and Utopia*. New York: Harvest Books, 1936.
Manpower Projections and Developmental Disabilities in the 1980's. Philadelphia, PA: Temple University Developmental Disabilities Center, n.d.
Marable, M. *Beyond Black and White*. New York: Verso, 1995.
Martin, T. *Race First*. Dover, MA: Majority Press, 1976.
———. ed., *African Fundamentalism*. Dover, Mass: The Majority Press, 1991.
Martinich. A. P., ed., *The Philosophy of Language*. New York: Oxford University Press, 1985.
Marwick, A. *The Nature of History*. London: Macmillan, 1989.
Masolo, D. A. *African Philosophy in Search of an Identity*. Bloomington, IN: Indiana University Press, 1994.
Matthews, G. *Philosophy and the Young Child*. Cambridge, MA: Harvard University Press, 1980.
Mazower, M. *Dark Continent: Europe's Twentieth Century*. London: Penguin Books, 1998.
Mazrui, A. A. *Africa's International Relations*. Boulder, CO: Westview Press, 1977.
———. *Political Values and the Educated Class in Africa*. London: Heinemann, 1978.
Mazur, L. A., ed., *Beyond the Numbers*. Washington, DC: Island Press, 1994.
Mbiti, J. S. *African Religions and Philosophy*. Nairobi, Kenya: Heinemann, 1969.
McBride, W. L. *Sartre's Political Theory*. Bloomington, IN: Indiana University Press, 1991.
McDermott, J. J. *Streams of Experience*. New Delhi, India: Asian Books Pvt. Ltd., 1986.
McGee, A. O. "Some Mathematical Observation on the Ifa belief System Practiced by the Yoruba People of Nigeria." In *Journal of Cultures and Ideas* 1: 95–114.
McKirahan, R. D. Jr. *Philosophy before Socrates*. Indianapolis, IN: Hackett Publishing Co. Inc., 1994.
Mclntosh, S. C. R. *West Indian Constitutional Discourse: A Poetics of Reconstruction*. Kingston, Jamaica: University of the West Indies School of Continuing Studies, 1994.
McLaughlin, B. and A. O. Rorty, eds., *Perspectives on Self-Deception*. Berkeley, CA: California University Press, 1998.
McClintock, A. *Imperial Leather*. New York: Routledge, 1996.
Mechamer, P. and M. Silberstein, eds., *The Blackwell Guide to the Philosophy of Science*. Malden, MA: Blackwell Publishing Inc., 2002.
Merelman, R. M. *Representing Black Culture*. New York: Routledge, 1995.
Meeks, B. and F. Lindahl, eds., *New Caribbean Thought*. Kingston, Jamaica: UWI Press, 2001.
Memmi, Albert. *The Colonizer and the Colonized*. New York: Beacon Press, 1965.
Menkiti, I. A. "On the Normative Conception of a Person." In K. Wiredu, ed., *A Companion to African Philosophy*. Malden, MA: Blackwell Publishing, 2004.

Messiha, K. et. al. "African Experimental Aeronautics: A 2000 Year Old Model Glider." In I. Van Sertima, ed., *Blacks in Science*. 1986, 140–56.
Mgadla, P. T. *Missionaries and Western Education in the Bechuanaland Protectorate, 1859–1905: The Case of Bangwato*. Gaborone, Botswana: Department of History and Department of Theology and Religious Studies, 1989.
Miller, E. *Jamaican Society and High Schooling*. Kingston, Jamaica: Institute of Social and Economic Research, University of the West Indies, Mona Campus, 1990.
———. ed. *Education and Society in the Commonwealth Caribbean*. Kingston, Jamaica: ISER, 1991.
Millikan, R. G. *Language, Thought and other Biological Categories*. Cambridge, MA: The MIT Press, 1991.
Mills, C. W. *Blackness Visible*. Ithaca, NY: Cornell University Press, 1998.
———. *The Racial Contract*. Ithaca, NY: Cornell University Press, 1997.
Moi, T. *The Kristeva Reader*. Oxford: Blackwell, 1986.
Mokhtar, G., ed., *Ancient Civilizations of Africa*. London: James Currey Ltd., 1990.
Momodu, A. G. S. *The Course of Justice and Other Stories*. Ibadan, Nigeria: Onibonoje Press, 1979.
Momoh, C. S., ed., 1989a. *Nigerian Studies in Religious Tolerance,* Vol. 3: *Religion and Nation Building*. Lagos, Nigeria: John West, 1989a.
———. *Nigerian Studies in Religious Tolerance,* Vol. 4: *Philosophy of Religious Tolerance*. Lagos, Nigeria: John West, 1989b.
———. *The Substance of African Philosophy*. Auchi, Nigeria: African Philosophy Publications Project, 1989c.
Moore, B. Jr. *Social Origins of Dictatorship and Democracy*. London: Penguin, 1991.
Moore, G. E. *Principia Ethica*. Cambridge: Cambridge University Press, 1992.
———. *Ethics*. Oxford: Oxford University Press, 1978.
———. *Some Main Problems of Philosophy*. London: Allen & Unwin, 1969.
Moore, T. and C. Carling. *The Limitations of Language*. London: Macmillan, 1988.
Moravia, S. *The Enigma of the Mind*. Cambridge: Cambridge University Press, 1995.
Moseley, A. G. *African Philosophy*. Upper Saddle River: Prentice Hall, 1995.
Moser, P. K., ed., *A Priori Knowledge*. Oxford: Oxford University Press, 1987.
Mudimbe, V. Y. *The Idea of Africa*. London: James Currey, 1994.
Nagel, T. *Mortal Questions*. London: Cambridge University Press, 1981.
Nelson, L. *Socratic Method and Critical Philosophy*. New York: Dover, 1965.
Nettleford, R. *Caribbean Cultural Identity*. Kingston: Institute of Jamaica, 1978.
———. *Dance Jamaica*. New York: Grove Press, 1985.
———. *Inward Stretch Outward Reach*. London: Macmillan, 1993.
———. *Mirror Mirror*. Kingston, Jamaica: LMH Publishing Ltd., 1998.
———. *Our Debt to History: Elsa Goveia Memorial Lecture*. Kingston, Jamaica: University of the West Indies, Mona Campus, 1995.
———. and V. Salter, eds., *Rastafari*. Kingston, Jamaica: Caribbean Quarterly, 2008.
Neugebauer, C. "Hegel and Kant: A Refutation of Their Racism." In *Quest: Philosophical Discussions* 4, (1991): 51–73.
Newsome, F. "Black Contributions to the Early History of Western Wedicine." In I. V. Sertima, ed., *Blacks in Science*. 1986, 92–99.
Newton, L. H. *Ethics and Sustainability*. New Jersey: Prentice Hall, 2003.
Nietzsche, F. *On the Genealogy of Morals: Ecce Homo*. New York: Vintage Books, 1989.
———. *Twilight of the Idols and the Anti-Christ*. London: Penguin, 2003.
Nigosian, S. A. *World Religions*. Boston, MA: Bedford/St. Martin's, 2000.
Nisbet, R. *Twilight of Authority*. Indianapolis, IN: Liberty Fund, 1975.
Nkomazana, F. and L. Lanner. *Aspects of the History of the Church in Botswana*. Pietermarizburg, South Africa: Cluster Publications, 2007.
Nkrumah, K. *Consciencism: Philosophy and Ideology, for Decolonization*. New York: Monthly Review, 1964.
———. *Neo-colonialism: The Last Stage of Imperialism*. New York: International, 1969.
Nolan, A. *God in South Africa*. Cape Town: David Philip. 1988.

Nwabueze, B. O. *Constitutionalism in Emergent States*: London: C. Hurst. 1973
Northrop, F. S. C. *The Logic of the Sciences and the Humanities*. Woodbridge, CT: Ox Bow Press, 1983.
Nwakeze, P. C. "A Critique of Olufemi Taiwo's Criticism of 'Legal Positivism and the African Legal Tradition.'" *International Philosophical Quarterly* 27 (1987): 101–105.
Nwala, T. U. *Igbo Philosophy*. Lagos, Nigeria: Lantern Books, 1985.
Nwonwu, F. and D. Kotze, eds., *African Political Elites: The Search for Democracy and Good Governance*. Pretoria, South Africa: Africa Institute of South Africa, 2008.
Nyerere, J. *Freedom and Socialism: Uhuru na Ujamaa*. Dar-e-Salaam, Tanzania: Oxford University Press, 1968.
———. *Man and Development*. London: Oxford University Press, 1974.
———. *Ujamaa: Essays on Socialism*. London: University of London Press, 1962.
Oba, A. A. "The Administration of Customary Law in the Post-Colonial Nigerian State" in *Cambrian Law Review* 37, (2006): 95.
Ochieng'-Odhiambo, F. *Conversations in Philosophy*. Newcastle-upon Tyne, UK: Cambridge Scholars Publishing, 2008.
O'Connor, D. J. *An Introduction to the Philosophy of Education*. London: Routledge, 1957.
Odinga, O. *Not Yet Uhuru*. New York: Hill & Wang, 1967.
Oduyoye, M. A. *Daughters of Anowa*. New York: Orbis Books, 1995.
Ogbogbo, C. B. N. "The Poverty of African Philosophy." In *Ibadan Journal of Humanistic Studies*, no. 7, (October 1997).
Ogden, C. K. and I. A. Richards. *The Meaning of Meaning*. San Diego, CA: A Harvest Book, 1989.
Oguejiofor, O. J. 1998. *Africa: Philosophy and Public Affairs*. Enugu, Nigeria: Delta Publications Ltd., 1998.
———. *African Philosophy and the Hermeneutics of Culture*. New Brunswick, NJ: Transaction Publishers. 2005.
———. *Has Bertrand Russell Solved the Problem of Perception?* New York: Peter Lang, 1994.
———. *Philosophy and the African Predicament*. Ibadan, Nigeria: Hope Publications. 2001.
———. ed., *Philosophy, Democracy and Responsible Governance in Africa*. Enugu, Nigeria: Delta Publications Ltd. 2004.
Oguejiofor, O. J. and G. I. Onah, eds., *African Philosophy and the Hermeneutics of Culture*. Munster, Germany: Lit Verlag, 2005.
Ogundele, S. O. "Man's Biological Genesis: A Review." In *Ibadan Journal of Humanistic Studies*, no. 7, (October 1997).
Ogungbemi, S., ed., *Philosophy and Development*. Ibadan, Nigeria: Hope Publications, 2007.
——— *God, Reason and Death*. Ibadan, Nigeria: Hope Publications, 2008.
Ogunyipe, O. "Universals of Language." *Oye: Ogun Journal of Arts* 3 (1990): 97–101.
Oha, Obododimma. "The Esu Paradigm in the Semiotics of Identity and Community," in Babawale, Tunde & Alao, Akin, eds., *Global African Spirituality, Social Capital, and Self-Reliance in Africa*. Lagos: Malthouse Press. 2008, 299–312.
Oheari, J. U. "Articulating a New Philosophical Basis for Traditional Medical Practice." *Journal of African Philosophy and Studies* 1, nos. 1&2 (1988): 1–12.
Ohiri, C. "Tribal Tongues: A Closed System of Communication?" In Okpaku, et al, eds., *The Arts and Civilization of Black and African Peoples* . Vol. 4. *Black Civilization and African Languages*. 1986, 42–59.
Okafor, F. U. "Legal Positivism and the African Legal Tradition." In *International Philosophical Quarterly* 33, (1984): 158–64.
Oke, M. "The Logic of Yoruba Conjunction" in *Oye: Ogun Journal of Arts* 2 (1989): 116-29.
Okere, T. "The Crisis of Governance in Africa: The Root of the Problem." In O. Oguejiofor, ed., *Philosophy, Democracy and Responsible Governance in Africa*. Enugu, Nigeria: Delta Publications, 2004.

Okigbo, C. C. and F. Eribo. *Development and Communication in Africa*. London: Rowman & Littlefield, 2004.
Okpaku, J. ed. *Nigeria: the Dilemma of Nationhood*. New York: The Third Press, 1972.
Oladipo, O., ed., *Remaking Africa: Challenges of the 21st Century*. Ibadan, Nigeria: Hope Publications, 1998.
———. *The Idea of African Philosophy*. Ibadan, Nigeria: Molecular Publishers, 1992.
———. *Philosophy, Literature and the African Novel*. Ibadan, Nigeria: Options Book and Information Services, 1993.
———. *Beyond Survival*. Ibadan, Nigeria: Hope Publications, 1999.
———. *Philosophy and the African Experience*. Ibadan, Nigeria: Hope Publications, 1996.
———. "Metaphysics, Religion and Yoruba Traditional Thought." In *Journal of Indian Council of Philosophical Research* VII, no. 2 (1990): 71-83.
———. *The Development Philosophy of Emanuel Onyechere Osigwe Anyiam-Osigwe*. Ibadan, Nigeria: Hope Publications, 2009.
Oladosu, A. "Higher Education and the Democratic Imperative." In S. Akinrinade, *Locating the Local in the Global: Voices on a Globalized Nigeria*. Ile-Ife, Nigeria: Faculty of Arts, 2004.
Olela, H. *From Ancient Africa to Ancient Greece*. Atlanta, GA: Select, 1981.
Olivier, B. "Gadamer, Heidegger, Play, Art and the Appropriation of Tradition." in *South African Journal of Philosophy* 21, no. 4 (2002): 242-57.
Oluwole, S. B. "The Rational Basis of Yoruba Ethical Thinking." *Nigerian Journal of Philosophy* 4, nos. 1&2 (1984): 14–25.
Onatunde, J. A. *Bewaji*. Ibadan, Nigeria: Onatunde and Co., 1981.
Onigbinde, A., ed., *Governance and Leadership in Nigeria*. Ibadan, Nigeria: Hope Publications, 2007.
Oruka, H. O. *Sage Philosophy*. Nairobi, Kenya: African Centre for Technology Studies, 1991.
———. and D. A. Masolo. *Philosophy and Cultures*. Nairobi, Kenya: Bookwise, 1983.
Orwell, G. *Homage to Catalonia*. London: Penguin Books, 1989.
Osei, R. N. *The Mind-Body Problem in Philosophy*. Ibadan, Nigeria: Hope Publications, 2006.
Osundare, N. *African Literature and the Crisis of Post-structuralist Theorizing*. Ibadan, Nigeria: Options Book and Information Services, 1993.
———. *Days: Upper Level*. Ibadan, Nigeria: HEBN Publishers Plc., 2007.
———. *Tender Moments*. Ibadan, Nigeria: University Press Plc., 2006.
———. *The Universe in the University*. Ibadan, Nigeria: University of Ibadan, 2005.
———. *The World Is an Egg*. Ibadan, Nigeria: Kraftgriots, Kraft Books, 2000.
Otakpor, N., ed., *Ezi Okwu Bu Ndu: Truth Is Life*. Ibadan, Nigeria: Hope Publications, 2006.
Otto, R. *The Idea of the Holly*. London: Oxford University Press, 1950.
Oyeneye, O. Y. and M. O. Shoremi., eds., *Nigerian Life and Culture*. Ibadan, Nigeria: Ogun State University Publications Committee, 1985.
Oyewumi, O. *The Invention of Women*. Minneapolis, MN: University of Minnesota Press, 1997.
Owoade, M. Adekunle. "Law and Justice." In Segun Gbadegesin, ed., *The Politicization of Society During Nigeria's Second Republic, 1979–1983*. Lewiston, NY: Edwin Mellen Press. 1991
Ozigi, A and L. Ocho. *Education in Northern Nigeria*. London: Allen & Unwin, 1981.
Pagels, E. *Adam, Eve, and the Serpent*. New York: Vintage Books, 1989.
Palmer, F. R. *Semantics*. Cambridge: Cambridge University Press, 1988.
Pannell, W. *The Coming Race Wars: A Cry for Reconciliation*. Grand Rapids, MI: Zondervan Publishing House, 1993.
Papineau, D. *Reality and Representation*. Oxford: Basil Blackwell, 1987.
Paris, P. J. *The Spirituality of African Peoples*. Minneapolis, MN: Fortress Press, 1995.
Parkinson, C. N. *The Law or Still in Pursuit*. London: Penguin, 1981
———. *Parkinson's Law or the Pursuit of Progress*. London: Penguin, 1970.

Parrinder, G. *West African Religion*. London: Epworth Press, 1949.
Partridge, S. H. *Cases in Business and Society*. Englewood Cliffs, NJ: Prentice Hall, 1982.
Passmore, J. *A Hundred Years of Philosophy*. London: Penguin, 1968.
P'Bitek, O. *African Religions in Western Scholarship*. Nairobi, Kenya: East African Literature Bureau, 1970.
Percesepe, G. *Introduction to Ethics*. Englewood Cliffs, NJ: Prentice Hall, 1995.
Peters, T. *Thriving on Chaos*. New Delhi: Tata McGraw-Hill Company Ltd., 1987.
Pfeiffer, R. *History of Classical Scholarship: From 1300–1850*. Oxford: Clarendon Press, 1976.
Phelan, J. W. *Philosophy: Themes and Thinkers*. Cambridge: Cambridge University Press, 2005.
Phillips, C. *The European Tribe*. London: Faber & Faber. 1987.
Pillay, N. "The Significance of Gadamer's Hermeneutics for Cross-cultural Understanding." In *South African Journal of Philosophy* 21, no. 4 (2002): 330–45.
Plant, R. *Modern Political Thought*. Oxford: Blackwell, 1993.
Plaskow, J. *Standing Again at Sinai*. San Francisco, CA: Harper, 1991.
Poe, R. *Black Spark, White Fire*. Rocklin, CA: Prima Publishing, 1997.
Pojman, L. P. *Ethical Theory*. New York: Wadsworth Publishing Co., 1998.
Polanyi, M. *Knowing and Being*. Chicago, IL: University of Chicago Press, 1969.
———. *Personal Knowledge*. London: Routledge & Kegan Paul, 1973.
Popper, K. R. *Conjectures and Refutations*. London: Routledge & Kegan Paul, 1963.
———. *The Logic of Scientific Discovery*. New York: Harper Torchbooks, 1959.
———. *The Myth of the Framework*. London: Routledge, 1997.
———. *The Open Society and Its Enemies*. Vol. 1. Princeton, NJ: Princeton University Press, 1950.
———. *The Poverty of Historicism*. New York: Harper Torch Books, 1964.
Post, L. V. D. *Jung and the Story of Our Time*. London: Penguin, 1978.
Potter, J. *The Origins and Development of Methodist Mission Work in the Area of Present-day Botswana*. Gaborone, Botswana: Department of History and Department of Theology and Religious Studies, 1975.
Poupeye, V. *Caribbean Art*. London: Thames and Hudson, 1998.
Powell, R. J. *Black Art and Culture in the 20th Century*. London: Thames and Hudson, 1997.
Praeg, L. *African Philosophy and the Quest for Autonomy*. Amsterdam, Germany: Rodopi, n.d.
Pribram, K. H. and M. M. Gill. *Freud's Project Reassessed*. London: Hutchinson, 1976.
Prior, M. *The Bible and Colonialism*. Sheffield, England: Sheffield Academy Press, 1972.
Pritchard, M. S. *Philosophical Adventures with Children*. Lanham, MD: University Press of America, 1985.
Quine, W. V. O. *Consequences of Pragmatism*. Minneapolis, MN: University of Minnesota Press, 1982.
———. *From a Logical Point of View*. Cambridge, MA: Harvard University Press, 1980.
———. *Indeterminacy of Translation again*." In *Philosophy* 84, (1987): 5–10.
———. *Philosophic Logic*. Cambridge, MA: Harvard University Press, 1970.
———. *Philosophy and the Mirror of Nature*. Princeton, NJ: Princeton University Press, 1979.
———. *The Structure of Language*. New Jersey: Prentice Hall, 1959.
———. *Word and Object*. Cambridge, MA: MIT Press, 1964.
Quine, V. W. O., and J. S. Ulian. *The Web of Belief* New York: Random House, 1970.
Rah, S-C. *The Next Evangelicalism*. Downer's Grove, IL: InterVersity Press, 2009.
Ramose, M. B. *African Philosophy Through Ubuntu*. Harare, Zimbabwe: Mond Books, 2002.
Rand, A. *Philosophy: Who Needs It*. New York: Penguin, 1984.
Raphael, D. D. *Concepts of Justice*. Oxford: Clarendon Press, 2003.
Rawls, John. *A Theory of Justice*. Cambridge, MA: Harvard University Press, 1971.

Reamer, F. G. *The Philosophical Foundations of Social Work*. New York: Columbia University Press, 1993.
Redner, H. *The Ends of Science*. Boulder, CO: Westview Press, 1987.
Reed, R. E. *Talking with Children*. Denver, CO: Arden Press Inc., 1983.
Reiman, J. *The Rich Get Richer and the Poor Get Prison*. Boston, MA: Pearson, 2007.
Rettová, A. "Symbolism in D. O. Fagunwa's *The Forest of a Thousand Daemons*." Universitat Leipzig. At: http://www.volny.cz/alena.rettova/rettova.htm. 1999.
Rescher, N. *Scepticism*. Oxford: Basil Blackwell, 1980.
Richardson, J. *Nietzsche's System*. New York: Oxford University Press, 1996.
Rivera, L. N. *A Violent Evangelism*. Louisville, KY: John Knox Press, 1992.
Rodney, W. *How Europe Underdeveloped Africa*. Washington, DC: Howard University Press, 1982.
Rorty, R. *Consequences of Pragmatism*. Minneapolis, MN: University of Minnesota Press, 1982.
———. *Contingency, Irony, and Solidarity*. Cambridge: Cambridge University Press, 1989.
———. *Essays on Heidegger and Others*. New York: Cambridge University Press. 1991.
———. *Objectivity, Relativism and Truth: Philosophical Papers I*. Cambridge: Cambridge University Press, 1991.
Rousseau, J-J. *The Social Contract and Discourses*. "Discourse on the Origin of Inequality." London: J. M. Dent Ltd., 1754, 1973.
Rowe, W. L. and W. J. Wainwright. *Philosophy of Religion*. San Diego, CA: Harcourt Brace Jovanovich Publishers, 1989.
Roy, P. K. "African Theory of Knowledge." *Nigerian Journal of Philosophy* 6, nos. 1&2 (1986): 1–10.
Ruch, E. A., and K. C. Anyanwu. *African Philosophy*. Rome: Catholic Book Agency, 1981.
Ruddock, R., ed., *Six Approaches to the Person*. London: Routledge, 1972.
Rue, L. *By the Grace of Guile*. Oxford: Oxford University Press, 1994.
Russell, B. *The Autobiography of Bertrand Russell*. London: Allen & Unwin, 1971.
A History of Western Philosophy. Oxford: Oxford University Press, 1945.
———. *Human Knowledge*. London: Routledge, 1992.
———. *Logic and Knowledge*. London: Allen & Unwin, 1977.
———. *Our Knowledge of the External World*. London: Routledge, 1993.
Sanders, A. *The Powerless People*. London: Macmillan, 1987.
Sartre, J-P. *Between Existentialism and Marxism*. New York: Pantheon Books, 1974.
Saunders, Cheryl and K. Le Roy, eds., *The Rule of Law*. Sydney: The Federation Press, 2003.
Schick, T. Jr. *Readings in the Philosophy of Science*. London: Mayfield Publishing Co., 2000.
Scholte, J. A. *Globalization: A Critical Introduction*. New York: Palgrave, 2000.
Seligman, B. B., ed., *Aspects of Poverty*. New York: Thomas Y. Crowley & Co., 1968.
Sen, A. *Identity and Violence: The Illusion of Destiny*. New York: W. W. Norton, 2006.
Sen, G. and C. Grown. *Development, Crises and Alternative Visions: Third World Women's Perspectives*. New York: Monthly Review Press, 1987.
Serequeberhan, T. *African Philosophy: The Essential Readings*. New York: Paragon House, 1991.
Shand, J. *The Nineteenth Century: The Central Works of Philosophy*. Chesam: Acumen Publishing Co., 2005.
Shapiro, H. L. *Race Mixture*. Paris: UNESCO, 1953.
Shepherd, V.. *The Ranking Game Discourses of Belonging in Jamaican History*. Kingston, Jamaica: Department of History, University of the West Indies, Inaugural Lecture, 2002.
———. *Transients to Settlers: The Experience of Indians in Jamaica 1845–1950*. Leeds: University of Warwick and Peepal Tree Books, 1993.
Shriver, D. W. Jr. *An Ethic for Enemies*. New York: Oxford University Press, 1995.

Shyllon, Folarin. *Freedom, Justice and the Due Process of Law*. Ibadan, Nigeria: University of Ibadan Press, 1987.
Singer, P., ed., *Applied Ethics*. Oxford: Oxford University Press, 1986.
Skagestad, P. *The Road to Inquiry*. New York: Columbia University Press, 1981.
Skyrms, B. *Choice and Chance*. Chicago, IL: Dickenson Publishing Co., 1975.
Smart, N. *The World's Religions*. Cambridge: Cambridge University Press, 1992.
Smith, M. *A Practical Guide to Value Clarification*. La Jolla, CA: University Associates Inc., 1977.
———. *Red & Black in Haiti*. Chapel Hill, NC: University of North Carolina Press, 2009.
Smith, P. J. O. "Making Words Sing and Dance: Sense, Style and Sound in Yoruba Prose Translation." In *Meta* XLVI, no. 4 (2001).
Soames, S. *Understanding Truth*. New York: Oxford University Press, 1999.
Sodipo, J. O. "Notes on the Concept of Cause and Chance in Yoruba Traditional Thought." In *Second Order: An African Journal of Philosophy*, no. 2. (1972): 12–20.
Soyinka, W. *Art, Outrage and Dialogue*. Ibadan, Nigeria: New Horn Press, 1988.
———. *The Forest of a Thousand Daemons*. Lagos, Nigeria: Nelson, 1968.
———. *Myth, Literature and the African World*. Cambridge: Cambridge University Press, 1978.
———. Ake. *New York: Vintage International, 1981.*
Spencer, M., ed., *Separatism: Democracy and Disintegration*. London: Rowman & Littlefield, 1998.
Stackhouse, M. L., ed., *God and Globalization*. Harrisburg, PA: Trinity Press International, 2000.
Staniland, H. S. "What Is Philosophy?" In *Second Order: An African Journal of Philosophy* 5, no. 2 (1979): 3–10.
Steel, T. B. and N. D. Belnap. *The Logic of Questions and Answers*. New Haven, CT: Yale University Press, 1976.
Stephens, G. L. and G. Graham. *When Self-consciouness Breaks*. Cambridge, MA: The MIT Press, 2003
Stevens, A. *Archetype: A Natural History of the Self*. London: Routledge, 1982.
Stevenson, L. *Seven Theories of Human Nature*. New York: Oxford University Press, 1974.
Stone, D. *Theoretical Interpretations of the Holocaust*. Amsterdam: Editions Rodopi B. V., 1994.
Strachan, L. S. *Confronting the Color Crisis in the African Diaspora: Emphasis Jamaica*. New York: Afrikan World Infosystems, 1992.
Strauss, D. F. M. "Understanding in the Humanities: Gadamer's Thought at the Intersection of Rationality, Historicity, and Linguisticality [. . .]." In *South African Journal of Philosophy* 21, no. 4 (2002): 291–305.
Strauss, L. and J. Crospsey. *History of Political Philosophy*. Chicago, IL: University of Chicago Press, 1981.
Stride, G. T. and C. Ifeka. *Peoples and Empires of West Africa*. London: Nelson, 1981.
Stuart, R. B. *Trick or Treatment*. Champaign, IL: Research Press, 1973.
Sumner, C. *Ethiopian Philosophy*. Addis Ababa: University Press, 1974.
Taiwo, O. *How Colonialism Preempted Modernity in Africa*. Bloomington, IN: Indiana University Press, 2010.
———. *Legal Naturalism*. Ithaca: Cornell University Press, 1996.
———. "Legal Positivism and the African Legal Tradition: A Reply." *International Philosophical Quarterly* 25, (1985): 197–200.
Tangwa, G. "Colonial Legacy and the Language Situation in Cameroon." *Quest* VI, no. 2 (1992).
Taylor, C., ed., *Multiculturalism*. Princeton, NJ: Princeton University Press, 1994.
Thagard, P. *Mind Readings*. Cambridge, MA: The MIT Press, 2000.
Teichman, J. and G. White. *An Introduction to Modern European Philosophy*. London: Macmillan, 1995.

Terris, M. "An Ancient Basis for African Philosophy." In *Second Order: An African Journal of Philosophy* 5, no. 2 (1979): 27-36.

The Republic of Uganda. *Education for National Integration and Development: Report of the Education Policy Review Commission*. Ministry of Education, Kampala, Uganda, 1992.

The Responsive Community 5, no. 4 (1995).

Thomson, J. *Rights, Restitution and Risk* Cambridge, MA: Harvard University PRess. 1986.

Thompson, L. *The Political Mythology of Apartheid*. New Haven and London: Yale University Press, 1985.

Tivnan, E. *The Moral Imagination*. New York: Simon & Schuster, 1995.

Toulmin, S. *The Uses of Arguments*. Cambridge: Cambridge University Press, 1958.

Toynbee, A. *Change and Habit*. New York: One World, 1992.

Trillin, C. *With All Disrespect: More Uncivil Liberties*. New York: Penguin, 1985.

Uganda Government White Paper on The Education Policy Review Commission Report, 1992.

Unger, P. *Identity, Consciousness and Value*. New York: Oxford University Press, 1990.

———. *Ignorance*. London: Oxford University Press, 1975.

Usher, R. and R. Edwards. *Postmodernism and Education*. New York: Routledge, 1994.

Van Hensbroek, P. B. *African Political Philosophy, 1860–1995.* Groningen, The Netherlands: University of Groningen, Center for Development Studies, n.d.

Van Sertima, I. *African Presence in Early Europe*. New Brunswick, NJ: Transaction Publishers, 1993.

———. ed., *African Presence in Early America*. New Brunswick, NJ: Transaction Publishers, 1992.

———. *The Came Before Columbus*. New York: Random House, 1976.

———. ed., *Egypt Revisited*. New Brunswick, NJ: Transaction Publishers, 1993.

———. ed., *Blacks in Science*. New Brunswick, NJ: Transaction Books, 1991.

———. ed., *Great African Thinkers: Cheikh Anta Diop* . New Brunswick, NJ: Transaction Books, 1992.

Vasciannie, S. *Us and Them: International Law in a Time of Trial*. Kinsgton, Jamaica: UWI, Mona Inaugural Lecture, 2004.

Vassell, L. *Voices of Women in Jamaica, 1898–1939*. Kingston, Jamaica: Department of History, 1993.

Veían, R. N. et al. *The Good Society*. New York: Alfred Knopf, 1991.

Vossler, K. *The Spirit of Language in Civilization*. London: Routledge and Kegan Paul Ltd., 1951.

Wa Thiongo, N. *Petals of Blood.* Cape Town, South Africa: Africasouth Paperbacks, 1986.

Ward, B. *Five Ideas That Changed the World*. New York: W. W. Norton, 1959.

Walcott, D. *Omeros*. London: Faber & Faber, 1990.

Walklate, S. *Victimology*. London: Unwin Hyman, 1989.

Wariboko, Waibinte E. *Planting Church Culture at New Calabar*. San Francisco, CA: International Scholars Publications, 1998.

———. *Ruined by "Race."* Trenton: NJ: Africa World Press, 2007.

———. *Race and the Civilizing Mission*. Trenton, NJ: Africa World Press, 2011.

Warner-Lewis, M. *Trinidad Yoruba: From Mother Tongue to Memory*. Tuscalosa, AL: The University of Alabama Press, 1996.

Watson, R. A. *La Mettrie: Man a Machine and Man a Plant*. Indianapolis, IN: Hakett Publishing Co. Inc., 1994.

Watts, B. K. R. *Business and Financial Management*. London: Pitman Publishing, 1992.

Weiner, P. P. *Charles S. Peirce Selected Writings*. New York: Dover Publications Inc., 1958.

Welsing, F. C. *The Isis Papers* . Chicago, IL: Third World Press, 1991.

Werhane, P. H. *Philosophical Issues in Art*. New Jersey: Prentice Hall, 1984

West, C. *Keeping Faith.* New York: Routledge, 1993.

Westlake, H. C. *Relationships*. Boston, MA: Ginn, 1972.

Westphal, J. and C. Levenson. *Time*. Indianapolis, IN: Hackett Publishing Co. Inc., 1993.
White, M. *The Japanese Educational Challenge*. Tokyo: Kodansha International, 1987.
Whitehead, A. N. *Science and the Modern World*. New York: The Free Press, 1967.
Whorf, B. L. *Language, Thought and Reality*. Cambridge, MA: MIT Press, 1962.
Wihl, G. *The Contingency of Theory*. New Haven, CT: Yale University Press, 1994.
Willett, Frank. *African Art*. London: Thames and Hudson, 1993.
William, B. *Morality: an Introduction to Ethics*. Cambridge: Cambridge University Press, 1972.
Williams, C. *The Destruction of Black Civilization*. Chicago, IL: Third World Press, 1974.
William, I. "How Globalization is Changing Citizenship." In S. Akinrinade, *Locating the Local in the Global: Voices on a Globalized Nigeria*. Ile-Ife, Nigeria: Faculty of Arts, 2004.
Williams, J. J. *Hebrewisms of West Africa*. New York: The Dial Press, 1930.
Williams, P. and L. Chrisman, eds., *Colonial Discourse and Postcolonial Theory*. New York: Columbia University Press, 1994.
Wilson, Brian. *Rationality*. Oxford: Blackwell, 1974.
Wilson, C. "Conceptualizing African Diaspora." *The Comparative Studies of South Asia, Africa and the Middle East* XVII, no. 2 (1997).
Wilson, J. *Moral Thinking*. London: Heinemann Educational Books, 1973.
Wiredu, K. *Philosophy and an African Culture*. Cambridge: Cambridge University Press, 1980.
———. *Cultural Universals and Particulars*. Indianapolis, IN: Indiana University Press, 1996.
———. "Philosophy, Humankind and the Environment." In Oruka, H. Odera, ed., *Philosophy, Humanity and Ecology, Vol. 1: Philosophy of Nature and Environmental Ethics*, Nairobi, Kenya: African Center for Technology Studies Press, 1995.
———. "Custom and Morality: A Comparative Analysis of Some African and Western Conceptions of Morals." In Mosley, Albert, ed., *African Philosophy: Selected Readings*, Englewood Cliffs: Prentice Hall, 1995.
———. *A Companion to African Philosophy*. Malden,MA: Blackwell Publishing, 2004.
———. "How Not to Compare African Thought with Western Science." In R. Wright, ed., *African Philosophy—An Introduction*. Washington, DC: University of America Press, 1977
Wittgenstein, L. *The Blue and Brown Books*. New York: Harper Torch Books, 1960.
———. *Zettel*. Oxford, England: Basil Blackwell, 1967
———. *On Certainty*. New York: Harper Torch Books, 1969.
———. *Philosophical Remarks*. Chicago, IL: University of Chicago Press, 1975.
———. *Philosophical Investigations*. Oxford, England Basil Blackwell, 1976.
———. *Tractatus Logico-Philosophicus*. London: Kegan Paul, 1981.
Wolff, R. P. *About Philosophy*, Englewood Cliffs, NJ: Prentice Hall, 1992.
Wolgast, E. H. *Paradoxes of Knowledge*. Ithaca, NY: Cornell University Press, 1977.
Wollheim, R. *Art and Its Objects* . Cambridge: Cambridge University Press, 1980.
Wolpe, H. *Race, Class and the Apartheid State*. Paris: UNESCO, 1988.
Womack, J. P. et al. *The Machine That Changed The World*. New York: Harper, 1991.
Wright, J. *Blood Secrets: The True Story of Demon Worship and Ceremonial Murder*. New York: Berkeley Books, 1991.
Wright, R., ed., *African Philosophy: An Introduction*. Lanham, MD: University Press of America, 1984.
Zack, N. *Thinking about Race*. New York: Wadsworth Publishing Co., 1998.
Zaitchik, Joseph A. and Roger E. Weihe. *Human Values: Perspectives on Six Themes*. Dubuque, LA: Brown and 1 Benchmark Publishers, 1993.
Zaslavsky, C. *Africa Counts: Number and Patterns in African Cultures*. Chicago, IL: Lawrence Hill Books, 1999.
Zobel, J. *Black Shack Alley*. London: Heinmann, 1980.

Index

abẹbẹ, 42
Abeokuta, 50–51
Abimbola, Kola, 98, 105, 125, 126, 127, 128, 132, 213, 216
Abimbola, Wande, 158, 159, 163, 206, 211
Abiodun, Roland, 181
abuku, 185, 186, 187
accountability, 8, 57, 65, 67, 74, 75, 76, 79, 202, 207, 217, 218
Adeleke, 198, 199, 200, 203, 207, 215, 216
Adimula, 90, 150
adversarial, 9, 16, 104, 110, 136, 214, 251
Africa's burden, 2, 4, 11; leadership, 2, 3
Africana, 32, 45, 57, 79, 107, 114, 201, 217, 252
African ancestry, 4, 161; civilizations, 13, 18, 28, 63, 65, 71, 84, 96, 103, 112, 114, 160, 204, 240, 248, 251; cultures, 5, 7, 32, 110, 160, 178; diaspora, 150, 179, 235; leadership, 3, 4, 7, 57; legal theory, 114; philosophies, 126; philosophy, 245, 248
African Union, 249
Agabi, 204
agba, 44, 68, 95, 134, 143, 158, 160, 163
agency, 3, 4, 74, 106, 121, 197, 207, 219, 234, 237, 248
aimo, 185, 187, 188, 253
Àjobí, 100, 132; *àjobí*, 81, 134, 138, 139, 144
Ajogbe, 40, 132; *àjogbé*, 46, 81, 100, 138, 139, 144
Ake, Claude, 3
Alaàfin, 36, 37, 90
Aladura, 150, 151
Alase, 65
Almeder, 171
Alo Ijapa, 93
àlọ, 52, 94
Amerindians, 18
Àparò, 96
Apostolic Church, 216
Appadorai, 156
Arabia, 2, 202
Arabian Desert religions, 10, 147, 215
Arabs, 59, 202, 240, 245
arbitrary authority, 60, 69, 70, 120, 141, 155
aristocratic, 18, 25
Aristotle, 63, 245
Ase, 216
Asia, 3, 240
asuwàdà, 33, 39, 40, 46, 100, 139
Asuwàdà ènìyàn, 33, 39, 46, 100, 139
Atlantic slave trade, 3
atonement, 5, 185
authoritarianism, 67, 230, 237
Awolalu, 149, 150, 151, 180, 196, 198
axiological, 8, 10, 81, 82, 103, 105, 120, 123, 183, 245

Baálẹ, 40, 42, 89, 90, 131, 158, 160, 161, 163
Babalawo, 52, 161, 216
Babalola, 93, 94, 130
Babangida, 78, 251
Babylon, 4
baloguns, 50
Bàrà, 90
Beauty and Culture, 94
Big Brother, 27, 197, 204, 205, 212, 214
black development, 254
Botswana, 222
brain drain, 239
Brazil, 80, 150, 225, 246, 254
Breton Woods, 231
British common law, 8, 103, 110

Buddhism, 150
Buhari, Muhammadu, 72
burden of survival, 88
Bush, George W., 77, 212, 248

capitalism, 15, 213, 222, 231
Caribbean, people of the, 32
Cartesian, 15, 47, 99, 108
Categorical Imperative, 16, 28, 171, 172
catharsis, 94, 248
Central Africans, 49
child labor, 222
China, 3, 225, 249, 254
Christianity, 4, 10, 67, 85, 98, 123, 147, 150, 151, 153, 163, 191, 194, 196, 197, 202, 209, 214, 215
Clinton, Bill, 212
collective malady of leadership, 249
colonialism, 3, 7, 32, 34, 45, 53, 57, 60, 66, 71, 74, 75, 77, 79, 82, 103, 111, 113, 115, 116, 120, 135, 151, 191, 204, 208, 230, 238; coloniality, 230
communal, 10, 29, 83, 234, 247, 248, 253
concept of law, 35, 37
conflict mediation, 192
conflict resolution, 95, 103, 120, 199
Consequentialism, 172
constituted authority, 69, 70, 72, 148, 149, 151, 153, 154, 156, 157, 158, 161, 162, 163, 165
conventions, 4, 24, 35, 38, 59, 60, 70, 140, 158, 171
corruption, 2, 5, 72, 74, 76, 78, 79, 100, 230, 253
customary 2.14 3.7 4.4 5.35 7.31

Declaration of Human Rights, 120, 137, 140
Deji of Akure, 67, 162
diaspora, 117, 120, 150, 179, 216, 235
Dicey, A. V., 60, 62, 245
dictatorship, 7, 40, 53, 67, 74, 77, 230, 247
Diop, C. A., 239
divination, 52, 91, 98, 99, 161, 174, 194, 207, 210
Divine Command Theory, 172
Divine Law, 171
divinities, 38, 44, 65, 81, 97, 126, 134, 158, 161, 162, 163, 165, 183, 185, 192, 193, 195, 196, 198, 199, 200, 203, 206, 207, 209, 210, 215, 217, 218
Dopamu, 149, 150, 151, 196, 198

educational subjugation, 45, 54, 82, 85
educational system, 2, 47, 85, 100, 114
eewo, 44, 48, 185, 186
EFCC, 54, 204, 252
Efunsetan Aniwura, 131
Egba, 50, 66
egoism, 147, 171, 172, 214
ẹjọ, 39, 42, 44
ẹkọ, 81, 93
ẹlẹri, 43
emi, 125, 126, 127
English common law, 5, 7, 9, 31, 45, 54, 101, 104, 108, 109, 110, 116, 118
enlightened self-interest, 2
enslavement, 1, 3, 4, 112
environmental protection, 222
epistemic responsibility, 108
epistemicide, 1, 2, 196, 197, 208, 213, 245, 255
epistemologies, 8, 34, 103, 105, 116, 117, 118
error, 26, 113, 125, 236, 237, 242, 253
eru, 38, 96, 112, 132, 246
ẹsan, 43
Èṣè, 38, 39, 125, 184
ẹsin, 43
Èṣù, 10, 38, 192, 193, 195, 196, 197, 201, 202, 203, 206, 207, 209, 210, 212, 213, 215, 217, 218
Èṣù agency, 197
ethical relativism, 171, 172
Ethical Subjectivism, 172
ethnophilosophy, 245
Eurocentric, 83, 151, 222
Europe, 6, 13, 18, 32, 36, 51, 60, 71, 73, 86, 87, 115, 116, 148, 162, 193, 242, 249, 250, 252
European Union, 15
evidence, 7, 15, 27, 31, 35, 39, 42, 59, 64, 65, 72, 77, 95, 97, 99, 103, 114, 133, 137, 138, 147, 150, 159, 175, 180, 198, 199, 210, 211, 221, 240, 242, 248, 251, 253

ewà, 81
Ĕwò, 38
Eyadema, 251

falsification, 78, 116, 196, 198
family, 23, 28, 29, 37, 39, 40, 42, 47, 50, 52, 58, 69, 86, 89, 91, 93, 96, 130, 156, 162, 164, 165, 177, 178, 186, 188, 198, 202, 209, 231, 234
Fanti people, 66
Federal Republic of Nigeria, 83
Fela Anikulapo Kuti, 50
female circumcision, 222
FESTAC 77, 86
Forbes, F. E., 50
fratricidal, 29
French, 32, 60, 103, 250
Freud, 123

Gbadegesin, 124, 127, 180
Ghana, 37, 51, 66, 73, 80, 86
globalization, 15, 32, 120, 153, 171, 197, 206, 208
Golden Rule, 28, 171, 172
Gordon, 85, 230
governance in Africa, 11, 245
governance systems, 2, 4, 7, 57

Habeas Corpus, 133
Haiti, 18, 32, 71, 150, 246
Hebrewisms, 245
Hegel, 248
Hegelian, 18
heterocultural, 224
Hinduism, 150
Hobbes, 6, 14, 15, 16, 17, 18, 19, 20, 26, 27, 28, 66, 71, 108, 245
human civilization, 1, 11, 58, 71, 119; culture, 71; nature, 16, 19, 20, 27, 60, 123, 124, 127, 129, 224; rights, 21, 54, 71, 103, 109, 113, 119, 120, 121, 123, 135, 137, 138, 139, 140, 141, 142, 143, 144
Human Development Index, 250
Hume, 107, 249

ibawi, 43
idajo, 43, 44
identity, 1, 4, 13, 25, 32, 53, 69, 81, 88, 91, 101, 107, 117, 127, 135, 137, 139, 143, 162, 176, 203, 230, 234, 236, 253
Idi Amin, 251
Idowu, William, 36, 37, 39, 111, 125, 127, 147, 152, 163, 180, 184, 196, 198, 202
Ifa, 36, 46, 52, 69, 81, 91, 98, 99, 119, 125, 135, 150, 151, 161, 163, 180, 192, 194, 207, 210, 213
Igbá Ìwà, 90
ihamọ, 44
Ìjàpà,, 93, 94, 131
Ìjàpà Tìrókò, 94
ìjòyè, 40, 42, 90
ikilọ, 43
Ile-Ife, 36, 134, 139, 143
Ìlẹkẹ, 42
IMF, 32, 253
impunity, 7, 54, 57, 62, 67, 71, 74, 75, 76, 77, 79, 118, 141, 207, 252, 255
incommensurability, 8, 103
independence, 2, 8, 22, 23, 32, 37, 57, 69, 73, 81, 86, 103, 135, 178, 214, 217, 230
India, 3, 80, 225, 254
indigenous: cultural jurisprudence, 9, 104; cultures, 81, 103, 114, 121, 137, 141, 194, 196, 243, 246; knowledge systems, 1, 3, 165, 242; leadership style, 245; legal systems, 4, 9, 34, 54, 83, 84, 105, 115, 117; moral education, 101; Yoruba society, 7, 10, 42, 44, 65, 67, 69, 81, 87, 100, 121, 135, 159, 191, 193, 215
individualism, 6, 14, 15, 16, 20, 45, 46, 86, 106, 147, 179, 213, 231, 234
individual material accumulation, 2
Indonesia, 80
innocent until proven guilty, 214
insurgencies, 63, 74
intellectual property, 220, 222
intellectual smuggling, 196, 198
Ipadí, 90
Iraq, 107, 112, 116, 141, 201, 224, 240, 248
Ìrùkẹrẹ, 42
Islam, 4, 10, 38, 85, 99, 104, 109, 112, 116, 147, 150, 152, 153, 191, 195, 197, 202, 214, 245

ìwà rere, 81, 97, 128, 184

Jamaica Constabulary Force, 73
Japan, 3, 79, 198, 211, 220, 225
Jesus Christ, 16, 28
Johnson, Rev. Samuel, 36, 41, 42, 81, 85, 90, 91, 98, 127
judicial education, 98
judicial system, 8, 46, 54, 83, 84, 100, 103, 117, 134, 135, 137, 193, 205, 214, 215
justification, 20, 26, 58, 121, 170, 172, 175, 221, 225, 233

Kabiyesi, 163
kangaroo, 226
Kantian Categorical Imperative, 16, 28
Kayode, 196
Kerekou, 251
Kgalagardi Desert, 227
Kingibe, Babagana, 248, 249
Kòso, 90

law and order, 42, 69, 81, 83, 87, 95, 100, 112, 148, 153, 157, 158, 160, 162, 163, 165, 193, 248
lawyer(s), 42, 46, 54, 83, 97, 114, 115, 121, 133, 204
leadership disaster, 189
legal : education, 48, 94, 95, 101, 115; power, 70, 154, 155; traditions, 4, 5, 10, 83, 193
legitimacy, 26, 29, 34, 37, 40, 45, 46, 69, 70, 77, 81, 87, 108, 118, 148, 149, 155, 156, 157, 159, 161, 162, 165, 183
Leviathan, 16, 18, 19, 26
liars, 42, 133
liberty, 17, 23, 48, 53, 62, 120, 127, 141, 168, 231
Lijadu, Pastor E. M., 194, 195, 196, 198, 207
liminal, 192, 196, 206, 217
Locke, 6, 14, 15, 19, 20, 21, 22, 27, 66, 71, 107, 108, 222, 245
Lorenz, 123

Machiavelli, Nicolo, 240
Makinde, M. A., 124, 125, 126, 127
Malaysia, 80
Marx, Karl, 18, 113, 123, 136
Marxism, 136
mathematics, 170, 192, 233, 250
Mbiti, J. S., 134, 153, 154, 159, 180, 198
Memmi, Albert, 108, 110, 113
metropolitanism, 238
Middle East, 4, 106, 150
Mobutu, 251
monopoly, 75, 223, 237
moral point of view, 171, 172
moral responsibility, 179, 181, 182, 235
Moses, 17

Naira, 78, 192
Narratives of Struggle, 1
National Electricity Power Authority, 73
National Power Holding Company, 73
native law and custom, 112
Negritude, 248, 250
New Zealand, 201
Nigerian Constitution, 9, 104, 109
Nile Valley, 65

Oba, 38, 40, 41, 42, 47, 52, 77, 83, 87, 89, 90, 95, 101, 112, 115, 138, 158, 161, 162, 163, 199, 200, 247, 248
Obabirin, 40
Obaluaye, 246
Obasanjo, Olusegun, 73, 214
obinrin, 134
obligation, 18, 20, 23, 29, 34, 35, 37, 40, 42, 44, 45, 52, 54, 72, 77, 81, 97, 129, 130, 134, 155, 174, 175, 177, 179, 181, 183, 188, 210, 212, 218, 234, 235, 236, 247
Oduduwa, 132, 139, 163
ofin, 38, 39, 43, 49, 81, 186
ogboni, 50
Ogun, 116, 134, 193
Ogunde, Hubert, 98
okodoro ọrọ, 43
okunrin, 134
Olagbegi of Owo, 67, 162
Olodumare, 37, 44, 81, 97, 158, 161, 163, 165, 184, 193, 195, 203, 206, 207, 209, 210, 213, 218
omode, 67, 68, 95, 134, 143, 158

Omoluabi, 39, 47, 51, 69, 88, 91, 130, 184, 213
Onisegun, 216
Ọọni Àdìmúlà, 90
ooto , 183, 210
Ọpa Aṣẹ, 42
ọràn, 43, 44
Ori, 125, 126, 127, 133, 207, 248
orisa, 65, 81, 158, 161, 165, 207
Orisha-nla, 163
Orunmila, 199, 200, 207, 210, 213
Osun, 134, 142, 199, 200
ours/theirs, 111
Òwe, 95
Oya, 199
oyibo, 36
Oyo, 36, 41, 79, 81, 90, 101, 150, 151, 161

P'Bitek, 126, 196, 198
Palestine, 141, 222
"Parallel Epistemologies", 117
Paris Club, 231
personhood, 32, 48, 59, 63, 65, 96, 113, 124, 126, 130, 162, 246
pharmacology, 192
philosophy of law, 1, 11, 248, 250
philosophy of religion, 194, 195, 196, 198
Plato, 63, 99, 123, 245
property, 1, 11, 16, 19, 20, 21, 22, 27, 29, 34, 45, 50, 52, 60, 76, 77, 120, 131, 138, 141, 174, 185, 205, 210, 220, 222, 242, 243
public education, 96
public order, 48, 193
punishment, 5, 20, 34, 37, 43, 45, 49, 52, 61, 63, 68, 75, 81, 92, 96, 97, 98, 99, 100, 108, 109, 118, 120, 127, 131, 141, 157, 159, 162, 163, 164, 185, 186, 192, 193, 211, 215, 252
pyramids, 65

Raphael, D. D., 14, 155, 157
Rastafarians, 4
Rawls, 14, 53, 77
religious institutions, 237, 245
reparation, 8, 96, 164
The Republic of Uganda, 85
research, 66, 115, 197, 210, 220, 221, 222, 223, 227, 228, 229, 230, 231, 236, 237, 238, 239, 240, 241, 242, 243; ethics, 221, 222, 226
respect for law, 5, 54
retribution, 43, 185, 204, 215, 217
risk, 220, 222, 226, 228, 230, 236, 237, 238, 239, 240, 241, 242, 243
Rome, 11, 248, 249, 250
Rousseau, 6, 14, 15, 22, 23, 24, 25, 26, 27, 66, 71, 108, 245
rule of law, 1, 5, 7, 13, 57, 60, 61, 62, 63, 66, 69, 72, 74, 79, 197, 212, 248, 252
Russell, Bertrand, 107, 155, 156

Sandhurst, 74
Sango, 90, 116, 134, 193
Saraki, 204
Sartre, Jean-Paul, 65, 113, 123
scandal, 77, 79, 96, 142, 191
Scripture of Yoruba, 52, 182
self-preservation, 17, 20, 23, 24, 28, 234
Semitism, 236, 245
Shagari, Shehu, 100
Sharia law, 5, 9, 104
Shyllon, Folarin, 48, 49, 50
Singapore, 80
Singer, Peter, 168, 169, 231, 233
social contract, 6, 14, 15, 19, 22, 25, 136, 140, 147
social order, 10, 22, 23, 37, 54, 167, 202
Socrates, 170, 174, 180, 210, 233, 234
Sodipo, J. O., 125, 127, 152, 187, 241
South Africa, 222, 254
South Korea, 80, 240
spiritual, 124, 125, 127, 158, 161, 207, 222, 250
sport fishing, 221
state of nature, 6, 15, 16, 17, 19, 20, 24, 25, 26, 27, 58, 61
statecraft, 7, 13, 27, 31
Supreme Being, 10, 37, 39, 109, 110, 125, 147, 180, 183, 184, 194, 195, 196, 203, 207, 209, 215

tabu , 38, 39
Taoism, 150
terrorism, 74, 253
theologians, 106, 110, 115, 122, 194, 202

Tocqueville, 60
traditional religion, 10, 148, 149, 150, 151, 152, 153, 157, 158, 165, 200, 216
traditional societies, 21, 147, 148, 151, 153, 156
trans-Sahara slave trade, 3
tripartite, 9, 10, 104
Trump, Donald, 231

ultra vires, 61
United Nations, 142; Charter of Universal Declaration of Human Rights, 120, 144
United States of America, 14, 15, 18, 20, 51, 73, 75, 77, 84, 116, 141, 150, 197, 201, 205, 211, 212, 216, 225, 240, 246, 253
universal, 15, 35, 111, 117, 119, 120, 121, 137, 140, 143, 171, 174, 176, 180, 221, 222, 250, 253
utilitarian, 85, 105, 154, 165, 171, 172, 176, 221, 223, 229

Vagabonds in Power, 78, 87, 248
Van Sertima, 239
vigilantism, 34, 51, 72, 74
Voudou, 246

well-ordered society, 35, 52, 141, 191, 192, 198, 248
Wiredu, Kwasi, 63, 68, 152, 180, 181, 182, 200, 251
World Bank, 32, 253
WTO, 32, 220

Yánníbo, 94
Yemoja, 199
Yoruba: civilization, 35, 87, 211; philosophy of law, 1; proverbs, 66, 95; religion, 37, 125, 133, 182, 193, 194, 196, 198, 200, 201, 207, 213, 216; traditions of law, 1

Zimbabwe, 51, 222

www.ingramcontent.com/pod-product-compliance
Ingram Content Group UK Ltd.
Pitfield, Milton Keynes, MK11 3LW, UK
UKHW041126071026
15587UKWH00009B/246

9 781498 518376